XINJIANG AND THE
MODERN CHINESE STATE

STUDIES ON ETHNIC GROUPS IN CHINA

Stevan Harrell, Editor

XINJIANG AND THE MODERN CHINESE STATE

Justin M. Jacobs

University of Washington Press

Seattle and London

Xinjiang and the Modern Chinese State was supported by a grant
from the Donald R. Ellegood International Publications Endowment.

UNIVERSITY OF WASHINGTON PRESS
www.washington.edu/uwpress

Names: Jacobs, Justin M., author.
Title: Xinjiang and the modern Chinese state / Justin M. Jacobs.
Description: Seattle : University of Washington Press, 2016. | Series:
    Studies on ethnic groups in China | Includes bibliographical
    references and index.
Identifiers: LCCN 2015044270 | ISBN 9780295995656 (hardcover : alk.
    paper)
Subjects: LCSH: Xinjiang Uygur Zizhiqu (China)—Politics and
    government. | Xinjiang Uygur Zizhiqu (China)—Ethnic relations.
    | Geopolitics—China—Xinjiang Uygur Zizhiqu. | Borderlands—
    China—Xinjiang Uygur Zizhiqu. | Imperialism—History.
Classification: LCC DS793.S62 J33 2016 | DDC 951/.604—dc23
LC record available at http://lccn.loc.gov/2015044270

In memory of Ernie Esser, the kindest, smartest, and most interesting friend I ever had. A mended boomerang and empty bottle of mead will always remind me of the good times, from Ninth Grade Island to the Channel Islands.

CONTENTS

FOREWORD BY STEVAN HARRELL ix

ACKNOWLEDGMENTS xiii

INTRODUCTION 3

1. Imperial Repertoires in Republican Xinjiang 17
2. Collapse of Empires and the Nationalist Threat 49
3. Rise of the Ethnopopulists 89
4. Raising the Stakes in Nationalist Xinjiang 127
5. The Birth Pangs of Chinese Affirmative Action 169
6. The Xinjiang Government in Exile 195
   Conclusion 228

NOTES 241

GLOSSARY OF CHINESE CHARACTERS 259

BIBLIOGRAPHY 263

INDEX 275

FOREWORD

Stevan Harrell

Xinjiang, or East Turkestan, as its independence activists call it, has been getting increasing attention in world political and journalistic circles. Once completely overshadowed by Tibet and Taiwan as margins of the Chinese political sphere, Xinjiang has attracted interest because of widely publicized riots in 2009, increased PRC government surveillance and repression of native populations, the incarceration of Xinjiang Uighurs in the U.S. military prison at Guantánamo Bay, and most recently, the arrest and conviction of Uighur economics professor Ilham Tohti for subversion and the repatriation of Uighur refugees by the Thai government. No longer is Xinjiang the conflict zone nobody but locals and specialists have ever heard of.

There are two pervasive ways of talking about today's Xinjiang. According to the discourse promoted by the world press and most governments, Uighurs are a Turkic-speaking, Central Asian Muslim people who resent heavy-handed Chinese rule and large-scale Han in-migration (some call it occupation), and have expressed opposition in forms ranging from private publications to exile websites to occasional riots and acts of terror, spurring further government repression in a vicious cycle. According to the official discourse of the PRC government and media, however, things are different. In this view, Uighurs are one of the fifty-six *minzu*, or national minorities, who make up the Chinese nation, they are progressing toward affluent modernity under Communist Party leadership, and only a tiny minority, probably manipulated by foreign powers seeking to weaken China, ever express opposition or cause any trouble.

What is missing from these discourses, and what Justin Jacobs's *Xinjiang and the Modern Chinese State* delivers in abundance, is the historical context of imperial governance. He stresses the important point that all three regimes that have ruled mainland East Asia in the last two centuries—the imperial Qing, the Republic of China, and now the People's Republic of China—have been empires, multiethnic or multinational countries whose central rulers have had to deal with the problem of governing the linguistically, culturally, religiously, and politically different peoples that inhabit their border regions. All three of these imperial regimes have recognized that ruling the ethnic peripheries presents different problems from ruling the Han core, and all three have employed a variety of strategies for what Jacobs refers to as the "strategic manipulation" of "the politics of difference" in governing their peripheries, particularly Xinjiang. Using the strategies that Jacobs calls "ethno-elitist" and "ethnopopulist," these regimes have attempted to win over the population of Xinjiang either through their traditional leaders or through appeal to the populace at large. They have done this while countering the appeals not just of local nationalism and independence sentiment, but also the ever-present threat of Russian territorial ambitions—Tsarist, Soviet, and post-Soviet. But under no strategy of governance has the region been at peace for long.

Today's rulers of Xinjiang are thus not facing a new problem. And like their imperial and Republican predecessors, they have not been very successful in solving it. There is local opposition from Uighurs and other local peoples, as there always has been. There are shifting policies and pressures from the central regime, as there always have been. There are external geopolitical interests, as there always have been. Through Jacobs's analyses of the successes and failures of Xinjiang's recent historical rulers, we come to appreciate not just the complexity but also the depth of its troubles. Perhaps we can better understand just why today's PRC leaders are at such a loss, and why they have not fulfilled their announced mission of helping Xinjiang advance harmoniously into the Chinese version of modernity. As long as Xinjiang is part of a state centered on China, problems of governance and conflict will come, literally, with the territory. But China will not grant any appreciable degree of autonomy, because there are geopolitical interests involved. We can only hope that lessons to be learned from Jacobs's stories of previous failures and occasional successes will somehow be useful in future attempts to solve the Xinjiang question.

ACKNOWLEDGMENTS

This book is the result of so many years of research and writing that I can hardly stand to look at it anymore. It has taken me from Seattle to San Diego, Taipei to Beijing, Urumchi to Kashgar, Istanbul to Nanjing, and London to Washington, DC. I long wished for a suitable analogy to convey this experience to friends and family, but I never found one. Then I came across the following entry in the diary of Wu Zhongxin, governor of Xinjiang during the mid-1940s. On March 1, 1946, Wu recalled the belated realization of his long desired dream: passage on a plane out of Xinjiang. The "plane experienced horrendous turbulence, and many passengers vomited in the cabin" as it passed through thick cloud cover and ferocious winds, the aged and battered aircraft lurching and weaving through mountain peaks, on several occasions nearly colliding with rocky outcroppings. Huddled uncomfortably in a drafty cabin without seats, Wu listened anxiously as the pilot cursed and sweated, wondering why they had taken off in the first place. "Though the weather was not conducive to flying today," the pilot later told him, "there were so many well-wishers at the airport, all giving us a grand and enthusiastic farewell, that it would have been a severe letdown to all if we had not taken off." When they eventually landed, they were many hours behind schedule.

That, in a nutshell, is the early life cycle of a professional historian and his monograph. For those of us fortunate enough to land safely, there are few greater pleasures than to thank the many well-wishers who paid for our tickets, saw us off at the airport, held our hands through turbulence, and forgave all our cursing and sweating. For putting me on that plane and giving me the tools to weather the storm, no one deserves more thanks than Joseph Esherick and Paul Pickowicz. Joe knows exactly when someone must be built up and when someone must be torn down. In deeming my immature scribblings "appalling," he ensured that later incarnations would not be such (at least, I can only hope). I thank Paul for many, many things, but none more than teaching me the importance of presentation and packaging. I now know that it is okay to have a PhD and still care about my audience. Sarah Schneewind is the intellectual equivalent of the legendary iron maiden, in which no bad idea goes unimpaled. Unlike the victims of the iron maiden, however, hers emerge much the wiser. For shepherding me through the intricacies of Russian and Soviet empires, I thank Bob Edelman. It is the rare scholar indeed who can impart trenchant insight with a book in one hand and a melting ice cream cone in the other. I am also grateful to Gary Fields and Hasan Kayali for their early enthusiasm and insights regarding my work.

No one has been as constant a friend or as reliable a critic in recent years as Judd Kinzley. I cannot think of anyone else in the world with whom I can discuss the careers of various Xinjiang governors while locking horns in *Mario Super Sluggers*. (And who else in our line of work can claim the pleasure of having heard him sing the entire score of *Mary Poppins*?) For smoothing my transition to San Diego and generously sharing their considerable wisdom and experience in the field, I am indebted to Jeremy Brown and Matt Johnson. I recall with fondness my many interactions with James Wicks and do not blame him for my failure to master the surfboard. Maggie Greene and Emily Baum are dear friends whose precocious accomplishments daily invert the hierarchy that once saddled them with the most unpleasant of camping duties. David Chang and Jeremy Murray are generous souls and worthy debate foes, even when they only debate each other. I owe a special thanks to Ernie Esser, who shipped a valuable book across the Pacific when I needed it most. I know he would have read this book with interest, despite its complete and unforgivable lack of algorithms.

I have been fortunate to benefit in a myriad of ways from the knowledge and expertise of many of the top scholars in the field of Xinjiang studies. Pride of place goes to James Millward, who read and commented extensively on two substantially different versions of this manuscript. He helped me think through and clarify some of the thorniest and most intractable theoretical problems in my work. I am also grateful to Linda Benson and Ingvar Svanberg for their early encouragement of my research and generous sharing of contacts throughout Eurasia. Victor Mair has likewise been steadfast and magnanimous in his support. I have benefited immensely from close collaboration with David Brophy and Charles Kraus, both of whom are always forthcoming with new sources, insights, and expert knowledge on all things Xinjiang. Much the same can be said of Eric Schluessel and Joshua Freeman, with whom I look forward to sharing many decades of intellectual stimulation.

My interest in China and its Central Asian borderlands was first stoked as an undergraduate at the University of Washington. Bi *laoshi* was relentless in her pursuit of tonal perfection, and Chris Dakin was my earliest and most companionable informant on all things China and Taiwan. I regret to note that my congenial Uighur-language instructor, who continually went above and beyond the call of duty, prefers not to be named. Daniel Waugh, who introduced me to the Silk Road and the Great Game, bears most of the responsibility for my unhealthy obsession with Xinjiang. Robert Stevick provided the professional and intellectual model for an academic, one that I have striven to emulate in my own career. Though I have left Old English and *Beowulf* far behind, I have never forgotten his useful adage that the -*es* declension always represents the masculine singular genitive—except when it doesn't. Kent Guy's enthusiasm for the Qing was so infectious that it was difficult not to want his job. When I told him this, he took me out to lunch and told me how to get it. I am grateful to David Bachman for overseeing my first attempt at conducting research, and for his early encouragement to try my hand in peer review. Few things can replace the sheer love of learning and intellectual discovery that characterized my interactions with Deborah Porter. No one lights a fire in the mind like she does. Stevan Harrell was an incisive and enthusiastic critic for my master's thesis and most directly responsible for my commitment to become a professional historian. I am very lucky to have had the opportunity to work with him at both ends of the academic spectrum, as both student and peer. His comments on this manuscript improved it immensely. It has also been an instructive delight to work with Lorri Hagman, who has made the publication process as painless as possible. From an earlier life, I recall with fondness time spent learning from Lynn Jacobson, who showed me how satisfying a life of writing and ideas could be. Last but not least, I thank Andrew Marble for tutoring me in the joys of grumpy editing.

At American University, I find myself blessed to have landed in an extraordinarily collegial and supportive department. From the very first day, Max Paul Friedman has served as an unfailingly supportive friend and mentor, from job talk blizzards to real estate in the suburbs and DC bicycling routes. As chair of the department, Pam Nadell has shown touching concern and steadfast support for the plight of a junior scholar. I could not have asked for better colleagues or a more supportive department.

An earlier version of chapter 6 appeared in the *Journal of Cold War Studies* as "Exile Island: Xinjiang Refugees and the 'One China' Policy in Nationalist Taiwan, 1949–1971." I am grateful to MIT Press for permission to reprint portions of that article here.

Last but not least is the family that has watched my life from afar this past decade and more, ever confident that the roots they laid down would one day bear fruit. From the day I was born, my parents, Jan and Candy, have devoted every possible attention and resource to my education, both within the classroom and without. Never did I lack for anything, and never were my crazy ideas and travel plans met with discouragement or derision. My elder brother Jeff blazed all the paths and erected all the signposts that a younger brother could possibly want. To fail when so much of the foundation had already been laid down would be most embarrassing.

Writing a book is a profoundly isolating and lonely experience. Having a supportive wife and noisy kids makes it slightly less so. Sasha and Lance give meaning to the life I lead when I am not in Rapunzel's tower. May they always scream at me to let down my hair. My wife, Cindy, has been with me through everything. Only for her do words do no justice. Here's to where we've been, and to where we're still going.

XINJIANG AND THE
MODERN CHINESE STATE

INTRODUCTION

O N JULY 1, 1911, YUAN DAHUA, THE GOVERNOR OF XINJIANG, sent a telegram to the central government in Beijing. The topic was empires and their modes of governance. "In administering their interior and exterior territories," Yuan wrote, "foreigners do not apply the same rubric of rule." The newly minted constitution of his very own Great Qing Empire, he noted, emulated that of Japan. But "the system of rule that Japan applies to its interior is not the same as that which it applies to Korea or Taiwan, and the system Japan uses to rule its prefectures and counties is not the same as that applied to Hokkaido." Why are there such differences? Yuan asked. "Because a system of rule must be suitable for that locality," he said in answer to his own question. "It cannot be otherwise." The point of Yuan's memorial was that the Manchu court in Beijing should emulate the governing tactics of neighboring empires that Yuan considered to be more advanced. He concluded, "Xinjiang is to China as Hokkaido is to Japan."[1]

This analogy resonated strongly with Han officials in Xinjiang. After all, they ruled over a vast Central Asian land of desert and steppe, home to a Mongol and Turkic demographic constituting more than 90 percent of the population. Just five years later, Yuan's successor, Yang Zengxin, felt compelled to remind Beijing of the virtues of learning from its rivals. Xinjiang, he noted somewhat more insistently, "absolutely cannot be managed in a fashion similar to that of the inner provinces." Yang emphasized that he, as governor, would be "reluctant to confine myself only to methods that are prescribed for China proper." Once more, the example set by Japanese administrators in their expanding empire served as a model for frontier officials in China. "In light of its special circumstances," Yang asked, "can we look into the possibility of allowing Xinjiang to be governed in the same way that Japan governs Hokkaido and Taiwan? Or perhaps in the accommodating manner that the Qing once stipulated for special administrations?" Yang's choice of words, some drawn from precedents set as early as the Tang dynasty (618–907), traced a consistent logic. Because the non-Han frontier evinced cultural, ethnic, economic, and political norms strikingly different from those in the Han heartland, "special conditions" (*tebie qingxing*) mandated adherence to a form of "loose rein" (*jimi*) governance imbued with the "spirit of accommodation" or "flexible arrangements" (*biantong*).[2]

During the first half of the twentieth century, Chinese officials in Xinjiang had good reason to question the wisdom of exporting to the Muslim frontier policies originally designed for the Han heartland. Incorporated into the Manchu empire by military conquest in the mid-eighteenth century, Xinjiang nonetheless remained an attractive military and economic target for states and empires along its western and northern borders. It shared with the peoples of these regions extensive linguistic, economic, cultural, ethnic, and religious ties. By the late nineteenth century, all these neighboring lands and peoples had become territories and subjects of the Russian empire, which knitted together its far-flung domains via the Trans-Siberian Railway. In 1884, owing both to the Russian threat and to the brief rise and fall of an independent Islamic state in Xinjiang, the Qing court decided to consolidate its rule in the northwest by turning Xinjiang into a province (*sheng*), as distinct from its former designation as an outer dependency (*shudi*). In this new provincial bureaucracy, Han officials with civil service examination degrees began to replace the long-standing military aristocracy of Manchu and Mongol bannermen, who had once regarded all the non-Han peripheries of China as their unique political preserve.[3]

Regardless of whether the officials in Xinjiang were Manchu, Mongol, or Han, however, they all confronted more or less the same problems along the non-Han frontier, be it Mongolia, Tibet, or Xinjiang. By the late nineteenth century, rival empires across Eurasia had begun to leverage their superior economic and military weight to siphon wealth and resources away from Beijing and to reorient the political and economic networks of the Qing empire toward their own metropoles. In response, during the last decades of the Qing dynasty prior to the 1911 revolution, the Manchu court undertook a vigorous program of reform. Just three years after Xinjiang became a province, so too did Taiwan, and that was followed by the carving of the Manchu homeland into what would eventually become the three northeastern provinces of the early twentieth century. Many previously closed frontiers were opened to Han migration, non-Han elites found themselves grossly in debt to Han merchants, and large contingents of modernized New Armies, staffed almost entirely by Han, were stationed outside the inner provinces. In Xinjiang, new Chinese-language schools encroached on institutions of Muslim pedagogy, much to the dissatisfaction of native elites. Most upsetting, however, was the ubiquitous imposition of new taxes to pay for the government's new policies, which for many felt like a form of sinification.[4]

The backlash visited on the Qing court and its Republican successors as a result of these reform efforts conformed to a political mold unique to the twentieth century. As the discourse of the nation-state increasingly lent itself to opportunistic application in the realm of geopolitics, Chinese elites quickly became aware of the ways in which discontent on their own non-Han borderlands could breed results drastically different from those engendered by discontent in the heartland. The last time Xinjiang had been wrenched from Beijing's control, for about a decade in the 1860s and 1870s, Beijing's political rivals in Central Asia could only produce a single slogan around which to rally the Turkic natives against Qing rule: holy war.[5] After the fall of the Manchus in 1911, the exclusionist discourse of the nation-state, premised on the novel ideal of ethnic self-rule, provided a new platform from which rival political elites could challenge Chinese rule. Yang Zengxin, governor of Xinjiang for seventeen years after the 1911 revolution, made clear what was liable to happen if China proved unable to keep the foreigners at bay. "Let us imagine," he wrote to Beijing in 1917, "that trouble was to break out in the southwestern provinces today. Eventually they would be reunified. But if there is even the slightest slip in Xinjiang, so important for national defense, it will fall under the control of a foreign power. Even if we then had an eternity, we would not be able to recover it."[6]

What Governor Yang was attempting to describe constitutes the narrative focus of this book. The creation of a putative "nation-state" by one empire on what was intended to become the former territory of its imperial rival was merely one permutation of a much larger phenomenon: the manipulation of ethnocultural difference. In the twentieth-century political history of Xinjiang, the only majority non-Han provincial-level unit of China never to have slipped from the hands of Han officials, we find the most complete case study for an interrogation of the legacy and inheritance of empire in the eastern Eurasian mainland after 1911. "Strategies of difference" consistently marked Xinjiang as a unique part of the Chinese state, a place where the normal rules of political discourse in the Han heartland ceased to apply. An extended analysis of what Han officials said and did *in* Xinjiang—as opposed to what Han intellectuals or politicians on the eastern seaboard merely said *about* Xinjiang—will thus bring us close to an understanding of the imperial foundation upon which modern Chinese political discourse actually operates.[7]

What are strategies of difference? The pronouncements of Governor Yang are instructive on this score. During his seventeen years (1912–28) in office, Yang made a habit of announcing surprisingly modest goals for himself. In 1925, he proclaimed as his highest ambition nothing more than the hope that "Xinjiang should not be delivered from our hands during my lifetime." Elsewhere, Yang would gloss this sentiment in more dramatic terms, declaring that only his policies would prevent Xinjiang from becoming "the next Outer Mongolia" (*wai Meng zhi xu*), "the next Tibet" (*Xizang zhi xu*), or "the next Urga" (*Kulun zhi xu*), the capital of Outer Mongolia. After the creation of the Japanese proxy state of Manchukuo in the 1930s, "the next northeast" (*dongbei zhi xu*) also entered the political lexicon of Chinese elites who concerned themselves with the fate of Xinjiang. As for the rest of the country, Yang occasionally voiced his hope that "two or three great and powerful men will rouse their consciences, get rid of predatory armies, and implement policies beneficial to the people." He did not, however, expect that any such savior would come from the non-Han borderlands. As governor of Xinjiang, Yang's job was to sit tight and "wait for the day when the central plains have calmed down." In the meantime, he wrote in 1919, "if I am able to maintain one portion [of the country], and the [central] government is able to maintain another, is this not for the best?"[8]

The novelty of Yang's words becomes apparent only with the realization that the deployment of this type of political discourse was largely restricted to those areas of China evincing the requisite ethnic, cultural, and linguistic criteria capable of allowing rival imperial elites to engage in strategic manipulation of the "politics of difference."[9] Unless a foreign power (such as Japan) actually invaded the Han heartland, a warlord who claimed as his highest ambition the preservation of Chinese sovereignty in Hunan or Jiangxi would have invited ridicule and scorn. For men like Yan Xishan, Feng Yuxiang, and Wu Peifu, some of the most prominent warlords of the inner provinces, such an "achievement" merely marked the starting line. They were further obliged, in a way Han officials in Xinjiang were not, to strive for "national salvation" (jiuguo), a task made impossible by the geopolitical conditions of the day. In other words, far out in Xinjiang and any other non-Han borderland of which the Chinese state might find itself steward, local officials could employ the politics of difference to support their bid for wealth and power in a way that officials operating in the heartland could not.

Governor Yang, aware of this, took the unusual step of publishing, while still in office, several thousand telegrams culled from his own government archives. Records from the Studio of Rectification (Buguozhai wendu), issued in handsome thread-stitched bound sets and available for purchase throughout the country, effectively showcased the governor's novel approach to self-legitimization on the non-Han frontier. The flip side of all this was that Yang's rivals, usually but not always foreign, could just as easily turn the politics of difference against him, provided they deployed such discourse in support of their designs on Xinjiang. Han officials in the heartland, though obliged to strive for the impossible goal of national salvation—and then watch as the inevitable denouement sapped the morale of all but their most ardent enthusiasts—generally did not have to worry about hostile charges of Chinese "colonialism" or "imperialism." Run-of-the-mill "autocrats" and "despots" they might be, but at least they were not characterized as chauvinist Han nationalists who "hated" their culturally alien subjects, as Russians officials once alleged of Yang. Viewed from this perspective, it should come as no surprise that Yang went to extraordinary lengths to select and publish for public consumption only those telegrams showing *his* manipulation of the politics of difference, while omitting entirely the hostile versions put forth by his many rivals.

This study is concerned not only with the abstract discourse of difference but also with the very real institutions of difference that continued to undergird Chinese rule in the former Qing imperium, long after the words *empire* and *monarchy* had succumbed to charges of illegitimacy. It is clear that Han officials in the new Republican state consciously revived selected rituals and modes of discourse from the Qing empire that had originally been designed for interaction with non-Han nobles, a tactic elsewhere described as "going imperial."[10] To probe the relevance of such a framework in Xinjiang during the first half of the twentieth century, it is necessary to shift our perspective from Beijing and Nanjing all the way to Urumchi,[11] the capital of Xinjiang and home of its Chinese governors. The perspective of Han officials resident in Urumchi is indispensable for this task, for the simple reason that no central government of the Republican era (1912–49) ever succeeded in enforcing its writ throughout the province. Indeed, most of our evidence will come from the approximately four decades in which Han officials held the reins of government in Urumchi but, owing to the chronic disunity and fiscal poverty of the inner provinces, found themselves perennially threatened with political disenfranchisement. Almost always, this latter threat came at the hands of foreign powers and domestic warlords peddling their own versions of the politics of difference.[12]

Thus, the contest for wealth and power in twentieth-century Xinjiang—and by extension, the rest of the non-Han periphery—was mediated both in name and in deed through the strategic manipulation of difference. That there was still such difference to exploit underscores the growing realization among scholars that the twentieth century in no way marked the transition from "empire to nation-state," in China or elsewhere. Yet if China did not become a Han nation-state, what did it become? Should we simply continue to refer to it as an "empire," or is some sort of intermediary term (e.g., *imperial formation*) more appropriate?[13] My analysis suggests that the phrase *national empire*—related to but distinct from the idea of the Soviet Union as an "empire of nations"—appears to be the most suitable label.[14] Even some late Qing intellectuals coined a strikingly similar phrase—*minzu diguo*—in Chinese.[15] The notion of difference is now regularly acknowledged as an indispensable feature of empires, and studies of the Ottoman, Russian, French, and other empires throughout history have all deemed the flexible institutionalization of ethnic and spatial difference as a defining characteristic of the largest and most enduring multiethnic states. In its most condensed form, the "politics of difference" is little more than the presumption "that different peoples within the polity will be governed differently" and that "distinction and hierarchy"—or the "non-equivalence of multiple populations"—will be maintained even as the state incorporates new people.[16]

Key to this interpretation is the distinction between empire as a type of state and empire as a type of power. As a type of power, empire is usually associated with an emperor or other absolutist monarch, who attempts to concentrate wealth and power in the hands of an exclusive elite whose ranks are often hereditary and usually closed to the mass of commoners who make up the taxpayers of the state. In its more lax and often popular usages, this interpretation of empire is almost always negative, concerned as it is with the use of brute military force, an elite dictatorship, and suppression of subaltern peoples. From this enduring paradigm, scholars and pundits have coined the phrase *divide and rule*, a concept usually imagined as the guiding ideology of a Machiavellian imperial elite. The idea of empire as a type of state, however, derives much of its explanatory power from scholarship conducted over the past several decades on the major Eurasian land-based empires: Ottoman, Russian, and Manchu.

The "new Qing historians" have shown the ways in which the Manchus forged an expansive empire during the seventeenth, eighteenth, and nineteenth centuries, one that drew its wealth from the Han heartland but was rooted in institutions of ethnic and spatial difference throughout East and Central Asia. Historians of China, however, have generally stopped short of adapting such insights toward the twentieth-century successor states of the Qing. In tracing this Eurasian legacy of political difference into the twentieth century, Soviet historians have done the most to complicate the enduring paradigm of empire as a type of power. In demonstrating how the Soviet state was more a "maker of nations" than a "breaker of nations," they have provided historians of modern China with the analytical tools necessary to reconsider the imperial legacy bequeathed to twentieth-century Republican and Communist administrators along the non-Han borderlands.[17] This in turn enables us to interrogate the ways modern China—as a type of state—still resembled its imperial predecessors. The study of ethnic classification projects in the southwestern province of Yunnan during the 1950s, for example, has illuminated our understanding of the modern *minzu* (or minority nationality) regime as well as the imperial legacy in postrevolutionary China.[18]

The present study provides a similar analysis of Xinjiang and much of twentieth-century China. In the interests of analytical precision, the word *empire* here will refer to a type of state that creates, maintains, and ultimately institutionalizes ethnic and spatial difference over a vast swath of territorial holdings. The actual exercise of power by Han officials in an ethnoculturally alien land will be captured by reference to strategies or politics of difference. Every effort will be made to avoid deploying politically charged and highly subjective terms such as *colonialism* and *imperialism,* unless they form part of the discourse of historical actors. In evaluating the increasingly liberal deployment of provocative words such as *imperialism* in the scholarly literature, Bernard Porter, a historian of the British Empire, writes that "currently there is no general agreement over what the word means or covers," and that "its negative connotations can make it difficult to use dispassionately or truly analytically."[19] In a very basic sense, the building blocks of empire are conscious performances of ethnocultural difference within a political arena. To describe something as "imperialist" or as the embodiment of "imperialism" is almost always to pass a negative moral judgment upon that performance.

In an attempt to drop an empirical anchor somewhere in this sea of partisan discourse, this study will confine its analysis of colonialism and imperialism to the contextual recognition of when and where it becomes rhetorically *possible* to affix one or both of these terms to the modern Chinese state. Less important than the ontological reality of such subjective and pliable terms is the recognition that only certain parts of the former Qing state were, in fact, suitable for their deployment by political elites. In practice, this meant only those places marked by a substantial "alien" ethnocultural demographic that lent substance to the definition of *empire* as a type of state built on the notion of difference. This study is not concerned with identifying or highlighting "victims" of imperialism, to the extent that such a phenomenon can actually exist outside the hypothetical abstractions of nation-states. Rather, it aims to identify and analyze the conditions under which rhetorical claims of ethnocultural victimhood can be made to sound plausible. For example, despite the fact that the vast majority of Han and Uighurs living in China today face similar restrictions in political, religious, and economic affairs, scholars do not generally refer to the "oppressed" or "restive" Han of Zhejiang or Anhui. Such "disenfranchised" Han are simply referred to as "exploited" but unmarked "people," "peasants," "prostitutes," and so on. But once the ethnocultural difference of the Uighurs or Tibetans has been foregrounded, near identical forms of "oppression" are habitually described as "colonialist" or "imperialist" in nature.

During the twentieth century, the presence of ethnocultural difference provided fertile ground for the introduction of a novel and unprecedented threat to extant paradigms of difference in East Asia: national determination. How did Han officials in Xinjiang respond to what they perceived as the nationalist threat? Despite a growing interest in Uighur unrest among mainstream intellectual and media circles, there is at present no historically informed interrogation of this important question from the perspective of those who exercised paramount power in modern Xinjiang: the Han ruling class. In part, this is due to a long-standing methodological bias within modern Chinese history. Because modern China is often portrayed first and foremost as a victim of Western and Japanese imperialism (both in the narratives of its own political elites and in those of foreigners), historians have been slow to recognize that not every significant region of ethnocultural difference managed to slip from Chinese control after 1911. Despite the permanent loss of Outer Mongolia, the lengthy estrangement of Tibet, and the brief emergence of the Japanese puppet state of Manchukuo, fully one-sixth of the present-day People's Republic of China remained subject to a handful of Han rulers who were grossly outnumbered by their non-Han subjects. That their writ continued to be observed in Xinjiang without break throughout the twentieth century could not be said of Han officials in Manchuria, Taiwan, Shanghai, or Beijing. And yet these latter locales are often called upon within the scholarly literature to serve as representative microcosms of the "Chinese nation-state" in toto.

Scholars of all persuasions will be better served by the recognition that twentieth-century China was much more than simply a nation beset by imperialists. Certainly, from the perspective of a great many residents of the Han heartland, this was an apt characterization, and scholars who study such communities exclusively can likely rest content with this framework. But when we shift our perspective from Shanghai to Urumchi, the historian of modern China encounters a case study substantial and continuous enough to illustrate the ways Chinese political elites continued to engage the rhetoric and realities of empire on the ground throughout the twentieth century. Owen Lattimore recognized as much during his travels along the northern borderlands in the 1920s, noting that "while the Chinese could rightly claim that they suffered from foreign imperialism, there was also a second level of Chinese imperialism against the Mongols."[20] The words and deeds of Han officials resident in Xinjiang constitute the missing link necessary to portray twentieth-century China first and foremost as an empire among empires, and later as a nationalizing empire among nationalizing empires. In this study, the empirical basis for such a portrayal is a detailed analysis of how Han officials in Xinjiang attempted to meet, counter, or otherwise defuse the nationalist threat over a period of five decades. In so doing, they drew from what we might describe as a comparative cabinet of imperial "best practices," borrowed and adapted from rival empires with which they were in direct geopolitical competition.

The link between the nationalist threat in Xinjiang and the idea of modern China as an "empire of difference" lies in the realization that the ideal of national determination has been manipulated for the purposes of geopolitical competition among rival empires since its very inception. The specter of the nation-state and the notion of ethnic self-rule first make their appearance in the documents of Han officials in Xinjiang in the form of offensive tactics deployed by rival Russian imperial elites. In response, successive Chinese governors formulated defensive tactical responses designed first to combat, and later to co-opt, nationalist politics among their non-Han subjects. Over time, the larger transformation in evidence here is a new form of the politics of difference: from an *ethno-elitist* alliance of culturally and politically conservative Manchu and Mongol bannermen, former imperial Han officials, and Turkic and Tibetan nobles, to an *ethnopopulist* alliance overseen by "progressive" and "revolutionary" cadres committed to the evolutionary development of ethnocultural and economic levels among a multitude of "backward" subjects. For Han officials in Xinjiang during the late Republican and early Communist eras, the appeal of the Soviet version of ethnopopulism was to be found in the realization that a preemptive sponsorship of national development within one's own state could do much to defuse the appeal of separatist platforms underwritten from abroad. From this awareness arose the impulse to nationalize the various territorial and human components of one's own empire before rival imperial elites succeeded in one's stead. Whoever managed to do so first could then orient that difference toward their own metropole.

The following chapters narrate this momentous shift in precise chronological detail, showing when and where twentieth-century China emerges as an empire within the world rather than a nation set against it. In constructing this narrative, I have primarily drawn upon Chinese archival sources in Taiwan and China, both published and unpublished. At key points, I also incorporate relevant insights from Soviet, British, and American archives, in addition to new and exciting research based upon Uighur-language source material. Some scholars may wonder about the utility of relying so heavily upon published Chinese archival sources, particularly those produced in and about a non-Han borderland. Yet for the historian who wishes to uncover the perspective of the Han governor and his ranking officials in Xinjiang, there are few alternatives. Of course, there are key moments when unpublished archival sources play a decisive role in filling in the gaps. But the idea that five decades of Han rule and contentious ethnopolitics in twentieth-century Xinjiang can be narrated primarily from source material made freely available to foreign researchers working in mainland Chinese archives is little more than wishful thinking. Fortunately, it has often been possible to corroborate sources published on the mainland with those made accessible in the less ideologically restricted political climate of Taiwan. In every available instance, published Chinese archival sources—even those of Governor Yang Zengxin, who personally edited his telegrams for publication while still in office—have aligned with unpublished and unedited counterparts in all but the most trivial of details.

Though we can be reasonably certain regarding the integrity of those Chinese archival sources that are published, we can only speculate about those that were not. The suspicion, of course, is that we are seeing only what Beijing wants us to see, and that these materials must somehow replicate or otherwise reinforce the official view of the Chinese government. If that was the goal, then we can only conclude that the censors somehow fell asleep on the job. How else to explain the inclusion of some of the most scathing and damning indictments of Communist ethnic policies ever seen, communicated by Uighur, Kazak, and Hui workers on the factory floors of Urumchi in the 1950s? Also on full and uncensored display is Governor Yang's unrelenting persecution of Uighur expatriates in the Soviet Union during the 1920s, along with rebel proclamations characterizing the Han people as "yellow filth" one decade later. Rare published archival documents from the Sheng Shicai era freely and openly admit the near total failure of the sort of ethnic policies the Communists themselves would one day try to implement. The facsimile edition of Governor Wu Zhongxin's handwritten diary reveals his chronic frustration and bitter disagreements with top Nationalist leaders, and includes every entry that he later attempted to cross out to protect both his reputation and that of his colleagues. Of course, it is true that these sources portray the most contentious instance of indigenous resistance to Han rule—the Ili rebellion of the 1940s—as entirely the result of Soviet manipulation and instigation. Fortunately, newly available Soviet archives and Russian-language scholarship on this topic yield the reluctant admission from behind closed doors that Han officials in Urumchi were right to be paranoid about Moscow's role in this uprising.

Last but not least, it is important to point out that the uses to which this source base have been put are about as far as possible from the "official line" of the Chinese government. To argue that postrevolutionary China continued to act as an empire while calling itself a democratic republic is to risk perennial ostracism and vitriolic denunciation in scholarly and political circles on the mainland. Many prominent foreign scholars of Xinjiang have been denied visas for even suggesting that modern China has been anything less than a harmonious multiethnic state for the past five thousand years.[21] Most recently, in April 2015, the Chinese Academy of Social Sciences described prominent American proponents of the "new Qing history" framework—which focuses on the eighteenth and nineteenth centuries—as "arrogant," "overbearing," and "imperialist." Their scholarship, from which much of the inspiration for this book was derived, was dismissed as "academically absurd." Their crime? Having the temerity to suggest that the Qing dynasty, which flourished more than two hundred years ago and fell from power in 1912, was an "empire" that had "conquered" non-Han peoples and the lands they occupied.[22]

It remains to be seen what the Chinese government will think of a scholar who argues for the extension of the empire paradigm into the twentieth century and is foolish enough to suppose that an imperial legacy can be identified and studied through Chinese archival sources published under its own watch.

CHAPTER 1

IMPERIAL REPERTOIRES IN REPUBLICAN XINJIANG

IN HONING THEIR TOOLS OF GOVERNANCE IN XINJIANG, HAN officials looked to both domestic precedent and foreign models. Their source for investigating the former is readily apparent: for the first two decades after the 1911 revolution, nearly all Han officials in Xinjiang were veterans of the Qing state, claiming extensive experience in the old imperial bureaucracy. Most of them were intimately familiar with Qing repertoires of rule and had an extensive literature of former imperial precedents at their fingertips. But what about their knowledge of contemporary European and Japanese models? The journey from Urumchi to Beijing, undertaken on camel and horseback well into the 1930s, could take upward of three months to complete. Clear into the 1940s, Xinjiang was notorious for the extent of the information blockade imposed upon its inhabitants by a series of Han warlords. The telegraph system was in perennial shambles, earning the derogatory nickname of "camelgraph" from the Russians. As a result, the conventional view of Han officials in Xinjiang has been that they were of a rather parochial and reactionary mindset, scarcely interested in the outside world. Writing about Governor Yang in 1917, Xie Bin, an envoy from the central government, concluded that "his mind is too steeped in the old ways of thinking and his convictions are too deeply imprinted. He has served as an official in the northwest for too long and knows nothing of intellectual currents in the outside world. He will prove unable to row his boat with the tides of progress."[1]

Xie may have been surprised to learn just how informed about the outside world both Yang and his former Qing colleagues in Urumchi

actually were. In 1909, Liankui, the Manchu governor-general for both
Gansu and Xinjiang and Yang's superior at the time, was tasked with
overseeing provincial elections and the formation of a parliament for
Xinjiang. After noting the miniscule proportion of Han in his province
and the almost total lack of educated Han gentry, Liankui proceeded to
regale the central government with his extensive knowledge of ethnopolitics in other contemporary empires. "In governing their dependent
territories," he wrote, "both Eastern and Western states employ special
methods. The British in India and the French in Vietnam, for example,
both maintain an autocratic form of government." After citing Herbert
Spencer's *The Study of Sociology*, Liankui outlined three types of government in European empires: settlement colonies subject to a monarch,
dependencies with representative organs but no cabinet, and those with
both representative organs and a cabinet. In those dependencies where
"white people are many but natives are few," the "degree of civilization"
made it possible for "the state to grant them self-governing powers."
Thus, according to Liankui, until Xinjiang made significant strides in
either developing education among the non-Han peoples or resettling
droves of educated Han to the northwest, the province was not prepared
to undertake elections.[2]

As was made evident in the discourse on Hokkaido and Taiwan, the
once prevalent view of Chinese officials on the frontier as doddering relics of an intellectual and cultural backwater is almost entirely baseless.
While they may have striven to limit the contact their subjects had with
the outside world, the Han governor and his ranking officials in Urumchi were fully enmeshed in the intellectual and political currents of a
cosmopolitan imperial elite. Wang Shunan (1851–1936), the provincial
treasurer of Xinjiang during the final years of the Qing dynasty, provides
us with an excellent example. Born into a literati family in Hebei, Wang
worked his way up through the traditional examination system before
serving as a magistrate in Sichuan for eight years. After coming to the
attention of Zhang Zhidong, one of the most vigorous reform officials
of the late Qing, Wang worked on various modernization projects in
the Yangzi delta, coming into frequent contact with Chinese students

returned from Europe. An ardent admirer of Japan, Wang was sent in 1898 to escort Western-style munitions to suppress a Muslim rebellion in Gansu, just southeast of Xinjiang. Wang would spend much of the next two decades in the far northwest, obtaining a transfer to Xinjiang in 1906.[3]

Just as important as his political career, however, were Wang's scholarly labors. During his time in Gansu, Wang wrote five books concerning the history of various European countries, with the goal of identifying the source of their wealth and power. By the time of his death, Wang had authored or edited histories of Greek philosophy and of great wars in European history, a massive gazetteer of Xinjiang, the official history of the Qing, and a history of Russia under Peter the Great. Among his voluminous publications, some are notable as the first-ever treatment of their subject in China. More germane to our purposes here, most of Wang's works on European history and culture were written during his time in Gansu and Xinjiang and published in Lanzhou, far from the traditional centers of Chinese scholarship. When the famous French sinologist Paul Pelliot passed through Urumchi in 1907, he was delighted to find so many cosmopolitan savants among Wang's entourage. Wang, "a man of great learning" and a "very esteemed scholar," asked Pelliot to lend him astronomical instruments for some scientific experiments. After noting a few places in need of revisions in Wang's history of Peter the Great, Pelliot was "overwhelmed" by local officials hoping to pick his brain. One asked Pelliot to write several pages summarizing the last two centuries of developments in European philosophy, while another asked him to pen an article describing the financial conditions of loans and interest rates in Europe, with an eye toward eliminating the usurious practices of Hindu moneylenders in Kashgar.[4]

Wang is so important because he presided over a patron-disciple relationship with Yang Zengxin, the future Republican governor of Xinjiang (1912–28). Indeed, over a relationship that would ultimately span more than three decades, Wang secured Yang's transfer to Xinjiang from Gansu, contributed several prefaces to Yang's *Records from the Studio of Rectification*, authored the epitaph for the tombstone of Yang's father, published a book of poetry in praise of Yang, and carried out a host of political assignments on Yang's behalf in Beijing. In return, Yang financially supported Wang and his entire family for nearly twenty years after the latter's departure from Xinjiang. Thus it seems safe to say that Yang, the governor of Xinjiang for nearly two decades after the 1911 revolution, was able to partake amply of the global knowledge economy of imperial governance as distilled in his patron's writings. Nor were Wang and Yang unique among Chinese officials in Xinjiang. The large volume of travel writings left by Western archaeologists and explorers who visited Xinjiang during these decades suggests that many—though by no means all—of Yang's subordinates were similarly eager to learn about the latest developments abroad. In 1906, when Finnish traveler and future statesman Gustaf Mannerheim passed through the southwestern oasis of Kashgar, he noted how "during our visits to the Chinese authorities they were interested in informing themselves about the political situation in Russia," and that they "expressed the conviction that H.M's government will not be long-lived and that their mighty neighbour is moving towards a republican form of government."[5]

Their interest in Russia was not misplaced. As with so many other areas of modern Chinese history, developments in the Russian empire often constituted a preview of social and political vicissitudes that were soon to shake China. Nowhere does this realization come through more clearly than in the response of Han officials in Xinjiang to the evolving imperial repertoires deployed by their Russian counterparts. Russian officials in and around Xinjiang first showed Han officials how to turn their newfound imperial liabilities into nationalized assets. Though political elites throughout China were closely attuned to strategies of difference practiced in the British, French, and Japanese empires, those practiced in the Russian empire would ultimately determine the geopolitical and ethnocultural configurations on display in today's People's Republic. Due to Russia's geographical proximity, superior military technology, transportation networks, and economic resources, Han officials posted along the northern and western borderlands ignored their neighbor at their own peril. In fact, more often than not, whenever Han rulers saw fit to import Russian political innovations into their own non-Han jurisdictions, they did so as part of a defensive strategy designed to counterbalance an offensive version of the same tactic first introduced by the Russians.

The concept of imperial repertoires is essential to understanding the specific types of institutions and strategies of difference employed in support of late imperial and early Republican rule in Xinjiang. These can be thought of not as "a bag of tricks dipped into at random nor a preset formula for rule," but rather the evolving tools of governance that imperial elites could envision on the basis of past precedents, cultural habits, geopolitical context, and rival innovations.[6] Flexible in nature, they tended to evolve from a pragmatic impulse to pursue the path of least resistance in securing the loyalties of diverse constituencies. At any given moment during the twentieth century, the changing repertoires of Chinese rule in Xinjiang are best viewed as a sort of administrative cabinet of "best practices," an imperial portfolio of governing tactics whose contents were culled from domestic precedent and contemporary foreign models. Successful Chinese rule in Xinjiang during the twentieth century depended upon up-to-date knowledge and innovative application of portable repertoires of differentiated rule then circulating through the various empires of Eurasia.

A number of specific precedents would have been familiar to Governor Yang as he assumed his new post in 1912, less than a year after the Wuchang uprising: territorial accommodation, dependent intermediaries, supranational civic ideology, deflection of ethnic tensions, and narratives of legitimacy.

TERRITORIAL ACCOMMODATION

The institutionalization of difference in units of territorial administration has long been a hallmark of empire. For most of the imperial era in China, the driving force behind such demarcations was the "northern hybrid state." These political entities combined the military advantages of an Inner Asian conquest elite with the cultural, economic, and administrative resources of the Han heartland. The largest and most successful empires in continental East Asia invariably evinced strong northern and northwestern associations.[7] Whenever pastoral peoples from the "northern zone" managed to incorporate the sedentary agricultural communities of the south into their state, however, they continued to treat the Han heartland as a distinct economic, cultural, religious, and political unit. While the "inner provinces" (*neisheng*) were intended to provide most of the wealth, labor, administrative knowledge, and cultural resources necessary to run a massive empire, Mongolia, Tibet, Manchuria, and Xinjiang were chiefly envisioned as strategic bulwarks unique to the geopolitical concerns of an Inner Asian conquest dynasty. As such, they were not expected to finance their own administrative and military expenses, and instead drew massive subsidies of silver—known as "shared funds" (*xiexiang*)—from the wealthy interior. Their special status was captured in the name of the government office tasked with their administration during the Qing: the Court for Managing the External (Lifanyuan). Whether envisioned as a "dependent territory" (*shudi*) or an "outer dependency" (*tulergi golo* in Manchu), the point was that Xinjiang and other non-Han territories were different, and this difference should be recognized in the territorial institutions through which they were governed.[8]

In practice, this meant that a political map of Qing Xinjiang would have evinced composite layers of jurisdictional units, which claimed varying degrees of autonomy and ties with Beijing. Some of these geographical units—Ili, Tarbagatai, and Khobdo among them—were governed by Manchu and Mongol bannermen dispatched from Beijing. Others, such as the Muslim khanates of southern and eastern Xinjiang, were hereditary fiefdoms granted by the Manchu court to the descendants of the indigenous Turkic supporters of the initial Qing conquest of Xinjiang in the 1750s. Muslim princes retained control over the tax-producing resources of their districts, the most prominent of which were located in Hami, Turpan, Kucha, and Khotan. Though cultural and social links persisted among these Muslim khanates, the relationship was ultimately oriented toward Beijing, where each prince and his entourage were expected to participate in a periodic round of pilgrimage to present tribute to the emperor. The end result very much resembled a so-called hub-and-spoke patronage network, "where each spoke was attached to the center but was less directly related to the others." Ideally, horizontal intercourse among the constituent parts—such as marriages—could be undertaken only through the center (Beijing).[9]

During the first decade of the republic, this patchwork legacy of territorial and administrative layering induced seemingly unending political headaches for Governor Yang Zengxin. Faced with numerous geopolitical crises in and around these semiautonomous regions, Yang found it almost impossible to force their officials to do his bidding. Making matters even more difficult for Yang was the fact that his rivals enjoyed their own lines of communication with Beijing, thereby allowing them to bypass the governor's censors in Urumchi. It should come as no surprise, then, to learn that Yang made it a high priority to eliminate these autonomous jurisdictions. From 1915 to 1921, the governor, aided by geopolitical crises occasioned by the Russian civil war, successfully lobbied for the abolition of the Ili general, Tarbagatai councilor, and Altay minister. In fact, the present-day borders of Xinjiang are largely a result of Yang's efforts to create an administratively homogenous provincial unit free from internal challenges to his rule.

Yet a crucial caveat is in order. Whereas Yang was only too happy to aggrandize the authority of those (mostly) Han officials sent by Beijing to fill military posts once reserved for the Inner Asian conquest elite, he did not apply the same model of aggrandizement to the indigenous non-Han nobility of the province. Partly this was for the simple reason that the Qing court had already done away with most of them. By the time Yang became governor, the Muslim princes of Turfan, Kucha, and Khotan existed in name only, having been divested of their economic and military prerogatives during the reforming zeal of the late Qing. Yet the prince of Hami, Shah Maqsut, still lorded over his khanate in both name and substance. Yang Zengxin, over a period of nearly two decades, never saw fit to continue the late Qing trend of depriving the indigenous

FIGURE 1.1. Yang Zengxin, governor of Xinjiang, 1912–28. The longest-serving governor in the history of Xinjiang, Yang consistently promoted a conservative ethno-elitist platform and was quick to suppress all nationalist platforms, including those that valorized "the yellow race." He was assassinated in July 1928, mere months after this photograph was taken. Sven Hedin Foundation collection, Museum of Ethnography, Stockholm.

Muslim nobility of Xinjiang of their hereditary privileges by eliminating the last Muslim prince of Hami. In fact, he often decried the integrationist thrust of late Qing reforms in Xinjiang, lamenting how Xinjiang had become a "colony" (*zhimindi*) of the inner provinces.

The cumulative picture to emerge from Yang's efforts, then, is as follows. Regarding as a mistake the designation of Xinjiang as a province in 1884, Yang moved to restore a foundation of institutionalized difference in Xinjiang, which he regarded as a land distinct from the inner provinces. To do this, he needed to eliminate those semiautonomous offices traditionally filled by appointees from Beijing, for these extended into Xinjiang a volatile continuity with the centralization and integrationist efforts of the late Qing state. In their place, Yang staffed his provincial bureaucracy with veteran Qing officials of the northwest and reserved criticism for those who ventured to govern the non-Han borderlands without prior experience in the field. In effect, he was recreating the principles of territorial accommodation once prevalent in Xinjiang prior to the last decades of the Qing, complete with a new occupational caste modeled on the Inner Asian conquest elite once assigned sole responsibility for the non-Han borderlands. These men were Han officials who had spent most, if not all, of their careers in the northwest.

Without a doubt, Yang manipulated this legacy of territorial difference for his own purposes. Yet part of the reason he managed to stay in power for seventeen years is precisely because he recognized the very real conditions of difference bequeathed him by his Qing predecessors. According to Yang, Xinjiang, though still a province in name, must be treated differently from the Han heartland. Otherwise, as he was fond of telling anyone who would listen, it just might become "the next Outer Mongolia." In 1955, the Chinese Communists, in repudiating Xinjiang's provincial status and designating it the Uighur Autonomous Region—effectively restoring the early Qing distinction between "inner" and "outer" domains—gave formal sanction to what Yang had long acknowledged in practice.

DEPENDENT INTERMEDIARIES

Closely associated with the aforementioned structures of territorial accommodation, dependent intermediaries generally belonged to one of four categories: indigenous elites from a conquered society (e.g., the Muslim princes of Xinjiang); members of the ruling caste intentionally displaced from their homeland (e.g., Manchu, Mongol, and Han bannermen); learned members of a previously marginal group who improved their lot by serving the new power (e.g., Jews, Armenians, Germans, Tatars, and Jesuits); and members of a stigmatized group suddenly placed in a position of authority (e.g., slaves and eunuchs).[10] What these groups had in common, however, was utter dependence on a transcendent authority, who in turn entrusted them with the most sensitive and strategic of tasks. Though certain types of dependent intermediaries were more prevalent in Han-dominated polities than in the northern hybrid states—the Ming emperors, for instance, employed at least five times as many eunuchs as did their Manchu successors—Qing emperors habitually made use of representatives from each of these four categories.

Due to the strategic nature of the posting, these dependent intermediaries played a particularly important role along the non-Han borderlands. In fact, until the late nineteenth century, the only post a successful Han graduate of the civil service examination system could hope to obtain was one located within the inner provinces. Mongols and Manchus, however, could serve in both the heartland and the non-Han borderlands. Thus, when Wang Shunan and Yang Zengxin were transferred to Xinjiang in 1906 and 1907, respectively, both were representatives of the first generation of Han officials to govern the non-Han borderlands in over a thousand years, all the way back to the Tang dynasty. Yet they quickly learned the tools of the trade. During the four decades of the republic in Xinjiang, Chinese governors would make full use of Tatar expatriates, Manchu bannermen (the Solon and Sibe), White Russian soldiers, the Muslim prince of Hami, Mongol and Kazak princes and chiefs, Turkic *begs*, and Hui (Chinese-speaking Muslims) soldiers.

Prior to the reassertion of central government control in Xinjiang during the 1940s, the goal of Han governors of the republican era was to redirect the loyalties of these dependent intermediaries away from their traditional orientation toward Beijing and recalibrate the relationship back toward the administration in Urumchi. Unlike the approach to rival Han generals stationed throughout the province, the goal was not to eliminate Xinjiang's dependent intermediaries. In the final analysis, Yang and his successors, in dealing with matters of religious, cultural, economic, or political import, aimed to position themselves as chief arbiters over the affairs of their dependent intermediaries, whom they generally recognized as continuing to play a critical role in mediating Han rule among their subjects. So long as they continued to acknowledge their vertical relationship within the hub-and-spoke network of the Chinese administration in Urumchi, their livelihoods were typically safeguarded.

When Shah Maqsut, the Muslim prince of Hami, attempted to break free of such constraints, he met with stiff resistance from Governor Yang. In 1914, the prince requested permission to make his scheduled pilgrimage to Beijing via the Trans-Siberian Railway in Russia, bypassing the costly and time-consuming camel paths through inner China. Yang begged the republican administration in Beijing not to set what he considered to be a dangerous precedent. "If the prince enters Beijing through Russia and traverses thousands of miles in a foreign land," he wrote, "he will see with his own eyes the material prosperity and superior transportation of the outside world. . . . It will then be very difficult for us to prevent him from becoming disaffected at heart."[11] When the central government seconded Yang's stance, Maqsut was forced to trod the well-worn caravan routes of the inner provinces. In overruling Shah Maqsut's request, the early republican government, not yet plagued by warlordism, was acting in a manner familiar to contemporary European empires. In 1919, when the paramount chief of Basutoland visited Britain for an audience with King George V, he was refused permission to proceed to Rome out of fear that he "might be unduly impressed by the pomp and state of reception at the Vatican, and might form the conclusion that the Pope was more important than the King."[12] Though both states had a vested interest in sponsoring initiatives that reinforced ties of politically conservative difference, such difference was beneficial to the state only if it was oriented toward its own metropole.

The Hami prince got his revenge in Beijing by circulating accusations of obstruction and sabotage against Governor Yang, who in turn directed his own brother, Yang Zengbing, to refute these accusations in the capital.[13] Whatever the truth of Shah Maqsut's grievances, however, it is important to note that Yang never saw fit to complete the course of late Qing reforms that had already divested Maqsut's fellow Muslim princes of their khanates. Quite the contrary: no matter how much trouble Shah Maqsut created for the Han administration in Urumchi, Yang seems never seriously to have considered abolishing his khanate. And yet the troubles Maqsut brought about were indeed serious. "The prince of Hami has treated his subjects so cruelly," Yang observed in 1915, "that in 1907 and 1912 the people twice rose against him in great rebellions." When the British archaeologist Aurel Stein passed through Hami in 1907, he too marveled at what the local prince could get away with. Describing Maqsut as "a Muhammadan local chief whom the Chinese have found politic to keep in power," Stein noted the ways he "squeezes his people far more than the most rapacious Amban [Qing official] would," resulting in "a little riot some weeks before my arrival, which, owing to the Wang's [prince's] possessing a supply of Mauser rifles, ended quickly with a good deal of needless bloodshed."[14]

Stein did not know the full story, however. A rebellion stemming from the misrule of Shah Maqsut did not constitute a piddling affair from which the Han governor in Urumchi could remain aloof. In the end, the Chinese administration in Urumchi took chief responsibility for costly military operations and the restoration of peace and order within the Hami prince's jurisdiction. After the 1912 uprising, Yang even went so far as to invite the chief rebel, Timur, to take up a minor military post in Urumchi. When Shah Maqsut reneged on his promise to reduce the corvée labor imposed on his Turkic subjects, Timur began to plot his return to Hami. Yang, apprised of the imminent renewal of hostilities, finally made his loyalties clear. Timur was arrested and executed, while Shah

Maqsut continued to lord over his khanate for another two decades, leaving this world much as he had come into it. Had Yang been looking for an excuse to rid himself of a troublesome Muslim peer, this was it.[15] In 1930, when Yang's successor, Jin Shuren, seized on Shah Maqsut's death as a pretext to finally abolish the khanate, a massive rebellion—one of the pivotal events of chapters 2 and 3—eventually broke out. Even then, envoys sent by the new Nationalist government in Nanjing managed to track down Maqsut's son and promise him the restoration of his father's khanate should the Nationalists emerge triumphant in Urumchi.

To Han officials in Xinjiang, the political value of retaining what many outsiders regarded as anachronistic relics of feudal administration extended far beyond a handful of khanates. Throughout the southern oases, Yang saw fit to keep in place the system of local Turkic *begs*, village headmen who assumed responsibility for the affairs of their communities. Formerly a hereditary post under the Qing, the *begs* under Governor Yang were a diverse group: some indeed inherited their positions, while others rose to prominence through economic or religious stature. One thing is clear, however. Despite the egregious corruption carried out under the cloak of their rank, Yang had absolutely no interest in undercutting *beg* privileges. Xie Bin, while acknowledging that Governor Yang was a "brilliant and level-headed administrator, perhaps foremost throughout the nation," nonetheless criticized him for "having made virtually no attempt to eliminate the manifold abuses and exploitative practices of these *begs*."[16]

In addition to the Muslim nobility and local Turkic notables such as *begs*, Yang Zengxin also presided over a vast hierarchy of Mongol and Kazak princes and khans who looked to the governor to secure their interests. The case of a merchant debt owed to the khan of the Torgut Mongols in Karashahr in 1919 will illustrate this point. Having sold seven hundred head of cattle to a Russian merchant who later defaulted on his payments, the khan looked to Chinese officials to pursue his debt. Yang's minister of foreign affairs, Zhang Shaobo, pestered the Russian consul in Urumchi, who wanted nothing to do with the case. "This was originally just a private business transaction between the khan and said Russian

FIGURE 1.2. Che Yuheng, magistrate of Khotan, with his Muslim *begs*, 1906. Though the office of the *beg* (local headsman) was formally abolished after 1884, they continued to serve as unofficial "dependent intermediaries" to Han and Manchu officials in Xinjiang throughout the late Qing and early Republican era. Despite the egregious corruption widely acknowledged to exist within the ranks of these *begs*, Yang Zengxin deemed it prudent to preserve their influence and functions during his tenure as governor. From M. Aurel Stein, *Ruins of Desert Cathay*, vol. 1, 220–21.

merchant," replied the consul, then besieged by the Russian civil war. "Seeing as my consulate did not purchase the cattle, this matter does not concern us." The temptation to lobby—and *to be seen* lobbying—on the khan's behalf, however, was simply too strong to pass up. Zhang continued to force the issue, demanding that the beleaguered czarist consul produce the debt. Most importantly, Zhang also made sure that copies of his protests were forwarded to Karashahr, so that the Mongol khan knew exactly who was looking out for his welfare.[17]

Last but not least were the services offered by "people who had earlier been marginal and could see advantages in serving the victorious
power."[18] In twentieth-century Xinjiang, this designation—which in
other Eurasian empires often denoted Jews, Armenians, and Germans—
referred to Tatars and White Russians. Members of both these groups
would find themselves violently displaced by the Russian civil war, and
both possessed invaluable skills and resources to offer Han rulers in
Xinjiang. By far the most famous Tatar under Governor Yang—as well
as under a staggering eight administrations, until his death in 1989—
was a man by the name of Burhan Shahidi. Originally a merchant and
fur trader, Burhan, fluent in Uighur, Chinese, and Russian, held countless job descriptions during his seven-decade career. He makes a cameo
appearance in the diary of Eleanor Lattimore, wife of the noted Inner
Asian historian Owen Lattimore. During her time in Turfan, Eleanor
notes how she and Owen were called upon by "a Tatar gentleman whom
Owen had met in Urumchi, some sort of an agent of the governor who
happened to be in Turfan on business, and who took it upon himself to
be our host, found us our cool room to live in and invited us to an all day
picnic at Grape Valley."[19] Six years earlier, Burhan had witnessed his
life and livelihood upended by the Russian civil war. Commenting on
his application to adopt Chinese citizenship—surely a novel experience
for a Han official at this time—Yang noted Burhan's "considerable family assets, his respectable bearing, and the high esteem he holds among
Russian merchant circles." Bringing this Tatar under Yang's wing, the
governor wrote, could only bring "numerous advantages for us."[20]

Men like Burhan were attractive to Chinese officials precisely because
they had nowhere else to go. Thus, much like the eunuchs of yesteryear, they could be entrusted with the most sensitive of tasks. Burhan
was not a Uighur, yet he spoke their language and could be accepted
as one of them. He was not a Russian, yet he could move seamlessly
through Russian social and political circles, and then share with Han
officials his knowledge of developments across the border. Whereas
the White Russians, bereft of an alternative sanctuary, offered modern
military armaments, organization, and battlefield tactics, someone

like Burhan offered invaluable intellectual and administrative services honed abroad. As a result of his unique background, Burhan was well equipped to adapt to one of the most significant developments to affect the politics of difference during the twentieth century. Prior to the Russian civil war and the unwelcome arrival of White and Red partisans across China's northern borderlands, the foundation of ethnopolitical difference both in China and elsewhere had been built upon a conservative alliance of ethnic and religious elites. This discourse, reflecting as it did the interests of Manchu and Mongol nobles, their Han civil servants, and a largely hereditary non-Han elite, will be referred to throughout this study as "ethno-elitism."

Yang Zengxin, though obliged to pay lip service to Confucian platitudes of patrimonial concern for "the people," relied heavily upon the high Qing discourse of ethno-elitism. The most concrete emblem of Yang's adherence to this platform is to be found in his Xinjiang Provincial Assembly, established as a concession to republican forms, if not substance. The job of this assembly, stocked with prominent Mongol princes and Muslim royalty, was to lend legitimacy to the words of a Han governor in Xinjiang by issuing sensitive or otherwise controversial decrees in its own name rather than that of the governor. When Jin Shuren, Yang's successor as governor (1928–33), encountered resistance from the Nationalist government in Nanjing regarding the assumption of his predecessor's titles, he trotted out the same Mongol and Muslim nobles to speak on his behalf. "It is said that the authorities are extremely anxious regarding the lack of a response from the central government," noted Xu Bingxu, the Chinese codirector of the Sino-Swedish Scientific Expedition then resident in Urumchi. "So today they sent a telegram to Nanjing under the names of the Mongol and Muslim princes requesting the confirmation of [Jin's] position."[21] The strategic calculus on display here is quite clear: if no dissent is evident among the Mongol and Muslim elite enjoying the patronage of the Han governor in Xinjiang—and the Provincial Assembly took great care to project just such an image—how could anyone from outside the province justify disrupting the status quo?

The answer lies in the realization that Yang's Provincial Assembly, like nearly every one of his tools of governance, could undermine only competing platforms of ethno-elitist difference, such as those put forth by czarist, British, or Japanese rivals. It had no answer for an entirely new discourse of difference that was soon to sweep across the political landscape of the former Russian empire, a form that we refer to in this study as "ethnopopulism." This new version of political legitimization shared with ethno-elitism the goal of justifying the rule of alien elites in an unfamiliar ethnocultural milieu. Where it differed was in its identification of the non-Han (in China) or non-Russian (in the Soviet Union) masses as the rhetorical pivot upon which alien rule would continue to be justified. Instead of claiming to secure and protect the interests of ethnic or religious elites—who in turn usually invoked some sort of divine or hereditary right to their position—the discourse of ethnopopulism claimed to champion the ethnopolitical enfranchisement of the indigenous common people, now portrayed as downtrodden and oppressed by corrupt and feudal ethnoreligious elites. The ethnopopulist platform, first institutionalized along the borders of Xinjiang by the Bolsheviks in the 1920s, attempted to cultivate a new narrative of political legitimacy. It did so via promises to help shepherd "backward" minority peoples toward their very own unit of territorial and political autonomy, be it a sizable republic within a federation or a smaller region within a republic.

That the ethnopopulist discourse of the Bolsheviks was related to the broader discourse of the nation-state is not in doubt. Yet there was a clear difference. Whereas the discourse of the nation-state was used by the Allied powers after World War I to dismember the German, Austro-Hungarian, and Ottoman empires along putative "national" lines, Soviet ethnopopulism was designed to "disarm" the national ideal by granting the forms of nationhood *before* potential rivals could do the same. In essence, the goal was to reconfigure the politics of difference away from its conservative origins and toward a progressive future, one defined in opposition to—and intended to defuse—the nationalist threat. Another way of looking at Soviet innovations to the politics of difference is to say that at the very moment when the idea of the "nation" was deployed as

an offensive weapon for the first time in systematic and coercive fashion—the Allied dismantling of the Central Powers—the Bolsheviks managed to devise a "defensive" strategy designed to combat the possibility
of just such a tool being used against their own multiethnic state.

In some ways, these ongoing innovations in the politics of difference
during the twentieth century in Xinjiang resemble the shifting criteria for
political legitimacy in the Han heartland after the Communist takeover
in 1949. The chief form of political capital in China prior to 1949—the
"expert" knowledge of long-standing social and cultural elites—vacil-
lated with a new form of political legitimacy after 1949, one that valorized humble origins, practical peasant knowledge, and unadorned
revolutionary enthusiasm. The "red" versus "expert" pendulum continued to swing back and forth until the Cultural Revolution, when the ideal
of the combined "red expert" finally emerged triumphant.[22] Similarly,
in the following narrative, we find a conservative ethno-elitist form of
difference, invoked since the earliest empires, forced to compete with a
progressive ethnopopulist form of difference imported from the Soviet
Union during the Russian civil war. Deployed against one another off
and on throughout the 1930s and 1940s, the progressive platform of
ethnopopulism would emerge the victor after 1949, but not before it
created a new class of dependent intermediaries scarcely distinguish-
able in class and occupation from their conservative predecessors. It did
not take long before the ethnopopulist intermediaries of the Communist
era, men like Burhan Shahidi and Saypiddin Azizi, mastered the art of
speaking for the people while partaking of the same elite power structure
that ensured their separation from those very people.

SUPRANATIONAL CIVIC IDEOLOGY

All large and diverse states need to develop a cosmopolitan civic ideology
capable of bridging those very differences that its own governing practices often serve to accentuate. In other words, the foremost goal of any
metropole is to hold itself up as a sponsor of difference—whether ethno-

elitist or ethnopopulist—while simultaneously orienting that difference toward its own center of political gravity. The tool used to facilitate this reorientation process is a supranational civic ideology that stresses real and imagined commonalities among the various subjects of the state, who otherwise may have little in common. Though the Qing court went to great lengths to institutionalize Manchu and Mongol privilege and to circumscribe areas of perceived Han dominance, its Manchu emperors made it clear from the start that their possession of the Heavenly Mandate—and their concomitant right to rule China—did not stem from any inherent birthright. Instead, it arose from their possession of "virtue" (*de*), an abstract political concept unbeholden to ethnic or national prisms. "The empire is not an individual's private empire," proclaimed the regent of the first emperor. "Whosoever possesses virtue, holds it."[23]

The revolutionary ferment of the late Qing dynasty, often expressed in the uncompromising discourse of militant Han nationalism, did much to undermine the supranational Confucian ideology that had long undergirded empires throughout East Asian history. In fact, we might say that, after 1911, the greatest threat to a successful reorientation of non-Han loyalties to an inner Chinese metropole lay in the widespread fear that the strident rhetoric of revolutionary Han nationalists might one day be translated into equally intolerant institutions of chauvinist Han rule. During the twentieth century, such fears were embodied via the widespread perception of a normative alignment of "nation" and "state." Both the Republic of China and the People's Republic of China chose to harness the Sinic compound *zhonghua* (lit. "central florescence") to represent the "China" of their official state names. Derived from the shifting and vague cognates of *zhongguo* ("the central states" or "central plains," i.e., "China") and *huaxia* (the "florescent and grand" community of civilized people), Zhonghua is the ostensible embodiment of the ideals of enlightened inclusion, not xenophobic exclusion. After all, there was no historical precedent for *zhonghua*'s linguistic derivatives, *zhongguo* and *huaxia*, to serve as fixed markers of rigid ethnic identities. Quite to the contrary, they served as flexible and ever-shifting points of reference for vague categories of political and cultural identification.[24]

The Han-led revolutionary struggle against the Manchus, however, initiated a dramatic reconceptualization of these terms that has continued for more than a century now. In attempting to bend an imprecise premodern intellectual inheritance into the rigid classificatory parameters of a modern national history, post-Qing Chinese theorists have effectively equated both *zhongguo* (China) and *huaxia* (the civilized culture sphere) with the ethnic—and virtually genetic—inheritance of a newly defined "Han" people. Prior to the twentieth century, such a strict and overt alignment of political and ethnic identity had never before been articulated for any group defined as "Han."[25] As a result, any Han official who found himself in power along the non-Han borderlands of the twentieth-century Chinese state had to deal with the common perception that he represented the very embodiment of chauvinist Han interests. One way to combat this perception was for Han officials to make a public show of protecting the livelihoods and customs of the non-Han peoples against the perceived assimilationist juggernaut of the majority Han. For Governor Yang Zengxin, cut from the ideological cloth of a loyal Qing civil servant, this was easily accomplished. Until his death in 1928, suppression of Han nationalism was the order of the day. In 1919, when a pamphlet of military songs exhorting the Han people to rise up and "wipe clean our national humiliation" was brought to Yang's attention, he ordered its immediate confiscation and destruction. The pride its authors took in their "yellow skin" was incompatible with the universalist teachings of the Confucian canon upon which he had consistently based his own narrative of legitimacy.[26]

The passing of Yang and the old imperial order in Xinjiang, however, coincided with the appearance of an innovative rhetorical tactic first peddled by Chiang Kai-shek's newly established Nationalist government in Nanjing. To one degree or another, each successive administration to occupy the Chinese metropole would attempt to defuse hostile charges of "Han chauvinism"—the kryptonite of any cosmopolitan civil discourse—by engaging in highly visible theatrics involving the public scapegoating of a Han villain associated with Xinjiang. Though such scapegoats were preferably Han men buried safely in the distant past, the most desperate administrations were willing to skewer anyone. Thus in the 1930s, the Nationalist government, shut out of Xinjiang entirely, pounced on the opportunity to arraign fleeing Han governor Jin Shuren on formal charges of exploiting and otherwise oppressing the non-Han peoples of Xinjiang. The trial, covered widely in the media and associated with expatriate Uighur intellectuals operating under Nanjing's umbrella, gave the Nationalists a stage on which to advertise their ethnopolitical enlightenment with respect to the non-Han borderlands. Just one decade later, they would push the envelope considerably farther by condoning Uighur periodicals that took "the bloodthirsty swords of the tyrannical Chinese butchers" and criticisms of then-governor Wu Zhongxin as their topics of discussion. Much like the early Soviet state, which found it expedient from time to time to make a grand show of criticizing Russian "chauvinism," the Chinese Communists similarly initiated periods of overt criticism directed at the majority Han. Common to each case, however, was the strategic desire to shore up the integrity of a supranational civic ideology by undercutting the novelty of rival charges of mainstream ethnic chauvinism.

DEFLECTION OF ETHNIC TENSIONS

As much as possible, it is in the interest of imperial elites to devise ways of deflecting the association of indigenous bloodshed with rulers considered to be ethnically and culturally different from their subjects. During much of their conquest of the inner provinces, for instance, the Qing prudently delegated prosecution of major battles to loyal Han generals, who shed the blood of other Han on the government's behalf. In early republican Xinjiang, Governor Yang Zengxin made it a guiding principle of his administration that Han commoners were best kept out of Xinjiang altogether, and that those who remained in the province should not be tasked with suppression of native discontent. Because this approach differed from that endorsed by late Qing reforms, which had fostered the establishment of Han-dominated New Armies in Urumchi and Ili, Yang justified his stance by reference to other successful empires of his day. "When the British conquered India," he wrote in 1913, "they did so by making use of native Indian soldiers. When the French took over Vietnam, they did so by making use of native Vietnamese soldiers. Under no circumstances did they make exclusive use of outside troops [*kebing*]."[27]

In Xinjiang, Yang attempted to mimic the British and French approach to their empires by organizing an army composed largely of Hui soldiers whose families and livelihoods were rooted in the province. According to Yang, not only were these Chinese-speaking Muslims "fierce by nature and excellent fighters," but they "all had property and family to which they could return," thus making it easy to decommission them. "Had I conscripted itinerant Han, however, it would now be very difficult to get them to disperse."[28] As a result, entrusting military bloodshed to loyal Hui, whose historical enmities with the Uighurs ran deep, carried logistical and tactical advantages for a Han governor. In addition to enlisting the Hui, Yang continued to call upon the Sibe and Solon, two military castes ensconced in the Ili valley whose members were descended from Manchu bannermen who had assisted in the initial conquest of Xinjiang in the eighteenth century. Perhaps most important were the various Mongol banners stationed in and around Karashahr, Altay, and Tarbagatai, whose fearsome cavalry was a reminder of the prominent role these Mongols once held as privileged "partners" of the Qing conquest elite. In 1931–32, the refusal of the Torgut Mongols in Karashahr to assist Governor Jin Shuren in suppressing the rebellion in Hami ultimately hastened his downfall. Thereafter, the armed mobility of the Mongols seems largely to have been supplanted by White Russian soldiers, who played key roles in the military battles of the 1930s and 1940s.

As for the Uighurs and Kazaks, who together constituted more than 80 percent of the population of Xinjiang, neither were deemed fit for formal military service. The Kazaks were occasionally tapped for light paramilitary duties, such as that witnessed by Owen Lattimore in Tacheng. He noted their obligation to "beat up any night wanderer who is not in a respectable sleigh or provided with a lantern; a duty they can perform all the better for not being able to listen to excuses." The Uighurs, however, referred to in Chinese documents of the day as "Turban Heads" (*chan-*

tou), were best kept away from arms and munitions altogether. Yang's official explanation was that they did "not possess knowledge or experience with regard to military service." Though this was largely true, it was mostly a by-product of the Qing's long-standing reluctance to arm their non-Han Muslim subjects rather than due to any innate characteristics of the Uighurs as a people.[29]

Thus far, the evidence seems to suggest that Yang did not maintain a Han army. He did. The difference, however, lay in the unique roles assigned to his Han soldiers. On the one hand, there were several crack contingents left over from the Qing era, formerly the pride of the New Armies or reformed secret society members. Into their arms Yang entrusted the most expensive and dangerous weapons, including the first machine guns ever fired by a Chinese soldier in Xinjiang. And yet, as any list of battlefield engagements in Xinjiang during Yang's tenure as governor will show, these elite Han units were deployed mostly against outside threats—in other words, against foreigners (i.e., Russians) and warlord armies from inner China.[30] The governor sent them to fight Russians and Mongols during a joint invasion of Khobdo in 1912, and he entrusted them with the governor's precious machine guns during the siege of Gucheng in 1921 by the White Russian general Boris Annenkov. Aside from these elite but seldom-used Han units, Yang also kept a tatterdemalion throng of Han toughs drawn from what he referred to as the opium-smoking vagrant population. Numerous foreigners commented on their disheveled and miserable appearance. By all accounts, the units to which this Han rabble were assigned appear to have functioned as little more than a holding ground for social undesirables that Yang wished to keep off the streets. They seem rarely, if ever, to have been ordered into action, and it is difficult to imagine that the native populace took them as a credible threat. More often than not, they were mocked and lampooned as dregs of the Han race whom the governor thought best to place under organized watch rather than let them roam free through the non-Han streets of Xinjiang.

During the nearly two decades when Yang Zengxin was in power, the most prudent military approach to a non-Han region cut off from metropole support was to ensure that organized attacks on the indigenous peoples of Xinjiang were not directly associated with the Han officials who had countenanced such violence in the first place. Off the battlefield, Han governors also had to consider the deleterious effects of the inevitable influx of Han migrants from the inner provinces. Manchu and Mongol officials had already found the regulation of such migrants—most of whom came illegally—to be a difficult task in the late eighteenth and early nineteenth centuries. The integrationist policies of the late Qing exacerbated this problem by promoting the "reclamation" of "wastelands" in the decades following Zuo Zongtang's reconquest of the region. By the time Yang Zengxin became governor, such migrants had become a threat to the stability of the province. "Over the past several decades," he lamented in 1914, "Xinjiang has become the colony [zhimindi] of the inner provinces." The following year the governor implored Beijing to stop sponsoring such aggressive policies. "What good can come from sending more vagrants beyond the pass?" he asked. "They bring with them nothing but trouble."[31] With the collapse of central authority in China following the death of President Yuan Shikai in 1916, Yang found it much easier to insulate Xinjiang from Han migrants. Indeed, though estimates vary, it seems likely that the Han population in Xinjiang did not exceed 10 percent of the population until well into the 1950s, and may even have been as low as 5 percent at times. Governor Yang, eager to downplay the Han presence, was wont to claim that the Han comprised less than one out of every hundred residents of Xinjiang.[32]

After a brief attempt in the early 1930s to resettle Han refugees from neighboring Gansu ended in disaster (see chapter 2), two more decades would pass before a central government emerged strong enough to enforce its authority in Xinjiang. When it did, however, one of the first items of business for the Communists—like the Nationalists before them—was to plan for a major influx of Han migrants, who were viewed as necessary to supply manpower for ambitious agricultural and industrialization projects (the subject of chapter 5). So long as rival powers such as the Soviet Union were strong and retained economic interests in the province, however, such plans were fraught with danger. As the Nationalist government would learn a decade before the Communists did, any blueprint for Han migration to Xinjiang offered a rhetorical tool—most often in the form of labels such as "colonialism"—with which rivals of the state could fan opposition to Chinese rule. Though it would not protect them from the application of such labels following the Sino-Soviet split—the Soviets immediately dusted off rhetorical salvos regarding "Han colonialism" that had proven so useful in the 1940s—the Chinese Communists did bring with them a more sophisticated rhetorical regime designed to justify the droves of Han migrants who arrived in Xinjiang after 1949. Much like Russian migrants to the non-Russian borderlands of the Soviet Union, Han migrants to Xinjiang were consistently presented as selfless "elder brother" guides who would bring prosperity to a poverty-stricken land. Whether anyone in Xinjiang actually believed this, from the historian's perspective, it merely constituted the latest attempt by Han rulers in Xinjiang to deflect association with ethnic tensions expected to arise as a result of policies their detractors portrayed as a repudiation of the politics of difference.

NARRATIVES OF LEGITIMACY

Han rulers in twentieth-century Xinjiang devoted inordinate time and resources to crafting personal narratives of legitimacy. Unlike a supranational civic ideology, which deals with ostensibly universal concepts of an abstract nature and may prove equally applicable to competing actors over many centuries, narratives of legitimacy were personal and specific to the person in office. Why should Yang Zengxin be allowed to govern Xinjiang, as opposed to one of his many rivals, some of whom were Muslim? What gave the Communists the right to march into Xinjiang and displace the Nationalists? Why, indeed, is one person more fit to rule over an ethnoculturally alien population than another? Because such narratives of legitimacy invariably color much of the discourse here, it is important to understand several characteristics common to each generation.

For Yang Zengxin, the first Han governor of republican Xinjiang, a narrative of legitimacy needed to accomplish two things. First, in an age saturated with the discourse of national determination, it had to explain why a Han official should be permitted to rule a non-Han land. Second, it also needed to explain why Yang was superior to other Han and Hui officials, both those who had come before him and those plotting to replace him. Yang accomplished the first goal by making a clear distinction between himself and those Han governors of the late Qing who had immediately preceded him. "When Xinjiang first became a province," he wrote in 1915, "the early governors . . . all excelled at administration, and their directives demonstrated familiarity with frontier conditions. Afterward, this all changed."[33] What Yang meant was that the earliest Han governors, posted to Xinjiang immediately after its provincialization in 1884, were cut from the same cloth as the Inner Asian conquest elite. These men justified their monopoly on power over the non-Han frontiers by pointing to their intimate familiarity with the northern and western peripheries. We might say that these early Han governors were, in Yang's view, a sort of "honorary" Manchu or Mongol, whose special qualifications made them more fit to rule Xinjiang than were Han who only evinced knowledge of the inner provinces.

Clearly, Yang intended to include himself in this category, as is evident from frequent mentions of his long experience and office in the northwest. In fact, Yang had never held a post in the inner provinces. Born and raised in the far southwestern province of Yunnan, he was posted to the northwestern province of Gansu—home to a large population of Hui—immediately upon passing the imperial examination in 1889. Once, while noting the approximately twenty years he spent as a magistrate in Muslim-dominated counties of Gansu, Yang referred to that province as his "second home." When he traveled to Beijing in 1907 for an audience with the Manchu court, the imperial censor classified Yang as a man uniquely suited to the peripheries, calling him "one of our more capable, important border officials."[34] In managing the process of official appointments in Xinjiang, Yang demonstrated a marked preference for veterans of the Qing state who had spent their entire careers in the northwest. Failing that, he often chose to arrange for the transfer to Xinjiang of Han officials familiar to him from his time in Gansu. Such men, in increasingly short supply as his career dragged on, were often permitted to retain their posts for many years at a time.[35]

More than anything else, Yang's narrative of legitimacy was founded on the notion that he alone represented a return to the politics of difference once practiced by the Mongol and Manchu rulers of Xinjiang during the high Qing era. In his view, those who eschewed the premise that Xinjiang and other borderlands were different—and thus should be governed differently—were largely responsible for the alienation of Tibet and Outer Mongolia during the last decades of the Qing. As he wrote in 1923, the Han "cannot simply blame the Tibetans for the error of their ways; it was the degeneracy of Han officials that first pushed Tibet toward autonomy. The British simply took advantage of our mistakes. Similarly, the autonomy of Outer Mongolia cannot be blamed entirely on the Outer Mongols; it was the degeneracy of Han officials that first pushed the Outer Mongols toward autonomy. The Russians simply took advantage of our mistakes."[36] Clearly, according to Yang, without someone like him in power—a man deeply versed in the conditions of the non-Han periphery—Xinjiang would go the way of Tibet or Outer Mongolia, with little hope of reclamation. So long as the politics of difference was practiced in Xinjiang by a man of the borderlands, however, Yang was confident he could "ensure that indirect rule by the Han is far superior to self-rule by the Muslims and Turbans."[37]

In his telegrams, public pronouncements, and official audiences, Yang constantly advertised his unique ability to understand and interact with his Muslim subjects. The validity of his claims rested largely on the fact that he had lived and served in some of the most difficult Muslim counties of Gansu for nearly two decades prior to his arrival in Xinjiang. During that time, he had forged deep and abiding ties with prominent local Muslim leaders and their families. In 1913, an envoy from the central government in Beijing traveled to Urumchi and recorded a few choice excerpts from his long conversations with the governor: "During his tenure [in Gansu, Yang] took the daughter of a Muslim surnamed Ma as his concubine. This Ma was a man of great talent and ability, well versed in the classics and history, proficient in the art of boxing, and an expert in swordplay. As a result, Yang enjoys harmonious relations with the Muslim people."[38] In practice, the logic of cause and effect was probably reversed here: it was unlikely that taking a Muslim concubine in itself had led to "harmonious relations" with the Muslim people. Rather, harmonious relations with the Muslims had most likely led to taking the concubine. Regardless, in arranging a strategic familial union with prominent Muslim families of the northwest, Yang was acting much as one of the most famous Qing emperors before him. In the late eighteenth century, the Qianlong emperor took the sister of a Muslim Turkic prince from newly conquered Xinjiang as one of his many concubines. In both cases, the abstract symbolism and political ramifications were clear to all.[39]

Yang rarely missed an opportunity to flaunt his detailed knowledge of Muslim scriptures and the complex relationships among the religious schools of the Hui and Uighur peoples under his rule. Not only that, but he frequently contrasted his intimate understanding with the ignorance of his predecessors and rivals. Anthony Garnaut notes that Yang had earned a reputation as a "capable manager" of Hui affairs in Gansu, something for which few late Qing officials won distinction.[40] In analyzing Yang's telegraphic directives to local officials and religious leaders in Xinjiang—subsequently published for the benefit of political observers on the eastern seaboard—one scholar concludes that Yang was "confident" in speaking on behalf of Islamic orthodoxy and evinced an "overriding interest" in "maintaining boundaries"—between natives and foreigners, among various *menhuan* and mosque communities, and between religious practice and other forms of social life.[41] Toward the end of his career, Yang was perceived by educated Han visitors, such as Huang Wenbi, the Chinese archaeologist, as possessing a unique and singular ability to defuse tensions among his Muslim subjects: "Last year [1927] rumors emerged among the Hui that the Han intended to slaughter each and every one of them, and the Hui religious leaders also announced this in their mosques. Fortunately, General Yang was able to adopt measures to defuse the situation, and nothing happened."[42]

It is surely not a coincidence that Yang's personal narrative of legitimacy, as a Han governor who was both a career northwestern official and an honorary Muslim "insider," also served him well in justifying several cases of unsavory bloodshed sanctioned during his time in office.

In 1916, when a group of republican loyalists from Yang's home province of Yunnan plotted his assassination, Yang was quick to arrest and execute them. In explaining his actions—around which much mythical embellishment would later accrue—Yang pointed to the conspirators' "ignorance of border affairs" as their chief retroactive sin, eliding altogether the issue of opposition to the governor's monarchist sympathies. "Had Xia and Li managed to overthrow me," Yang explained one year later, referring to his victims, "there is no guarantee that the Mongol and Muslim tribes would have submitted [to their leadership]. It would then have been very difficult to prevent a war of the races." Therefore, "in the interest of maintaining our borderlands," Yang had "no choice but to execute" the conspirators.[43] He would deploy a similar pretext in 1924 when he decided to send an army to Kashgar to kill Ma Fuxing, a Hui general who Yang had learned was in intimate communication with warlords in Beijing. Rather than acknowledge the bald power politics that lay beneath his actions, Yang chose instead to highlight Ma's oppression of the native Uighur populace, an ongoing tragedy ignored by the governor for nearly a decade. "Now that Ma Fuxing and his son have been eliminated," Yang reasoned after the affair, "the outrage of the Turbans has been appeased, and there will be no further cause for any incidents."[44]

Much of Yang's narrative was premised on simple preservation of the status quo, in opposition to rivals who he alleged would disrupt it. Absent the silver subsidies that Beijing had once directed to Xinjiang from wealthier provinces in the interior, and lacking resources with which to maintain a respectable army, Yang's strategy was basically to circle the wagons and then warn about what might happen if they somehow became uncircled. When his successor sparked a massive civil war interpreted by many of its participants as a war of the races, however, aspiring Han rulers of Xinjiang could no longer champion the existing order, nor could they look to the discredited past for models of narrative legitimacy. As a result, conditions were ripe for a major overhaul of existing ideological paradigms. The twelve-year tenure (1933–44) of Han warlord Sheng Shicai, a man with no experience whatsoever in the non-Han borderlands, witnessed the first steps toward importing a narrative of legitimacy first designed in the Soviet Union. The "affirmative action empire," as historian Terry Martin characterizes it, provided a ready-made model for Han rulers to justify the retention of ethnoculturally dissimilar peoples and their lands. Treated in depth in chapters 3 and 4, the guiding tenets of Soviet affirmative action obliged Han officials to take a proactive role in shaping national identities.

In brief, this new narrative of legitimacy, successively adapted by Sheng, the Nationalists, and later the Communists, cast the Han-led state as an evolutionary sponsor of "less advanced" nationalities toward their fulfillment of "mature" nationhood and some form of political autonomy. A Nationalist official from the Ministry of the Interior put it best when, in 1945, he criticized the tendency in recent decades for Han rulers to shun policies of intervention among the non-Han masses of Xinjiang. "Most countries, in their governance of minority peoples," he wrote, "intervene in all aspects of their affairs, leaving nothing untouched." As a result of Yang's hands-off ethno-elitist approach, however, the non-Han masses, increasingly aware of the ways the Soviets claimed to shepherd their non-Russian masses toward socialist modernity, had begun to "make demands on us to nurture them and get involved in their affairs." Otherwise, "they will simply look to a foreign power to take our place and nurture them in our stead, thereby bringing about progress and modernization." The conclusion was inescapable. "We must completely overhaul our past attitude of letting [non-Han peoples] rise and fall at their own volition, and strive with all our might to nurture their development."[45]

Although this may sound like a blatant repudiation of the politics of difference, it was in fact simply a new innovation within a familiar imperial model. It was certainly true that Han rulers were now intent on "intervening" in the cultural lives of their non-Han subjects. But, as will become clear in the following chapters, such intervention was still carried out in accordance with the tenets of difference. In this case, it was embodied through an ethnopopulist narrative of political legitimacy. As Thomas Mullaney has shown, this process would ultimately culminate in the Communist "fathering" of fifty-six distinct nationalities, united in recognition of the metropole that had institutionalized their nationhood. In Xinjiang, this process had begun under Han warlord Sheng Shicai two decades before the arrival of the Communists. Both Sheng and the Nationalists had taken the unprecedented step of placing non-Han figures into government positions of conspicuous—yet often hollow—authority. Thus, when the Communists decided in 1949 to leave in place the Tatar politician Burhan Shahidi as governor, they were merely building upon the ethnopolitical foundation first constructed by the Soviets and imported across the border by Sheng Shicai and the Nationalists. In fact, the latter own the distinction of appointing the first-ever non-Han governor of Xinjiang.

As is evident in the above quote from a Nationalist official in 1945, by the time the Communists took over in Xinjiang, Han narratives of political legitimacy along the borderlands had become firmly dependent upon promises to keep pace with the latest global trends in ethnocultural engineering—or, as the ministry official put it, the "nurturing" of "minority peoples." After 1949, the Communist state was also able to inject credibility into claims that they alone were capable of bringing economic prosperity to Xinjiang. Among the more novel additions to Han narratives of legitimacy about this time, however, were Communist proclamations that they were responsible for having rectified a century of "national humiliation" (*guochi*). Though the Nationalists were acutely aware of their "humiliation" and frequently promised its imminent reversal, the geopolitical conditions of the day did not allow them to succeed in this endeavor.

For the Communists, however, the discourse of national humiliation—and their purported role in negating it—would become an invaluable strategic tool along the non-Han borderlands. Without fail, on nearly every occasion after 1949 in which Uighurs or Tibetans have engaged in political dissent against the Chinese state, their motives are impugned in a way that Han protests in the heartland are not. As Yang Zengxin recognized nearly a century ago, it is only in those regions of China that Han elites "would not be able to recover" even if "we had an eternity" that Beijing can expect accusations of foreign meddling to sound plausible.

*   *   *

The ethnopolitical milieu into which the first Han governor of the Republic found himself thrust after the 1911 revolution was far from auspicious. British archaeologist Aurel Stein, who began his third expedition and second circuit of the province in 1913, the year after Yang's hasty promotion, recorded a terse summary of the conditions he faced near Kashgar: "Kichik Beg, of Kashgar origin, deplores uncertain condition since there is no Emperor. Though all harvests since 1908, with exception of one were excellent & water abundant, no new lands opened. Want of labour felt. Great drain of labour to Farghana. High prices since a year or two attributed to uncertain political outlook."[46] And yet Yang Zengxin would ultimately remain in power for another sixteen years, all the while lacking a single credible military asset. Writing just four years after Stein, the central government envoy Xie Bin was surprised to find a seemingly anachronistic Chinese administration still ruling over such a vast non-Han land. "When the race of those who wear caps and sashes," Xie observed, referring to Han officials, "rules over a people whose language is unintelligible and with whom no communication either via speech or writing is possible, it has no choice but to use interpreters to reach the people, while relying on local chiefs to implement their policies."[47] In the best of times, Han officials in Xinjiang already faced considerable impediments to the deployment of ethnopolitical policies not detrimental to the peace and stability of the region. To achieve their goals, these officials leveraged every new idea in the transnational global economy of imperial repertoires to buttress their rule. Governor Yang, however, did not rule during the best of times. How he dealt with the nationalist threat to Chinese rule in Xinjiang during the worst of times is the subject of the next chapter.

CHAPTER 2

COLLAPSE OF EMPIRES
AND THE NATIONALIST THREAT

T HE NARRATIVE OF CHINA THAT MOST HISTORIANS ARE FAMIL-
iar with recounts that following the death of President Yuan Shikai in
1916, "warlords" and "ideas" take center stage. In such tellings, the
warlords, charged with having "made national politics look like a game
of musical chairs with guns,"[1] provide the backdrop against which purveyors of progressive ideological agendas begin to lay the foundations
for a new China. More often than not, the landmark political events of
this decade are scrutinized less for their contemporary geopolitical relevance than for the ostensible influence they were believed to exert in
stimulating a new revolutionary movement, the realization of which lay
far in the future.[2] Thus the Treaty of Versailles is linked to the May Fourth
Movement, the Bolshevik revolution to the establishment of two Leninist
party-states, and the May 30th Incident to the Northern Expedition. For
those whose interest in China is limited to the lives and livelihoods of its
ethnocultural majority—Han resident in the inner provinces—this framework of China as a nation beset by imperialists has long proven serviceable. In fact, even when historians look to complicate or otherwise
interrogate this narrative, they still tend to proceed from a conceptual
premise that takes the Han narrative of the nation-state as its normative
focus.

When we adopt the perspective of a Han governor in Xinjiang, however, it quickly becomes apparent just how inadequate the concepts of
"revolution" and "nationalism" are to an understanding of developments outside the Han heartland. As we saw in chapter 1, Governor Yang

Zengxin (1912–28) repeatedly justified his policies in terms of their suit-
ability to "empire," understood to be a type of state that privileges the
institutionalization of ethnic and spatial difference. Seen from this point
of view, the era of the warlords in China (1916–28) and the prolonged
course of the Bolshevik revolution in Russia (1917–23) were marked less
by ideological ferment than by the contest for geopolitical power in Eurasia. In other words, the fate of Han rule in Xinjiang after 1916 allows
us to reframe the following four decades in China not in terms of the
success or failure of the revolution—often viewed as a vehicle for Chinese
nationalism—but rather as the collapse and reconstitution of imperial
authority across Eurasia, as brought about through competing strategies
of difference. When the Bolsheviks, free from the entrenched colonial
interests of outside powers, managed to reconstruct their empire first,
the stage was set for the exportation of a new form of difference to the
non-Han frontier of China, with which the former czarist empire shared
an extensive border.

In Xinjiang, the collapse of imperial authority both in China and in
Russia was experienced almost simultaneously. The stage on which the
initial collapse played out was the Kazak and Kyrgyz refugee crisis of
1916. Long exempt from forcible integration into the political projects
of European Russia, the Turkic-speaking nomads of Russian Turkestan
responded to calls for their conscription to the European war front by
organizing armed resistance throughout the Karakul region. The decision to renounce a long-standing czarist policy of ethnic privilege for
the empire's non-Russian peoples was a repudiation of the politics of
difference, implemented in response to a geopolitical crisis in the metropole: manpower shortages along the Russian front during the Great
War. When the consequences of Saint Petersburg's actions spilled over
into Xinjiang, Governor Yang was able to obtain his first glimpse of the
deterioration of central government authority in the Russian empire. In
attempting to manage the fallout from the Russian collapse within his
own province, however, Yang would also come to realize just how frag-
mented his own Chinese republic had become in the brief time since
President Yuan passed.

RUSSIAN COLLAPSE AND RECONSTITUTION

"Countless Kyrgyz lie dead in the passes, piled one on top of the other. Their frozen corpses, stuck solid to one another, obstruct the mountain roads. It is a sight too horrible to describe."[3] This was the gruesome report forwarded to Governor Yang's desk on October 2, 1916. It described the fates of thousands of Kyrgyz and Kazak nomads who had fled Russian reprisals and ventured up into the Pamir Mountains of western Xinjiang. Informed that Russian authorities had no intention of sparing the remaining 300,000 Kazak and Kyrgyz refugees from a similar fate, Yang Zengxin reflected on the depths to which the Russian state had suddenly plunged. "The mountains are littered with corpses," he wrote. "Russia is supposed to be a great civilized country, with respect for human life. How can they let this happen?"[4] The answer to the governor's question was to be found in the shivering bodies of innocent bystanders, snatched as strategic collateral by fleeing nomads. "When the Kyrgyz fled from Russia," Yang later learned, "they took with them a countless number of white-skinned women and children as hostages. These women and children are now howling from starvation and cold in the passes, their plaintive cries for help unanswered." Before long, Russians armed with machine guns and bayonets were streaming over the border at will, in frantic search of wives and children, descriptions of whom were posted as "missing persons" signs throughout the province.[5]

For Yang, the crux of the crisis was its timing. Just a few months before the first refugees and their heavily armed pursuers crossed into his jurisdiction, President Yuan Shikai passed away in Beijing. With his passing went all semblance of central authority in China, with no clear successor in his wake. In the absence of Yuan's unifying presence, Han officials had only discredited institutions to work with. Whereas the revolutionaries had undermined the authority of the monarchy, Yuan's abolition of the republic, suppression of parliamentary bodies, and attempt to establish his own monarchy had all done irreparable damage to the integrity of the republic. Both of these processes were ultimately rooted in the foreign presence in China, in the face of which neither the Manchu court nor its Han successors had proven able to protect domestic interests. As a result, after Yuan's passing, Chinese officials lacked a clear consensus regarding whom they could entrust to coordinate the affairs of the former empire. In Xinjiang, the loss of support from the Chinese metropole spelled trouble for Governor Yang, who could no longer look to a higher authority to enforce his writ throughout the province. The Kazak and Kyrgyz refugee crisis thus constituted the geopolitical context through which Yang would witness the collapse of imperial authority in both China and Russia.

Outside the provincial capital of Urumchi, the governor's political authority was severely circumscribed. Among those regions of Xinjiang still retaining their own military units and the right of direct communication with Beijing were the Altay minister (*zhangguan*), Tarbagatai councilor (*canzan*), Ili general (*jiangjun*), and Kashgar commander (*titai*). As any glimpse at a map of contemporary Xinjiang will show, the jurisdictions of these four semiautonomous offices were all situated in strategic regions sharing a border with the Russian empire. As a result, the vast majority of Kazak and Kyrgyz refugees fled into mountain strongholds directly under their administration. Over the next year, Yang engaged in a three-way struggle among himself, Beijing, and the members of this semiautonomous quartet to determine who held ultimate authority for coordinating government policy toward the Russian refugees. To Yang, the threat to provincial security was self-evident. "For each chief, there are roughly one thousand subordinates under his rule," Yang explained. "Even the lesser chiefs claim the loyalties of several hundred men. If Russian troops cross the border and begin to hunt down these chiefs, untold numbers of their subordinates may rise up in resistance."[6]

One by one, each member of the semiautonomous quartet proceeded to adopt a martial solution to the refugee crisis, deploying troops or other coercive measures to round up Kazaks and Kyrgyz and deliver them to the nearest Russian consulate. When Yang's provincial rivals began to justify their actions via recourse to directives issued in Beijing, the governor responded by insisting on the superiority of policies bred from long experience in China's northwest—in other words, his own. "Even though these are the Ministry [of Foreign Affairs]'s orders," Yang wrote on one occasion, "it appears that they simply do not understand the situation on the borderlands. We must act in accordance with local conditions and avoid rash actions that will lead to incidents."[7] As heavily armed Russians tramped across the land and Xinjiang's officials prodded cornered nomads like so much cattle, the governor made frantic efforts to regain control of the situation. When some twenty to thirty thousand Russian Kyrgyz holed up in the mountains of Aksu—the only region in Xinjiang sharing a border with Russia but not subject to the rule of one of the governor's provincial rivals—Yang decided to make a stand.

Aksu was the only region within Xinjiang to which Yang had ever been posted outside the capital, having served as *daoyin* (circuit intendant) there for three years following his transfer from neighboring Gansu. Just as important, its current *daoyin*, Zhu Ruichi, was, like Yang, a veteran Qing official who had spent the greater part of his career in the non-Han borderlands. The two men implicitly trusted one another, viewing themselves as a distinct class of frontier official whose areas of expertise were increasingly impinged upon by carpetbagging Han sent from Beijing. When a telegram from Semireche informed Yang that a Russian punitive expedition to Aksu was imminent, he and Zhu coordinated a united front in response. Much to the surprise of both men, Beijing had secretly authorized the Russian expedition. "When the Russians arrived here," Zhu reported, "the first thing they told me was that our government had already approved the capture of Russian criminals."[8] Zhu, firmly in Yang's camp, continued to drag his feet, prompting a formal note of protest. "The unwillingness of your officials to assist us in the apprehension of these criminals resulted in a host of problems," the Russian consul in Urumchi later complained to Yang. "Please order the *daoyin* of Aksu to help us in capturing these bandits."[9] With the Russians frustrated in Aksu, Yang sent Zhu to take up the post of *daoyin* in Kashgar, where Zhu and Yang's brother coordinated a pacifist campaign in contravention of the forward approach advanced by Ma Fuxing, the Kashgar commander.

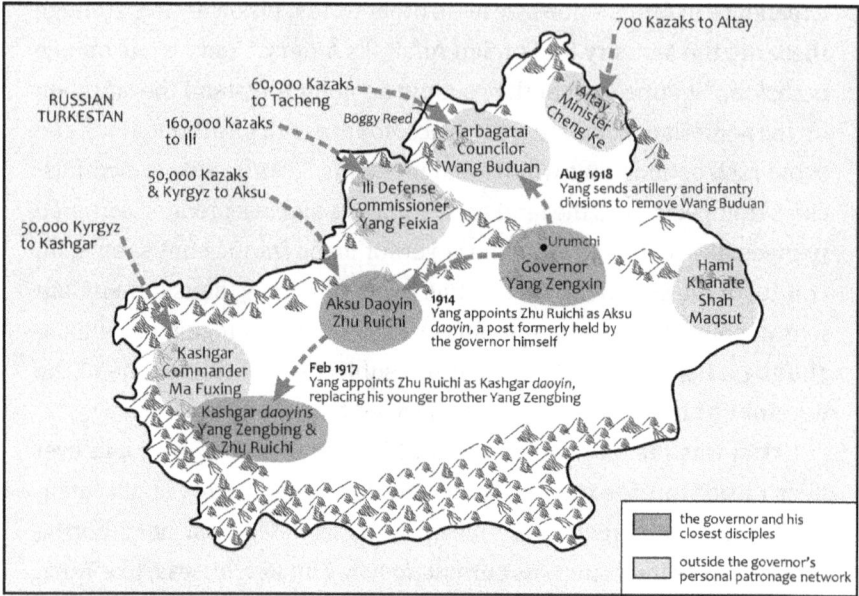

FIGURE 2.1. The Kazak refugee crisis and the autonomous quartet, 1916–18. Cartography by Debbie Newell.

Zhu's transfer to Kashgar coincided with the February Revolution in European Russia, followed just nine months later by the Bolshevik revolution. In Xinjiang, the impact of the former was felt immediately. The transitional government in Saint Petersburg, now consumed with far more serious matters closer to home, no longer had the time or resources to devote to the situation in Xinjiang. Before long, a general amnesty was issued, and both sides agreed to peacefully repatriate all remaining nomads. As this was what Yang had lobbied for all along, he jumped at the chance to usher fugitive Kazaks and Kyrgyz back over the border. To his surprise, however, the governor soon came face-to-face with an unfamiliar feature of the new political landscape. In short, while the Russian central government in Saint Petersburg may have lost all appetite for confrontation, vigilante Russians stranded on the ground in Central Asia most certainly had not.

The first tangible signs that Russian imperial authority was in freefall came in June 1917, in the form of a report to Kashgar *daoyin* Zhu Ruichi. Eyewitnesses recounted a chilling scene. Approximately seven hundred Russian Kyrgyz, armed with little more than consulate-issued amnesty papers from Kashgar, had been gunned down as they passed through an alpine valley. Vigilante Russians equipped with machine guns were almost certainly responsible for the massacre. "What is the meaning of all this?" Yang thundered to Beijing. "First they issue a general amnesty, then they execute every last one of them!" Getting these nomads to return in the first place had been a nigh-impossible task, Yang observed, one that required vast amounts of provincial funds and labor. "Not only has this inhumane action resulted in the deaths of those who ventured to return, but it also ensures that those still remaining will not risk a similar fate." Throughout the summer of 1917, additional reports of massacres and poisonings continued to reach an exasperated Yang. The Russian ambassador in Beijing, Prince Nikolai Kudashev, could not have cared less. "Before they fled to Xinjiang," the prince patiently explained, "the Kazaks pillaged and ravaged the people of Russian Turkestan. It is only natural that the people will enact their revenge upon their return."[10]

The response from the Russian ambassador, while certainly cold, was also a tacit admission that Saint Petersburg was now powerless to put a stop to the carnage in Xinjiang. For Yang, this was uncharted territory. Never before had a Chinese official of his generation witnessed the wholesale collapse of the authority of a European power in China, unless the vacuum created by its retreat was immediately filled by the advance of a rival. But no one stepped in to fill the Russian void in Xinjiang. Similarly, Yang was not accustomed to a Chinese metropole that proved unable or unwilling to help him coordinate policy among his nominal subordinates in Xinjiang, as had been the case while President Yuan Shikai was in office (1912–16). As such, the grim reality of the situation soon dawned on the governor: even prior to the outbreak of the Bolshevik revolution in late 1917, the political authority of both the Russian and Chinese empires throughout Eurasia had already suffered irreparable damage. What partial structures of authority still remained would be swept away entirely by the Russian civil war, whose bloody partisan battles everywhere spilled over into China's northern borderlands.

Both developments are on remarkable and candid display in a telegram issued by Governor Yang during the dark days of November 1919. The catalyst was the sudden appearance of White partisans in the vicinity of Kashgar, heretofore a relatively quiescent front in the civil war. "I see that these Russian troops are equipped with machine guns," Yang observed. "Yet my own government has not only never issued a single machine gun for the defense of Xinjiang, but likewise has never even provided a single gun or bullet for the most fundamental of tasks." Reminding Beijing of his innumerable requests for weapons that had gone unanswered over the past two years, the governor then questioned the patriotic credentials of his own central government. "I do not know whose land you think Xinjiang belongs to, nor whose government rules over its people. Every time I reflect on this matter, it pains me deeply." Yang addressed this telegram to then president Xu Shichang, who, like Yang, had served under Yuan Shikai. "Back when President Yuan was still in office, you were then state councilor. In those days, we all worked in tandem to address the affairs of Xinjiang, like the pulse of a body in synchronized rhythm. You were not yet afflicted by your current state of apathy and indifference." Yang signed off with a plea to look beyond warlord politics. "I beg you to look upon Xinjiang as part of the Republic of China and under the jurisdiction of its central government. Do not look upon Xinjiang as simply the domain of one man, Yang Zengxin, and thus beyond your purview."[11]

But that was exactly what it had become. Moreover, it could not be said that the governor was entirely displeased with this state of affairs. After all, it was precisely this volatile political environment that allowed Yang to spin an elaborate web of isolation about his province. At every step of the way, Yang justified his retreat from the outside world in terms of the "difference" he—and he alone—knew best how to manage in Xinjiang. Already in 1917, Xie Bin reported that Yang maintained regular communication almost exclusively with the Ministries of Foreign Affairs and Finance, only rarely corresponding with the Office of the President.[12] For Yang, the world outside Xinjiang offered nothing but sabotage for the "sanctuary" of which he now saw himself as the sole and wisest steward. "In Kashgar alone," Yang warned Commander Ma Fuxing in late 1919, "we must be on guard against the British and Russian consuls, Japanese intelligence agents, and investigative teams from China's Military Advisory and Border Defense departments. Every little thing we do is being monitored by foreigners and Chinese alike."[13] In 1920, China's postmaster-general complained to the governor that "inspection procedures in Xinjiang have become quite unnecessary. Some items, such as newspapers, have not seen a single copy delivered in three years."[14]

Not content merely to censor all forms of media, Yang also began to thoroughly vet all officials who ventured outside Xinjiang in the course of their duties. In 1927, Owen Lattimore crossed paths with several such men, including one who had served as the governor's parliamentary representative in Beijing for some time. "He was now returning to Urumchi, to take up a new post as Chief of Police," Lattimore learned. "But so strict is the control that the old Governor lays on all subordinates that he had been delayed for days at Chuguchak [Tacheng], while his application to reënter the province and proceed to the capital was being considered; in other words, while other equally confidential agents of the Governor were ascertaining that he had not returned from Peking tainted with unsuitable ideas, or contaminated by extra-provincial affiliations." In addressing those rivals whom Yang imagined intent on recruiting such intermediaries, the governor did his best to advertise his province in the grimmest of hues. "Some ignorant people like to wax poetic about how lush and fertile Xinjiang is," the Mongol and Muslim-dominated Provincial Assembly once wrote on Yang's behalf. "Perhaps they do not know how emaciated our oxen are, how their skin clings to their bones, and how even this meager ration is fought over both tooth and nail. Perhaps they do not know how catastrophic is the state of our finances."[15] In the event anyone remained in doubt as to the identity of these so-called ignorant people, Yang was elsewhere more explicit. "If [Xinjiang] were to fall into the hands of some eminent person from the inner provinces, he would find that it is not possible to maintain even a single brigade of troops here."[16]

By 1921, it would not be an exaggeration to say that Yang stood among the ashes of Russian and Chinese imperial authority in Central Asia. And since no one in either metropole had yet demonstrated the ability to put the pieces of the former empires back together again, Yang had little incentive to relax his control over provincial security, which remained tight. At a minimum, the governor could take solace in the fact that, during the past five years, he had managed to cull Xinjiang's semiautonomous quartet down to one remaining member: Kashgar commander Ma Fuxing. On the other hand, Yang's long-standing commitment to an ethno-elitist alliance composed of Muslim and Mongol nobles presented an institutional legacy of difference that foreign rivals could attempt to reorient in alignment with their own agendas. As it turned out, White partisans fleeing the battlefields of the Russian civil war were the first to try this. In 1919, Viktor Lyuba, the Russian consul in Ili, "printed several hundred pamphlets in the Muslim script and disseminated them all over the place," according to a report delivered to the governor. "He is trying to incite the Muslims and Turbans so he can form a new army." Not to be outdone, Red agents on the other side of the border adopted the same strategic approach, reportedly paying a group of Hui agents 300,000 rubles to return to Ili and inform the local Muslims that their day of "liberation" was at hand, and that they should rise up in response.[17]

These overtures to the non-Han peoples of Xinjiang posed a sort of threat qualitatively different from anything Yang had encountered before. He was, of course, intimately familiar with various incarnations of national determination platforms that had long circulated throughout the region. "At present," Yang observed in 1920, "the issue that most requires our attention is this doctrine of Muslim independence."[18] Initially, however, Yang had less reason to worry about such doctrines in Xinjiang than he did those aimed at the Russian colonial presence across the border, whose hand fell much heavier on their Turkic subjects than did the Chinese on theirs. In fact, many of those who criticized Russian rule in Central Asia professed a sympathetic attitude toward Chinese rule in Xinjiang, which was viewed as more "hands-off" than that of the

Russians.[19] Thus, from Yang's standpoint, the goal was not so much to suppress widespread Muslim discontent with Han rule in Xinjiang as it was simply to prevent nationalist agitations incubating elsewhere in the Muslim world from taking root in his province. "Calls to throw off the foreign yoke grow stronger day by day," he wrote in 1920, assessing global politics. "Whether in China or elsewhere, everybody now harbors such thoughts." To Yang, the implications of such trends were clear and disturbing. "The Turban people are gradually gaining more knowledge about the world. In the future, there is little doubt that those in Russian Turkestan . . . will drive out the Slavic race of Russians, and restore their own Khoqand Khanate."[20]

To prevent the Han race from being driven out of its non-Han lands, Yang did everything in his power to prevent nationalist propaganda from infiltrating Xinjiang. In 1918, when a British tract urging Arabs to throw off the yoke of Ottoman rule in the Middle East suddenly showed up in Xinjiang, Yang praised "its originally benevolent intent" in furthering the aims of one of China's wartime allies. At the same time, however, he ordered any copies of the pamphlet that might surface in Xinjiang to be confiscated and destroyed. After all, he wrote, "the tract encourages people to extricate themselves from alien rule." For Yang, there was nothing wrong with "the Arabs seeking independence from Turkish rule." What he was afraid of, however, was that "Muslims in other countries will then be misled by their actions, and seek to overthrow the ruling government in their states."[21] Here we see Yang dealing with the double-edged sword of nation-building efforts harnessed for offensive purposes. In other words, Yang had finally come face-to-face with the propensity since the late nineteenth century for empires to create nations not on their own territory but "preferably on another empire's territory."[22] Assuming such a fate did not befall the former Chinese empire, Yang was perfectly happy to watch it befall the Ottoman Empire.

So long as calls for national liberation in Xinjiang produced little more than a paper trail, Yang's countermeasures were relatively straightforward and effective. When they entered on the backs of heavily armed White Russians, however, the governor faced a crisis of unprecedented proportions. In 1920–21, Yang's worst fears came to pass. First came General Andrei Bakich (1878–1922), a Montenegrin Serb who made camp at Tacheng with eight thousand soldiers and another five thousand refugees in tow. One month later, Cossack Ataman Boris Annenkov (1889–1927) followed him into the Ili valley, still commanding a force of about one thousand battle-tested troops. Through equal parts diplomacy, subterfuge, and military coercion, Yang managed to imprison Annenkov and his men in the desert wastes of Dunhuang, where they proceeded to deface ancient murals in the Thousand-Buddha Caves. Bakich, however, heartened by the arrival of one General Novikov and his men in Tacheng, began to prepare for a counterattack on Red positions just over the border. In May 1921, the Reds delivered an ultimatum to Yang outlining the consequences in store for him should he continue to harbor an enemy combatant in Chinese territory. The governor, unable to call on Beijing's support or confront a militarily superior Russian foe, informed the *daoyin* of Tacheng that "[I] must row my boat with the current." Heaven, he declared, "has presented us with an opportunity to destroy the Whites by borrowing the strength of the Reds. We cannot go against the will of Heaven."[23]

On May 24, the Reds, with Yang's blessing, burst into Tacheng and opened fire on the Whites. Much to the governor's dismay, nearly two-thirds of the White force managed to escape and flee toward Altay, putting the men in close proximity to Outer Mongolia, itself a major battleground in the Russian civil war. Here General Bakich first deployed the national idea via the barrel of a gun. "For too long now you have been wantonly abused and violently oppressed by your Han overlords," he announced in July. "Now I have driven them out and taken control of Altay." Bakich's goal was join forces with Baron Roman von Ungern-Sternberg, who had just captured Urga, the capital of Outer Mongolia. Bakich outlined his preferred denouement in Outer Mongolia while calling for Mongol and Kazak assistance in Altay. "The Boghd Khan will soon lead forth an army of Mongols to help you loosen your shackles of oppression," he promised, referring to the spiritual leader of Outer Mongolia. "Since all of you stand to benefit from such developments, I am requesting each and

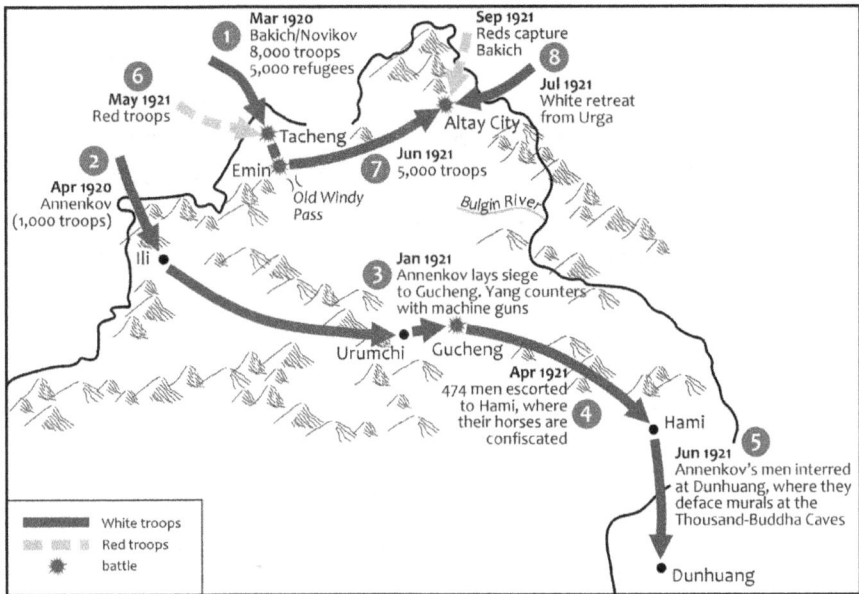

FIGURE 2.2. Annenkov and Bakich in Xinjiang, 1920–21. Cartography by Debbie Newell.

every person to provide cattle, sheep, and horses, as well as rice and grain rations."[24]

His calls appear to have fallen on deaf ears. Prince Ailin, one of the most important members of Yang's ethno-elitist alliance in Xinjiang, remained loyal to the governor and promised to steer his Kazaks away from Bakich. And once Red armies invaded Urga and succeeded in capturing Ungern-Sternberg —over the futile protests of Beijing and other northern Chinese warlords, who had promised to drive him out themselves—Yang knew what he had to do. "The ancients teach us: cure poison with poison."[25] On September 12, representatives of the governor met with Red agents in Tacheng and negotiated new terms for a Red assault on Altay. A second attack flushed Bakich out of Altay, and he was captured in Outer Mongolia soon thereafter. The Bolsheviks then kept to the agreement they had signed with Governor Yang and withdrew their soldiers from Xinjiang. In contrast, they elected to remain in Outer Mongolia, where they cast themselves as stewards of an independent Mongol nation, free at last from Chinese "oppression." Though this new Mongol "nation-state" posed a perennial geopolitical threat to Yang, the fact that his Han contemporaries in the heartland had failed where he had succeeded provided the governor with one of his most cherished platforms of strategic difference. "If we were to implement the rapacious policies of inner China in Xinjiang," Yang warned in 1927, "the people would surely rebel, and Xinjiang would go the way of Outer Mongolia and Tibet."[26]

Yet Yang still had to live with the "poison" of the Bolsheviks, who now surrounded his province in some form on three sides. Rumors regarding their tactics for soliciting political support, both among Russian Turks and Chinese expatriate Turks, had been trickling into Xinjiang for several years. "The strength of the Reds is growing fast in Tashkent," came a February 1920 report from Kashgar. "Without regard to nationality or ethnicity, they are holding elections that are open to Hui, Turbans, Kazaks, and Russians." An uprising in Bukhara emboldened a group of expatriate Turkic workers from Kashgar to declare that "the Turbans in Kashgar have been the victims of unbearable exploitation by Han officials, and that an armed battalion should be sent to drive the Chinese officials out of Kashgar so that they may enjoy the same freedoms" as did the Turkic peoples of Russian Turkestan. In Andijan, émigré Turkic laborers from Xinjiang set up a committee and "issued pronouncements concerning independence." Though the situation across the border was far more complex than the governor could have imagined, for Yang, the bottom line was clear. Such slogans, he lamented, "cannot be suppressed by force, nor can we neutralize them with countermeasures." By May 1920, Yang's spies informed him that "formal autonomy has already been implemented in Turkestan. They have established a republic, with organized elections, and a seventy-four-member senate. All power rests with the Turkestan government." The governor's commentary on this report is telling. "It is frightening to see these Muslims and Turbans handling their own affairs of state during this time of chaos."[27]

Initially, Yang found that there was very little he could do about these alarming developments across the border. Mostly, he seems merely to have seized upon the threat of a national liberation movement among Turkic expatriates across the border to justify his own attempts to further consolidate his power in Xinjiang. In 1924, Yang learned that the fourth and only remaining member of the semiautonomous quartet, Ma Fuxing, the Kashgar commander, had initiated a suspicious correspondence with the Cao warlord faction in Beijing. The governor's response was to march a Hui army on Kashgar and execute Ma.[28] In justifying Ma's death to the outside world, however, Yang said nothing about the commander's shady dealings with other Han warlords. "He abused his power and deprived the people of their wealth and women," announced the Xinjiang Provincial Assembly on Yang's behalf. "Knowing no restraints, he styled himself a *pasha* and incurred the deep enmity of the people, who longed for his execution."[29] But it was not just any "people" who longed for the commander's death: it was "Chinese and Russian Turbans," who had "gathered in Andijan, proclaiming their intent to lead an army on Kashgar and get rid of Ma Fuxing." In other words, the threat of a national liberation movement from abroad—a pretext that only the Han governor of a non-Han land could invoke—had motivated Yang to kill one of his own officials. "Now that Ma Fuxing and his son have been eliminated," he reasoned after the affair, in a telegram later printed in his *Records,* "the outrage of the Turbans has been appeased, and there will be no further cause for any incidents."[30]

It is, of course, possible that Yang truly believed the continued presence of Ma Fuxing in Kashgar would invite the unwelcome attentions of radicalized expatriates operating in what had once been Russian Turkestan. After all, consolidation of the new Soviet state in Central Asia certainly gave Yang much to reflect upon. "Ever since Russia reorganized its polity, it has become a federation of autonomous parts," the governor observed. "There are now over twenty republics within this federation, which looks quite different from the Russia of the imperial era." Within each republic, representatives of the majority ethnic group had been installed in prominent government offices, in an attempt to make each republic look as though it "belonged" to the majority of people who lived within its borders. "The governor of Semireche is a Kazak," Yang explained to the *daoyin* of Altay. "Though still a part of Russian territory, officials in this 'Kazakstan' are drawn mainly from the Kazaks themselves. Similarly, they let Kazaks serve in their own army." According to Yang, such a novel state of affairs was born not of compassion but of pragmatism. "It is not as though the Soviet government is reluctant to use military force to suppress their Russian Muslims and Kazaks. But the situation in which it finds itself makes it impossible to do certain things [*qi shi you bu neng*]." That is why, according to Yang, they allowed "the Russian Muslims in Andijan and Tashkent to set up an autonomous Muslim state, and the Russian Kazaks in Semipalatinsk and Zaysan to set up an autonomous Kazakstan."[31]

What Governor Yang was attempting to describe has been the subject of much research by Soviet historians over the past two decades. One scholar characterizes the Soviet transformation of its non-Russian borderlands as "a strategy aimed at disarming nationalism by granting what were called the 'forms' of nationhood." In other words, it was a preemptive strike against the ideal of national determination, an attempt to make nationalism work for the empire, not against it. In much the same way as a vaccine protects its host from a fatal disease by injecting a less potent version of the same disease into the bloodstream, Soviet policymakers similarly "midwifed" silhouette versions of independent nationhood, hoping to dissuade non-Russian elites from seeking national independence outside the umbrella of Soviet stewardship.[32] Governor Yang knew exactly what the Soviets were up to, and he cared for it not one bit. "Bolshevik promises of independence for Muslims do not respect national borders," the governor noted with alarm. "The effect in Xinjiang cannot be underestimated. . . . The independence of their Muslims will spark an unstoppable tide of radicalism, with a political crisis sure to follow."[33]

The problem for Governor Yang was essentially one of geography. "We have no choice but to maintain an active relationship with the Soviet Union," he conceded in 1925. "But their policies of governance are not

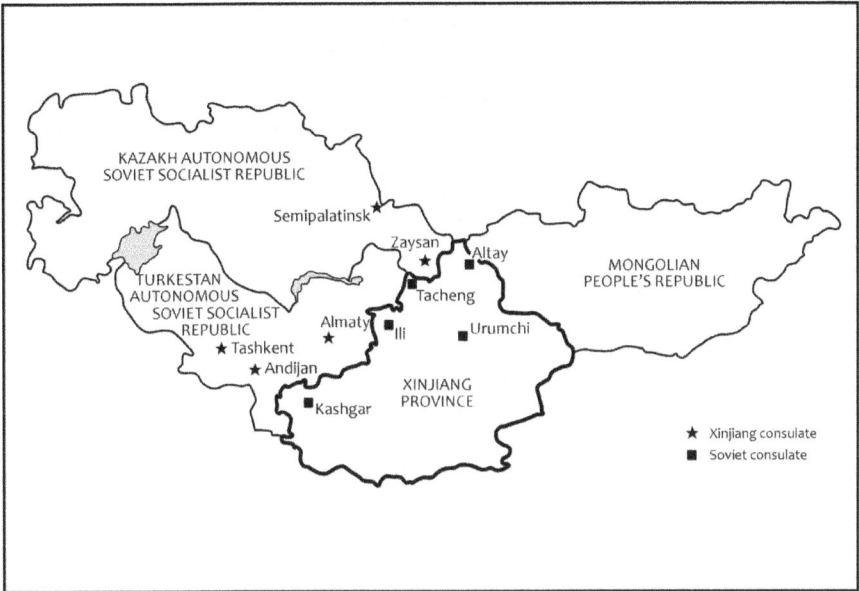

FIGURE 2.3. Soviet national republics: the view from Xinjiang, c. 1924. By 1924, Governor Yang was surrounded by Soviet nationality projects. Responding to the new republics on his western, northern, and eastern borders, he predicted that "the Kazaks of Russian Kazakstan will collude with Chinese Kazaks," the Mongols of "Russian Mongolia will collude with Chinese Mongols," and the "Muslims of Russian Turkestan will collude with Chinese Muslims." As a countermeasure, he bargained for the establishment of five Xinjiang consulates in Soviet Central Asia, intending to monitor the dissemination of Soviet affirmative action ideas among his own subjects. "If I let Xinjiang's Turbans cross the Soviet border with impunity and without any restrictions whatsoever," he wrote, "the ten thousand seasonal expatriate laborers of today will become the ten thousand agitating returnees of tomorrow." Source: Yang, *Buguozhai wendu sanbian*, vol. 2, 15–16; and vol. 1, 33. Cartography by Debbie Newell.

welcome in Xinjiang." Soviet ideology, Yang wrote on another occasion, was "a lurking menace to the entire world. How can we expect Xinjiang, which everywhere shares a border [with the Soviet Union], to be able to resist the gradual infiltration of extremism?" Yet no matter how vigilant the governor may have been against Soviet affirmative action policies, he could not silence its most enthusiastic promoters. "The Kazaks of Russian Kazakstan will collude with Chinese Kazaks," Yang wrote with resignation in 1924. "The Mongols of Russian Mongolia will collude with Chinese Mongols. The Muslims of Russian Turkestan will collude with Chinese Muslims." And on and on. The governor, rarely one to admit defeat, finally conceded the brilliance of Soviet policy. "It is now a matter of Russian policy to make aggressive use of their Mongols, Kazaks, Hui, and Turbans [*liyong Meng Ha Hui Chan wei zhuyi*]. In response, Chinese policy must now turn to defending against Mongols, Kazaks, Hui, and Turbans. The Russian position, however, is far superior. All our counter-measures are destined to fail."[34]

Although Yang rarely provided specifics regarding the nature of the "collusion" (*goujie*) he envisioned, Owen Lattimore, who traveled throughout Xinjiang in 1927, was quite adept at pinpointing the source of the governor's malaise. "The Qazaqs on the Russian side of the frontier," Lattimore wrote, "are able to purchase modern arms, a liberty not allowed by the Chinese," who confined most Chinese Kazaks—the Altay tribes, bordering Outer Mongolia, being an exception—to lightweight paramilitary duties. "Moreover, that part of the old province of Semirechensk adjoining the Ili territory is now the Autonomous Soviet Socialist Republic of Qazaqistan. The Russian Qazaqs therefore have a dash and initiative to which their kinsmen who are subject to the Chinese cannot aspire. Consequently the triumph of the Russian Qazaqs in all encounters of border thieves and cattle lifters has a galling effect of attrition on the Chinese prestige."[35] In 1924, reports streamed in to Urumchi that Mongols from the new Mongolian People's Republic, under Comintern direction, were encouraging Xinjiang's Mongols to take up arms and "unite" with their "motherland." Yang read these reports with interest. "They are telling all Mongols under our jurisdiction to shed the shackles of abusive government and endless toil, and join the blissful path of development." Before long, Yang found that the Mongols were expanding their irredentist claims beyond the Altay region, declaring, on the basis of historical demographics, that Ili, Tacheng, and even Urumchi should also "return" to the Mongol embrace. "Ever since the Outer Mongols began to receive

Soviet financial and military backing," Yang lamented, "their ambition knows no bounds."[36]

Governor Yang could not similarly promise his Kazaks or Mongols their own "motherland," nor had his career as a late imperial official taught him the virtues of sponsoring the development of mass nationalisms. "If ethnic boundaries are excessively distinguished from one another [*zhongzu jiexian guoyu fenming*]," Yang argued in 1920, "this will cause fish to be separated from water and birds from their flocks."[37] Instead, all Yang could think to do was to reduce the tax burden of the nomads in question and broadcast stock Confucian platitudes. "We can no longer sanction the treatment of our Altay nomads as so much fish and meat," Yang wrote to one of his officials. "Otherwise, their hearts will open up to foreign intervention, and our borders will never know a day of peace."[38] Elsewhere, he addressed the threat of "self-government" more directly:

> If we do not fix our own internal affairs first and effect a fundamental resolution, then it will prove impossible to make the Muslims and Turbans forever endure the rule of Han officials, and the compact among our peoples will break. The tide of calls for self-government rises day by day. It is not something that machine guns nor artillery can stop. If good government and noble instruction cannot be upheld, if virtue is absent and principles are not just, then all I can do is eradicate corrupt governance, punish greedy officials with extreme severity, strengthen the resolve of the people, and eliminate lurking threats.[39]

For Yang and other Han officials educated during the imperial era, the very idea of national determination represented a perversion of the natural social order. Though all Chinese officials were exhorted to "love" or otherwise "cherish" the common people, there was to be no question of who was in charge. In 1913, Yang Zuanxu, a Han general sympathetic to the revolutionary movement, told the Muslims of Kashgar that "the age of ignorance has ended" and anyone could now aspire to become governor of the province.[40] In response, Yang Zengxin shut down the "new method" Muslim schools of Kashgar and arranged for Yang Zuanxu's transfer out of the province. He was fortunate to leave Xinjiang with his life, a luxury not accorded some of his allies. The discourse of social mobility promised by such an ethnopopulist platform was simply not welcome in Governor Yang's Xinjiang. From his perspective, the job of those in charge was to ensure that a pretext for political agitation—or even mere political engagement—did not percolate down to the commoners.

As Yang must have been painfully aware in the face of Soviet financial and moral support for national determination across the border, his actions came off as decidedly feeble. Though the governor regarded Soviet affirmative action institutions with strong distaste, even he was ready to acknowledge that they represented a "superior" (*yousheng*) adaptation to the storehouse of imperial repertoires with which he had been long familiar. Now that the Soviets were "making aggressive use" (*liyong . . . wei zhuyi*) of the non-Russian peoples of Central Asia, Yang needed to be equally proactive or risk the extinction of the conservative order he so fervently championed. He was not about to cast himself as a sponsor of mass ethnic nationalisms. What he was prepared to do, however, was search for a way of neutralizing the Soviet ethnopopulist "poison" at its source. To do so, he would first need to grab hold of one of the most potent institutions of Western political subterfuge in China— the consulate—and attempt to turn it back on its creators.

"THEY CALL THEM CONSULATES . . ."

The Bolsheviks were newcomers to Xinjiang, and it took them some time to discover that Ili and Tacheng were not cities in Outer Mongolia.[41] On the other hand, Governor Yang, despite getting on in years, did everything he could to educate himself about socialism and its doctrines, even going so far as to attend weekly tutoring sessions with a Soviet consular aide. "Wherever there are poor people," Yang reflected in early 1923, "this so-called doctrine of common property [*junchan zhuyi*] will find ready converts."[42] His marked distaste for Soviet economic and ethnic policies notwithstanding, Yang made it a point to attend to each and every diplomatic courtesy expected of an official in his position. "The days of the Russian empire are over," Yang wrote in 1920. "In the realm of international diplomacy, we are starting anew on equal footing, leaving behind the aggressive policies of the autocratic era."[43] As such, the governor paid lip service to the new relationship by extending personal condolences to Foreign Commissar Chicherin upon "the early death of the great leader, genius, and scientist V. I. Lenin," while making it a point to congratulate the Soviet consul in Urumchi upon the anniversary of the October Revolution.[44]

For their part, the Soviets, while privately disparaging the Han governor of Xinjiang in their internal reports, were actually quite willing to engage Yang on terms to his liking. Perhaps most importantly for the governor, the Soviets promised not to propagate socialist ideologies within the borders of Xinjiang. Though it is still unclear precisely to what degree they managed to uphold this promise during the time Yang was in office, at least in principle, the Soviets do appear to have been committed to this end. That is, while the Turkic expatriates of Xinjiang could expect sympathetic treatment and perhaps even an "autonomous" Uighur political unit of their own while living *within* the boundaries of Soviet Central Asia, they could not expect Soviet sponsorship of a Uighur nationalist platform to accompany the return of expatriates to Xinjiang.[45] In other words, the moment Soviet affirmative action threatened to make the leap from domestic to international policy, Moscow's geopolitical interests would ultimately determine whether that leap would be made. In the final analysis, pragmatism trumped ideology.

The problem for Yang, however, lay in his realization, as early as 1920, that "Bolshevik promises of independence for Muslims do not respect national borders." After all, the very definition of *expatriate* is someone who resides outside the borders of their country of citizenship but retains cultural, social, economic, and sometimes political ties to their homeland. Thus, even if the Soviets refused to formally sanction the designs of some of Xinjiang's Turkic expatriate community toward their homeland, they had little control over what these same Chinese subjects might do once they returned to Xinjiang filled with new ideas about nation and state. During his fourth expedition to Xinjiang in 1930, archaeologist Aurel Stein summarized his discussions about this problem with a Han official in Kashgar: "Difficulty from Soviet propaganda and how to meet it. Encouragement to be given to those who after visit to Farghana report true facts."[46] Yet the Soviets had nothing to hide: their institutions of affirmative action were intended to be publicly visible and rhetorically omnipresent. No one who left Xinjiang as a "Turban Head" could fail to notice that such ethnonyms were now regarded as racist and derogatory by Soviet intellectuals, and that, as newly christened Uighurs, they were entitled to some form of political autonomy such as that bestowed upon their ethnic brethren across the border. All in all, the number of Uighur expatriates who resided in Soviet Central Asia—variously estimated at anywhere from fifty to several hundred thousand—was considerable, and their potential collective political power certainly posed a threat to the governor of Xinjiang.[47]

It should therefore come as no surprise that Yang's next demand, right after his insistence that socialism not be propagated within Xinjiang, was that the Soviet state refrain from transmitting its ideologies among "Chinese subjects traveling in Russian territory." To this the Bolsheviks could not agree. Characterizing Yang's request as compelling the Soviets to "prohibit Chinese expatriates from reading the newspapers," the Bolshevik representative responded with a simple rebuttal. "The newspaper offices in socialist countries propagate socialist ideas as a matter of course." As their content involved merely "the guiding principles of science and socialism," Yang had nothing to fear from any incendiary political content he may have imagined to exist within their pages. As for the governor's specific request that the Soviets "prohibit Chinese citizens from joining various Russian organizations, where they will be exposed to speeches and publications, while also forbidding the sons of Chinese citizens from enrolling" in Soviet schools, Yang was roundly castigated on these points. The Soviet response was that to act thus "would be to deprive expatriate Chinese citizens of their rights and freedoms, including their right to receive an education while in Russia. Not only would this prove difficult to enforce, but it would also infringe upon the laws of our country."[48]

This was unacceptable to the governor. He knew what his Turkic subjects were exposed to while abroad, and he knew that it would be his responsibility to deal with them if and when they returned to Xinjiang. By then, however, it would already be too late, obliging Yang to resort to coercive measures against his indigenous subjects, the likes of which—incarceration and execution—he was not eager to associate with his isolated and vulnerable Han administration. What Yang needed was a forward base of operations in Soviet Central Asia to head off the threat before it crossed the border. He got his first chance in March 1920, when Bolshevik agents agreed to meet Han officials in secret at Khorgas Pass near Ili. The result, two months later, was the Ili Provisional Trade Accord, the first equal treaty to be signed by a Chinese official and a foreign government in over seventy years. The accord was, first and foremost, an acknowledgment of the extensive economic interests merchants on both sides of the border had in free passage, the obstruction of which during the long years of the civil war had meant famine and hardship for large portions of the population.[49]

Even more important from the governor's perspective, however, was the stipulation that the Bolsheviks and the Chinese would each be permitted to install a "commercial representative" within the other's border. For the Bolsheviks, who chose to establish their commercial office in Ili, this was merely a stepping-stone toward the recovery of all five former czarist consulates in Xinjiang. For Governor Yang, who chose to send Ili County magistrate Zhao Guoliang to Semipalatinsk, this was an unprecedented concession. Prior to Zhao's appointment, the Xinjiang expatriate community across the border had been overseen by wealthy Turkic merchants and notable Muslim religious figures who had been formally recognized as aqsaqal by the governor in Urumchi.[50] In the face of ubiquitous Soviet propaganda, Yang could no longer trust these men. Now, however, for the first time, Yang was permitted to station abroad a permanent Han official who would send back regular reports about "commercial affairs" in Semipalatinsk.

Not surprisingly, Zhao Guoliang seems to have been far more interested in keeping tabs on the radicalization of Chinese citizens in Russian Turkestan than he was in facilitating the movement of trade caravans.

In one of his very first reports to Urumchi, Zhao noted that the Soviets had already begun to make overtures to émigré laborers and merchants from Xinjiang, hoping to train them for clandestine missions back into Xinjiang.[51] The governor's suspicions appeared to be vindicated. "More than half of these men," Yang wrote, referring to the thousands of itinerant Turkic laborers who crossed the border in search of seasonal work each year, "are involved in hard labor. They are an uneducated floating population, and are extremely susceptible to instigation by foreigners."[52] Convinced of expatriate radicalization abroad, Zhao's first cable from Semipalatinsk advised Xinjiang's local officials "to conduct thorough background checks on any future military conscripts, so as to avoid allowing any man who has performed seasonal hard labor abroad from filling our ranks."[53]

Yang was thrilled to have finally established a forward base in Soviet territory, modest though it was. From the Bolshevik perspective, however, their one commercial representative office in Ili was still a far cry from the generous political representation their czarist predecessors had once enjoyed. Thus it was only a matter of time before the Soviets lodged a formal request with the governor allowing them to reopen the five consulates of the imperial era. Yang surely expected this move, and likely knew that he could not hope to keep the Soviets at bay forever. And yet, in contrast to the troubled decades of the late Qing, this time Yang was determined to get something of substantive value in return for the concession of so powerful an institution. "They call them 'consulates,'" observed Aksu *daoyin* Zhu Ruichi in 1926, "but in reality they are bases from which a monopoly on all commercial transactions is forcibly imposed."[54] It is unlikely that Yang thought he would be able to impose his own economic monopoly on commercial transactions anywhere in Soviet territory. But if he could manage to set up a consulate or two of his own, he might just be able to impose a political monopoly on suspect émigrés who hoped to return to Xinjiang.

In the end, Yang reached for the stars: he insisted on a regime of absolute parity, proclaiming that the Soviets would get the keys to the five czarist consulates only if he was allowed five sister consulates in Soviet Central Asia, all managed by Han appointees from Urumchi. In acting thus, Yang was attempting to export to virgin territory the institutional embodiment of a foreign ideal: reciprocal diplomatic representation among ostensibly equal states. Though some late Qing statesmen had eagerly lobbied for the liberal establishment of consulates abroad and could point to a brief but encouraging precedent set by the first Qing officials to be stationed permanently in Korea, Yang's initiative represented the most innovative and aggressive adaptation of all.[55] The Soviets were clearly taken aback. "The five consulates that the old Russian government maintained in Xinjiang," came the reply, "are not to be compared with the sudden establishment of [Chinese] consulates in Soviet territory, in a region that has never before hosted such consulates."[56] Yang turned such logic right back on its head: Xinjiang, the governor pointed out, had likewise never hosted a single foreign consulate until the Russians had bullied their way into the province half a century earlier. Initiative had a way of forging its own precedent.

In October 1924, much to Yang's delight, the Soviets relented, leading to the distinctly odd phenomenon of a Chinese province establishing and managing its own consulates entirely independent of the Chinese central government in Beijing.[57] Yang Zengxin touted his diplomatic victory as "an opportunity to look after our expatriate merchants and obtain compensation for their financial losses" during the long years of the Russian civil war.[58] No doubt there is some truth to this statement. Yet it is clear from the surviving documentary record that Yang was most intent on doing unto the Russians as they had long done unto him. If the Soviet consuls made it their business to extend the influence of their state into Xinjiang, then Yang would make it his business to export the most pressing items on his agenda into Soviet Central Asia. "If I let Xinjiang's Turbans cross the Soviet border with impunity and without any restrictions whatsoever," he concluded, "the ten thousand seasonal expatriate laborers of today will become the ten thousand agitating returnees of tomorrow."[59]

Alarmed at seeing the tools of imperial competition turned back against themselves, the Soviets hatched a plan to eliminate the Chinese expatriate community altogether, in order to deprive Xinjiang's five consulates of their raison d'être. In July 1925, before any of Yang's consulates had managed to open their doors, Xinjiang's trade representative in Semipalatinsk informed the governor that the Soviets were forcing all Xinjiang émigrés to adopt Soviet citizenship unless they managed to obtain a consulate-issued passport within the next three months. At that time, the only consular posting even remotely prepared to issue such paperwork was the office of the former Semipalatinsk commercial representative, which also happened to claim jurisdiction over the smallest number of Xinjiang expatriates. Yang sensed an ulterior motive. "Our expatriate workers are mostly composed of Kazaks and Turbans, who share ethnic and religious ties with the people living all along the Soviet border," Yang observed. "If the Soviets succeed in laying claim to our unregistered expatriates, they will be able to expand their network of socialist infiltration and avoid all claims for financial restitution by our aggrieved merchants."[60]

By mobilizing the printing presses, eliminating the six-*yuan* application fee, and threatening to treat Xinjiang's exiled White Russian population in similar fashion, Yang's five consulates appear to have averted the wholesale elimination of their non-Han constituencies—both those on whose financial behalf they hoped to lobby and those who they hoped would remain vulnerable to Chinese surveillance and other political countermeasures, should the need arise.[61] For our purposes here, what is most fascinating about Yang's interactions with the post-czarist state is the way he adapted to Soviet innovations of the Russian imperial repertoire, carefully selecting only those tactics and institutions he deemed most suitable for deployment in Xinjiang and its immediate environs. For someone of Yang's education and temperament, the Western consulate and its ability to facilitate political subterfuge abroad proved most useful in combating the institutions of Soviet affirmative action. Because Yang viewed himself as steward of the last bastion of conservative imperial authority in all of China, he found utility only in those repertoires that he could deploy to keep disruptive revolutionary innovations at bay.

With the collapse of the regime, however, future Han governors of Xinjiang would find far more to admire in the Soviet approach to empire.

THE CHINESE COLLAPSE IN XINJIANG

If the morning of July 7, 1928 was like any other for Governor Yang, then he most likely rose from bed at four o'clock in the morning, as was his routine. He probably ate his standard fare of plain tofu and cabbage for breakfast, meditated for an hour, perused a text on Daoism, and made his way to the governor's office to tend to the day's affairs of state.[62] It was going to be a gorgeous summer day, complete with soaring July temperatures. On Yang's desk was the usual pile of reports and telegrams requiring his attention. At some point in the morning he decided to reexamine a directive that he had written up five days prior, on July 2. The matter concerned a caravan of Turkic merchants from Xinjiang who, owing to bad weather and a host of other difficulties, had requested permission to make a detour from the usual border crossing at Nilka Pass and instead enter the Soviet Union by another route. For Yang, there could be no debate on this issue. "The appointed border crossing for trade transactions with the Soviet Union is at Nilka Pass," Yang wrote, still determined to paper over widespread transgressions of the 1920 Ili Provisional Trade Accord. "We cannot make an exception to this long-standing precedent simply for the sake of a few merchants." The governor had already sent this reply to his officials in Ili, but he had not yet forwarded his decision to the provincial commissioner of foreign affairs—a bureaucratic oversight he was about to correct. "Print and distribute this directive, and make sure your ministry follows up on this matter," Yang wrote. "This is an order."[63]

It was the last order the governor would ever issue. After Yang completed the mundane paperwork of the morning, he retired to take his daily nap. That afternoon promised to offer a respite from the morning's bureaucratic drudgery, for today graduation ceremonies were to take place at the Xinjiang Academy of Russian Law and Politics. After his nap, the governor likely saw to it that sufficient copies of his complete works, *Records from the Studio of Rectification*, had been prepared as gifts for that year's graduating class, along with his favorite Daoist treatises, as was his habit. He then made his way several blocks to the academy. Pomp and circumstance proceeded without a hitch, and everyone took their seats. Lunch was about to be served. It was two o'clock in the afternoon.

"Suddenly we heard the sound of multiple gunshots," remembered one witness. "Amid the ensuing chaos, someone shouted out, 'The governor has been shot!'"[64] Most of the guests thought they were hearing firecrackers set off in joyous celebration. But soon the truth emerged. Several waiters garbed in formal attire had approached the governor's table with spirits in hand. Yang rose for the expected toast. Instead of opening their bottles, however, each waiter pulled out a revolver and fired repeatedly into the governor's chest. He doubled over, gargled the words "What the—?!" (*ganma*), and collapsed onto the ground. Yang Zengxin was dead. He was sixty-four years old.

Once shrouded in mystery, the details surrounding the assassination of Governor Yang are now gradually coming to light. A growing body of scholarship in Chinese suggests the likelihood that Feng Yuxiang—the peripatetic "Christian warlord" in perennial search of a rearguard base from which to "save" the nation—somehow managed to orchestrate the dramatic events of the Triple Seven Coup, so named for its occurrence on the seventh day of the seventh month in the seventeenth year of the republic. How Feng's agents could have plotted beneath the watchful eye of the governor—reputed to know of a snake's fever in Hami—remains something of a mystery. Nevertheless, the broad outlines of the assassination are clear. The head of the academy where the shooting took place, Zhang Chunxi, apparently maintained covert connections with Feng. In 1927, with the establishment of a new Nationalist government under Chiang Kai-shek, warlords like Feng scrambled to shore up their defenses against the newly acknowledged central government in Nanjing. Feng needed an additional rearguard base from which to engage the Nationalists, and Xinjiang had long fit his geopolitical criteria for such a base.[65]

By 1928, it had become widely known that Yang was about to retire. "I've worked my 'stratagem of the empty citadel' [*kongcheng ji*] in Xinjiang for seventeen years now," Yang told a visitor in 1928, referring to an ancient strategy for deterring enemies through the art of illusion. "But it won't work much longer."[66] The spectacular resurgence of the Nationalists in the south, helmed by conservative leaders hostile to socialist ideologies, initially appeared to be a most welcome development for the old governor. On March 17, four months before his passing, Yang told a visitor from the inner provinces that "if the southern armies were to take Beijing today, he would fly the [Nationalist] white sun and blue sky flag tomorrow."[67] Just a few weeks earlier, Yang had sent three cables of support for Chiang Kai-shek's new government at Nanjing. "The Nationalist revolution has now succeeded," Yang wrote. "The good fortune of the rest of the country is also the good fortune of Xinjiang." On July 5, just two days before the assassination, the Nationalists wrote back, expressing fulsome admiration for the preservation of peace in Xinjiang and optimism that the coming transition would proceed apace. Meanwhile, the governor's designated envoy, Liu Wenlong, arrived in Nanjing and began to initiate concrete discussions regarding the handover.[68] On July 6, the governor let it be known that "he was very excited about national unification. As for his own exit, he said it would not be a problem."[69]

Unfortunately for Yang, that exit came the very next day, quite ahead of schedule. In a gesture of good will, the Russians provided free berth for his coffin on the Trans-Siberian Railway, destination Beijing. Today, Yang is buried in a handsome tomb in the northern suburbs of the national capital, bypassed unawares by millions of tourists every year en route to the Great Wall ticket booth at Badaling. More importantly, his death initiated a deadly chain reaction that would eventually tempt his successor, Jin Shuren, into a decisive breach of Yang's ethno-elitist strategy of difference. The assassination represented much more than a simple change in leadership. Rather, it was a geopolitical crisis of the sort that is almost always responsible for repudiation of policies that privilege the institutionalization of ethnic and spatial difference. Though Yang had managed to insulate Xinjiang from rival Chinese warlords for a full twelve years following the death of President Yuan Shikai in 1916—a year generally acknowledged as marking the inauguration of warlord politics in China—the continuing inability of the warlords in the inner provinces to reconstitute a strong central authority almost guaranteed that sooner or later someone would manage to infiltrate Yang's inner circle.

When the dust finally cleared, Jin Shuren, a career northwestern official whom Yang had taken under his wing during his tenure in Gansu, emerged as the new governor of Xinjiang. Since Jin was cut from the exact same geopolitical and ideological cloth as Yang—a former Qing official from Gansu—he, too, evinced little interest in implementing Soviet affirmative action policies in Xinjiang. So long as the land was at peace and isolated from outside disturbances, maintaining the status quo bequeathed to him by Yang was a viable strategy, as the latter's seventeen-year tenure as governor had amply demonstrated. But that was no longer the case. Yang's once formidable cocoon had been breached, and anyone who wished to avoid following him to his grave needed to find a way to raise an army capable of deterring warlords such as Feng Yuxiang from marching a full-fledged army on Xinjiang. As the Chinese archaeologist Huang Wenbi learned in 1928, just months before Yang's assassination, there was no easy solution to this problem: "It is said that Yang harbors a mortal fear of Feng, and is terrified that he is plotting to come and take over his land. He wants to raise an army, but is afraid of the consequences that may bring. But if he doesn't raise one, there is no way he can defend against an outside enemy. He knows only too well that his own military forces are insufficient to engage in battle."[70]

To bring these forces up to par, the new governor had to extract more resources from the people of Xinjiang than Yang had ever dreamed possible or prudent. Jin embarked on a state modernization project, heavily weighted toward the military and its ancillary accoutrements. The problem faced by Governor Jin would be faced by the Chinese Communists some thirty years later: in the pursuit of wealth and power in Xinjiang, the politics of resource mobilization all too often end up resembling a Han-led nationalization project by default, if not always by design. In his understandable rush to extract capital from his subjects, Jin systematically repudiated the ethno-elitist alliance that had once undergirded his predecessor's rule. Though not his original intent, such a result was scarcely avoidable. Had Yang Zengxin survived the Triple Seven Coup and remained in office to confront his warlord rivals head on, it was likely a blueprint he would have had to follow as well, though with considerable distaste and likely under a formidable rhetorical smokescreen. After all, in sparsely populated and fiscally anemic Xinjiang, bereft of outside support, there were only so many ways to build an army: tax the peasants, squeeze the wealthy, or initiate mass conscription. Jin pursued all three measures at once. As Yang had noted more than a decade before, the major handicap of a Han governor of Xinjiang during the republican era was the lack of a strong central government capable of financing the institutions of empire. "Since the establishment of the Republic of China," Yang once wrote, "the disbursement of shared funds from the inner provinces to Xinjiang has been cut off entirely. We have not been issued a single penny with which to cover administrative and military costs." As a result, Yang continued, "I have had little choice but to print unbacked paper currency simply to make ends meet. The dangers of such a practice are too great to speak of."[71]

Jin would do this and more, extracting from the peasants in his province the long-absent fiscal subsidies once provided by Beijing. That the peasants of Xinjiang were Uighurs, not Han, only exacerbated the problem. As Yang Zengxin had been fond of pointing out, in the Han heartland, disgruntled peasants constituted little more than a domestic disturbance: either they were suppressed by their Han rulers or they replaced their Han rulers, but outside forces were unlikely to get involved. Discontent among non-Han peasants in the borderlands, however, would facilitate a form of political discourse largely unavailable to discontented Han within the pass. In other words, leaders of a Uighur uprising could advocate for the realization of exactly what Yang had warned against to justify his continued rule in Xinjiang: national liberation from Han rule. This could now be glossed—with more than a little encouragement by Soviet intellectuals—as "colonialist" or "imperialist" in nature.

When the British archaeologist Aurel Stein passed through the southern oases in the winter of 1930–31, he witnessed Jin's creative exactions firsthand. After noting the "popular apprehension that a tax of 1M. is to be imposed on every tree cut," Stein learned that "every sheep killed in honour of a guest is now taxed S. 3½!" Several days later, he talked at length with his old *aqsaqal* friend Ghulam Muhammad, who "tells of increased exactions of Chinese administration. Bribes extorted in a way which [Stein's Chinese companion] Chiang could not have thought of."[72] In return, Jin had nothing to offer either by way of material compensation or ideological justification, such as an ethnopopulist discourse of development might have supplied. The Uighurs sat on agricultural wealth, and that was precisely what the governor targeted, in greater quantities than ever before. None of Jin's predecessors had viewed the Uighurs as fit for military service, and precious few could be integrated into the Chinese bureaucracy. As Han peasants elsewhere in twentieth-century China knew only too well, the impoverished yet industrializing state offered its rural residents—Han or non-Han—but a single role: as producers of agricultural surplus for expensive modernization projects, in a process known as "primitive accumulation."

Yet Jin did not stop at the Uighur peasantry. He also took aim at the Russians, who operated the only viable trade network in the region, albeit at the expense of the Chinese administration. In September 1928, the governor issued orders to deport illegal Russian traders in Tacheng and Altay, followed eight months later by the detention of Soviet merchants in Turfan, all accused of participating in illegal cotton transactions.[73] "Recent directives from the provincial government have transgressed the long-standing policy of friendly relations between neighbors," wrote the Soviet consul in Urumchi in late 1928. "As a result, the Soviet Union has been forced to scale back its commercial operations." By "illegal," of course, Jin meant any activity not permitted by the 1920 Ili Provisional Trade Accord drawn up by Yang Zengxin and the Bolsheviks, a document both Soviet and Chinese authorities had been winking at for years. The Russians called foul. "Today is nothing like the friendly policies of yesterday," the consul lamented.[74] Though Jin knew full well the risks of alienating the Soviets, he deemed the bark from the west to be of far less consequence than the bite from the east. In the end, the governor got his fair share of the merchant cut but paid for it with far more ill will than

FIGURE 2.4. Jin Shuren, governor of Xinjiang, 1928–33. Following the assassination of Governor Yang in 1928, Jin's attempt to revisit some of the integrationist and extractive policies of the late Qing state without the support of the central government led to a devastating collapse of the ethno-elitist order. The political vacuum produced by Jin's ouster in 1933 was filled by a host of belligerents peddling nationalist platforms of every sort. Sven Hedin Foundation collection, Museum of Ethnography, Stockholm.

the Russians alone could muster. After all, it was the Mongol and Turkic entrepreneurs of Xinjiang who composed the chief clientele of the Russians, and they suffered the most when the Russian market contracted.

Last but not least, there was the Mongol and Turkic nobility, long spared the rod of reformation under Yang. Initially, Jin gave every impression of continuity with the policies of his predecessor. "I promise to observe the principles of our departed governor," he informed Tsetsen Puntsag Gegeen, the Incarnate Lama of Karashahr and regent for the khan-wang of the Torguts, "implement a just and fair administration, and maintain the peace."[75] In return, the khans, princes, and other non-Han nobles of Xinjiang had backed Jin's accession to the governorship in the wake of Yang's death and stood beside him in a united front against the warlords of inner China.[76] Once he obtained the governor's seal, however, Jin gave free rein to his reforming zeal. He imposed a personal monopoly on lambskin, long a bartering staple of Xinjiang's nomads, thereby forcing the Lama of Karashahr to close several processing factories operating under his wing. By infringing upon the time-honored perquisites of the Mongol nobility, Jin alienated one of the most important members of Yang's ethno-elitist alliance. Several years later, when Jin called upon the lama to supply Mongol cavalry for the eastern front, Tsetsen Puntsag Gegeen instead laid siege to the Chinese garrison at Karashahr, a move that ultimately cost him his head.[77]

The fiasco involving the Incarnate Lama of Karashahr just four years into Jin's reign is a powerful testament to the swift deterioration of the ethnopolitical compact that had once existed between Yang Zengxin and the non-Han elite of Xinjiang. There was, however, a clear purpose behind it all: the creation of a military force capable of ensuring that Jin did not join Yang in his grave. And in that, the new governor had largely achieved his goal. Less than five months after Yang's death, Jin had expanded his standing army to a mind-boggling thirty thousand troops, more than three times what Yang had grudgingly maintained and far more than Xinjiang could support on its own. Just one year later, the army had again doubled in size, with 74 percent of the provincial budget allotted to the military. To facilitate movement of soldiers throughout the province, along with a reliable communication network, Jin poured money into road construction and telephony services, with several steam-rollers imported from—and a handful of students exported to—Germany. Most importantly, Jin undertook to finance, in fits and starts, a pair of massive arms shipments from British India and the Soviet Union.[78]

Jin's new conscripts were mostly Han of Gansu and Shaanxi stock, the two provinces providing the most direct path of migration into Xin-jiang. Yang Zengxin had always deplored the admission of Han migrants into Xinjiang, and he did his best to seal off the border at Xingxing Gorge, just east of Hami. But times had changed. For much of Yang's tenure, the most destabilizing battles among Chinese warlords had occurred far from Xinjiang's borders, with contestants setting their sights on strategic Beijing or affluent Shanghai. But now, with Chiang Kai-shek's Nationalist Party in command of the Yangzi delta and presiding over a new capital in Nanjing, some of the most vicious wars, fought far from the eyes of Western diplomats and donors, were occurring right on Xin-jiang's borders. And that meant a flood of refugees, impossible to stop no matter what the governor's stance on Han migration might be. Jin tried to make the best of the situation, employing many tens of thousands of refugees in his newly bloated armies. But what to do with the rest, espe-cially those trailed by women and children? Jin's solution owed much to a fateful turn of events that he could not have anticipated. Ultimately, it would serve as the stage upon which the governor managed to alien-ate the entrenched interests of the Turkic nobility at Hami—the gateway from inner China to Xinjiang that no governor could afford to antagonize. When combined with the loss of his Mongol allies at Karashahr, this move would eventually lead to the end of Jin's brief and ignominious tenure as governor.

"Found large party of Hajis en route via Chitral," wrote Stein in late 1930, as he descended into Kashgar over the Pamirs. "Among them men from Kumul & Turfan. Report of Hami Wang's recent death."[79] The death of Shah Maqsut in March 1930 set off a concatenation of events that would ultimately end with a coup against Governor Jin in Urumchi, a briefly independent East Turkestan Republic in Khotan, and a Japanese-

trained Han warlord as the new governor. The spark igniting the fuse
was Jin's decision to abolish the Hami khanate, reclaim the prince's
vast landholdings for the state, dispossess his heirs of their inheritance,
and resettle some Gansu and Shaanxi migrants on the defunct khanate's land. This bold move has often been misinterpreted by historians.
To begin with, it is clear that the prince's subjects widely chafed under
his rule, twice taking up arms during the late Qing, the last time under
Governor Yang's watch. In addition to the words of Governor Yang on
this point, we also have the testimony of two envoys from the Chinese
central government, Xie Bin and Lin Jing, who visited Xinjiang in 1917
and 1919, respectively, and studied local conditions. Xie noted how the
Turkic peasants of Hami, hearing of the abolition of the Muslim khanates in Shanshan and Turfan during the late Qing, "twice circled the
city walls to protest the corvée obligations imposed upon them by the
Muslim prince, and demanded to be placed under the jurisdiction of
Han officials." Xie thought it a "pity" that Yang refused to accede to their
request. Two years later Lin Jing described much the same situation,
adding further details about how Yang resisted the demands of both his
own local Han officials and the Turkic peasants in Hami for the abolition
of Shah Maqsut's prerogatives.[80] Yang not only refused to impinge on
Shah Maqsut's prerogatives, but even went so far as to aid him in brutal
suppression campaigns, all the while continuing to claim the prince as
a Muslim ally of the Chinese state. The Hami prince had his ethnicity
and strategic geographic location to thank. Elsewhere in Xinjiang, Yang
was perfectly happy to undertake the systematic dismantling of every
other semblance of Han or Hui autonomy. The Tarbagatai councilor, the
Altay minister, the Ili general, and the Kashgar commander had all been
victims of Yang's consolidation of power during the chaos of the Russian
civil war and its immediate aftermath.

Each time Yang took out one of his provincial rivals, however, a spell
of military tension and political uncertainty had always followed. Such
periods of brief instability had proven manageable so long as the person deprived of his power remained geographically isolated from the
southeastern passes connecting Xinjiang with warlords in the inner

provinces. Shah Maqsut and his Hami khanate, however, straddled the border with Gansu, the sole gateway to inner China and its warlords after the loss of Outer Mongolia. Simply put, there was no way an invading army from the east could skirt around Hami and strike straight for Urumchi. Thus, if Hami was at peace, warlords from Gansu would be hard pressed to justify its occupation, but neither could they choose an alternate stepping-stone to target. If Hami was not at peace, however, it was an open invitation for aspiring warlords from the inner provinces to try their luck in Xinjiang, with Hami as a rhetorical and strategic foothold. Yang Zengxin, knowing this, opted to leave Shah Maqsut and his retainers in place, no matter how much trouble they brought him. Jin Shuren, pressed for funds and inundated by Han refugees, viewed the timely death of the prince as a convenient pretext to kill three birds with one stone. He could gain control of the khanate's tax revenue, resettle destitute Han refugees, and appease the long-suffering Turkic peasants of Hami, who had never ceased to pine for the khanate's departure.

There were problems of implementation, to be sure. Minor skirmishes resulted from the perception that legitimate Turkic landowners were being dispossessed of their land to make way for Han migrants. The surviving documentary record shows that these initial conflicts were easily redressed or suppressed and did not pose a serious challenge to Jin's administration. Far more threatening, however, were the actions of those who had the most to lose from the abolition of the khanate. These men were Shah Maqsut's longtime retainers. Much like the Incarnate Lama of the Torgut Mongols, who laid siege to the garrison at Karashahr in response to Jin's intrusions into his lucrative lambskin trade, it was the most powerful members of the Hami prince's inner court who took the lead in organizing armed resistance against the governor: Khoja Niyaz Haji, captain of the palace guard; Yolbars Khan, the palace *ordabegi* (major domo); and Beshir Wang, a claimant to the throne. According to Jin, these men, "realizing that land reform was not in their interests, spread malicious rumors among the people, saying that the government was going to give Turban wealth and women to the Han."[81] From 1931 to 1933, Khoja Niyaz and Yolbars solicited and received military assis-

tance from Outer Mongolia, while variously allying or fighting with a
Hui warlord from Gansu, a brash twenty-something-year-old named Ma
Zhongying. They may even have colluded with insurgents as far afield
as Karashahr, Khotan, and Kashgar, who needed no further inducement
to take up arms against Jin's relentless impositions.[82]

By the end of 1932, every corner of Xinjiang was aflame. "The bones
of the dead lie heaped in piles, steaming blood is everywhere plastered,
the earth is scorched dry, and no matter where you look, your heart
aches," wrote Ma Zhongying, observing some of his handiwork. "The
celestial garden of refuge has become nothing more than the home of
tearful gods and wailing spirits."[83] The battlefield machinations of the
various contestants during these years were decidedly byzantine, to say
the least, and have been explored in much greater detail elsewhere.[84]
More germane to the issue at hand is how the chief belligerents justified
their claims to political authority in Xinjiang. Khoja Niyaz and Yolbars,
both creatures of the non-Han nobility and its elite Han stewards, quickly
mastered the discourse of the nation, invoking the prospect of a "republic" populated entirely by what even they referred to in Turkic as the
chanto ("Turban") peoples.[85] Even though they once represented some
of the most important pillars in Yang Zengxin's ethno-elitist alliance—
Yolbars would speak highly of Yang for the rest of his life—they were
now determined to forge new careers by borrowing from the discourse
of mass ethnic nationalisms. In other words, they hoped to reclaim their
former ethno-elitist class privileges under an ethnopopulist guise.

Insurgents in Khotan broadcast the shrillest pronouncements.
"Henceforth, we will have no need to the employ the language or place
names of outsiders," declared one such call to arms. "The black and yellow filth [Hui and Han] have stained our land for far too long. We must
cleanse ourselves of this filth, and drive out the yellow and black barbar-
ians. Long live East Turkestan!" For his part, Ma Zhongying, a Hui, distributed leaflets urging Muslims and Kazaks to "rise up and cease being
slaves of the Han."[86] Such inflammatory rhetoric eventually reverberated
all the way to Nanjing and Moscow, where the Chinese ambassador to
the Soviet Union recorded his alarm. "The Muslim groups are all calling

for national determination," he wrote, "and saying they will not tolerate Han rule anymore." In Nanjing, Zhang Fengjiu, the Xinjiang liaison to the Nationalist government, cast a wary eye over the new political discourse now saturating the non-Han lands of the northwest. "In recent years," Zhang wrote in 1933, "the notion of a great independent Muslim unity has gained widespread currency throughout the northwestern regions."[87]

By alienating the non-Han nobles and their peasant constituencies, Jin Shuren ensured the destruction of the old order bequeathed him by Yang Zengxin. Like Yang, Jin was a former Qing official steeped in the ideology of the Confucian classics, and words from his brush read much like those from Yang's. Unlike Yang, however, Jin could not claim the slightest alignment of word and deed. Though he pursued a roughshod agenda of resource extraction and military modernization, Jin was not an intolerant racist, nor did he "hate" his Turkic or Mongol subjects, as is often alleged. It was simply that in Xinjiang the greatest concentration of pliable wealth happened to be in the hands of sedentary Turkic peasants, while the most glaring conservative political arrangements just happened to be draped around the shoulders of the Muslim and Mongol nobility. In a similar vein, the most plentiful and vulnerable prospects for mass military conscripts intimately familiar with modern warfare just happened to be destitute Han migrants from war-torn Gansu and Shaanxi. Unfortunately for Governor Jin, this particular constellation of initiatives lent itself all too easily to charges of a bulldozing Han assimilationist project. And that in turn facilitated the articulation of its mirror opposite: national platforms for the non-Han peoples of Xinjiang.

As the old imperial order everywhere disintegrated around Jin, replaced by a bewildering variety of nationalist platforms, it became clear that the eventual victor, whoever it might be, would no longer find it possible to rule Xinjiang as Yang and Jin once had. After the events of the early 1930s, the political imagination of any future ruler in Xinjiang would need to encompass tactics from an imperial repertoire already familiar with the appeasement of expectations for political autonomy from each and every putative "nation." And in Xinjiang, that meant taking a page from the Soviet Union and its affirmative action regime, of which Yang and Jin had been so wary. Ultimately, if Xinjiang was not to separate from the Chinese state, its reconstruction would most likely fall to politicians born and bred in the inner provinces, men who did not feel ill at ease with the progressive rhetoric of revolution so characteristic of Han nationalist movements in the heartland. Such men, of course, would be denied recourse to a narrative of political legitimacy that stressed long-standing ties to, and intimate knowledge of, the northwest.

The battle for Xinjiang reached its apex in 1933. The pool of potential victors had shrunk to just three, all Han or Hui and all provincial outsiders: Sheng Shicai, a Japanese-trained Han general from the northeast; Ma Zhongying, the Hui warlord from neighboring Gansu; and the Nationalist government of Chiang Kai-shek and Wang Jingwei in distant Nanjing. In April, their efforts would gain an added impetus when a coup backed by White Russian soldiers in the capital drove Governor Jin Shuren out of the province. With that, the stage was set for a political showdown. Regardless of who prevailed, one thing was now certain: with Jin Shuren went any hope of reconstructing the old ethno-elitist order upon which two millennia of East Asian empires outside the Han heartland had once rested.

CHAPTER 3

RISE OF THE ETHNOPOPULISTS

I N EARLY 1933, MOU WEITONG, HEAD OF THE XINJIANG CON-
sulate in Tashkent, received a pair of disturbing telegrams from Ili
and Tacheng. The military commanders stationed there had asked
him to "procure, without delay, a large amount of military weapons,"
in exchange for raw commodities. "Wherever there are many troops,"
Mou promptly wrote to Governor Jin Shuren, "there will be chaos. And
wherever one finds many weapons, there he will find rebellion. I cannot
stop the chaos in Xinjiang, but neither will I contribute to a rebellion."
Reports of raging violence across the border convinced Mou that Jin's
days as governor were numbered. The consul-general decided to send
out feelers to the Nationalist government in Nanjing. "Various agents
have recently arrived in the Soviet Union to purchase a massive quantity
of firearms," he reported in April. "But Xinjiang is Muslim territory. If
we suppress popular uprisings with force, it will be sure to create hatred
and enmity with the Han." He ended his report with a vow to take action.
"So long as I am in office, I cannot bring myself to just sit here and watch
quietly as foreign munitions are used to lay waste to our borderlands."
To Jin, Mou advised a swift exit. "I beseech my governor to sacrifice himself for the sake of Xinjiang. I hope you do not sacrifice all of Xinjiang
for the sake of one man." He assured Jin that if "you were to explore
exit strategies, the central government would be sure to give you one."[1]

Mou took care to forward all these telegrams to Nanjing, where
Nationalist officials reached an ominous conclusion. "There is no single person capable of putting all the pieces back together," noted one
assessment.[2] Of course, not all of the belligerents in Xinjiang *did* want
to put all the pieces back together. The Nationalists, however, could be

counted among those who did. To do so, they would need to draw upon a vision far more inclusive than the narrow Han nationalism that had fueled the revolutionary movement ever since the late Qing. On April 12, 1933, opportunity knocked. Former confidantes of Jin, supported by a White Russian contingent, chased the governor out of Urumchi and elected General Sheng Shicai as military governor (*duban*) of Xinjiang. Sheng was confined to the vicinity of the capital, now under constant siege by Ma Zhongying, the Hui warlord from Gansu. When word of these developments reached Nanjing, the Nationalists decided that the time had come to make their presence felt. Their means for doing so was to send a "pacification commissioner" to Urumchi, for the ostensible purpose of mediating among the various battlefield contestants. The real purpose, however, was to identify possible allies and attempt to seize power.

Suggestions for the formulation of an ethnopolitical message appropriate to Xinjiang came pouring into Nationalist offices. Consul-General Mou counseled Nanjing to send "a prestigious, high-ranking official who holds no prejudice against either Han or Muslim." Though he thought it best to send an official who was not prejudiced against Muslims, Mou was adamant about the composition of any new cabinet in Urumchi. "Above all else, you cannot allow any Muslim figure to obtain a position of real authority in Xinjiang." The Nationalists heard the opposite from Muslim associations in Beijing and Nanjing. "We should send a loyal Muslim official who thoroughly understands the Nationalist political platform, and who is capable of obtaining the trust of people in the northwest." Others, such as Shandong governor and former warlord Han Fuju, only recently integrated into the Nationalist fold, strained to conceal personal ambitions. Han begged Nanjing to allow him to "march my armies on the northwest, where I will first quell the rebellion, then cultivate the wastelands."[3] Based on these representative samples of advice, Nanjing had much to choose from: an inclusive multiethnic administration led by Han officials, a Muslim-led coalition premised on the tenets of nationally subordinate self-rule, or a muscular platform of Han-dominated economic development.

By early May, the Nationalists had made up their mind. Wang Jing-wei, head of the civil government and Chiang Kai-shek's chief rival for control of the party, took the lead. Noting how difficult it was to "communicate the reputation and prestige of the central government to the distant borderlands," Nanjing announced that it had selected Huang Musong, the vice-minister of foreign affairs, as "pacification commissioner" to Xinjiang. Huang, who would be sent on a similar mission to Tibet the following year, found Urumchi in shambles. "Though the residents appear calm," he wrote back to Nanjing, "the streets of the city resemble a riverbed, with filth and garbage strewn all about. . . . If we do not thoroughly renovate the government here, the situation will soon be beyond repair." The message Huang brought was one that Yang Zengxin likely would have approved, with minor modifications: an ethno-elitist alliance subordinated to Han rule. While searching for "a powerful general upon whom I can bestow a title and work together with," the vice-minister also visited the Urumchi prison, where he sought out the dispossessed heir to the Hami throne. In accordance with Wang Jing-wei's instructions, Huang promised the hapless heir to restore his noble titles, plus compensate him for any wealth confiscated by Jin—that is, should the Nationalists take control of Xinjiang.[4] In other words, had Huang had his way, real power would have continued to be concentrated in the hands of a few Han and Hui strongmen, with a supporting cast of symbolically important Muslim elites drawn from the hereditary nobility and united under recognition of a larger umbrella organization situated in China proper: the Nationalist Party.

Huang, however, did not have his way. Without a single soldier to his name, the vice-minister's attempts to meddle in Xinjiang's civil war quickly led to his ouster. As Huang himself admitted, "the details are exceedingly complex, and the general situation is far more complicated than I had expected. There is much that I simply do not understand. If I slip up even slightly, conflict is sure to break out." Sure enough, after backing an unsuccessful coup attempt against General Sheng, Huang found himself under house arrest and his co-conspirators executed. The price of the vice-minister's release was nothing less than the humiliating confirmation of Sheng Shicai as *duban* of Xinjiang, a man with whom no one in Nanjing wanted to work.[5] With Huang's ignominious departure from the northwest, Wang Jingwei formulated new plans in Nanjing for a second attempt to infiltrate Xinjiang. The pretext revolved around the need to formally inaugurate Sheng's position as *duban*, an occasion in which the Nationalists had a legitimate excuse to participate.

This time, Wang sent Luo Wen'gan, the minister of foreign affairs, to Urumchi to oversee the oath of office. On September 7, immediately after the ceremony, Luo made overtures to Zhang Peiyuan, a Han general in Ili, and Ma Zhongying, the Hui warlord then based in Turfan. Once again, General Sheng's nose for conspiracy began to twitch, and he launched a preemptive attack on Turfan. Luo tucked tail and fled to the Semipalatinsk consulate. On October 12, he cabled Wang in Nanjing: the time to act had come. "The way I see it," Luo wrote, "Sheng cheated us to get his title, and the central government conceded it only to keep the peace. Because Sheng still has not reformed his immoral ways, we have no choice but to take him out and remove a pox on our nation and people. Otherwise, no one will have any respect for the central government anymore."[6]

On December 29, 1933, Nanjing's endgame was revealed. Zhang Peiyuan set off from Ili with several thousand troops, intent on reducing Urumchi to rubble. Two weeks later, on January 12, 1934, Ma Zhongying set seven thousand of his best men against the walls of the capital. Had either Zhang's or Ma's armies survived for more than a week, there is little doubt that Urumchi would have fallen. Sheng Shicai, outnumbered and outgunned, had absolutely no chance of surviving the coming pincer attack. Then, as promised by Minister Luo, Ma Zhongying would have received jurisdiction over southern Xinjiang, while Zhang Peiyuan would have been given the northern half, both men paying something more than lip service to Nanjing.

But it was not to be. On December 30, only one day after General Zhang had set forth from Ili, seven thousand Soviet soldiers, under cover of tanks, warplanes, and massive artillery, sneaked up behind Zhang and decimated his battalion. Six days later Zhang committed suicide, brain-flecked shrapnel staining the snow. Back in Urumchi, Ma Zhong-ying continued his assault on Sheng. Two weeks later he was on the verge of breaking through the city gates. Then, on January 18, Soviet planes appeared in the sky and rained a hail of bombs on his encampment. Ma and a smattering of survivors fled south, never to threaten Urumchi again. In a dizzying change of fortune, Sheng *duban*, instead of lying maimed beneath the rubble, somehow stood triumphant atop it. There was only one question on everyone's mind.

What had just happened?

THE RISE OF SHENG SHICAI

To fully understand this dramatic turn of events, let us take a look at a page from the Chinese customs ledger at Nilka Pass for a single winter's morning in early 1934, drawn at random from the Xinjiang Uighur Autonomous Archives in Urumchi:

> A convoy arrived at 10:30 a.m., with 9 vehicles, 18 drivers (lead driver named Qurban), 625 blocks of tin (27,500 pounds), 164 rounds of ammunition, 272 empty iron canisters, and 7 empty wooden canisters. Released at 11:30 a.m.
>
> At 11:30 a.m. another convoy arrived, with 57 vehicles and 103 drivers (en route to Xingxing Gorge), 640 barrels of oil (97,428 kilograms, 53,466 kilograms less than before), 11 rifles, 36 "seven star" revolvers, 8 turtle guns, 1,100 bullets, and 56 Soviet commercial representatives.[7]

The resources described on this ledger represent only a piddling fraction of the enormous amount of industrial and war matériel that Sheng had managed to procure from the Soviet Union against the credit of his *duban* office.

But why would the Soviets choose to support Sheng, a relatively unknown Han general, against any number of Muslim leaders in the field? After all, in an age that valorized national determination, any one of them could construct a narrative of political legitimacy in Xinjiang far more convincing than that of Sheng, who was an ethnic and political outsider to the region. To answer this question, we must reconstruct the early days of the Soviet state in Central Asia with the aid of Russian archival documents. In 1921, when White Russian general Andrei Bakich occupied the Altay region and Turkic expatriate laborers in Andijan were openly calling for an attack on Ma Fuxing in Kashgar, the Soviet Politburo broached the idea of creating two separate states in Xinjiang: the Republics of Kashgar and Jungaria, to be set up in the southern and northern parts of the province. They would be modeled on the national republics then being molded throughout Soviet Central Asia. Lenin overruled the proposal, sparking a decade-long debate with the Comintern regarding Moscow's proper stance toward the revolutionary potential of "subjugated" peoples the world over. The Comintern viewed the Chinese administrators in Xinjiang as purveyors of a "greedy and barbarous colonization" and described its Han rulers as "slavemasters."[8] As a result, in 1931, all eyes were on the uprising in Hami. The Comintern saw in the movement led by Khoja Niyaz and Yolbars the "characteristics of a national liberation movement" and urged dispatching Soviet-trained Turkic expatriates into Xinjiang to help direct its course. "We must resolutely oppose any platform that provides assistance to the Chinese authorities in their suppression of the uprising."[9]

Stalin vetoed the Comintern proposal. Instead, on June 23, 1932, the Politburo decided to approve sales of US$200,705 worth of munitions to Governor Jin Shuren for use against the rebels, a preview of the much larger aid package given to Sheng less than two years later. Turkic supporters of the rebels were demoralized and lodged complaints with the Soviet consulate in Tacheng. Aware of how the Soviet state claimed to empower formerly subjugated, colonized people elsewhere via affirmative action policies, the protesters expressed disbelief. "We were quite sure that if oppressed peoples rise up against their oppressors for the sake of liberating their nation and homeland from occupation," the petition read, "the Soviet state would treat such peoples with sympathy, and defend them from oppression. . . . We believe that these rumors are false, because the Soviet authorities profess to be defenders of the oppressed."[10]

This they certainly professed. But profession is several steps short of implementation. The problem is that Soviet nationality policies were designed for exclusive use within the sovereign borders of the Soviet Union and its socialist satellites. In other words, Uighur expatriates living within Soviet Central Asia had every right to expect the creation of a Uighur autonomous entity of some sort, whether as a region, a county, or some other such administrative unit, lodged within the boundaries of a much larger national republic (such as Kazakhstan or Kyrgyzstan) under Soviet control. For people resident in Xinjiang yet envious of the ostensible political autonomy conferred upon their transnational brethren, however, Comintern blueprints for national liberation movements could not compete with Soviet realpolitik.[11] Throughout the 1930s, Soviet economic and political interests in East Asia translated into support for a Han warlord who would neither secede from China nor be subject to the dictates of a resurgent central government. After all, an independent Xinjiang—or any single portion of Xinjiang—might encourage secessionist sentiments among Moscow's national republics next door, while the installation of Nanjing's preferred ally in Urumchi would surely bode ill for the Russian economic monopoly in the province.

Cognizant of the real power behind Sheng's office, the Nationalists quickly attended to damage control. Once it became clear that the armies of Ma Zhongying and Zhang Peiyuan had been eliminated or otherwise marginalized, Fu Zuoyi, the governor of Suiyuan and nominal ally of the Nationalists, rushed to his telegraph. "The entire nation is rejoicing now that the central government has discovered a pillar of loyalty and administrative talent [in the northwest]," Fu wrote to Sheng. "During these times of trouble along our borderlands, we must place absolute trust in Chiang and Wang . . . and pay no heed to the inevitable rumors." Nanjing strained to squelch precisely those rumors that described how the Nationalist government had tried to destroy the same *duban* upon whom it had conferred its own reluctant blessings just six months earlier. "The central government is fully aware of your extraordinary concern for the nation," came a telegram from Tianjin, "and Chiang and Wang trust you completely. Do not listen to malicious rumors." From Qinghai, Ma Lin, a distant relative of Ma Zhongying, told Sheng not to believe anything he read in the newspapers. "Due to obstructions in communication and transportation, rumors have circulated unchecked throughout the nation, often appearing in the newspapers. Such things are truly regrettable, like gnat droppings in an otherwise flawless piece of jade."[12]

What Sheng thought of these disingenuous telegrams we do not know, only that he did not destroy them. As records from the Soviet archives show, Sheng was far more preoccupied about this time with trying to impress his Soviet patrons. In telegrams addressed to Stalin, Sheng highlighted his lifelong interest in socialist ideologies, a crude understanding of Marxist-Leninist dialectics, and a burning desire to join the ranks of the Communist Party of the Soviet Union. Incredibly, he even laid out an elaborate plan to foment a new communist revolution from Xinjiang, link up with the beleaguered Chinese Soviet in Jiangxi, and overthrow the Nationalist government in Nanjing. Stunned by Sheng's fawning confessions and reckless proposals, Stalin informed the Soviet consul in Urumchi that Sheng's letter had "made a depressing impression on our comrades." Concluding that only a "provocateur" or a "hopeless leftist having no idea about Marxism" could have written it, Stalin issued a blanket repudiation of each of Sheng's points, warning that "if our instructions are not taken into consideration we will be forced to deny aid to Sheng." Sheng wisely retracted his original telegram, assuring Stalin that "the instructions you have given me are unquestionably correct."[13] With that, an uneasy alliance was born.

Meanwhile, back in Nanjing, the industrious Wang Jingwei returned to the drawing board and planned for his next assault on Xinjiang. This was part of a larger strategy designed to increase his influence within the party vis-à-vis Chiang Kai-shek. This time, however, frustrated by Soviet intervention, Wang would change tack, set aside the ethno-elitist blueprint of Governor Yang, and begin to formulate his own ethnopopulist approach to Xinjiang.

Jin Shuren was to be its first target.

FIGURE 3.1. Sheng Shicai, military governor (*duban*) of Xinjiang, 1933–44, with Swedish explorer Sven Hedin, c. 1934. Trained in Japan but excluded from Nationalist circles in Nanjing, Sheng Shicai rose to power in Xinjiang on the strength of a comprehensive alliance with the Soviet Union. To justify the continued monopoly on power by an ethnic and political outsider to the province, Sheng imported and adapted a Soviet platform of ethnopopulist affirmative action for the non-Han peoples of Xinjiang. Sven Hedin Foundation collection, Museum of Ethnography, Stockholm.

SHOW TRIAL IN NANJING

On July 12, 1933, Jin Shuren, the now disgraced governor of Xinjiang, completed an exhausting three-month journey from Urumchi to Tianjin. After the April coup, he had traveled first via military escort to Tacheng, then by rail from Novonikolayevsk to Vladivostok, and finally by boat to Tianjin. "Due to hardships incurred during my journey," he wrote to Wang Jingwei in Nanjing, "my old illness has flared up once more. After I have recovered, I will call upon your office and dutifully submit my report in person."[14] Wang, however, had no intention of listening to Jin's story over a cup of tea. On October 30, the day after Jin arrived in Nanjing, Wang ordered his arrest and indefinite incarceration while awaiting trial on four counts: signing an unauthorized trade pact with the Soviet Union in 1931 (the arms purchase); absconding with provincial funds; wanton destruction of Xinjiang; and forced appropriation of peasant land. When Jin hired an expensive lawyer from Shanghai and began to defend himself in the press, the stage was set for a cause célèbre.[15]

Yet the Jin Shuren trial actually had little to do with Jin Shuren. Its real point was to put on public display the Nationalist government's newly enlightened stance regarding the ethnopolitical future of Xinjiang. In practice, Nationalist emissaries Huang Musong and Luo Wen'gan, in their attempts to seize power in Urumchi in 1933, had acted much like Hami rebel leaders Khoja Niyaz and Yolbars two years prior. That is, in the name of the nation and the common man, each had secretly formed alliances with political figures from the old ethno-elitist order. Despite a liberal helping of revolutionary discourse, in practice they looked much like Governor Yang. If the Nationalists wanted to challenge the Soviet grip on Sheng Shicai and Xinjiang, they would need to do a lot more than simply talk like the Soviets. They would need to act like the Soviets, too.

In practice, this meant taking under their wing prominent Uighur intellectuals from Xinjiang who were willing to broadcast the language of ethnopopulism on behalf of their Nationalist sponsors. In 1933, Muslim councils in Beijing had urged Nanjing to pay more attention to its image in Xinjiang. "The key to national defense lies not in military armaments but in the minds of the people." This job was entrusted to Isa Yusuf Alptekin, a former translator in the Tashkent consulate. For reasons not entirely understood, Isa left the consulate in 1931 and made his way to Nanjing. Once there, Huang Musong saw the value of an educated native from Xinjiang and decided to include Isa on his mission to Urumchi. Upon his return to Nanjing, Isa began to refer to himself as a "representative of Xinjiang" and was allotted funds to publish a host of periodicals concerned with border affairs.[16] In these, Isa advocated for the political enfranchisement of Muslim peoples in Xinjiang under the "enlightened" stewardship of the Nationalist government. He was also given license to criticize any Han ruler in Xinjiang, past or present, who was not an ally of Nanjing. Isa's agenda proved immensely useful for the new image Wang Jingwei hoped to project to the people of Xinjiang: by locating political sovereignty in the common Muslim masses, Isa positioned himself and his Nationalist patrons as ethnopopulist allies of the poor and downtrodden non-Han peoples of the northwest.[17] As Yufeng Mao has shown, Wang's Xinjiang initiatives were part of a much larger propaganda campaign waged by the Nationalists during the 1930s and 1940s, designed to leverage China's Muslim peoples to cultivate goodwill throughout the Middle East.[18]

Isa also served as a magnet for other educated Uighurs from Xinjiang who had been excluded from the old ethno-elitist order. In 1934, Isa managed to bring Masud Sabri—a future Nationalist governor of Xinjiang—to Nanjing. A native of Ili who had spent more than a decade abroad completing a medical degree in Istanbul, Masud was well known throughout Xinjiang. His tenure in Istanbul, against the backdrop of World War I, turned him into an intransigent Russophobe, an endearing quality for the Nationalist brass. But he was also considered to be a progressive advocate of cultural modernization among "his" people. From 1917 to 1928, Yang Zengxin twice shut down Masud's Uighur schools, twice threw him into jail, and thrice interrogated him—all clear signs that he represented a threat to the conservative ethnopolitical order. In 1931, when Jin's administration began to crumble and Turkic militants established a short-lived separatist state in Khotan, Masud forsook medicine for good and plunged into politics. Before long, disillusioned with the movement in Khotan, Masud crossed the Himalayas into India, where he accepted Isa's invitation to begin a new career in Nanjing.[19]

In 1934, Wang Jingwei gave the public profile of both men a significant boost when he allowed Isa and Masud the strategic honor of bringing formal suit against Jin Shuren. The courtroom proceedings for Jin's trial were dominated by the theatrics of Isa and two of Masud's sons, who portrayed the Hami uprising as a revolutionary Turkic national liberation movement, much like Khoja Niyaz and Yolbars had before them. They also provided the newspapers with a deluge of sentimental grandstanding that made Jin look like an insensitive lout. "The judge then showed Jin a photograph of an akhund [killed in the fighting] and asked him if he knew this man personally. Jin replied, 'Lots of people were killed in the fighting. I didn't know any of them.'" Though ostensibly a forum in which to broadcast the ethnically neutral justice of the Nationalist government, no one could fail to miss the potent symbolism of Uighur prosecutors excoriating a Han defendant. From the beginning, Jin's conviction was a foregone conclusion. On June 29, 1935, the court pronounced his guilt, labeled him a "national traitor," and handed down a sentence of three and a half years in prison. Upon his release, Jin retired from politics and returned to his hometown in Gansu. A lifelong devotee of the opium pipe, he died in 1941, at sixty-two.[20] He has not been remembered fondly.

The Jin Shuren trial in Nanjing had proven to be the perfect stage for Wang Jingwei to showcase his increasingly sophisticated strategy for the future recovery of Xinjiang. The key elements would remain part and parcel of the Nationalist approach to Xinjiang for the next two decades, long after Wang ended his career in disgrace and ignominy. The formula was simple: elevate non-Han figures to positions of conspicuous prestige, then permit them to criticize the frontier policies of anyone who was not the Nationalists. More often than not, Isa's rhetorical targets were Han or Hui officials. As the years wore on, however, he and his Turkic colleagues increasingly took aim at the Nationalists. The limits of such criticism thus had to be constantly renegotiated, usually through trial and error. In the context of Nanjing's attempt to infiltrate Xinjiang in the early 1930s, the ethnopopulist rhetoric of Isa and Masud proved most useful as a counter to Soviet affirmative action, which, all along Xinjiang's borders, located sovereignty in poor and "downtrodden" non-Russians. But the Nationalists were nothing if not flexible, and they continued to cultivate aristocratic non-Han elites as well, so long as they learned to speak in the name of the nation. After all, Japan, with its entrenched interests in China's northeast, consistently peddled a conservative politics of difference: Tokyo's answer to Soviet populists of "humble" origin in Outer Mongolia was to elevate men like Puyi, the last emperor of the Qing dynasty, to the throne of Manchukuo.

Shut out of the northwest for the next decade, the Nationalists had plenty of time to determine the proper balance of progressive ethnopopulist and conservative ethno-elitist strategies of difference for Xinjiang. In 1937, Yolbars, a representative of the latter, fled Hami and joined Chiang Kai-shek in Nanjing. Mohammed Emin Bugra, a Uighur politician living in exile in Afghanistan and a representative of the former, accepted an invitation to join Isa and Masud in the wartime capital of Chongqing. The next time the Nationalists marched into Urumchi, this cabinet of non-Han personages, both conservative and progressive, would all have major roles to play and bigger Han scapegoats to skewer.

AFFIRMATIVE ACTION IN XINJIANG

Back in Urumchi, Sheng Shicai had a decision to make. What, if any, posture should he evince toward the kangaroo court then vilifying his predecessor in Nanjing? Sheng had every reason to gloat over Jin Shuren's downfall. Four years earlier, during a scouting mission in Nanjing, Jin's agents had recognized Sheng's superb martial qualifications and urged the governor to offer him a job training soldiers in Urumchi. Sheng accepted, but Jin, ever wary of this Japanese-trained mercenary in his midst (prior to his arrival in Nanjing, Sheng had served a Manchurian warlord named Guo Songling and studied in Tokyo), used him sparingly. Even in disgrace and exile, Jin could not bring himself to say anything nice about his former general. "Sheng Shicai is merely of ordinary talent, a man whose ambitions far outstrip his abilities," Jin wrote to Nanjing in 1933. "He will not be able to maintain peace along the borderlands."[21] So, in 1934, when the Nationalist courts sent a formal request to Sheng for damning evidence against Jin, he might have been expected to leap at the chance to consign his former boss to the gallows.

He did not. Certain incivilities, of course, were in order. "Jin has a corrupt mind, and his worldview is outdated," the High Court of Xinjiang informed Nanjing in December, undoubtedly with Sheng's approval. "He delegated tasks poorly and left office without any accomplishments to speak of." Speaking ill of Jin was one thing, appropriately relished; condoning a Nationalist show trial against a one-time governor of Xinjiang was quite another. "As for the present accusations against him . . . we find that all of his actions were proper and justified by the circumstances at the time, and do not constitute grounds for legal culpability." The High Court of Xinjiang proceeded to defend the 1931 land reform efforts in Hami as "in accordance with the doctrine of our late premier Sun Yat-sen that we should eliminate systems of feudal governance," and reminded the courts that the Turkic peasants of Hami had themselves long petitioned for the abolition of the khanate. Those who sought to accuse Jin of anything other than gross incompetence were engaged in "nothing more than malicious slander."[22] In the final analysis, any initiative with the potential to ingratiate the Nationalists with a popular audience in Xinjiang boded ill for Sheng. It was thus little wonder that he chose to repudiate the charges against Jin.

Moreover, Sheng scarcely could have failed to note the uncomfortable parallels between his own precarious position and the current Nationalist posture toward Xinjiang. Sheng and the Nationalists were responding to an apocalyptic war waged in response to what was widely perceived— or at least widely propagandized—as a Han colonization project. Both needed to come to terms with an unprecedented outburst of anti-Han vitriol in the public sphere, and both found themselves facing strident calls for the expulsion of all Han from the northwestern borderlands (even some Hui subscribed to this platform, as the pronouncements of Ma Zhongying revealed). Yet try as they might, there was simply no way to disguise the fact that both Sheng Shicai and Chiang Kai-shek belonged to an ethnocultural community regarded by Khotan insurgents as "yellow filth." For his part, Sheng, unlike Yang and Jin, was not even a career northwest official. "Sheng is from the northeast," a central government report noted. "With respect to a platform of national determination, he is not qualified to fill the post of either *duban* or chairman in Xinjiang."[23] If the *duban* hoped to last even half as long as his predecessor, he would have to justify the installation of yet another Han governor in Urumchi, and he would need to do so in the aftermath of substantial bloodshed directed against its reoccurrence. He needed exactly what the Nationalists were slowly cultivating in Nanjing by means of Isa and Masud's association with the Jin Shuren show trial: a Han narrative of ethnopopulist legitimacy.

Yet Sheng was in a hurry. He needed an *instant* narrative of legitimacy. Fortunately, the Soviets were prepared to sell him precisely that. The "goods" came in the form of a rehabilitated Han administration newly legitimized by a modified application of Soviet affirmative action policies and economic stimulus packages. The "price" was to turn Xinjiang into an exclusive sphere of Soviet interest, with a near complete monopoly over the extraction of the province's agricultural and mineral wealth. Of necessity, the first few years of Sheng's tenure as *duban* were marked by providing the promised "goods." As early as May 1934, a team of Soviet engineers drew up plans for four thousand miles of highways, bridges, and tunnels, all oriented westward toward the Turksib Railway in Soviet Central Asia. From 1935 to 1937, Moscow extended eight million U.S. dollars in loans to the *duban,* while welcoming more than three hundred students from Xinjiang to study in Soviet universities (by contrast, Jin had sent five students to Germany). On the ledger of somewhat less savory initiatives, Sheng also received instruction in the ways of a Stalinist police state, quickly recruiting a network of secret police and plainclothes informants to go along with Urumchi's expanded prisons and execution grounds.[24]

In 1934, and again in 1937, the Soviets also undertook three separate military operations designed to destroy Sheng's rivals: Zhang Peiyuan in Ili, Ma Zhongying in Urumchi, and Ma Hushan in Khotan. The

Soviet treatment of Ma Zhongying—who, unlike Zhang Peiyuan, survived the battle for Urumchi in early 1934—is one of the enduring mysteries of modern Xinjiang history. For the past several decades, the only thing historians knew for certain was that he willfully crossed over into Soviet territory in July 1934, leaving behind one of his generals, Ma Hushan, to take command of their Hui army at Khotan. Though no reliable evidence ever emerged to support the theory, it was simply assumed that the Soviets had somehow managed to convince Ma to enter the Soviet Union in hopes of using him as a bargaining chip against both Sheng Shicai and Ma Hushan. Recently declassified Soviet archives now confirm this strategic calculus beyond a doubt. Documents dating from 1935 to 1937 reveal at least eight references to Ma and whether he should be "released" back into Xinjiang. These discussions reached a climax in the summer of 1937, when the Politburo announced that "the Soviet government is ready to permit the departure of Ma Zhu-ying" upon the condition that Ma Hushan lay down his arms and agree to work within the new Sheng-led order. Instead, Ma Hushan's decision to renew hostilities with Sheng soon thereafter likely sealed Ma Zhongying's fate, especially if he was suspected of playing a role in Ma Hushan's return to the battlefield. Following a terse Politburo decree of July 29, 1937 ("Do not release Machuin [Ma Zhongying]"), his name does not surface in the archives again. It is interesting to note, however, that as late as January 1944, Han officials stationed in the Xinjiang consulates in Soviet Central Asia continued to believe that Ma Zhongying was still alive and capable of being "released" back into Xinjiang.[25]

The most visible transformation, however, came with the introduction of Soviet nationality policies. To assist Sheng in implementing affirmative action in Xinjiang, Moscow sent to Urumchi a sizeable contingent of Han and Turkic expatriates who were already familiar with the Leninist-Stalinist line. These men included Han members of the Chinese Communist Party undergoing education and indoctrination in Moscow, along with former residents of Xinjiang's southern oases. The latter were long resident in Soviet Central Asia and long hopeful of exporting Soviet nationality policies back to their homeland. Yang Zengxin had maintained the utmost vigilance against their return. These expatriate Turkic activists championed replacing the ethnonym *Turban* with *Uighur,* and they agitated vociferously for the political enfranchisement of Xinjiang's non-Han peoples along Soviet lines. Until now, Moscow had kept them on a tight leash, forbidding the exportation of affirmative action policies intended for use only within the Soviet Union and its satellites. Now that Xinjiang had become precisely that—a Soviet satellite—these "Uighurs" were at last permitted to cross the border. Yet they were saddled with one very ironic caveat: they could apply their knowledge of Bolshevik nationality policies only in support of the Han warlord whom Moscow now regarded as one of its most important strategic allies: Sheng Shicai.[26]

In adapting Soviet nationality policies for Xinjiang, Sheng eschewed one long-standing condition: that every nationality be institutionally tethered to a physical plot of land bearing its name. In omitting this cherished stipulation of Stalin's, Sheng hewed closer to what was known as the Austro-Marxist line than the Bolshevik line. Thus, unlike the Soviets before him and the Chinese Communists after him, Sheng made no attempt to establish "autonomous" regions, counties, or other such administrative units in Xinjiang, and certainly not in the name of the Kazaks, Kyrgyz, Uighurs, or Tajiks. Xinjiang was still a "province" formally indistinct from any other province of China, and Ili County was still Ili County, not the Ili Kazak Autonomous County (as the Chinese Communists would label it). The defining feature of Sheng's administration was ethnocultural autonomy, not territorial autonomy. Other than this, however, Sheng's approach, with some other slight variations, generally aped that of the Soviet Union. His chief advisers were Garegin Apresov, the Soviet consul in Urumchi, and Yu Xiusong, a Han member of the Comintern. Yu urged Sheng to preside over "national representative conferences," where leading nobles and community leaders traveled to Urumchi for an audience with the *duban.* The idea was to convince the people of Xinjiang that Sheng was genuinely interested in sharing power and that the days of exclusive Han governance were over. Nothing embodied this promise more than the appointment of Khoja Niyaz Haji, the former rebel leader of Hami, as deputy governor of the province.

After the Hami rebellion, Han narratives of political legitimacy in Xinjiang hinged on ostentatious demonstrations of political equality with non-Han peoples. As a result, Khoja Niyaz was by no means the only such representative to be incorporated into the new government.[27]

Unlike those of his predecessors, however, the viability of Sheng's regime depended upon much more than merely a pragmatic alliance of non-Han personages, many of whom had only recently begun to speak in the language of revolutionary ethnopopulism. To reach the mass of indigenous commoners ignored by Yang and Jin, Sheng sponsored two new organizations: the Anti-Imperialist Society (Fandihui) and the Association for Ethnocultural Advancement (Minzu Wenhua Cujinhui). The Anti-Imperialist Society was the official mouthpiece of Sheng's administration, and it constituted the first and only organization into which a resident of Xinjiang could gain admission as a card-carrying party member. The very name of the organization was strategic: if Sheng defined himself as an enemy of "imperialism," it became much harder for his rivals to tar him with the brush of "colonialism." (Two decades later, the Chinese Communists would adopt the same rhetorical approach, even going so far as to insist that those who participated in an anti-imperialist national liberation movement were fundamentally incapable of practicing imperialism.)

Under the direction of the Anti-Imperialist Society, residents of Xinjiang experienced a revolution in print culture. Every time they went to the market, they paid in bills displaying both Chinese and Uighur script. By 1936, there were 260 different booklets, magazines, journals, pamphlets, and newspapers available for purchase on the streets. Later, the society consolidated operations into a single flagship monthly journal, *Anti-Imperialist Frontline* (Fandi zhanxian), which soon tallied a print run of 5,000 to 15,000 copies, in both Chinese and Uighur editions. To reach distant nomads and rural residents, the society organized "back to the homestead" work teams, composed of students and low-level government functionaries who spent their summers circulating Sheng's message to their hometowns and tribes. Hoping to hone the persuasive capabilities of these work teams, the society sponsored speech competitions and training sessions in public rhetoric. "Though we have many kinds of print materials . . . if we want our message to penetrate to the farthest corners of the province and take root in villages and marketplaces, we must hone our skills in public speaking and household persuasion, and communicate via the simple language of the streets."[28]

Those literate in both Chinese and a native language suddenly saw their political stock skyrocket. One Mongol official was targeted for promotion based on the fact that "he is fluent in Chinese, thoroughly conversant in the government's policies, and has spent much time translating the speeches of the *duban* and other important figures."[29] Any man so linguistically endowed would have been sent to the annual national representative conferences, where he—or, for the first time, she—would be able to learn the ins and outs of Soviet affirmative action policies. "Other than the Soviet Union, which is the only country in the entire world to have completely and correctly solved its nationality problems," Yu announced in 1937 to a group of Mongol representatives, "Xinjiang is the only place to have adopted a correct nationality policy."[30] Yu was determined to prove that, thanks to the "scientific" remedies of the Soviet approach, ethnic tension in Xinjiang was a thing of the past. Such a miracle was supposed to have been achieved by revoking "the special privileges of former ruling groups such as the Han" and elevating into visible positions of authority representatives of all fourteen nationalities now determined to populate the province. As Yu frequently reminded his audiences, "from the deputy chairman to provincial committee members, from deputy departmental heads to deputy bureau heads, from deputy divisional heads through various organizations throughout the government, everywhere are representatives of the various nationalities."[31]

The work of the Anti-Imperialist Society was largely relegated to the realm of discourse, in that it attempted to shield Sheng from hostile charges of "Chinese imperialism" or "Han chauvinism." By contrast, the tasks assigned to the Association for Ethnocultural Advancement tell us much more about the concrete transformations the *duban* intended to pursue on the ground. The association, compartmentalized into nine sub-bureaus devoted to the affairs of one or more closely related nationalities (Han, Uighur, Hui, Mongol, Kazak-Kyrgyz, Sibe-Solon-Manchu, White Russian, Tatar, and Uzbek), was charged with bringing the cultural levels of "backward" peoples up to par with those of "advanced" peoples. At least, that is what it claimed to do. In reality, the available archival evidence—admittedly lean—suggests that the association and its nine sub-bureaus were committed to an extractive economic agenda couched in the language of ethnocultural populism. If successful, the association would help Sheng accomplish two pressing goals. First, he would be able to pay off his Soviet creditors with surplus agricultural product culled from "unproductive" nomadic pastures. Second, he would succeed in breaking the power of entrenched non-Han elites by investing the non-Han masses below them with political agency. In other words, Sheng would become the first governor to develop Xinjiang's natural resources on the basis of an inclusive progressive platform rather than an exclusive conservative one.

The Association for Ethnocultural Advancement was tasked with the creation and promotion of attractive pretexts with which to lure non-Han commoners to Urumchi. Once there, they enrolled in new institutions designed to indoctrinate them in the Soviet-inspired policies of the *duban*. In his drive to foster a mass non-Han ethnic constituency, Sheng poured sizable resources into cultural and educational initiatives. In missives exchanged among Sheng and the heads of the various sub-bureaus, for example, the expense of a Mongol Lama temple in Urumchi—a symbol of the old order—is justified for its potential in converting Mongol youth. "The Mongol people are simple-minded adherents of the Lamaist faith, and are steeped in superstitions," wrote a man named Saliq, head of the Mongol Association for Ethnocultural Advancement, to Sheng. Therefore, "it would seem best to establish a Lama holy site in Urumchi, which would then give Mongol youth a reason to come to the capital. Once here, they can worship freely as they please, while simultaneously being compelled to enroll in a course of study that will introduce them to the new education." This way, the Lamaist religion would "naturally dissipate," and Mongol youth would become "fully cognizant of the government's policies." In another directive, Sheng made it clear what he expected of anyone—in this case, a nomad—who received food and board in Urumchi. "In the future they are to return to their pastures and thoroughly indoctrinate their people's minds with our policies."[32]

Education offered an important venue for attracting non-Han recruits capable of eroding the authority of their elders back home. Within a year of taking office, Sheng approved compulsory student quotas for each nationality and region of the province. In the spring of 1935, one of the first groups of Kazak and Mongol youth enrolled in an elementary school designed specifically for the children of nomads. The Bureau of Education, working in tandem with the association, initially expressed satisfaction at the fulfillment of the quotas. Before long, however, the students' lackluster performance became cause for concern. Four students left school without explanation, three returned home due to "special circumstances," and a staggering thirteen—nearly half the class—showed up on the first day with festering ulcers and boils covering their bodies. After these were sent home, only eight students remained to attend classes. Clearly their Kazak and Mongol elders back home had not sent the most fit and promising youth to Urumchi. Why? For many, it was a simple economic calculus. "Some people say," a newspaper editorial observed, "'Our family is poor and we live on a day-to-day basis. Our children must stay home to help, making it impossible to send them elsewhere to study.'"[33]

For others, however, an alarming pattern had begun to emerge. When young men and women ventured out to the provincial capital, they tended to return home with ideas threatening to the old ethno-elitist order. This was not a coincidence: Sheng's policies were deliberately designed to undermine the conservative status quo and create an ethnopopulist politics of difference centered on the non-Han masses. At first, some younger non-Han elites, such as Manchuqjab, khan-wang of the Torgut Mongols, thought it possible to stave off Sheng's antagonism by aping his rhetoric. In late 1936, when Manchuqjab made the momentous decision to relocate to Urumchi—a decision he would live to regret—he offered an assessment of his peers back home that was tailor-made to please the *duban*. "The current chief is a doddering old man, who spends his days reciting the scriptures and ignoring matters of state," the khan-wang wrote to Sheng. "To carry out our tasks of improvement, we must promote a talented new person. The current incumbent is not the man for the job."[34]

For those who did not come to the capital, Sheng chipped away at their authority from afar. One such opportunity came in early 1936, when Sheng learned of the plight of eleven-year-old Patima, a Uighur girl whose prepubescent marriage in a southern oasis had culminated in injuries to her genitalia. "The marrying off of adolescent girls is an age-old custom among the Kazaks and Uighurs," the report noted. Sheng's response was firm. "Post bulletins banning this custom, and convene all village heads and tribal chiefs to explain to them that this practice is henceforth to be strictly forbidden."[35] Though we are more likely today to side with Patima and Sheng than with the wealthy Uighur clerics implicated in her abuse, we should note that such a decree undermined precisely those conservative power holders with whom Sheng saw himself in competition: men of long-standing wealth, title, or both. Unfortunately for Sheng, his agents searched in vain for signs of compliance with the new decrees. "[The people here] know nothing of official government policies," reported a downcast official from Karashahr in late 1938. "Though our various leaders have enthusiastically propagated government policies, speaking until our tongues are dry and wisdom depleted, we can claim less than one enlightened convert out of every hundred people."[36]

Faced with a gradual circling of the ethno-elitist wagons, Sheng shifted to less admirable tactics. A Soviet historian has described the "soft-line" and "hard-line" policies deployed in support of the new affirmative action platform in the Soviet Union.[37] While he takes pains to stress the synchronous nature of the two (i.e., executions for nationalist zealotry did not necessarily preclude further stimulation of nationalist pride), in the case of Sheng Shicai, a clear progression from soft to hard-line tactics appears to be in evidence. The turning point came in 1937.

DEPLETE AND REPLENISH

"On December 4, 1937, at two o'clock in the afternoon," came a report from Wulungu Lake County, in the Altay region, "we convened a meeting of approximately five hundred people. We explained the sentences of death for the most heinous offenders and announced the liquidation of their property. The audience responded with thunderous applause." Throughout the late fall and early winter of 1937, the people of Xinjiang were repeatedly regaled with harrowing accounts of traitorous officials occupying the highest echelons of power. These officials were said to have been "bought off by the imperialist powers," to have served secretly as "running dogs of the imperialists," and to be bent on "the mass murder of our compatriots."[38] The endless meetings were necessary not only because the charges were so fantastic but also because the purported offenders were so well known. In the three months from August to October 1937, more than eight hundred government officials received invitations to political gatherings held throughout the province. Upon their arrival, agents from Sheng's security network placed them under arrest and escorted them to a jail in Urumchi. Among the most prominent were deputy chairman Khoja Niyaz Haji, former Kashgar *daoyin* Ma Shaowu, Soviet consul Garegin Apresov, and Comintern agent Yu Xiusong. All four men were eventually executed.

The immediate context for the political drama of 1937 was the hysteria of Stalin's great purges in the Soviet Union. We know very little of the substance—if any—behind Sheng's accusations. It is clear, however, that the men and women tossed into prison included nearly everyone who had risen to positions of power during the past three years. Seemingly the only people immune to arrest were members of the *duban*'s own patronage network, most of whom dated their relationship with Sheng to the days of Jin Shuren. It was not a purge directed toward any particular nationality; if anything, by the time he left Xinjiang, Sheng probably had more Han blood on his hands than that of any other ethnic group. Shrewdly parroting the discourse of "Trotskyites" and "running dogs of imperialism" then in vogue across the Soviet border, the *duban* saw an opportunity and pounced. After years of warfare, the rehabilitation of a viable government administration in Xinjiang had led Sheng to incorporate numerous Han and non-Han adversaries into office. Once enemies on the battlefield, Sheng did not trust any of them in the halls of power. Therefore, just as Soviet affirmative action had expertly disguised the recrudescence of Russian imperial power, so too did the Stalinist show trials in Moscow deftly legitimize Sheng's consolidation of power in Urumchi.

The terror of the "great purge" in Xinjiang fundamentally shifted the balance of power between Sheng and the entrenched non-Han elites of the province. The latter now knew exactly what the *duban* was capable of and what might happen to them if they continued to resist his intrusions into their communities. Furthermore, it was apparent to all that the Soviet Union stood firmly behind Sheng, as clearly demonstrated by Moscow's acquiescence in the execution of Consul Apresov. As a result, models of appropriate demonstrations of loyalty to Sheng were duly circulated. In 1938, the Incarnate Lama of Tacheng received praise for "voluntarily stepping aside and letting the pastures bordering Heshi County undergo household registration and be donated for urban construction." Conversely, held up for vilification were those tribal chiefs who "do not let any outsider settle on their pastures. As a result, no one is able to commit to serious cultivation, and the land lies fallow for decades."[39] Progressive local leaders were those who welcomed Soviet-trained veterinarians and their vaccines, and did not begrudge the collection of "surplus" sheep resulting from projected increases in herd size.

Still, compliance with the new directives from Urumchi could only go so far. In the end, Sheng was determined to take out all vestiges of the old ethno-elitist order, erecting in their stead the structures of ethnocultural populism, if not its substance. Less than a year after the purges, Qiu Zongjun, Sheng's father-in-law and the minister of provincial administration, urged his daughter's husband to abolish the hereditary titles of the non-Han aristocracy. "It would be best if this tribe could request the implementation of a local administration and dissolution of the old titles of nobility on its own initiative," Qiu wrote of one Mongol community. "Then, after we carry out their request in accordance with the relevant statutes, those who are upset with the administrative change will have no pretext [to retaliate]."[40] Just one year earlier, such a request likely would have gotten nowhere. After 1937, however, local power holders who chose not to emulate Urumchi's depictions of model behavior did so at their own risk. By the time Sheng had left Xinjiang, not a single non-Han eminence from the days of Yang and Jin still retained his liberty. Among those languishing in jail, regretting their decision to meet with the *duban* in Urumchi, were Manchuqjab, the khan-wang of the Torgut Mongols; Prince Ailin of the Altay Kazaks; and the descendants of the Muslim princes of Kucha, Hami, and Turfan.

If Sheng's promises of Soviet-style affirmative action turned out to be hollow, his desire to develop the resources of Xinjiang was not. Partly it stemmed from his promise to bring the fruits of socialist modernity to his subjects. Mostly, however, the impetus came from Moscow, to whom Sheng was grossly in debt. In 1938, Mao Zemin, the younger brother of Mao Zedong, passed through Xinjiang en route to Moscow, where he hoped to receive medical treatment. Ten days after his first meeting with Sheng, Mao, working under the pseudonym Zhou Bin, was named deputy director of the Ministry of Finance. He was appalled at what he saw. "In little more than five years," he wrote to his brother in April, Sheng "has recklessly printed thirty billion silver taels and taken out twenty million *yuan* in foreign currency loans. Who knows what other unconscionable acts have been committed here?"[41]

The problem was not that Xinjiang lacked a tax base capable of financing its government, provided its rulers—like Yang—were in a position to refrain from investing in the military. The problem was now the Soviets themselves, who acted in a capacity analogous to the Qing government half a century earlier: as a financial wet nurse for a fiscally famished province. Unlike Beijing, however, which dreamed of wealth but settled for sovereignty, Moscow wanted nothing but wealth. As such, it expected to receive a lucrative return on its investment. And that meant sooner or later, Sheng would have to pay his bills—or else. "If we had a

similarly vast revenue in northern Shaanxi," Mao noted, referring to the
Chinese Communist headquarters in Yan'an, "we would find ourselves
with an enormous surplus. But when we consider the unconscionable
size of the foreign debt here, the situation is simply unsustainable."[42]

Mao appears to have spared no effort in trying to relieve Sheng of his
Soviet creditors, who continued to finance one-third of Xinjiang's annual
budget. But the late 1930s witnessed the rise of the wartime economy in
Moscow, and Mao simply could not capture enough "floating capital" to
satisfy Sheng's creditors. Had he done so, it is unlikely the *duban* would
have placed Mao in charge of one of his least reputable organizations:
the Rebel Assets Committee. Having failed to sate the Soviet behemoth
by "soft" economic initiatives, Sheng and Mao turned to "hard" methods. The Rebel Assets Committee, though injurious to Sheng over the
long term, proved a seductive short-term salve. Charged with seizing and
managing the wealth of anyone deemed a "rebel" by the state, the committee soon found itself in charge of considerable assets. To take just one
example, the confiscated estate of former deputy chairman Khoja Niyaz
Haji consisted of seventy-six camels and four thousand sheep in Urumchi; five irrigation canals, one factory, and a hundred wells in Turfan;
five thousand sheep and sixty irrigation canals in Hami; a house and
tillable fields in Wushi; and one flower garden in Kucha.[43]

During Sheng's tenure as *duban*, anyone who went to jail could
expect the majority of his family's assets to be confiscated. Though estimates vary, a veteran of Sheng's security force later put the number of
executions in Urumchi at 14,000. As this does not include the many
more people who were imprisoned but later released or anyone outside
the capital, we can probably concur with the assessment of another former official, Guang Lu, that the total number of people jailed during
Sheng's tenure as *duban* was likely close to 80,000—in other words, 2 to
3 percent of the population of Xinjiang.[44] So many people were thrown
into prison on trumped-up charges that visitors to elementary schools in
Urumchi began to comment on the striking prevalence of female teach-
ers. Half the students said they had no father at home. In 1944, with
Sheng's departure, his Nationalist successor was inundated with twenty

to thirty petitions per day from relatives of the *duban*'s victims. While Sheng was in office, urban residents had been known to recite the following maxim: "Whether you go to jail now or go to jail later, only one thing is certain: sooner or later, you will go to jail."[45]

The evidence suggests that Sheng's security apparatus identified prominent subjects of some means, then lodged trumped-up charges against them to facilitate confiscating their wealth. Education and the military, two of the most costly institutions funded by Sheng and the Soviets, seem to have been the chief recipients of these confiscated assets. In 1939, poor classroom conditions in Khotan prompted a local official to register his intent to "move the entire current group of students to the seized courtyard of the rebel Ablajan, where they will hold class and assume lodgings." Another school received 150,000 taels worth of auctioned-off "rebel assets" for "educational and cultural expenses."[46] In Hami, rebel assets helped purchase sixty-three camels for the local military garrison, while seized buildings were used to quarter troops.[47] Anything not funneled into the military or schools appears to have found its way straight into the coffers of Mao's Rebel Assets Committee in Urumchi. "We have taken possession of former magistrate Chen's rebel assets," reported an official in Yarkand in May 1940, "and auctioned off his interests in copper and steel for $1,477.26 in foreign currency. We will soon transfer these funds from the branch bank in Yarkand to the Rebel Assets Committee in Urumchi. The remaining five hundred pounds of copper will be delivered on the next truck out."[48]

Sheng extracted financial capital from the people of Xinjiang in another way, too, this one more tactfully disguised. Donation campaigns were run for almost anything that could be construed as a public cause. When the streets of Urumchi turned into a muddy morass in the spring, municipal authorities launched a "public hygiene" campaign. Though the Sino-Japanese War was being fought far from Xinjiang's borders, the patriotic slogan exhorted residents to maintain "healthy bodies if we are to drive out the Japanese bandits!" In late 1936, a devastating earthquake in Lanzhou, the capital of neighboring Gansu, provided the pretext for a "disaster relief" campaign. The residents of Kucha County submitted 122,000 silver taels for the victims, while thirteen wealthy donors in Weili turned in 250,000 taels.[49] Despite the supposedly "voluntary" nature of these donations, clear quotas were imposed. In Urumchi, all public servants were told to donate two days' salary for the front line in Suiyuan. During the public hygiene campaign in 1941, an Urumchi shopkeeper observed that, due to a lull in business, "I am unable to submit my donation. I beg you, sir, to look upon me with pity, and order your subordinates to collect my donation in accordance with the lowest possible household regulations, as relief for your people."[50]

In those cases where overt quotas did not apply, a measure of subtle coercion did. In late 1937, one of Sheng's generals turned a covetous eye on the property of native-place Han guilds from Hunan and Hubei. "Currently, these buildings stand as the private possessions of a minority of the population, and provide no benefit whatsoever to the general masses," he noted. "Without instigating any suspicions, I propose that we send someone out to make contact with the guild heads, convince them of the greater good they will be serving, and explain to them that we are not confiscating their property."[51] Of course, the guild heads were free to decline the general's entreaties. But in a climate where any person of means was liable to be thrown into prison on imaginary charges, they did so at their own peril. The clearest indication of the use of coercion, however, is to be found in the preemptive justifications of the collectors. "The donations I collected this time were solicited without an ounce of forceful coercion," wrote an agent for the Mongol Association of Ethnocultural Advancement in September 1939. "I took only from rich nomads who were willing to assist. No poor nomad was compelled to donate." Collection agents working for the Anti-Imperialist Society also denied any wrongdoing. "These donations of sheep and jewelry were offered without the slightest bit of coercion, and every one of them was entirely voluntary."[52]

That Sheng's agents in the field now felt compelled to defend their collection methods suggests that the *duban* had experienced a backlash of sorts, one sufficiently worrisome to prompt a modest retrenchment of operations. By this point, after years of imprisonments, executions, and compulsory donations, Sheng had every reason to be anxious. After all, in resorting to shady tactics for the repayment of Soviet largesse, he had inadvertently endangered the most precious thing Moscow had given him: a convincing narrative of Han political legitimacy in Xinjiang. The acute pushback Sheng felt from the residents of Xinjiang in response to his incessant donation campaigns forced the *duban* to try to rein in his officials. That, of course, was easier said than done. "In every district, despite repeated directives to the contrary, [local officials] continue to run rampant donation campaigns among the masses," Sheng wrote in 1940. Henceforth, there would be no more mercy for offenders, and "anyone who proposes or advocates donation campaigns must be assumed to be a running dog of the imperialists, intent on sabotaging the policies of our government."[53] Local officials, who had grown dependent upon such "donations," resented Sheng's change of heart. Attributing any and all misunderstandings to "errors in translation," they appealed to Sheng with the justness of their cause. "I was just about to proceed with collection duties for this year's famine preparation donations," wrote the magistrate of Korla County in the fall of 1940, "when I received your orders that all donation campaigns should stop." The magistrate appealed for an exception. "Can I continue to collect these donations or not?"[54]

By the late 1930s, the view of Sheng among the people of Xinjiang could not have been anything but negative. His avowed commitment to a program of ethnocultural populism had merely been a political façade designed to help him break the power of the non-Han elites and confiscate their wealth. His highly touted program of economic development for the masses turned out to be a thinly veiled siphon of provincial wealth, payable to the Soviets, who themselves had betrayed their own oft-publicized principles by propping up a power-hungry Han warlord. For non-Han intellectuals who had bought into the first three years of the new administration, the Sheng-Soviet alliance turned out to be an unholy union. Thus far, however, Sheng had proven himself merely a proponent of equal opportunity exploitation for the people of Xinjiang. Now, bereft of administrative talent and in desperate need of qualified candidates to fill government vacancies, Sheng was at the point of no return. During his last few years in office, the *duban* would embark on a series of initiatives that would make him look very much like the harbinger of Han colonialism that the Comintern had always believed him to be.

After the purges of 1937, lack of administrative talent, always a problem in Xinjiang, became even more acute. Not only had Sheng removed his provincial rivals, Han and non-Han alike, but he had also imprisoned much of the Han and Uighur personnel sent to him by Moscow. As a result, complaints about unqualified officials and widespread vacancies began to flood the *duban*'s office. "Ever since these two officials fled their posts," wrote a Mongol from Karashahr in May 1938, "affairs of state have gone untended. I alone certainly cannot assume the burden."[55] Sheng's security agents began to scour the countryside for suitable replacements, at one point embarking on a weeklong search for talent in the Altay region. The local security bureau reported on "mannerisms of speech and body language" and cast in a positive light youth born of mixed Han-Mongol marriages. "Since they are Han, they are completely loyal to the government." Other candidates were required to undergo an exhaustive vetting process designed to ensure complete political reliability. One candidate was ready to depart, but his local handlers "await the *duban*'s detailed investigation and directives before we send him to Urumchi."[56]

As is evident from these quotations, the cultivation of non-Han talent not connected to the old ethno-elitist order of Xinjiang took considerable time and resources. Meanwhile, there was a great temptation to install locally prominent Han in vacancies throughout the province. After all, in republican Xinjiang, only Han were likely to meet all the criteria established by the Sheng administration: humble birth, ample education, and lack of ties to existing religious or tribal institutions. "The positions of deputy county magistrate and deputy bureau magistrate should all be filled with Han officials," wrote the district magistrate of Karashahr in early 1939. "This will enable us to carry out our work."[57] Even better for Sheng would be if they were vulnerable outsiders entirely dependent on his patronage. Such was precisely the criteria fulfilled by several hundred Chinese Communist cadres sent from their base in Yan'an to lend fraternal assistance to the Soviet Union's favored *duban*-in-arms. Between 1938 to 1940, upon the explicit instructions of Sheng's Soviet advisers, they were posted throughout the southern Uighur oases. "Ever since taking office as magistrate of Moyu County," Sheng observed in late 1940, referring to a suburb of Khotan, "Nasirjan has not had any accomplishments to his name. Relieve him of his post and fill the vacancy with Chen Jiexu, deputy director of the Khotan Tax Bureau." Ten Han cadres were sent to Khotan alone, where they undertook the delicate task of divesting the locals of the very firearms they had used to shoot Han like themselves just five years earlier.[58]

Of course, Sheng turned to the Chinese Communists because they were educated, resourceful, and vulnerable, not necessarily because they were Han. This last point cannot be emphasized enough. In fact, the clearest indication that Sheng was not engaged in a Han-led disenfranchisement of indigenous leaders lies in the fact that he eventually executed a considerable number of the Yan'an cadres, including Mao Zemin, the younger brother of Mao Zedong. All that, however, occurred behind closed doors. As far as the non-Han peoples of Xinjiang were concerned, the Han governor had marginalized or killed every one of their established leaders, replacing a visible majority of them with Han officials. By the time Sheng left Xinjiang, virtually no Turkic or Mongol official—or any Han whose influence predated Sheng's rise—occupied a position of political substance. Very few of Sheng's subjects had the means to resist him, if for no other reason than that they knew the Soviets still stood behind the *duban,* warplanes and machine guns at the ready.

Even had the Soviets withdrawn their support for Sheng, what hope was there? Moscow had already helped Sheng collect his subjects' firearms, destroy their armies, imprison or execute their leaders, deprive them of the next generation of talent, and insulate the province from any outside force with whom they might possibly form an alliance. The only place in Xinjiang where one or more of these conditions still failed to apply was Altay, home to several tribes of Kazaks and Mongols. Not surprisingly, then, it was in Altay that many of the pivotal events of the next decade were to occur.

THE BIRTH OF A KAZAK ETHNOPOPULIST

Long the least integrated and most remote region of the province, Altay lacked even a rudimentary road connecting it to the provincial capital. Yang Zengxin once called it the "most desolate and remote region" (*juedi*) in all of China. Though Altay's steeded nomads could reach Urumchi in mere days, convoys of mechanized transport could take weeks to go in the other direction. Clear up until the 1950s, access from Urumchi was typically achieved not in a straight beeline to the northeast but via a roundabout journey first to Tacheng in the northwest, then east to Altay City (formerly Chenghua Si). Faced with the unlikely prospect of defending Altay with soldiers from Urumchi, Yang Zengxin had attempted to curry favor with the Altay Kazaks by decreeing a lower tax burden for them than for any other nomadic group, along with the right to bear arms—a rare privilege—in the event the Outer Mongols crossed the border. And since Altay had played only a marginal role in the warfare preceding Sheng's rise, it was not devastated in subsequent mopping-up campaigns. As a result, as the new decade approached, anyone looking for a viable source of resistance to the status quo would have done well to look toward Altay.

The first signs of trouble arose in 1937, when Sheng issued a blanket order abolishing the nomads' right to hunt. "We have always depended on hunting to survive," protested a Kazak chief. "If we cannot hunt, we will be unable to maintain our livelihood."[59] Though Sheng was not bent on starving the nomads of Xinjiang, he was determined to deprive them of firearms. And since Sheng was now a close ally of the Soviets, the nomads of Altay in theory had nothing to fear from the Mongolian People's Republic, which deferred to Moscow in all matters of foreign affairs. Therefore, if deprived of the legal right to hunt, Kazaks and Mongols no longer had any pretext to retain their firearms. Unfortunately for Sheng, the Kazaks and Mongols of Altay did not see things this way, and no weapons were forthcoming. In response, the *duban* invited their chiefs to Urumchi for a "meeting," where he promptly placed them under house arrest. The game was blackmail: chiefs for guns.[60] The plan backfired when one leader defied the *duban,* gathered his followers, and fled the capital. Though Sheng sent emissaries out to assure him that his "life, wealth, and status would be safeguarded," most of the *duban*'s entreaties fell on deaf ears.[61] In early 1940, under cover of night, a team of Kazak raiders laid siege to a security bureau in Koktogay and ambushed a firearms liquidation depot. Their message to the *duban* was carved on the bodies of their victims, dumped unceremoniously at the gates of Altay City: corpses without eyes or tongues, and hearts and intestines dangling from their torsos.[62]

Sheng responded by strafing the Altay steppes on repeated flyby missions. The Kazak rebels, soon fifteen hundred in number, shot down several warplanes. In September, Sheng brokered an uneasy peace with a series of concessions. He promised to close down local security bureaus, release imprisoned leaders, and cease confiscating firearms. Yet Kazak unease continued, fueled by the increasing presence of Soviet prospectors. The wartime economy of Europe had altered Moscow's priorities in Xinjiang. No longer did the Soviets demand only cotton, sheep, leather, silk, and oil from Sheng. Now they wanted the building blocks of industrial war munitions: tin, aluminum, copper, gold, silver, wolfram, and beryllium.[63] For Lu Xiaozu, the onetime *daoyin* of Altay during the days of Governor Yang, this explained the sudden surge of Soviet interest in the region. "Its rich deposits of metals are known throughout the nation," Lu observed in 1945, a year after being released from the *duban*'s prisons. According to Lu, the departed governor had long ago recognized Altay's importance in an industrial world: "[Yang] said, 'Northern Xinjiang is more important. Even though southern Xinjiang has an abundance of agricultural products, their accumulated value still comes nowhere close to the worth of the Altay mountains.'"[64]

Moscow's response to the *duban*'s reports of Kazak unrest was to push Sheng aside and further enshrine its access to the mines of Altay. In November 1940, the Soviets submitted for Sheng's approval a document that would allow them the right to unearth tin and other "ancillary minerals" in Xinjiang for a period of fifty years. Sheng, swimming in debt, duly affixed his seal. In later years, the Xinjiang Tin Mines Agreement (formerly referred to as the "Sin-Tin" accord) would be described by Chinese policymakers and historians as the most humiliating, unequal treaty to be signed in China since 1915, when Japan submitted the Twenty-One Demands to Yuan Shikai. For Sheng, the increased Russian presence in Altay only made things worse. The following summer, Koktogay flared up yet again. This time the Kazaks took aim at Russian convoys prospecting for gold, beryllium, and other precious metals. Altay officials begged Sheng to send reinforcements. "Because we lack any authority capable of keeping the peace out here," wrote an alarmed official in Burjin in 1941, "our ability to develop agriculture has been compromised."[65] Sheng reverted to familiar tactics. He invited those still willing to risk a meeting to proceed to Altay City, where officials there convinced them to fly to Urumchi. Not surprisingly, Sheng had them arrested on touchdown.[66]

Left to his own devices, Sheng likely could have contained the Altay rebellion. Incarceration and machine guns had silenced previous rivals, and there is no reason to think they would have proven any less effective in this case. By the summer of 1941, however, the Soviets, besieged on the European front, were more desperate than ever before for war matériel. Sheng, deeply in debt to Moscow, could no longer drag his feet. In the following years, as Soviet mining expeditions continued to agitate the Kazaks, mounting bills for other expenses came due. Most of them were paid for with Altay minerals and the products of animal husbandry. In 1942, Sheng was forced to authorize the ruinous sale of 50,234 horses at basement prices. An additional ten thousand were taken in 1943 as "donations" to the provincial government, this time entirely from Altay pastures. The following year, Sheng repaid an aeronautics debt with 400,000 head of sheep from Tacheng and Altay, purchased at prices well below market value.[67] While the Soviets bled the turnip white, Sheng could only exhort his public servants to be more frugal, write on both sides of the paper, fix broken office chairs, ride bicycles to work, and stop drinking tea. Before long, the *duban* ordered everyone in Urumchi to turn off the lights, an austerity measure implemented during working hours.[68]

By 1942, Sheng was a pauper. Not only was the treasury bankrupt but so too was his vaunted ethnopopulist platform. Indeed, by this point, the only non-Han ethnopopulists of any substance to be found in Xinjiang were those that had taken up arms against the *duban*. After Sheng jailed the second batch of emissaries from Altay, a Kazak shepherd named Osman stepped into the void. Openly hostile to Sheng, Russians, Mongols, and any Han settlers in his midst, Osman quickly earned a unique calling among his Kazak peers: *batur*, an honorific bestowed upon self-made "heroes" of non-noble birth. Several years later, when Osman's social "betters" were finally released from prison, they looked down upon this Kazak upstart with scarcely concealed scorn. "Osman is a shepherd from Koktogay," noted the wife of Prince Ailin. "He is a nobody."[69] Yet it was precisely such non-Han "nobodies" that Sheng had vowed to elevate to positions of true wealth and power. When that wealth instead flowed to Moscow and all power gravitated toward Sheng, the hollow ethnopolitical rhetoric of the *duban* became ripe for appropriation by others.

The most famous of these "others" was Osman Batur, whose charisma and presence soon won him the mass Kazak constituency Sheng had once promised to cultivate. "Over the past four or five years," Osman announced in 1943, with charismatic aplomb, "I have toiled without cease and have not slept at night. I have endured the cold of winter and the heat of summer. When I sleep, it is on a bed of horse droppings, with a hard rock for my pillow. All day long, I spur my steed across riverbeds and do battle with the enemy." For those not yet resigned to Orwellian compliance with the Soviet-inspired rhetoric of Sheng, Osman was an exhilarating breath of fresh air. "We are not animals," he continued. "We are the same as any other people. And when we see that the actions of the *duban* do not match his words, how can we not rise up and fight for the interests of the Kazaks?" For many, Osman was the embodiment of everything Sheng had promised but failed to deliver. He called for local Kazak self-government, the formation of a Kazak militia, an end to Han settlement of Kazak pastures, and active resistance to the Han officials in Sheng's government. The pride that Osman felt in his imagined community of Kazak braves was tangible. "If, among you, there are any heroes who wish to fight for the future of our people, then come with me. Grab your guns and mount your horses. Otherwise, you may as well turn your back on the customs and traditions handed down to us from our ancestors."[70]

Osman would not go away. Invited to Urumchi for "negotiations," he instead fled south to the Bulgin River. Though Sheng continued to pursue Osman, events in Europe soon overtook developments in Xinjiang. With the Soviets fighting for their lives at Stalingrad, Sheng sensed an opportunity to divest himself of his creditors. In July 1942, the *duban* pulled off an astonishing about-face. Without warning, he executed those Chinese Communists still in his employ, invited to Urumchi a delegation of Nationalists from their wartime base in Chongqing, and offered to cede all authority for the foreign affairs of Xinjiang to Chiang Kai-shek. The Generalissimo was understandably thrilled. "For all matters pertaining to Xinjiang," Chiang rushed to inform the Soviet ambassador, "your government must now deal with the central government of China. You are not permitted to discuss anything with Sheng *duban*." In his diary, Chiang referred to the recovery of the northwest as "the greatest accomplishment in the history of the Nationalist government."[71] For Moscow, it was an astonishing affront, all the more so due to the many outstanding bills on Sheng's ledgers. It did not surprise anyone, then, when the Soviets turned to Osman to recover Sheng's debt.

THE HAMI REBELLION DEFERRED

Sheng Shicai was the first Han official to pursue a platform of ethnopolitical populism in Xinjiang, one designed to unite its Soviet-defined nationalities under a single Chinese roof. When the discourse is stripped away, however, it is apparent that Sheng pursued the same agenda of intensified resource extraction and industrial development to which his reviled predecessor, Jin Shuren, had once aspired. To the extent that Jin and Sheng countenanced the imposition of a Soviet economic monopoly in the province, Moscow supported this agenda, as evidenced by its arms sales to Jin and comprehensive aid packages to Sheng. As long as such outside support was tendered with interest, however, the entire enterprise merely constituted a deferred reckoning. When the bills finally came due—as they did, with a vengeance, at the turn of the decade— Sheng began to look remarkably similar to Jin Shuren, only with a vastly superior regime of rhetorical sophistication and coercive machinery at his disposal. In both cases, the impetus for change was the same. That is, the moment Xinjiang became enmeshed in larger geopolitical competition, the inability of the Chinese central government to finance a competent standing army necessitated raising an army with provincial resources. As Xinjiang's resources were invariably insufficient, their diversion to the military quickly destabilized the ethnopolitical balance.

Jin Shuren was a casualty of the first destabilization. For a time, Sheng Shicai avoided being a casualty of the second by adapting the ethnopopulist discourse and institutions of Soviet affirmative action into Xinjiang. When those institutions proved to be window dressing on a program of resource extraction far more intense than anything Jin had ever attempted, Sheng resorted to the tools of a Stalinist police state to safeguard his position. But when the Soviets began to take by force what Sheng and Mao Zemin repeatedly proved incapable of producing, the day of reckoning finally arrived. Its poster child was Osman Batur, a Kazak ethnopopulist entirely of Sheng's making. At this point, the only way to avoid a repeat performance of the Hami rebellion—this time in Altay—was to write off the balance owed to the Soviets by transferring the bill to the Nationalists. This is precisely what Sheng tried to do in the summer of 1942, while the Soviets were preoccupied with the Germans. But someone had to foot the bill of costly modernization projects in Xinjiang, and Moscow had no intention of letting the Han stewards of Xinjiang fly the coop. By his act of stealth and ingratitude, Sheng had merely gotten himself off the hook.

Now it fell to the Nationalists to reap what Sheng had sown. In so doing, they would find themselves pulled into an elaborate ethnopolitical bluffing match marked by a degree of Kazak and Uighur agency unique in the twentieth century.

CHAPTER 4

RAISING THE STAKES IN NATIONALIST XINJIANG

SHENG SHICAI WAS THE FIRST ETHNOPOPULIST TO SERVE AS governor of Xinjiang. But he was by no means alone in his admiration of Soviet affirmative action policies. In the summer of 1941, as German panzer divisions raced across the Ukrainian steppe, Sheng invited a Nationalist diplomat from the Chinese embassy in Moscow to visit Urumchi. En route to Xinjiang, the envoy passed through the Soviet national republics of Kazakhstan and Uzbekistan. "Though native peoples are installed in office," he wrote in his report, "every important lever of decision-making is controlled by the Russians." The envoy, noting that Sheng had adopted a similar approach in Xinjiang, was duly impressed. "In just two years he achieved impressive results, and there appears to be no downside to this approach. In the future perhaps we can employ similar tactics for our own profit."[1] For his part, Chiang Kai-shek needed little encouragement on the matter. Now that Wang Jingwei, who had become a Japanese "collaborationist," was out of the picture, the Generalissimo, charged with governing actual non-Han borderlands for the first time in his career, had adopted his rival's one-time ethnopolitical portfolio. Of paramount importance were the lessons of the Jin Shuren trial: the idea that an ostentatious display of non-Han ethnopopulists in the public sphere could help construct a narrative of Chinese political legitimacy along the borderlands.

It should therefore not surprise us in the least to learn that Chiang Kai-shek, far from begrudging the *duban* his decade of estrangement from the central government, instead took great pains to enshrine a legacy for Sheng far more positive than that accorded to Jin Shuren. In

1945, when Isa Yusuf Alptekin and Masud Sabri attempted to use the Sixth Party Congress to treat Sheng in much the same manner as they had Jin a decade earlier, the Generalissimo would have none of it. "Yesterday one of our colleagues accused Comrade Sheng of wanton mass murder during his time in Xinjiang," Chiang announced. "Yet the fact that Comrade Sheng was eventually able to use his talents to deliver Xinjiang back to the central government is a contribution to both nation and party. Everyone here needs to understand this. Let us look at the larger picture, and stop fixating on culpability for the past."[2] Part of Chiang's statement can simply be attributed to the discourse of national humiliation, embodied along the non-Han peripheries by the fate of Outer Mongolia and Tibet: so long as Xinjiang did not become "the next Outer Mongolia" (wai Meng zhi xu), incidental unpleasantries accrued during the course of Sheng's rule could all be forgiven.

But there was more to Chiang's support of Sheng. The Generalissimo was among the most determined of advocates for granting Isa and Masud their own prominent ethnopopulist platform in Xinjiang. But he was also supremely envious of the political discipline and organization evinced by the Soviets and Chinese Communists in their bid to mobilize the common masses. When Chiang studied Sheng's time in Xinjiang, he saw someone who had taken the best of what the Soviets had to offer and used it to great effect against its original innovators. In short, Chiang saw in Sheng an ideal version of himself, before the trials and tribulations of the past fifteen years had stripped his party of all cohesion and discipline. As a result, Isa and Masud were free to criticize the abstract sins of past Han officials like Jin Shuren, in addition to advocating for Uighur ethnocultural autonomy in the present. But they were not allowed to tear down the entire ideological edifice that held together the diverse peoples and lands of China. With a few key adjustments, Sheng's ethnopolitical platform represented the future of Chinese stewardship over the non-Han borderlands. Much like Khoja Niyaz Haji under Sheng, men like Isa and Masud were a pragmatic means to an end. They were not an intrinsic source of pride for their patrons.

In emulating much of what passed for political engagement in Xinjiang during the era of the *duban*, the Generalissimo put himself at odds with the conservative wing of the party. Wu Zhongxin, a founding member of the party and the man chosen to replace Sheng as governor in 1944, was one such person. Wu's sympathies are evident in his diary, where he constantly ruminated on the actions of those who preceded him. For Wu, Yang Zengxin was a surprising source of pride, given the old governor's demonstrated hostility toward revolutionaries of all stripes. Conversely, when Wu reflected on Sheng Shicai and his methods of keeping the peace, he was far more judgmental. While the *duban* earned full merit for "his ability to preserve Xinjiang as part of Chinese territory," Wu wrote, "his means of conducting foreign and military affairs, in addition to economic and political matters, were so extreme that they have made it quite difficult today to resolve their complex legacies." Wu eagerly recorded every rumor and piece of gossip about Sheng that came his way, only to cross them out later while preparing his manuscript for publication. For his true feelings toward Sheng and his political career, we need only read Wu's musings after bumping into the former *duban* in Chongqing, where the stresses of life after Xinjiang had taken their toll. "It seems that, in accordance with the tenets of Buddhism," Wu concluded, "he has descended to the lowest depths of hell as recompense for his past crimes."[3]

These two very different interpretations of the legacy of Sheng Shicai represent the tensions within the Nationalist Party over the ethnopolitical posture best suited to governing Xinjiang. On the one hand was Chiang Kai-shek, who thought Sheng's progressive ethnopopulism and use of provincial outsiders had facilitated "the greatest accomplishment in the history of the Nationalist government." On the other end of the spectrum was Wu Zhongxin, who reserved heartfelt praise for Yang Zengxin, the architect of an ethno-elitist alliance composed of conservative non-Han personages and career northwest Han officials. In his day, Yang had despised men like Sheng. Sheng returned the favor, ritually scorning the "feudal" mindset of his robed predecessors. Though the Nationalists were avowed revolutionaries (and thus closer in spirit to Sheng than Yang), by the early 1940s their motto tended to be a pragmatic "whatever works." What brought together the two poles of Yang and Sheng—or Wu and Chiang—was the discourse of national humiliation, evident in the jarring loss of Outer Mongolia. Staring down the Soviet Goliath in Xinjiang would require both conservative and progressive ethnopolitical postures. What neither Wu nor Chiang yet knew, however, was just how far beyond their comfort zones they would have to push their respective agendas.

For their part, the Soviets engaged in deep introspection following their betrayal by Sheng. No longer would they commit resources to constructing a Chinese narrative of political legitimacy in a non-Han land. Instead, the time had come to tear down the very edifice of ethnopolitical enlightenment they themselves had once taught the Han to build in Xinjiang.

MANUFACTURING AN INSURGENCY

The origins of what would eventually become known as the Ili rebellion have long constituted one of the most scrutinized and contentious subjects in the history of modern Xinjiang. Under the microscope is the question of agency—in other words, who bears the brunt of responsibility for the initial outbreak of the rebellion and its subsequent expansion? Was it mostly an "organic" Uighur and Kazak rebellion against Han misrule, or was it largely concocted and manipulated by Moscow? Using contemporary Chinese-language news reports, memoir literature, and the archives of the British and American consulates, previous scholars have proposed a wide range of answers, running the gamut from "justified" Muslim resistance to a Soviet puppet state.[4] None of these studies, however, has been able to draw upon documentation of the rebellion from the perspectives of Soviet and Chinese archives. The remainder of this chapter will do precisely that. Taken in isolation, the unwavering conviction of Han officials in Xinjiang that the insurgency was conceived, implemented, and manipulated by the Soviets from start to finish naturally invites a healthy skepticism. When the evidence presented in the Chinese archives is consistently corroborated by the Soviet archives, however, it becomes increasingly difficult to maintain a stance of agnosticism regarding the causes and course of the rebellion.

On May 4, 1943, the Politburo of the Central Committee of the Communist Party of the Soviet Union passed a new resolution regarding the Chinese province of Xinjiang. According to the minutes for this meeting preserved in the Soviet archives, it called for the creation and support of "national revival groups" along the Soviet borders with Xinjiang. The types of aid envisioned, openly acknowledged by the authors of this document as "illegal," were staggering in scope: comprehensive propaganda efforts, covert infiltration and aggressive sabotage, military education and logistical support, and large-scale operations on the battlefield. Moreover, these "national revival groups" would be created "on the territory of Xinjiang among Uighurs, Kazakhs, Kirgiz, Mongols, and others composed of both local ethnic personnel as well as specially trained personnel from Soviet Central Asian republics." Three years later, Stalin and Lavrentii Beria, the Soviet minister of internal affairs, conferred medals on everyone who had helped carry out the May 4th directive. During the planning and execution stages, the neighboring Soviet Central Asian republics of Kazakhstan, Uzbekistan, and Kyrgyzstan were ordered to allot a fixed amount to be used for training, arming, and transporting non-Han insurgents. The goal was simple: drive Sheng Shicai out of the province and install in his place an administration composed of indigenous Xinjiang residents loyal to the Soviet Union.[5] In other words, the Soviets wanted to return to the early days of Sheng, when Uighurs and Kazaks had briefly occupied visible positions of authority in his cabinet. Only this time, there would be no Sheng. In fact, there would be no Han officials at all.

Such a monumental project was to be inaugurated by an unabashed flaunting of what John Muccio, an American diplomat in Urumchi, referred to as Soviet "swank." "The Soviet Consul-General has two very large FAS limousines," he wrote. "[They] gain face with their cars and the pretentious consular compound—one large block square—they maintain, housing about 180 members of the consular, Sino-Soviet airlines, Sino-Soviet cultural institute, and hospital staffs."[6] This swank was particularly useful for convincing potential recruits that Moscow would reward those who labored on its behalf as well as protect them from any backlash their activities might engender with the Chinese authorities. Soviet archives reveal that, in 1943, the five Soviet consulates in Xinjiang were tasked with canvassing their corners of the province to determine which site offered the best conditions for fomenting an insurrection against Han rule.[7] While the detailed findings of the consul in Ili—the future capital of the East Turkestan Republic—have not come to light, reports from Kashgar have, thanks largely to the efforts of clandestine Nationalist agents who managed to track down Soviet recruits.

As it turned out, swank had its downside. To unravel the trail of Soviet plots in Xinjiang, Nationalist agents needed only shadow conspicuous symbols of Soviet power. "I was chatting with Ibrahim at the entrance to the Kyrgyz school," reported a Kashgar security agent in August, "when suddenly an official Soviet car drove quickly past us, heading toward Tokkuzaq Street. We immediately followed the vehicle to Gulshdin, where it stopped briefly, then sped away. A man appeared where the car had stopped, so I rushed forward to apprehend him. As we struggled, a bag attached to his waist came undone and flyers fell into the gutter. After I yelled for Ibrahim to come help me, we were able to tie the man up and collect all the flyers."[8] The man they caught went by the name of Sadiq, the head of the local Uighur Association for Ethnocultural Advancement. He was typical of the men targeted by the Soviets. A product of Sheng's Soviet-inspired ethnocultural institutions, Sadiq was familiar with Soviet rhetoric yet thoroughly disillusioned with Sheng's vow to realize such promises on the ground.

According to Sadiq, his contact in the Kashgar consulate was a short, fat man he referred to as "Shapin." In exchange for generous sums of cash, Sadiq carried out assignments on Shapin's behalf. Shapin was most interested in determining what the Uighur masses of the southern oases thought of the Chinese government. Shapin ordered Sadiq to canvas village sentiment toward government conscription efforts and rumored immigration plans. "When you go to the countryside this time, I want you to pay close attention to whether the people are talking about these matters, and then report back to me," Shapin allegedly told him. When Sadiq failed to find evidence of local discontent, Shapin opted for more proactive measures. Handing Sadiq a stack of Uighur-language pamphlets, he ordered his spy back to the countryside. "Take these leaflets to the people and disseminate them among the peasants and akhunds." This time, Sadiq's mission was to "wake the people."[9] Upon the conclusion of this meeting with Shapin, Sadiq was ushered into a vehicle, dropped off on Tokkuzaq Street, and immediately apprehended by the Kashgar police.

The Soviets apparently pursued similar tactics with other recruits. A Uighur man by the name of Ariz was told to "investigate public opinion and write up a report," then hand it over to a man who would utter the phrase, "Two fewer books, please." A Tajik man by the name of Zemi, tasked with smuggling firearms into Tashkurgan, was assured that "the Soviets are not just recruiting you alone to go to the Soviet Union. We have people all over the place disseminating propaganda." In Khotan, a Soviet agent working under the cover of a geological mission conducted a social experiment. "Twenty days after I depart, under cover of night, post ten billboards in public that read as follows: 'Our akhunds have sold us out to the Han, our extinction is imminent.' . . . Pay attention to the public response, and report immediately to Kashgar. Then, after another ten days have passed, post more signs, under cover of night, that read: 'There are 800,000 of us Khotanese living here. Why do we not wake up and fight for our rights?' Again, pay attention to the public response, and send your reports along to Kashgar." Only when the Kashgar Police Bureau forwarded this stack of confessions to Urumchi did it finally begin to dawn on the Nationalists just how industrious the Soviets had been. "It is evident from these reports," wrote Wu Zexiang, a special agent sent to Xinjiang by the Ministry of Foreign Affairs, "that the Soviets have dispatched a considerable number of spies who are agitating all over the province."[10]

What was their message? A Kazak-language brochure seized near Tacheng provides an apt summation:

Following the invasion and occupation of Xinjiang by China over a period of many centuries, there came a decade of colonial policies by Sheng Shicai. The people have been oppressed, cheated, exploited, subjugated, and made ignorant. Our leaders have been eliminated, and now the Han and their armies control the entire province. The Solon, Kazak, Kyrgyz, Mongols, Tatars, Uzbeks, and other oppressed peoples have all become the slaves of Sheng Shicai and his running dogs. We cannot take this anymore. Let us initiate a glorious battle for freedom and equality.

From the street corner scuffle with Sadiq in Kashgar, the following critique was gleaned from one of his pamphlets: "Sheng *duban* proposed the concept of national equality and established the shells of cultural organizations in various districts. These organizations were just a means to an end, a veil, and one that everyone has now seen through. . . . At the locality, are there any district or county magistrates today who are Muslim? No, they are all Han, and no matter what crimes they commit, they always go unpunished." Additional leaflets drew attention to the prospect of mass Han immigration and mocked Sheng's affirmative action platform. Back in Urumchi, there was little doubt that such handbills were the products of Soviet presses. "These Kyrgyz, Kazak, and Uighur pamphlets," observed the same ministry official, "are printed on the presses of 'a certain party,' and are absolutely not something that could be produced in Kashgar."[11]

After canvassing their corners of the province, the Soviet consulates in Kashgar, Ili, and Altay submitted their reports to Moscow. The Kashgar consul, convinced that his spies were missing ubiquitous signs of anti-Han discontent, reported on the intense hatred for Han in his district. He added, however, that any uprising in Kashgar "must allow the participation of the Muslim clerical establishment; otherwise we will not be able to develop the struggle for national liberation." Since a movement united by nothing more than religion could turn just as easily against the Soviets as against the Han, Kashgar was promptly removed from the list. The consul in Ili submitted a much more positive report, drawing attention to the sizable community of Soviet-educated intellectuals living in the area. Promoted to office during the early days of Sheng's reign but now thoroughly embittered at their expulsion from government, these men would serve to offset the influence of Muslim clerics, who were viewed as key but unpredictable allies.[12]

So it passed that Ili was selected as the most promising site for a Soviet-led rebellion against Han rule. Just as the pro-Soviet outlook of Ili's Muslim elite worked substantially in its favor, so too were most other clandestine recruits culled from among those familiar with Soviet politics and culture. The chief training grounds for the insurgency appeared to be in Tashkent and Almaty, the capitals of Soviet Uzbekistan and Kazakhstan.[13] In January 1944, Feng Zuwen, the consul-general for all five Xinjiang offices in Central Asia, reported on the "frequency last year of suspicious Uighur expatriates applying for a visa to pass through Irkeshtam Pass on their way to Kashgar." After further inquiries revealed intimate dealings with the Soviets, Feng ordered all such applications to be rejected. The Andijan consulate compiled a list of twenty-four agents whose covert dispatch to Xinjiang was known to be imminent, and forwarded it to Urumchi for future reference. The consul in Zaysan kept tabs on twenty expatriates believed to have been sent to Moscow for training, then whisked back to Tacheng and Altay for undercover missions.[14] If Yang Zengxin would have been pleasantly surprised to learn of the pro-Chinese mission assigned to Uighur expatriates during Sheng's reign, his paranoia would have been fully vindicated by the subversive tasks finally entrusted to them during the 1940s.

Back in Xinjiang, Soviet consular staff continued to make overtures to the non-Han commoners. In Ili, they set up free Russian-language schools, hospitals, and film venues. They drove to the distant countryside and steppe to hand out candy and consumer goods, inquire into the health of the locals, and disseminate Soviet citizenship papers. "Whether these actions constitute the first steps toward initiating a major conflict along the borders," the Ministry of Foreign Affairs warned Chongqing, based on reports from its men in the field, "it is too early to surmise." In Urumchi, the Soviets targeted battle-tested White Russians, many of whom would become key generals for the insurgency. Tracts designed to tug at the heartstrings of expatriate Russians in Xinjiang were placed between the pages of books sold at the Soviet International Bookstore. The same store also distributed leaflets in Uighur extolling "how wonderful life is for Uighurs in the Soviet Union." Yaqub Beg, the leader of a briefly independent Islamic state in Xinjiang during the nineteenth century, was presented as a national hero.[15] Those inspired by these tracts were assured that the Soviet consulate would protect them should they need protecting. In the spring of 1944, when Chinese police in Urumchi tried to escort a White Russian to prison, their route happened to pass by the Soviet consulate. "Suddenly the consulate opened its front gates, and the criminal broke away and rushed into the compound," a police report read. The Soviets refused to produce the man in question, instead accusing the Xinjiang authorities of "provocative" behavior.[16]

The five Soviet consulates in Xinjiang could do little to stop the meticulous documentation of their clandestine activities by Nationalist agents deployed throughout the province. If Moscow wanted to retaliate before the formal outbreak of the rebellion, the natural place to direct their retribution was toward the five Xinjiang consulates in Soviet territory. Aware that all five consulates were submitting detailed reports to Chongqing regarding activities in their jurisdictions, Moscow decided to make life miserable for their staffs. "I went to the local foreign relations office to pick up our monthly provisions," wrote Sun Wendou, an employee in the Zaysan office, in early 1944, "and was told that they had not yet arrived. . . . This is nothing more than an excuse." Repeatedly rebuffed, Sun soon found himself with provisions barely sufficient to last two weeks, with similarly diminishing supplies of horse feed. In Semipalatinsk, the situation was similar. "Ever since we returned to the central government," wrote Wen Songling in August 1944, "the attitude of the local authorities has changed considerably toward us." Wen detailed sudden resignations of hired help, denial of firewood, refusal of foodstuffs, broken door locks, derailed telegrams, and disconnected telephone wires. "The weather is still warm now, so we can bear such neglect at present," Wen observed. "But if this situation continues into the winter, our lives will become miserable."[17]

It did, and they were. By October, a downcast Sun submitted his resignation, adding, "We are waiting here to die." His resignation rebuffed, Sun and his colleagues were soon forced to prepare their own meals and sweep their own floors. But mealtime pickings were scarce. "They will not even give me a single potato or head of cabbage here."[18] When the temperature dropped below freezing indoors, Sun was forced to scavenge for cow dung to light a fire. Faced with a struggle for mere survival, Xinjiang's consular staff no longer had any time or energy to report on Soviet activities, which, of course, was precisely the point. "My entire staff is shivering from the cold," wrote Wen Songling in Semipalatinsk. "We cannot get any work done." Based on the posture of their Soviet handlers, Sun Wendou was decidedly pessimistic about the future. "Since it seems that this is all being done for the sake of revenge, there is little hope that the situation will change." Fu Bingchang, the Chinese ambassador in Moscow, came to the same conclusion. "Whenever I forward our reports to the Soviet foreign ministry, the manner of their response suggests that this is all being done in the spirit of revenge."[19] Not to be outdone, Sheng Shicai appears to have tried to make life equally intolerable for Soviet consular staff in Xinjiang.[20]

By the spring of 1944, preparations for the Ili rebellion were nearly complete. And if that meant Sheng's days as *duban* were numbered, then it was Osman's job to initiate the denouement. "Under favorable conditions," wrote the Soviet consul in Altay, "Osman's Kazaks can play a decisive role in preparations for an uprising in Altay." Once conquered, an Osman-controlled Altay would be expected to merge with the coming movement in Ili. If handled correctly, Osman, the Soviets believed, could eventually "contribute a large portion of the district's population." In 1941, after spurning Sheng's offer to negotiate a peace treaty in Urumchi, Osman took refuge along the Bulgin River, near the border with Outer Mongolia. In late 1942, petty disputes between his Kazaks and local Mongols over grazing rights suddenly faded when Russian generals appeared on the scene. For the next two years, Osman received generous helpings of arms and military training, the only stipulation being that he direct both at Sheng. Osman's favorite tactic was to launch a surprise attack on one of the *duban*'s garrisons, then flee into Outer Mongolia. If just one of Sheng's men crossed the border—as they did in March 1944—the Soviets had all the excuse they needed to rain down a hail of bullets and bombs from the sky. After this, Osman struck north and, with twelve Soviet planes providing cover, occupied the town of Chingil with ease. Taken prisoner in retreat was a young Mongol soldier who confirmed Nationalist suspicions that the Soviets were responsible for Osman's sudden resurgence. "We were told that we were here to help the Kazaks resist government troops," he informed his captors.[21]

For his part, Sheng had seen enough, and demanded to know when the Nationalist government was going to file a formal note of protest with the Soviet ambassador. Chongqing, however, had little to gain by sticking out its neck for the *duban*. If the Generalissimo raised a fuss, "naturally the Soviets, via pretty phrases and misleading words, will deny all involvement, and then we will have no other recourse." The Soviet response to such protests could be predicted with distressing regularity. "We are currently investigating the matter and will get back to you shortly," Chongqing was duly informed in September. "But we have encountered such problems before, and our investigations have never confirmed the accusations brought forth," the memo read. "The Sino-Soviet border is extremely long," it continued, "and investigations over this vast area are extraordinarily difficult to undertake."[22] What the Nationalists did not want Sheng to know was that troubles for the *duban* were blessings for Chongqing. After the Osman fiasco, Sheng figured this out for himself and attempted to pull off one last reckless return to the Soviet fold. In the summer of 1944, he placed under sudden arrest more than seventy Nationalist officials posted to Xinjiang, accusing them of spying for the Chinese Communists in Yan'an. To Stalin, Sheng character-ized his Nationalist prisoners as Japanese spies. Both accusations were painfully outlandish, a sign of just how desperate Sheng had become. In August, the Generalissimo responded with a simple message, hand-delivered by Nationalist emissaries to Urumchi: Sheng was to report to Chongqing to take up the post of minister of forestry and agriculture. In the event the subtext was not obvious enough, Chiang also moved several fighter jets to the Gansu border and ordered Nationalist armies to march on the provincial capital.[23]

Sheng's eleven-year tenure as *duban* was over. He duly submitted his resignation and boarded a plane to Chongqing. In a letter delivered to Sheng upon his resignation, Chiang Kai-shek aired his assessment of the *duban*'s decade in Xinjiang. "For over ten years now you have maintained and protected the borders, keeping them perfectly intact," he wrote. "Words can hardly describe the unspeakable hardships you have endured. Since the founding of the Republic, no one has succeeded as you have in preserving the nation's borders."[24] Unfortunately for the Nationalists, however, Sheng's departure had no discernible effect on covert Soviet activities in Xinjiang. This they had long feared. According to one of Chiang Kai-shek's top generals, "The question of personnel is only secondary. The chief concern is still the Soviet Union itself. . . . If the Soviets have no intention of improving relations with us, our removal of one major official will have no impact."[25]

He was right. The border raids, training camps, weapons smuggling, and Soviet denials continued apace, in spite of Sheng's departure.

THE ILI REBELLION

Mere days after he stepped off the plane in Urumchi, new governor Wu Zhongxin received what he later referred to as a "cryptic" report from Kashgar. "Just before the last consul in Kashgar returned to the Soviet Union, he told his staff not to talk to anyone. When the new consul arrived, he also told his employees not to talk, assuring them that they would know why in two months' time." Several weeks later, Wu learned of a Kazak uprising in Nilka County, just south of Ili. Those reports, full of suspicious details, seemed to confirm the words of the departed Kashgar consul. According to intelligence passed along to the governor, thirty Kazak bandits had suddenly morphed into six hundred well-heeled soldiers. As they approached provincial garrisons, the rebels waved flags brandishing the words *East Turkestan Republic*. Further sleuthing led Wu to believe that professional Soviet soldiers had been disguised within their ranks, and that poor vagrant men had been recruited with free cloth, eggs, tea, and sugar. A few days later, after broadcasting strident anti-Han propaganda throughout the countryside, the bandits, now clearly made up of Kazaks, Tatars, and White Russians, moved toward the affluent oasis of Yining, the urban jewel of the Ili valley. There they picked off Han policemen in a wave of sniper attacks. At the same time, the Soviet consulate in Ili unveiled a machine gun on its roof, ostensibly for "defensive measures."[26]

On the morning of November 7, 1944, with disconcerting reports from Ili on his mind, Governor Wu made his way to the Soviet consulate in Urumchi to celebrate the twenty-seventh anniversary of the Bolshevik revolution. The Soviet consul bent over backward to accommodate Wu, adjusting the ceremonies to the governor's schedule and giving Wu the honor of first toast. Afterward, he escorted Wu to his vehicle, where the governor praised Stalin as a "remarkable leader." Had he known of the horrific bloodshed then taking place in the streets of Yining, Wu might have tempered his praise. Several hours prior, a well-armed force composed of White Russians and Kazaks had fanned out onto the streets of Yining and proceeded to occupy a middle school. From there they fought their way into several key buildings, chosen with an eye toward waging an extended siege. Confronted with state-of-the-art machine guns, heavy artillery, and ample vehicular support, approximately two thousand Han residents, officials, and officers retreated to three defensive locations: an air force training camp, a Chinese temple, and the municipal airport. According to eyewitness reports, those captured were stripped of their clothing, then shot in the head.[27]

For Governor Wu, there could be no doubt that the Soviets were responsible for the mayhem in Ili. Multiple eyewitness accounts confirmed the participation of Soviet soldiers and generals, the latter directing all major offensives. The rebels were frequent visitors to the Soviet consulate in Ili, where they held meetings and procured weapons. From a mountaintop perch, one witness described a view of "endless convoys of vehicles traveling back and forth between Yining and Khorgas Pass both day and night." Armed with such intelligence, Wu cabled Chongqing to request antiaircraft weapons capable of defending the capital. "The insurgents have no planes and no aircraft personnel," Chiang's befuddled secretary wrote back, on the logical assumption that these must be indigenous rebels. "How can they bomb Urumchi?" Wu scrambled to organize reinforcements but knew full well they would prove insufficient. "Xinjiang does not have the resources to deal with this problem all on its own," he wrote in his diary. The governor's pessimism proved well founded. Long before his reinforcements reached the outskirts of Yining, the rebels pinned them down and cut off their retreat. Many lost limbs to frostbite, while others were forced to eat leather.[28]

Over the next two months, the defenders trapped in Ili found themselves in increasingly desperate straits. In late January, the survivors, having retreated from the temple and air force training camp, converged on the airport. When food ran out, they slaughtered camels, dogs, and horses to eat. The last telegrams from Yining, sent at the end of January, crushed Wu's heart. "We have no more blood to spill or bones to break," the governor read. "When are reinforcements due to arrive? Should we continue to starve and await our deaths, or is there a chance that we might be able to link up with reinforcements if we were to break out of our encirclement?" Once the suicide attempts began, the surviving generals made plans for a desperate break through enemy lines. On the evening of January 30, 1945, over a thousand survivors charged through the encirclement and headed straight for the wintry countryside. Three days of frantic pursuit ensued before the rebels caught up, opening fire indiscriminately. The last few survivors scattered to the wind. By the time Wu learned of these developments a week later, all vestiges of Chinese authority had disappeared from the Ili valley. "The bodies of over a thousand of our revolutionary soldiers are now buried beneath endless heaps of snow," Wu concluded.[29]

The loss of Ili introduced a sense of urgency into Nationalist deliberations on the ethnopolitical future of Xinjiang. If the wanton bloodshed was not enough to give pause, the shrill rhetoric emanating from Ili certainly was. "Before long we will march on Urumchi," declared Ali Han Tore, the leader of the rebels, after the fall of the city. "We will overthrow the Han government and drive all the Han out of this province."[30] An Uzbek mullah who had fled the Soviet Union in 1931, Ali Han Tore rose to power as part of a broad Soviet coalition that included both secular intellectuals and Muslim religious leaders. Captured Kazaks later reported that the original rebel leaders were "elected by local Islamic gentry." Real military power in the field, however, was placed in the hands of Soviet or White Russian generals.[31] The Soviets viewed Ali Han Tore as a charismatic Muslim cleric from the Ili valley who could bring legions of foot soldiers on board. During the early stages of the insurrection, his fire-and-brimstone rhetoric provided a clear rallying cry: drive the "heathen" Han from "our" land. "God is on our side," he told his followers. "To my Muslim brethren, I say this: you must be on guard and you must be brave. When the time comes for our final victory, we will drive the barbarous Han out of our homeland. We will throw them out of our precious ancestral land of East Turkestan." To hear Ali Han Tore tell it, the Han, "a people of little culture themselves" who "consider us a lower race," were "the enemy of God." It goes without saying, then, that the idea of Xinjiang belonging to China was an "absurd fallacy."[32]

Soviet archives largely confirm the preceding account of the Ili rebellion as documented by Governor Wu and his agents in the field. V. A. Barmin, the only historian to have gained sustained access to Soviet archives on this subject, concludes that there is "no doubt" early rebel success was due in large part to "the assistance provided to them by the Soviet state." Barmin openly laments these actions as "illegal." Formally, of course, all such assistance was "undertaken at the request of the Prime Minister of the ETR, Ali Han Tore." In reality, however, it was common knowledge that the Soviets were providing copious weapons, equipment, instructors, and soldiers to the insurgency. Barmin, based on his reading of available Soviet archives, describes "sustained, serious, and tangible support."[33] Other documents that emerged only recently from the Soviet archives paint a similar picture. Stalin and Beria corresponded over the precise number of officers and soldiers of "Central Asian nationalities" to be decommissioned from the Red Army and spirited into Xinjiang, along with the number of serviceable fighter aircraft (nine) to be stationed in Ili. Their avowed goal was to create "intolerable conditions for the Chinese troops in Xinjiang." A general-major by the name of Yegnarov, sent to Xinjiang by the People's Commissariat for

Internal Affairs, surfaces in these files to report on his personal direction of rebel forces in the field and the brisk traffic back and forth across the border. Ali Han Tore also appears, writing personal letters to Stalin thanking him for "giving us comprehensive aid in this cause."[34]

In April 1945, two months after Ali Han Tore became a household name in Nationalist circles, Chiang Ching-kuo, the Generalissimo's Soviet-educated son and minister of education, stopped in Urumchi on his way to Moscow. Governor Wu played the role of host. "He suggested that we might now adopt the idea of some of our comrades in other clans, and try to appoint some of their talented people to government positions," Wu noted in his diary, adhering to the official party line of "clans" (*zongzu*) and "tribes" (*buluo*) rather than "ethnicities" (*minzu*). Ching-kuo also recommended "placing representatives from other clans as heads of government bureaus, with a Han occupying a secondary post." Eventually, he told Wu, the Nationalists might even consider appointing someone from another "clan" as deputy governor of the province. Wu might have been forgiven for thinking that he was talking to a Soviet adviser rather than the Generalissimo's own son. Wary of just whom Ching-kuo and his father were considering for such posts, Governor Wu assured his guest that he had already made considerable progress toward the cultivation of non-Han personnel. He then laid out all the details of his ethnopolitical vision for the future of Xinjiang. As the Generalissimo and his son were about to learn, Wu was an avid sponsor of an ethno-elitist platform of political difference.[35]

Over the past six months, Wu told Chiang, an illustrious group of non-Han figures had joined the governor's camp. Just a week after his arrival in Urumchi, Wu had scoured Sheng's prisons for signs of the old hereditary elites. "Among the imprisoned are many Kazak leaders," Wu noted. "If we used men like Prince Ailin in a prudent manner, we just might be able to quell the Kazak uprising." The incarceration of Prince Ailin had sparked the first Kazak uprising in 1940 and opened the door for Osman Batur. Wu sent Ailin numerous gifts in jail before eventually securing his release. "From here on out," Wu told the prince, doing his best impersonation yet of the long departed Governor Yang, "I will take the moral policies of Confucius as my guide, supporting and caring [for the Kazaks] as if they were my own younger brothers." Visibly touched—according to Wu—Ailin promised to rein in the insurgents. He then told Wu all about the good old days under Yang Zengxin. "In the past, we Kazaks lived peacefully and without incident," Ailin told his newfound patron. "It was only when the government started to imprison Kazak leaders that a handful of bad elements took the opportunity to incite a rebellion." Before long, Ailin and his wife began to make overtures to some of their followers in the Altay region, where they achieved instant results. "The nomad bandits have been deeply touched by the return of Prince Ailin to Altay," some Kazaks reported back to Urumchi, "and are submitting in droves. . . . They are calling Governor Wu the 'savior of the nomads.'"[36]

Next up were the Mongols. Wu learned that Manchuqjab, khan-wang of the Torguts, was still languishing in an Urumchi jail cell after seven long years of incarceration. With the departure of Sheng, droves of Mongols from Karashahr lined up to petition Wu for his release. The new governor was only too happy to comply and in return received declarations of loyalty from the representatives of seventy thousand Torgut Mongols. Manchuqjab, bitter and depressed, took somewhat longer to warm up to Wu. When he finally did, however, Wu promptly returned all the khan-wang's wealth, property, and armaments, which had been confiscated during the Sheng era. According to reports from the newly appointed Han official in Karashahr, the rehabilitation of Manchuqjab and his wife had encouraged their substantial following to turn a deaf ear to Soviet overtures. "The magnanimous overtures of Governor Wu have greatly moved us," Wu learned from a Mongol emissary. For the remainder of his tenure in Xinjiang, Karashahr and its Mongols, which had once played an integral role in the downfall of Governor Jin, were staunch allies of the Nationalist government. "It was said that there had been much restlessness among the Karashahr Mongols previously," Wu observed in early 1945. "But the release of Manchuqjab Khan and the return of his wife . . . have put their minds at ease and quelled their unrest."[37]

Looking to complete the resurrection of Governor Yang's non-Han cabinet, Wu next sought out Burhan Shahidi, the Uighur-speaking Tatar "dependent intermediary" whom Yang had once rescued from the Russian civil war. Wu found him, like so many others, wasting away in an Urumchi prison, his home ever since the *duban* had him recalled him from the Zaysan consulate and placed him under arrest. "He is just the sort of educated professional that Xinjiang needs more of," wrote Wu in his diary. "During his seven years in prison, he spent his days translating the 'Three Principles of the People' and the works of the Generalissimo into Uighur. This is most commendable." Recognizing his value—and fortuitous dependence on the Chinese state—Wu offered Burhan the prestigious posts of commissioner and head of public security in Urumchi, making him the first non-Han ever to hold these posts. "[His appointment] clearly shows the government's commitment to ethnic equality and public welfare." It also reinforced the governor's belief that the Nationalists had no need of ethnopopulist posturing derivative of the Soviet experience.[38]

Wu rested his case with a plea to utilize only "local Xinjiang leaders of real influence and power," who are "loyal to the nation." Such men, which Wu was convinced could be found "all over the province," were worthy of an invitation to Chongqing, where Wu would "escort them . . . for a personal audience with you." For Wu, the reason his entreaties all seemed to fall on deaf ears was because so few of the Nationalist brass had actually visited Xinjiang. "A small number of uninformed people in the central government," he wrote in his diary, "knowing little about the actual situation, mistakenly believe that all of Xinjiang's problems are rooted in ethnicity." To hear Wu tell it, it was these "uninformed people" who had "irresponsibly condoned and encouraged Masud." If Wu's colleagues would only listen to him, they would learn that Xinjiang's real problems stemmed from nothing more than shoddy transportation infrastructure and incessant foreign meddling. Wu thought it of the utmost importance for "senior officials from inner China to make a trip out here and live in Xinjiang for a few months. Then they would experience a great awakening."[39] They would see, he hoped, that the ethnopopulist discourse of Masud, Isa, and their Soviet foils was an artificial and deceptive political agenda that lacked resonance on the ground.

According to Wu, such a platform paled in comparison with the tangible prestige and influence of conservative upper-class non-Han elites, who exerted a real presence among their communities and had long leaned toward the Chinese central government.

Unfortunately for Wu, one of those "uninformed people" who had "irresponsibly condoned and encouraged Masud" was Chiang Kai-shek. As far back as 1942, just two months after Sheng had turned his back on the Soviets, the Generalissimo went out of his way to condone the increasingly bold pronouncements of his Uighur protégés in Chongqing. When Chiang's inner circle of strategists became alarmed at reports that Masud and Isa—then in Lanzhou—were calling for self-government or even independence for Xinjiang, one of his aides took the liberty of drafting a directive recalling the pair back to Chongqing. According to the report, such inflammatory rhetoric was old hat for Masud and Isa, who had "demanded independence for Xinjiang a decade before, when they openly called China an imperialist country." Wu had agreed back then with the decision to recall Masud and Isa. And yet, the Generalissimo "alone holds a dissenting opinion, and has simply instructed [the governor of Gansu] to keep an eye on them."[40]

Before long, Chiang went even farther, instructing the Ministry of Foreign Affairs to devise a plan that featured Masud and Isa in a prominent role in Xinjiang. The ministry, having already received early reports on clandestine Soviet activities, considered "a set of principles on ethnic equality" that would "inspire patriotic sentiment among Xinjiang's Muslim peoples, so as to combat the detrimental effects of foreign propaganda." Bu Daoming, head of the West Asia Division, submitted a draft proposal to Chiang for "making the nationalities content both in their political and daily lives, so that the Soviets cannot instigate them from the sidelines." One of Bu's proposals was for a "provincial senate in which representatives of the nationalities could participate." Though the Generalissimo urged caution on the idea of a senate, his belief that the Nationalists needed their own proponents of a non-Han ethnopopulist platform in Xinjiang remained firm. "I have already received notification from the Generalissimo himself," noted Wu in late 1944, as Ili lay in a state of siege. "He has instructed [Chen] Guofu and [Chen] Lifu to find a way to use Masud."[41]

Two months after Chiang's son departed from Urumchi, Wu traveled to Chongqing for an audience with the Generalissimo. On June 15, 1945, Wu did his best to convince his boss of the folly of sending Masud and Isa back into Xinjiang. Chiang wasn't listening. "Can Masud and the others return to Xinjiang now?" he asked Wu over tea. "They can return any-time," Wu replied. "But they harbor incorrect 'East Turkestan' thoughts. We must first rectify this shortcoming." In the notations following this incident in his diary, later to be crossed out, Wu vented his frustration. "Whenever border figures are treated too generously during their time in the central government, I fail to see any good come out of it. Quite the contrary, they bring nothing but trouble to the state."[42] Wu could scarcely believe his ears. Perhaps with an eye toward posthumous vin-dication, the governor took great care in his diary to record the "absurd proposals" of his Uighur colleagues, all of which were sure to "sabo-tage national unity": that Xinjiang be renamed East Turkestan; that the people of Xinjiang govern Xinjiang; that the central government not be permitted to station troops in, or sponsor migration to, Xinjiang; and that the various nationalities of Xinjiang all be considered part of the Turkic—not Chinese—race.[43]

As Wu and Chiang sparred over the ethnopolitical face of the Nation-alist government in Xinjiang, events on the ground continued to develop. After a dark and miserable winter, Wu Zhongxin welcomed the summer snowmelt. "The cold spring beyond the pass is something those living in inner China simply cannot imagine," he wrote. "The snow does not melt, and everywhere the ground remains an endless expanse of white."[44] In the summer of 1945, however, the long-awaited thaw simply brought more heartache. In May, several thousand Kazaks joined forces with Mongols and raided the Altay region. Soviet planes were spotted every other day or so, and one Kazak detachment was sent south to attack Barikol. In June, Ali Han Tore ordered the armies of the East Turkestan Republic back on the warpath. A thousand rebels made a beeline south through the Heavenly Mountains, toting heavy artillery behind them.

Though their sights were set on Kucha, the severed heads of ten Han men were found strung up along the road outside Aksu as well.[45]

Then, on July 2, officials in Tacheng sounded the alarm. Bandits had appeared in the surrounding countryside, and entire villages had defected to their side. Vast caravans of pillaged livestock headed toward the Soviet border, where their cargo was exchanged for firearms. Lacking reinforcements, Wu watched from afar as the bandits took over the countryside and approached Tacheng. A White Russian general led the assault, on orders signed by Beria and approved by Stalin. Though most Nationalist officials managed to escape to the Soviet Union, ten thousand Han civilians were not so lucky. Trapped behind the city walls, they soon met a gruesome fate. On July 31, Wu received his last telegram from the Tacheng authorities, marked "extremely urgent." "Their weapons are state-of-the-art and they have heavy artillery. The sound of wailing shakes the earth. . . . Lacking appropriate words, I send my tears with this telegram."[46]

With the fall of Tacheng, the Ili rebels continued toward Altay. By now, Osman's Kazaks were expected to play only a supporting role. The latter struck first, however, raining heavy artillery upon the streets of Altay. In one sustained succession of six assaults, more than three hundred bombs cascaded over the city walls. The only bodies on the battlefield were Han, as "the Kazak warriors tie their feet into their saddles, so that their horses transport the dead riders away." The regional *zhuanyuan*, Gao Boyu, informed the governor that "if no bomber planes come to our assistance within the next twenty-four hours, the entire district will be lost." Three days later, the Ili army from Tacheng finally drew near, stopping along the way to occupy Burjin. On September 5, Gao *zhuanyuan* sent his final telegram. "If you were planning on sending any reinforcements, it is now too late," he wrote. "Soon there will be nothing more to report from Altay. This is my last telegram." Altay fell to the rebels two days later, and it was reported that every Han resident not married to a Kazak was slaughtered.[47]

Before he fled the city, Gao warned Wu that "unless you fight back, the same suffering will be visited upon you. Before long, Urumchi will become the next Altay." Rebel movements appeared to confirm Gao's prediction. In late July, the Ili march on Tacheng was matched with an eastern drive toward Jinghe, the first town out of Ili on the road to Urumchi. After a heavy artillery attack on Nationalist forces at Jinghe, the Ili rebels struck forth for the Manas River.[48] Then the Japanese surrendered to the Allies, and the rebels paused. During the interlude, Chongqing and Moscow signed the Sino-Soviet Friendship Treaty, a document containing wide-ranging implications for China's northern borderlands. In exchange for Stalin's pledge to refrain from intervening in the affairs of Xinjiang and Manchuria, the Nationalists formally recognized the de jure independence of the Mongolian People's Republic, long known to them as Outer Mongolia.[49] "As far as China is concerned," Wu wrote after learning details of the accord, "the recovery of the northeast is of paramount importance. This should also make it easier to settle the situation in Xinjiang."[50]

It thus came as a profound shock to the governor when, less than a week later, the Ili rebels renewed their advance on the Manas River. "The bandits are now vigorously expanding, obviously in fulfillment of some planned and organized joint movement," Wu observed. Though the Soviets had promised not to meddle in the affairs of Xinjiang, "in reality, they are still unwilling to release their grip." During the first week of September, as the rebels closed in on the approach to Urumchi, General Zhu Shaoliang ordered his men to make a stand. By all accounts, the fighting was intense. The Soviets rose to the challenge. "There are frequent reports of heavy weaponry and brand new firearms among the rebels," Wu wrote. "Vehicles transport grain and ammunition, and new soldiers appear in their ranks." On September 4, the rebels reached Dushanzi, where the Soviets had once operated lucrative oil rigs under Sheng. The next day, two bombers strafed the approach to Wusu, less than two hundred miles from the capital. Refugees poured into Urumchi, and Nationalist officials sent their relatives out of the province. By contrast, the American consul, typically skeptical of Chinese charges of foreign instigation in Xinjiang, was baffled. "He first expressed extreme concern over the recent bombings," Wu noted, "and then asked me, 'Where did the planes come from?'" The day after the bombings at Wusu, Liu Zerong, a Nationalist official from the Chinese embassy in Moscow, arrived in Urumchi. Convinced that the Sino-Soviet Friendship Treaty—which he had helped broker—would lead to an immediate ceasefire, Liu met Wu with a smile on his face. It fell to the governor to bring him down. "You place too much trust in other people, my friend."[51]

The imminent threat to Urumchi finally pushed Chongqing into decisive action. Prior to that, Wu lamented, the central government had not sent a single bullet for the defense of Xinjiang, echoing a similar complaint broadcast by Yang Zengxin more than a quarter of a century earlier. Pushing the melodramatic envelope, General Zhu threatened to commit suicide if the Generalissimo did not send help. If tangible supplies or troops could not be sent, Wu begged Chiang to at least send a "big official." On September 13, his prayers were answered: General Zhang Zhizhong stepped out onto the runway at the Urumchi airport. Zhang, then the head of the political department in the Military Affairs Commission, was one of the most respected figures in all of China. He had distinguished himself in several high-profile, tense negotiations with the Chinese Communists, rightfully earning an epithet as China's "peace general." He was briefed on touchdown. Rebel armies were two days from Urumchi, and the capital was on the verge of starvation. Under no illusions regarding the chief force behind the rebels, Zhang walked straight to the Soviet consulate and delivered an ultimatum. "The rebel army must halt its military movements immediately. This will allow both sides to send representatives to engage in formal peace talks," he said. "If military operations continue to expand, I am afraid that there will be no opportunity for a peaceful resolution."[52]

In exchange for their services as "mediator," the Soviets asked that Chongqing submit a proposal for Sino-Soviet economic cooperation in Xinjiang. Zhang agreed. With that, hostilities came to an abrupt halt. In London, Molotov informed Wang Shijie, the Chinese minister of foreign affairs, that the situation in Xinjiang "was simply transitional in nature, and that we should not overly concern ourselves with it." Wang himself

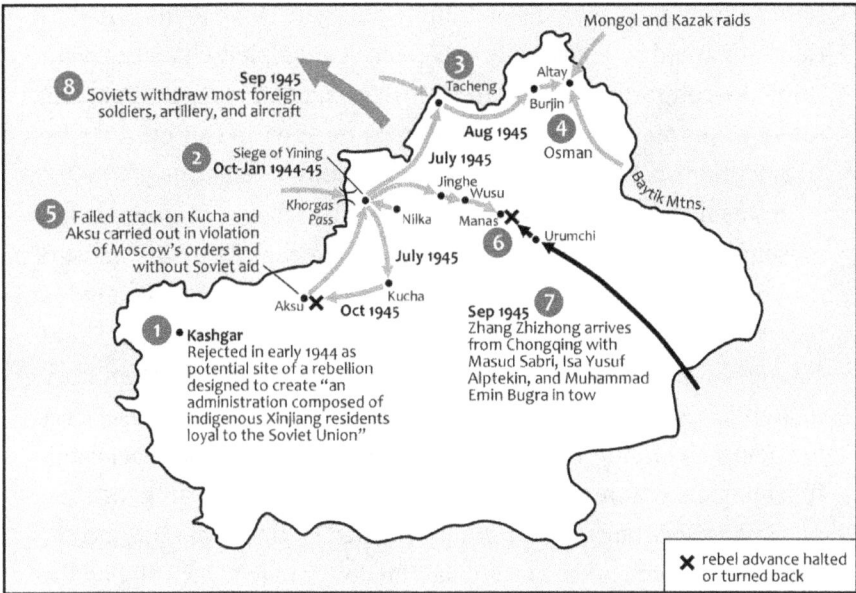

FIGURE 4.1. The Ili rebellion, 1944–45. With the fall of Altay and advance to Manas in September 1945, the boundaries of the East Turkestan Republic encompassed the oil rigs at Dushanzi and the mineral and pastoral wealth of Ili, Tacheng, and Altay. Cartography by Debbie Newell.

suspected that recent events "had all been planned prior to the signing of the Sino-Soviet treaty."[53] In other words, the military aggression on display in late August and early September belonged to an earlier Soviet blueprint, and the fulfillment of its provisions trumped any promises made in the Sino-Soviet Friendship Treaty. After the meeting in London, less than twenty-four hours were to pass before the Soviet consulate in Ili made an astonishing announcement. The Ili rebels, he said, had asked the Soviets to mediate peace talks with the Nationalists. As other historians have pointed out, had this truly been the case, it would have been a coincidence of cosmic proportions. There had not even been enough time for a single telegram to make a round trip from Moscow to Chongqing, much less to Urumchi and Ili.[54] Furthermore, having sliced through

Nationalist armies like steel on tinfoil, it beggars belief to think that Ali Han Tore would have suddenly experienced a complete change of heart. Quite the contrary, it is clear that Moscow, having pushed Chongqing into a compromising position, had now decided to call off the rebel advance and wait for the economic concessions to roll in.

It was no mystery to Governor Wu why the rebels had stopped their advance. "According to reports," he wrote in early October, "most of the Soviet members of the Ili army returned to the Soviet Union in late September." In fact, following the arrival of Zhang Zhizhong in Urumchi, not only had Soviet personnel been recalled from the front lines. In addition, every last scrap of heavy artillery and modern weaponry, including all aircraft bombers, had been pulled from the rebel camp. What remained were Uighur and Kazak foot soldiers sporting the same rusty rifles and ramshackle artillery wielded by their Nationalist counterparts. In other words, just enough firepower to fend off a Nationalist advance, but nothing that might enable them to further their gains. The reason was simple: the Soviets had achieved their goals. The gold and mineral mines in Altay, the beryllium mines in Koktogay, the trade hubs of Ili and Tacheng, and the oil fields of Dushanzi—all had been wrested from Nationalist control. Viewed as collateral damage were the deaths of fifteen thousand Nationalist soldiers and ten thousand civilians, most of whom were Han.[55]

To consolidate its newfound gains, Moscow now needed to put out the fire. The original rebel leaders in Ili, however, having been promised sovereignty over all of Xinjiang, refused to lay down their arms. Tasked with sending representatives to the peace talks in Urumchi, Ali Han Tore informed his followers that they were to ignore the ceasefire.[56] At the same time, his men laid siege to Aksu, the only city in southern Xinjiang to come under sustained attack. This offensive was carried out in direct violation of Moscow's directives, which focused on the mineral-rich steppes of the Kazak north rather than the agriculturally rich Uighur oases of the south. Three weeks after rebel armies in northern Xinjiang halted their advance, the battle for Aksu continued, but this time without Soviet aid. On October 6, after a month of encirclement,

Nationalist forces lifted the siege. Without Soviet help, the tide quickly turned. President Ali Han Tore openly criticized the fickle calculus of the Soviets. His profound disillusionment with his once magnanimous patron echoes through the Soviet archival record. In letters to Beria and in meetings with General-Major Yegnarov, he warns that the people of Ili are starting to believe Chinese claims that "wolves in sheep's clothing" are acting as "champions of Islam" in Ili, and that they had been "sold out by the Bolsheviks."[57]

In response, Moscow, likely suspicious that Ali Han Tore was the real instigator of such rumors, facilitated his swift replacement with a new crop of leaders. It was time for secular ethnopopulist intellectuals to take over. By early 1946, Ali Han Tore had exited the scene, seemingly without a trace. Though a Chinese source asserts that he continued to reside in Soviet Uzbekistan until his death in 1976, the only thing known for certain is that he was never seen again in Xinjiang.[58]

THE NATIONALISTS FIGHT BACK

By the autumn of 1945, the Soviets had achieved what they had set out to achieve: to re-create the era of Sheng Shicai without Sheng—or any Han replacement, for that matter. To legitimate its newfound gains, Moscow needed the Chinese central government to acknowledge that the rebellion was essentially indigenous in origin. And that meant negotiations, in which the Soviets offered to act as "mediators" for the Kazak and Uighur leaders who had only recently replaced Ali Han Tore. On September 11, General Zhang Zhizhong wrote to Governor Wu from Chongqing. "The Generalissimo is very concerned about recent events," he told Wu. "If the rebels are willing to send a representative to talk with us, then I will bring Masud, Isa, and Emin [Mohammed Emin Bugra] to Urumchi to facilitate communications. What is your opinion?" Wu, despite his conviction that Masud, Isa, and Emin—the latter active in Nationalist circles ever since accepting Isa's invitation to emerge from exile in Afghanistan in the early 1930s—were peddlers of a "narrow-minded ethnic nationalism with ulterior motives," was powerless to object. "If the arrival of Masud and company will benefit the situation," he replied, "then by all means they are welcome."[59]

Try as he might, Wu never understood just how Zhang's team of Uighur ethnopopulists was supposed to benefit the situation in Xinjiang. "If the talks [with the Ili representatives] proceed smoothly," Wu learned after their arrival, "then we will not let Masud and company meet with the bandit representatives. If the talks experience difficulties, however, then we can consider using them as intermediaries."[60] From Wu's perspective, this made little sense. Wouldn't the strident anti-Han rhetoric of the Ili rebels become even worse once Masud and Isa joined its chorus? Foremost in Wu's mind were the belligerent pronouncements of Ahmetjan Qasimi, the secular, Soviet-educated successor to Ali Han Tore. "The current era is an era in which invaders get punished," he wrote in early 1946, in the midst of the talks.[61] What Wu failed to realize was that Masud, Isa, and Emin had not been brought to Xinjiang to be used as grist for the Soviet mill. Instead, they were intended to buttress Nationalist claims to speak on behalf of a mass non-Han constituency in Xinjiang. Their job was to demonstrate to the people of Xinjiang that the Nationalists were not as intolerant and chauvinistic as the anti-Han rhetoric from Ili had made them out to be, thus negating the sole claim to political leadership proffered by the rebel leaders.

For how could anyone accuse the Nationalists of Han chauvinism when they sponsored and condoned the sinophobic activities of Uighur dissidents operating within their own party? John Hall Paxton, the American consul in Urumchi, was one of those impressed by Nationalist demonstrations of ethnopolitical tolerance in Xinjiang. In a confidential report dated November 20, 1947, and entitled "Charges by Secretary General Aisabek [Isa Yusuf Alptekin] of Chinese Oppression of the Natives of Sinkiang," Paxton highlighted the remarkable way the Chinese administration suffered "a considerable party . . . among the Muslim natives that is restless under Chinese control, critical of its abuses and eager for increased liberties for the native inhabitants of the area, without any reason to suppose that it is under Soviet influence." During an extensive interview with Paxton and Eric Shipton, the British consul, Isa "stated over and over again that he was without any hope that the Chinese would do anything to redress the grievances of the Turki people or grant them any real liberty." Taken aback by Isa's tirade, Shipton characterized the rest of his talking points as "an indictment of Chinese rule in the province." For their part, Chiang Kai-shek and Zhang Zhizhong were fully aware of Isa's truculent critique of Han rule in Xinjiang but regarded his statements as "exaggerated" and "not shared by the majority of the Turki people."[62] And yet this was precisely the sort of person they wanted to hold up as the non-Han face of the newly "enlightened" administration in Xinjiang: an intractable pessimist who never missed an opportunity to excoriate the Nationalist government to anyone and everyone who would listen. This was the sort of Uighur ethnopopulist with whom they wished to associate themselves, even if his views were not, according to Zhang and Chiang, representative of the majority of Uighurs in Xinjiang.

Governor Wu was a nervous wreck. "Since the middle of last month," he wrote in November, "these three people have been running around instigating the populace and exhorting young people to demand high-level autonomy. . . . Masud tells the Muslim clergy to take up the issue in their weekly sermons, and counsels the people not to be afraid of speaking up anymore. Our detractors now openly insult the government and say that the Han have lost their strength. They demand the transfer of power and threaten to take up knives, axes, clubs, and rocks to exterminate us." Wu could hardly contain himself. "When General Zhang invited them to Xinjiang, he intended for them to help resolve the Ili affair. Instead, they have organized and incited the masses, and stirred up a wave of discord." Editorials in the Nationalist press echoed the governor's concern. "On the surface they follow the central government," opined a Shanghai pundit, "but behind the scenes they are collaborating with the Ili rebels. Uighur akhunds who used to gravitate toward the central government have now joined their ranks." Wu concluded his analysis by lamenting how "the rhetoric of Masud and company is exactly the same as that of the Soviets and the Ili bandits."[63]

That, of course, was precisely the point. How far were Chiang Kai-shek and Zhang Zhizhong willing to push the envelope of ethnopopulist posturing? "It is said that Masud will be given the post of an inspector-general of Xinjiang," Wu learned in February, with no small distress. "I have nothing against him personally, but he propagates a pan-Turkic doctrine that will split our country apart." Two days later, the governor learned that his paranoia did not run nearly deep enough. The inspector-general post had been intended merely as a stepping-stone. Masud's ultimate destination was the governor's quarters.[64] This realization created considerable friction between Wu and Zhang, whose personal friendship dated to the earliest days of the Nationalist Party. When Wu urged Zhang to exercise extreme caution with Masud, Zhang finally had to reprimand his friend. "You and I agree on 80 percent of our ideas on how to rule Xinjiang," Zhang replied. "But our viewpoints regarding Masud and the others are different. I still intend to use them, as a counterweight to the Soviet Union."[65]

General Zhang dominated Xinjiang politics for the remainder of the republican era, first as successor to Wu (1946–47) in Urumchi, then as northwestern commissioner (1947–49) based in neighboring Gansu. Zhang led negotiations with Ahmetjan Qasimi and the rest of the Ili camp, while trying to implement economic and political concessions pleasing to their Soviet patrons. Once Moscow was satisfied with the progress of the talks, Ahmetjan began to sing a radically different tune. In 1946, he assured Zhang that "our national liberation movement is not directed at any particular ethnic group, but only at that group's ruling class and its authoritarian government." These mild statements were worlds apart from the fire-and-brimstone pronouncements of Ali Han Tore. They were also considerably tamer than the anti-Han sentiments now routinely expressed in Uighur-language periodicals published under the liberal forbearance of Zhang's administration in Urumchi. In 1946, one such journal, *Khan Tengri*, lionized several departed heroes of the Uighur intellectual elite by decrying their deaths at the hands of "the bloodthirsty swords of the tyrannical Chinese butchers." Other articles decried the "oppressive imperialist and colonialist policies" of the

FIGURE 4.2. The Nationalist cabinet of Uighur ethnopopulists, 1947 or 1948. Throughout the latter half of the 1940s, the Nationalist government countered the Soviet patronage of Uighur and Kazak leaders in the East Turkestan Republic by raising the stakes and elevating non-Han personages into conspicuous positions of political authority throughout the province. From left: Isa Yusuf Alptekin (general-secretary, 1947–49), Masud Sabri (governor, 1947–48), Burhan Shahidi (governor, 1949), and Mohammed Emin Bugra (deputy governor, 1949). Also pictured on the far right is the Han official Liu Mengchun. John Hall Paxton Papers (MS 629). Manuscripts and Archives, Yale University Library.

Chinese government, which had kept the people of Xinjiang in a "state of ignorance and slavery." One even went so far as to lump Governor Wu Zhongxin with Sheng Shicai, labeling him as a proponent of oppressive policies that had denied "political freedom" to the non-Han peoples of Xinjiang.[66]

This was all very surreal for Wu, who began to complain of a weak heart and begged the Generalissimo for a transfer out of the province. His wish was granted in the summer of 1946, as Ili representatives relocated to Urumchi to join a coalition government under Zhang. Wu left his successor with a cabinet of non-Han personages steeped in the imperial regalia and titles of a bygone era. They were delivered to General Zhang as a symbol of what a conservative politics of difference could still accomplish in Xinjiang. Zhang and his team of Uighur intellectuals were committed to an ethnopolitical vision of Xinjiang that located legitimacy in progressive representatives of the "people," not in their social "betters." Wu, however, wanted nothing more than to show Zhang that the "people" were little more than a deceptive pretext, and that the living embodiments of the old order still exerted very real power on the ground. To make his point, Wu drew attention to his crowning achievement while in office, one that bore fruit just as he departed Xinjiang for the last time.

COURTING OSMAN BATUR

"If I could just get these Altay bandits to submit," Wu wrote in early 1946, "it would bring succor to the people, considerably weaken the Ili camp, and constitute a devastating blow to the Soviet Union, the bandit manipulator."[67] For the governor, the insurgencies of Altay and Ili represented entirely different phenomena. Ili, guided by the "bandit manipulator" from Moscow, merited an international response orchestrated at the highest levels of the Chinese government. There was little that Wu, the governor of a single province, could do about it. But Osman had shed his blood long before it became useful to Moscow, reacting "purely against the oppressive policies of the former *duban*." In fact, the only reason Osman even became a *batur* in the first place was due to the specific policies of Sheng Shicai, who had imprisoned two rungs of hereditary Kazak leadership before him. Whereas the Soviets had recruited an ethnopopulist constituency from scratch, Osman merely stepped in to fill the shoes of a departed noble. Handled correctly, therefore, he just might prove receptive to "trading in his weapons of war for silks and jade." Wu's plan was to imitate the tactics of imperial administrators throughout history: in return for demonstrations of loyalty to the Chinese state, Wu would confer upon Osman and his descendants entry into an exclusive and conservative club of hereditary elites.[68]

Initiating contact with Osman proved more difficult than Wu had expected. Watched closely by his Soviet handlers on the Mongol border, Osman did not learn of Wu's arrival in the province until nearly four months after Sheng Shicai had left Urumchi.[69] Prior to the creation of the East Turkestan Republic, Osman's chief appeal to Moscow lay in his ability to inflict damage on Chinese military forces. In other words, he was the only self-made ethnopopulist in Xinjiang who commanded a martial following. But the Soviets wanted native non-Han leaders indebted to themselves. Self-made men who had facilitated much of their own rise could not be reined in easily once strategic objectives were met or altered, as had been the case with Ali Han Tore. After Sheng left the province, Soviet support for Osman lost its raison d'être. In mid-1944, Moscow brought in a Kazak named Delilhan Sugurbaev to serve as a more pliant version of Osman, consigning the one-time *batur* to house arrest in Mongolia.[70]

Governor Wu, catching wind of developments across the border, encouraged Prince Ailin and his wife to send their agents back to the Altay steppe. In just one month, they achieved encouraging results. Three of Osman's top leaders, disheartened by their *batur*'s dramatic demotion and confronted with the imminent return of the prince, indicated their desire to submit to the government. Wu was ecstatic. "Without firing a single bullet, our pacification efforts have already succeeded. The eastern marches may soon be at peace." Immobile and abandoned, Osman began to look for an exit strategy. He slipped messages across the border, conveying his greetings to Governor Wu. "The people do not listen to my rallying cry anymore," he admitted to one of Wu's agents. "I am fully aware of how the Outer Mongols intend to treat me. Before long, they will throw me in jail or they will kill me." At the same time, two of his former comrades-in-arms made a pilgrimage to Urumchi, where they vowed to initiate their own pacification missions. "In the past we used to fight against the Communists," one of them said. "And now we are supposed to listen to them and act on their behalf? Just think for a moment how stupid this is." Taking aim at the separatist rhetoric of the East Turkestan Republic, he spread the message that "no country in the world can be composed of so few people [as us]. We were born in China. We are Chinese."[71]

Alarmed at the sudden success of Kazak recruiting efforts inspired by the return of Prince Ailin, the Soviets abandoned their ethnopopulist posturing and tried to match Governor Wu move for move. In early 1945, Osman, fearing the rapid eclipse of his once promising career, tried to curry favor with Prince Ailin, sending him a tribute of eight horses, fifty sheep, and two yurts. The Soviets responded by urging the Mongols to bestow upon Osman the title of khan, something that only an ostensible descendant of Chinggis Khan—the embodiment of the nomadic aristocracy—could do. Wu believed the Soviets were using the title of khan "to cheat and deceive" Kazak youth. We might describe their tactics more dispassionately as resorting to a conservative politics of difference, deployed to parry the conservative assault of Governor Wu and Prince Ailin. The fact that the Soviets felt the need to rehabilitate a Kazak ethnopopulist with the trappings of imperial conservatism likely came as sour vindication to Wu. It was also a shrewd strategic move, one that put Wu back on the defensive. Before long, Osman "Khan" sent out orders to apprehend Prince Ailin's emissaries and deliver them to the Mongol authorities.[72]

Although the Soviets had outmaneuvered Wu, the governor refused to admit it. "Osman is an incorrigible man," he fumed in August. "We are now resolved to exterminate him." Over the coming weeks, however, Wu's anger gradually abated as new details trickled in regarding the siege of Altay City, the final offensive of the Ili rebels. The presence of Osman "Khan" notwithstanding, the Soviets had entrusted logistical command of the operation to Delilhan Sugurbaev, with Osman's men confined to a less prestigious supporting role. Apparently, the manipulation of Osman was merely a ploy to contain Wu and Ailin's conservative brand of influence in Altay. Moscow was still not willing to trust a self-made man like Osman. The final insult came in early September, when the city fell. "When Osman arrived at Altay, he heard that a Soviet official had been sent from Ili to assume control over the city," Wu learned. "He turned away and left immediately." The realization that his *khan* moniker had been a sham all along finally disabused Osman of any further illusions regarding the Soviets. "We fought the government for many years, long before the uprising at Ili," he announced. "They were inspired by our lead. We were the original vanguard. So how can we just sit by and allow them to come in and take over our affairs in Altay?"[73]

Osman's open defiance of Delilhan and the Ili rebels was quickly brought to the attention of Soviet officials in Moscow. Beria, the Soviet minister of internal affairs, observed that the "Kazak Robin Hood" does "not intend to recognize the government of East Turkestan ... and believes himself to be Khan of the Altay." Though Osman ultimately accepted a face-saving post in the new coalition government as *zhuanyuan* of Altay, the days of exposing himself to the whims of great power politics were over. Instead, Osman raided Nationalist and Ili garrisons alike, in the process recruiting a new Kazak constituency from scratch. Governor Wu, while deploring Osman's methods, could not help but admire his pluck. "He was the earliest of all the rebels," he wrote, "and the Altay Kazaks love him." More than anything else, it was Osman's uncanny ability to re-create a loyal following seemingly at will that most impressed the governor. "The people are embracing Osman with enthusiasm," Wu learned after the fall of Altay, "and turning their backs on Delilhan." One month after accepting the *zhuanyuan* post, Osman withdrew his men from Altay, sent an exposé of illegal Soviet mining activities to General Zhang, and commenced large-scale raids on their camps.[74] He was now a loyal ally of the Nationalists.

Osman's successful recruitment to the Nationalist fold stood as supreme vindication for Governor Wu. Born into a shepherd's family in Koktogay, Osman was a nobody whose rise to power was made possible only by Sheng Shicai's sidelining of the traditional Kazak elites. Having based his legitimacy as *batur* on a form of Kazak ethnopopulism that no longer reflected new sociopolitical realities under Prince Ailin, however, Osman quickly faced the limits of his potential. When the Soviets transferred their support to Delilhan Sugurbaev, an ethnopolitical creature even more artificial and dependent than Osman, the prestige of the latter suffered. The return of Prince Ailin's emissaries to Altay ultimately forced Osman to salvage what little remained of his self-made name by taking a subordinate yet prestigious position under Governor Wu's reconstituted conservative order. In response, the Soviet decision to designate Osman as khan was an attempt to beat Governor Wu at his own game. It worked, for a time. Ultimately, however, Osman came face-to-face with the hollow authority of his khan title and opted to embark on the re-creation of a new ethnopopulist constituency unbeholden to either the Nationalists or Soviets. His ability to do just that allowed him to join the Nationalists voluntarily from a position of strength, owing nothing to the Mongols, Prince Ailin, the Soviets, or Governor Wu.

As Osman's tumultuous saga clearly demonstrates, the clash of conservative and progressive platforms of political legitimacy in 1940s Xinjiang offered tremendous potential for an ambitious non-Han actor such as himself. In 1943, when the Soviets made the fateful decision to exploit, rather than conceal, the Han crisis of political legitimacy in Xinjiang, they effectively fired the opening salvo of an ethnopolitical tug-of-war in which each side endeavored to sponsor as much non-Han agency as possible. On every point of contention, there was room for two at the table: Osman and Delilhan, Masud Sabri and Ahmetjan Qasimi. As Russian and Chinese officials competed to prove just how enlightened they were in all affairs susceptible to charges of colonialism or imperialism, a brief window of upward mobility and access to resources opened up for their Uighur and Kazak beneficiaries. In a game of constant one-upmanship, however, it was only a matter of time before the possibilities of harmless ethnopolitical bluffs exhausted themselves. By 1947, anyone who understood the rules of the game must have started to wonder: just how much farther could the envelope safely be pushed?

ZHANG ZHIZHONG'S COUP DE GRÂCE

On May 28, 1947, Zhang Zhizhong resigned his post as governor. For his successor, Chiang Kai-shek appointed Masud Sabri, the first-ever native-born governor of the province.[75] The impact was immediate. Halfway around the globe, in Southern California, the *Los Angeles Times* called Masud's appointment "unprecedented," while Zhang, claiming that Nanjing was bowing to native wishes to see "a Xinjiang man rule Xinjiang," portrayed it as a demonstration of Chinese "respect for the political rights of minorities."[76] As governor, Masud remained remarkably true to form and continued to issue incendiary statements regarding Chinese rule in Xinjiang. "Today, the government of China is telling the world: 'We are democrats and are struggling for democracy.' But regardless if imperialism is white or blue, it always oppresses minority nationalities or even tries to annihilate them and wipe them out."[77] To his detractors, General Zhang played down Masud's well-known separatist rhetoric and instead highlighted the benefits of a Uighur figurehead adored by the non-Han masses of Xinjiang. "Masud is a highly virtuous gentleman, who enjoys a senior position of authority among the Uighurs," wrote an anonymous journalist in *China News*. "But in truth, even though Masud has ascended to the governorship, he wields very little real power." Assuring his Han audience that Zhang, "the real power behind the throne," was still in command, the author characterized Masud as Zhang's "ace card."[78] The political calculus on display here is almost identical to that of the Nationalist report on Soviet affirmative action six years earlier, with which this chapter opened.

Masud's appointment was the banner event of Zhang's elaborate propaganda campaign against the Soviet-directed rebellion in Ili. With Masud's presence effectively negating the novelty of Ahmetjan Qasimi as leader of the Ili camp, Zhang felt secure enough to hit the road to publicize his ethnopolitical "enlightenment" to audiences in inner China. With a Uighur and Kazak dance troupe in tow, Zhang embarked upon a three-month tour of Shanghai, Nanjing, Hangzhou, and Taiwan. His colorful entourage initiated a frenzy of media reportage. To his Han audiences, Zhang played up the idea that long-estranged branches of the Chinese family were about to reconnect. For their part, Isa and Emin were given free rein to propagate a pan-Turkic agenda designed to appease their constituencies back in Xinjiang. A striking example of just such a dichotomy appeared in the pages of the official party newspaper, the *Central Daily News,* which reprinted a sample of Uighur calligraphy likely provided by Isa on behalf of the dance troupe. The Uighur version, penned in Arabic script, read as follows: "Let us forever develop our national art of Turkestan" (*Türkistanniñ milliy sänitimizni abadi rawajlanduraili*). A classic expression of Isa and Masud's pan-Turkic platform, this message was reinforced elsewhere with ubiquitous images of mosques in Turkey. In its Chinese translation, however, the Uighur message was rendered somewhat differently: "Develop the culture of Xinjiang" (*fazhan Xin[jiang] wenhua*). In a similar vein, the Chinese newspapers, instead of focusing on Turkish mosques, chose to print pictures of Uighur performers paying homage to Sun Yat-sen's shrine in Nanjing.[79]

The Soviets, recognizing Zhang's multifaceted campaign for the threat it was, attempted to cast the new governor as an ultraconservative "reactionary" associated with the chauvinistic "CC Clique" of the Nationalist Party. As Masud took the oath of office in Urumchi, rebel authorities in Ili organized massive protests through the streets of Yining demanding his immediate resignation. According to internal reports, the Ili rebels had much to fear from Masud's appointment. Uighurs were heard to claim that "good things will happen during the era of Masud," and many proceeded to thank the central government for giving them the "blessing" of Masud. As a result, Ahmetjan decided to expose the Nationalist plot for what it really was. "To those who do not understand how the colonialists operate, here is what they do. They say: 'We have given you a leader from among your own people.' They say this to attract people to their side and fracture our indomitable,

FIGURE 4.3. This sample of Uighur calligraphy was provided to the *Central Daily News* in Shanghai in December 1947 by a member of Zhang Zhizhong's Xinjiang Youth Song and Dance Troupe. It is most likely that of Isa Yusuf Alptekin, who traveled with the dance troupe and oversaw its daily affairs. The Uighur text reads, "Let us forever develop our national art of Turkestan" (*Türkistanniñ milliy sänitimizni abadi rawajlanduraili*). The Chinese caption below, however, translates the same passage as "Develop the culture of Xinjiang" (*Fazhan Xin[jiang] wenhua*). Kai Lei, "Xinjiang gewutuan canguan ben bao ji," *Zhongyang ribao*, December 18, 1947, 4–5.

united front of national liberation." According to Ahmetjan, Masud was nothing but an ambitious careerist, a man who "babbles manure" for a living. He had deceived himself into thinking the Nationalist authorities would allow the realization of his pan-Turkic "fantasies." On the contrary, Ahmetjan claimed, he was simply doing the work of the Han colonialists for them.[80]

What is most fascinating about the reaction from Ili is its call to reinstate Zhang Zhizhong as governor of Xinjiang. Nearly a year into Masud's governorship, long after the Ili representatives had withdrawn from the coalition government, Ahmetjan still demanded "the dismissal of Governor Masud as a precondition for any return to Urumchi for further talks." Nothing can better illustrate the futility of taking seriously the charges of "Han chauvinism" and "Chinese colonialism" levied by the Ili camp. Because the goal had never been to bring about "enlightened" Han rule in Xinjiang, but was rather to facilitate the perpetuation of a Soviet economic monopoly in the geologically rich regions of the north, nothing the Nationalists could do would ever satisfy the Ili rebels. The unprecedented level of vitriol directed at Masud—the living embodiment of a Chinese commitment to precisely the sort of ethnopolitical tolerance demanded by the rebels—was in direct proportion to the severity of the blow Nanjing had managed to land against the ethnopopulist platform of the Soviet proxy government in Ili. The irony of the situation must have been apparent to many: in calling for a demonstration of Nationalist commitment to indigenous sensibilities in Xinjiang, Ahmetjan insisted on the reinstatement of a Han governor from Anhui. As such, there was simply no way Chiang Kai-shek would consider withdrawing Masud. According to the Ministry of Defense, the call for Masud's removal was "the most difficult demand to meet, and the primary source of the current impasse."[81]

If Masud served as an antidote to the rebel mind, then Osman offered Zhang an opportunity to strike at the rebel heart. By 1947, the Kazak *batur* had successfully negotiated his entry into an elite club of conservative Kazak allies formally aligned with the Chinese state. "I am an official in service to my country, and I have a duty to defend its territory," he announced in 1947. "To protect our national territory, we Altay Kazaks must deliver a severe blow to any evil power attempting to destroy national unity."[82] Among his newfound peers, however, Osman was perhaps the least dependent upon resources from Urumchi for his continued political survival. This fact would become more and more apparent as time wore on. In April, Osman set up camp in the Baytik Mountains, four days northeast of the capital. He immediately clashed with Mongol border patrols, from whom he took eight hostages. In June, the Mongols announced that severe repercussions would ensue if the hostages were not released within forty-eight hours. Osman ignored the order. As promised, four or five unidentified aircraft crossed the Chinese border and laid waste to Osman's camp. For the next two months, Osman and the Mongols traded bullets and casualties all along the mountainous border. Kazaks flocked to Osman's banner in droves. In just four months, he increased his following more than eightfold, peaking at 1,700 warriors.[83]

The aerial assault on Osman—executed by the Mongols but almost certainly countenanced by the Soviets—coincided with Masud Sabri's appointment as governor. As the Soviets knew all too well, the two phenomena were intimately related. For his part, Osman, emboldened by his success over the summer, set his sights on Altay. Though Zhang told him to stay put, Osman again ignored the order. In late August, Osman reconquered Chingil and drove out Soviet mining camps in Koktogay. Several weeks later, he laid siege to Altay and drove Delilhan from the city. Nationalist authorities declared that Osman was "acting entirely on his own initiative," a rhetorical move that made the recovery of rebel territory appear to enjoy the spontaneous support of Kazaks desirous of a more proactive Nationalist role in the province.[84] Faced with the stunning loss of Altay, the Ili camp fell into disarray. Then, in a move that surprised almost everyone, Osman continued to ride westward to conquer Tacheng, far outside his customary route of pastoral migration. At this point, Moscow, now deeply committed to mining operations in Altay, had no choice but to rearm Delilhan Sugurbaev and send him back into the fray. He returned to Altay at the head of an army with six tanks. Confronted with such an onslaught, Osman wisely abandoned his gains and retreated to the Baytik Mountains.

As expected, Osman soon received the same vitriolic treatment accorded to Masud. In his speeches, Ahmetjan condemned Osman as a "dog," "rapist," "enemy of the people," and an "agent of Nationalist fascism."[85] As with criticisms of Masud, the goal was not to explore any sort of common ground between potential non-Han allies, but rather to neutralize a rival narrative of ethnopopulist legitimacy in Xinjiang. Viewed from this perspective, Ili's hyperbolic response bears testament to the blow that Zhang's Kazak and Uighur allies had managed to land against the Soviets. The Ili camp demanded both "the arrest of the so-called 'Altay bandit Osman'" and his arraignment before the people "for a public trial as a precondition for any return to talks in Urumchi." Judging by their "tone of language and grotesque posturing," Zhang concluded, "I do not see any willingness to meet us halfway. Thus the situation will only get worse, and the current deadlock is likely to intensify."[86] Zhang could not have been much surprised by these developments. Like the Soviets, the Nationalists had little intrinsic interest in fostering non-Han agency for its own sake. The goal was simply to stop the rhetorical bleeding of the Chinese body politic begat by the Ili rebellion and little more. Judged by that standard, by late 1947 the Nationalists had met the Soviet test in Xinjiang.

Nevertheless, the incessant raising of the ethnopopulist stakes in Xinjiang carried troubling implications of its own. With Ahmetjan Qasimi president of the East Turkestan Republic and Delilhan in nominal control of its armies, Moscow had placed "proletarian" Uighurs and Kazaks at the top of a "national" republic, thus violating its own taboo against replicating the principles of affirmative action outside the borders of the Soviet Union and its satellites. With Governor Masud in Urumchi and Osman Batur on the field of battle, the Nationalists had aped the Soviets to perfection, in the process completing their transition from a conservative to a progressive brand of the politics of difference. In the back-and-forth struggle to construct and deconstruct narratives of Han political legitimacy in Xinjiang, both the Nationalists and the Soviets had finally exhausted their capacity for innovation.

Everyone knew where the script of national determination was supposed to go from here. For fifteen years, the people of Xinjiang had been promised an ever greater share of the ethnopolitical pie. These mostly hollow pledges nevertheless gave rise to a very real logic of rising expectations, one with a momentum all its own. Therefore, if independence for the non-Han peoples of Xinjiang was not in the offing—and it most certainly was not—then some sort of surrogate compensation must be found. In the event, it would fall to the Chinese Communists to determine just what sort of compensation would be offered.

CHAPTER 5
THE BIRTH PANGS OF
CHINESE AFFIRMATIVE ACTION

I N OCTOBER 1949, THE CENTRAL COMMITTEE OF THE CHINESE
Communist Party received a report from Deng Liqun, a special agent
sent to infiltrate the Ili valley two months prior. "Some of the young
people out here," Deng wrote, "are wondering why the new Chinese
leadership is not adopting the Marxist-Leninist principles of national
determination as a means to national liberation." Instead, "they say we
are merely implementing regional autonomy. How do I respond to such
queries?"[1] Deng's report highlights the thorny legacy of rising expectations in Xinjiang that would confront the new leadership in Beijing after
1949. Over the past two decades, the Soviets had alternately concealed
and exploited the Han crisis of political legitimacy in Xinjiang by playing
various permutations of the affirmative action card. The general trajec-
tory, however, was toward an ever larger political role for the non-Han
masses of Xinjiang. Thus ethnocultural autonomy under a Han warlord
bereft of territorial claims had gradually given way to a sinophobic East
Turkestan Republic firmly wedded to the administrative boundaries of
Ili, Tacheng, and Altay. The Nationalists, negotiating from a position
of weakness, were forced to engage the Soviets on their own terms. As
a result, they too did their part, however reluctantly, to reinforce the
notion that men like Masud Sabri and Osman Batur represented the real
ethnopolitical future of the province.

During the latter half of 1949, the Chinese Communists, for reasons
entirely unrelated to anything that took place in Xinjiang, gradually supplanted Nationalist authority throughout the northwestern regions. In

nearly all matters of ethnopolitical import, however, the people of Xinjiang could have been forgiven for thinking the Nationalists had never left the province. Both parties were committed to placing Kazaks and Uighurs in prominent positions of largely symbolic authority. For example, Burhan Shahidi, the Uighur-speaking Tatar appointed to succeed Masud as governor in early 1949, was retained in that post for another six years by the Communists. Though both parties were determined to rein in the Ili rebels, the Communists, aided by the Soviets, had a far easier time of it. In the end, the East Turkestan Republic would be recast by party historians as the Three Districts Revolution (*sanqu geming*), whose leaders had always intended to merge with the progressive forces of Chinese Communism. In line with this retelling, the anti-Han pogroms carried out in Ili, Tacheng, and Altay were largely written out of official narratives.[2]

Most importantly, however, the Nationalists and Communists were both committed to some form of administrative autonomy as a surrogate compensation for the national ideal. (In the Nationalist version, this was glossed as *gaodu zizhi*, or "high-level autonomy.") The only difference is that the Communists could dial back the rhetoric of the past two decades from a position of strength, a distinction of no small significance. Let us recall for a moment the specific causal agent of the political malaise that had undermined every single central government administration since the late Qing: foreign powers, who deprived China's ruling class of the opportunity to harness domestic resources for domestic consumption. In a sense, the great misfortune of the Nationalists was their precocious rise to power. Simply put, until the foreign powers left China, whoever held custody of the central government was destined to bear the brunt of repeated onslaughts on the very foundation of their narratives of political legitimacy. For the Nationalists, the enormous expenditure of capital and resources necessary to meet the Western and Japanese threats saddled them with an additional handicap, one largely evaded by the Communists: the superficial but necessary incorporation of numerous warlords, whose independent bases of support severely undercut the ideological and organizational cohesiveness of the party.

By contrast, the early setbacks of the Communists and their retreat to the margins of inner China proved to be a blessing in disguise. As Jay Taylor has shown, unlike the Nationalists in Nanjing, Mao Zedong, holed up in the hinterlands of Shaanxi, was not forced to watch his considerable investments in German industry and munitions destroyed by the Japanese. Nor was he obliged, as a show of good faith to the Allies, to send his best fighting forces to the Burma theater, where, under the command of Joseph Stilwell, far too many perished. In Yan'an, Mao did not have to engage in protracted conventional warfare against vastly superior Japanese forces, nor did he have to integrate capricious warlords into his chain of command. As the Communist Party expanded by leaps and bounds during wartime, Mao was able to maintain an organizational discipline and ideological purity of which the Generalissimo could only dream.[3] In 1945, when the Communists finally emerged from Yan'an, they could maneuver their forces without fear of succumbing to foreign assaults on their narratives of political legitimacy, as had already happened to the Nationalists. The surrender of Japan and the Allied renunciation of extraterritoriality two years prior had taken care of all that.

The same conditions that allowed Mao to achieve a swift victory over the bruised and battered Nationalists also enabled the Communists to adopt a less concessionary approach to matters of ethnopolitical import. In response to the concerns of Ili youth expressed in Deng Liqun's telegrams, Premier Zhou Enlai was sympathetic yet firm. "Without a doubt, every nationality has a right to self-determination," he explained. "But now the imperialists are attempting to split Tibet, Taiwan, and even Xinjiang from our country. Under such circumstances, we will call our state the People's Republic of China, and not a federation." Wang Enmao, the new party secretary in Xinjiang, seconded Zhou's statement. The idea of a Chinese "federation," he added, "in which Xinjiang would become a republic within the People's Republic of China," represented "incorrect" thinking.[4] It was that easy. No need to sponsor public demonstrations of public penance for the suffering of non-Han frontier peoples, as Wang Jingwei and Chiang Kai-shek had once felt obliged to do. No need to convene contentious conferences that gave non-Han officials like Isa and Masud a platform to berate their "chauvinistic" Han colleagues and demand "high-level autonomy" for Xinjiang, as the Nationalists had felt compelled to do in 1945. With foreign patrons for disaffected non-Han figures now in short supply, the Communists no longer feared what a spurned successor of Masud or Isa might do. After 1949, those who disagreed with Zhou's and Wang's statements were confronted with a short list of options: flight (Isa, Emin, and Yolbars), imprisonment (Masud and Manchuqjab), or execution (Osman and Janimhan, the Kazak provincial minister of finance for the Nationalists).

The profound disparity of resources available to the two parties along the non-Han borderlands also illuminates the tone of pronouncements for public consumption. As anyone familiar with the official writings of Chiang Kai-shek and other top leaders is well aware, the Nationalists were not known for progressive statements regarding non-Han peoples and their eventual integration into the Chinese state. The most famous distillation of the official party line can be found in *China's Destiny*, ghostwritten by Tao Xisheng and published under the Generalissimo's name in 1943. In it, Chiang concluded that the differences among China's various ethnicities were attributable to "regional and religious factors, and not to race or blood," and that the "various clans actually belong to the same nation, as well as to the same racial stock." Wu Zhongxin, an enthusiastic promoter of the Chinese melting pot, once told Masud that "those peoples who followed the Han have risen high, while those who turned their back on the Han have disappeared."[5] As we have seen, however, the words and actions of these same "chauvinist" Han look very different when viewed from the unpublished archival documents they did not intend for public consumption. As we saw in the previous chapter, behind closed doors the Nationalists evinced a remarkable degree of flexibility, pragmatism, and compromise.

In stark contrast to the Nationalists, the Communists have cultivated a reputation for being far more "enlightened" than their predecessors. After all, they formally recognized the existence of fifty-six official nationalities within China, making sure that representatives of each group filled seats in the National People's Congress. It was also the Communists who finally enshrined the Soviet ethnopolitical model along the borderlands, unveiling the Xinjiang Uighur Autonomous Region (Xinjiang Weiwuer Zizhiqu) in 1955. But if we confine our analysis to substantive action rather than abstract discourse, it soon becomes apparent that there is a direct relationship between the strength of the state and the ethnopolitical discourse it chooses to broadcast. For example, in 1884, when imperial administrators conferred provincial status upon Xinjiang for the first time in history, they did so in an attempt to project a centralizing reach that the state did not actually possess. Similarly, the Nationalist refusal to recognize distinct ethnic groups, preferring talk of subordinate "clans" and "tribes," was a rhetorical strategy rooted in weakness. After all, why give China's border peoples yet another pretext to collude with foreign powers by formally acknowledging their lack of historical ties with the Han race? With the Communists, the opposite was true: Beijing could afford to recognize a multitude of non-Han nationalities and grant them some form of regional autonomy on paper precisely because they no longer feared that such concessions could be realized on the ground.

There is a great deal of irony in all this. The Communists, while talking a more progressive talk, walked a far less permissive walk. The National People's Congress, which included representatives of each newly recognized ethnic group, was never anything more than an ornamental government body whose job was to rubber-stamp whatever legislative proposal came its way. The Communist equivalent of Masud Sabri berating his Han colleagues in 1945 was a staid political ritual exactly one decade later in which fifty-seven delegates to a conference in Urumchi submitted their views on the proposed designation of a Xinjiang Uighur Autonomous Region. The first words out of the mouths of thirty of them were "I completely agree" (*wanquan tongyi*). Eleven others expressed their "firm" or "complete support," while two decided to hedge their bets by both "completely agreeing" and "firmly supporting" the proceedings.[6] Would that Chiang Kai-shek had enjoyed such ideological and political conformity! As for the Xinjiang Uighur Autonomous

Region, time would eventually make a mockery of the very name, which today describes a region lacking either a Uighur majority or any semblance of political autonomy.

And yet the Nationalists, who talked an embarrassingly chauvinistic talk, had walked a comparatively progressive walk. They did so out of necessity, to be sure, but with tangible implications nonetheless.[7] In the more than six decades since the Nationalists withdrew from Xinjiang, no Uighur or Kazak figure has ever managed to exert as much influence on Chinese policy as did Isa, Masud, or Osman. It is now clear that the Nationalists were obliged to tolerate a degree of non-Han agency that their successors would never seek to replicate. Conditioned by the geopolitical crises of the 1940s into a brand of "progressive" ethnopolitical pragmatism, the Nationalists, had they somehow emerged victorious from the civil war, might well have found that they had no choice but to bow to certain elements of the logic of rising expectations that they themselves had helped to foster.

Ultimately, however, this is all an exercise in counterfactual speculation. By early 1950, the Communists had extended their writ throughout the province and were eager to prove the superiority of their ethnopolitical platform. Not surprisingly, this would entail dramatic structural and rhetorical transformations. First and foremost, the Communists attempted to pick up where the late Qing state had left off. In practice, this translated into a revival of the integrationist thrust that the beleaguered Manchu court had tried but failed to implement more than half a century earlier. Then, as now, the goal was to guard against rival foreign empires who might use the pretext of "national liberation" to further their economic interests in Xinjiang. From a structural perspective, the key innovation was the creation of the Xinjiang Production and Construction Corps (Xinjiang Shengchan Jianshe Bingtuan). Described by one scholar as "an empire almost to itself," subordinate only to Beijing, the *bingtuan* represented the reassertion of political, economic, and cultural ties between Xinjiang and the Han heartland. It was an overwhelmingly Han-dominated organization, composed in its early years almost entirely of demobilized Communist and captured Nationalist soldiers.[8]

The Production and Construction Corps fulfilled every political and economic goal once aspired to by the late Qing court. By funneling millions of Han migrants into Xinjiang, it strengthened cultural and demographic ties to the inner provinces and struck a blow at any attempt by political dissenters to portray Xinjiang as "deserving" its own Uighur nation-state on the basis of ostensible ethnocultural homogeneity. It also oversaw massive agricultural reclamation projects and the development of new boomtowns in areas of the region rich in natural resources. In addition, the Production and Construction Corps received enormous investments of capital from the central government. None of this had been possible during the late Qing or republican eras, when the center had no money to give and chronic political disunity discouraged the cultivation of ties between the Han governors of Xinjiang and the rest of China. But even during relatively quiescent times, few Han governors possessed the wherewithal to manage the fallout sure to ensue as a result of such a bold repudiation of the politics of difference. The cultural, economic, and political integration of Xinjiang with the rest of China, while deemed essential, was a very risky proposition. After all, the last time a Han official had overseen large-scale Han migration to Xinjiang—Jin Shuren in the early 1930s—the apocalyptic Hami rebellion was the result.

Thus it was the job of Chinese Communist ethnopolitical discourse to mitigate the inevitable backlash to its integrationist thrust in Xinjiang. But before we examine how this integrationist approach was experienced on the ground, let us examine the response of top Communist leaders to the delicate question posed by Uighur intellectuals to Deng Liqun in Ili: why is Beijing giving us less than the Soviet blueprint allows for?

JUSTIFYING REGIONAL AUTONOMY

Examined in light of the legacy of the Qing empire, the decision to turn Xinjiang Province into the Xinjiang Uighur Autonomous Region makes perfect sense. Quite simply, it was an attempt to recapture the spirit of differentiation inherent in the administrative status originally assigned to the province prior to 1884: a non-Han dependency (*fanshu* or *shudi*) of the Qing empire, sharing little in common with the inner Han provinces (*neisheng*) of the heartland. The Communist move was merely a formal recognition of what had long been apparent in practice. In 1909, when the Qing court oversaw China's first-ever general elections, all provinces were allowed to nominate and elect candidates for their assemblies—all provinces, that is, except Xinjiang, whose "special conditions" precluded its participation. Later on, even as Nationalist officials duly referred to Xinjiang as a province in official paperwork, some policymakers despaired over the ways Xinjiang remained "special," and thus resistant, to integration with the rest of the country. Governor Wu's refusal to elevate Uighur expatriates to prominent office in Urumchi had been based on his adamant belief that such appointments made Xinjiang appear even "more special" than it already was. In fact, he and some of his colleagues reasoned, the Nationalists should be trying to make it less special, so as to guard against Soviet plots aimed at exploiting its unique conditions.[9]

So Xinjiang clearly had always been special. In and of itself, this was not necessarily a bad thing. Indeed, the politics of difference depends upon the preservation and often valorization of ethnic and spatial distinction to achieve its strategic goals. Difficulties arise only when the Chinese state no longer proves capable of acting as the sole source of mediation and legitimization for the special conditions in Xinjiang. This is a crucial point. Chiang Kai-shek had no problem placing men like Masud Sabri in the governor's seat, so long as the Nationalists—and the Nationalists alone—had put him there. But the Soviet installation of Ahmetjan Qasimi in Ili was totally unacceptable, even though many of his public pronouncements were less provocative than those of Masud. The Chinese Communists picked up where the Generalissimo had left off. In practice, this meant that Beijing would need to find a way of reinforcing certain categories of difference while orienting that difference toward the Chinese state. This is a tricky balancing act for any state. Writing about the Soviet Union, Francine Hirsch has called this process "double assimilation": by subscribing to a set of characteristics allegedly common to all members of a particular ethnic group, the members of that group acknowledge their subordination to the state that defines and institutionalizes such categories in the first place.[10]

The People's Republic of China was that new state. In place of Nationalist "clans" and "tribes," the Communists went to great lengths to codify fifty-six nationalities, each of which acknowledged its allegiance to Beijing by participating in institutions designed to reinforce a sense of state-sponsored difference.[11] Whether created from scratch or simply inherited from republican forebears, each nationality was to regard itself as one of fifty-six fraternal twins: different in appearance (culture, language, etc.) but identical in paternity (the Chinese state). All were united in looking to Beijing to sponsor their collective progress toward socialist modernity. It is for this reason that the phrase *empire of nations*, first coined by Hirsch for the Soviet Union, is nearly as applicable to the People's Republic of China as it was to its Eurasian neighbor. The goal was to see how the politics of difference could facilitate the acquisition of wealth and power for the metropole. The only difference lay in what was meant by *difference*. In place of the conservative ethno-elitism championed by imperial administrators and some of their republican admirers, we now find the language of progressive ethnopopulism. This was well suited for justifying the encroachment of the state into the economic and private lives of its subjects, much as it had for Han warlord Sheng Shicai two decades earlier.

Thus far the Communist approach looks very much like the Soviet approach. The chief distinction is to be found in the obligation of the fraternal nationalities of China to recognize a Chinese rather than Soviet father. That single distinction would make a world of difference. Though many of these fifty-six nationalities could ultimately trace their institutional genesis to a Soviet blueprint, no one but the Chinese Communists could now claim the authority to regulate and legitimate their affairs. This was the political breakthrough eagerly sought but never achieved by the Nationalists. For the Communists, recovering national sovereignty enabled the creation of a unique political discourse still with us today: "socialism with Chinese characteristics." Though this phrase dates from attempts in the post-Mao period to reconcile the contradictions of Lenin-

ist governance with market economics, we can see its rhetorical forebears in the ethnopolitical platform of the 1950s. Such a convenient and
flexible discourse allows the Chinese state to claim that it is only doing
what more developed states have already done, but in accordance with
the special conditions of China. Simply put, unlike the Soviet Union, the
People's Republic had no intention of giving its nationalities their own
"national republics," complete with the right of secession. This radical
departure from the Soviet affirmative action blueprint needed to be justified, not least because the peoples of Xinjiang—more than any other
region of China—were intimately familiar with the Soviet model.

The discourse brought to bear upon this problem is best described as
Soviet affirmative action with Chinese characteristics. Its messenger was
Premier Zhou Enlai, who delivered a sweeping lecture on the subject two
years after the creation of the Xinjiang Uighur Autonomous Region. The
reason the Bolsheviks had given some of their non-Russian peoples their
"own" national republics, Zhou said, was because the Russian state had
emerged from the same "colonialist" impulse that characterized other
European empires. To make amends for the "imperialist" legacy of the
czarist era, the Bolsheviks needed to prove that they were different from
other Western powers. The creation of national republics, along with
their associated right of secession, were thus tangible demonstrations
of ethnopolitical progressivism, without which no one would have taken
seriously the Bolshevik commitment to a new world order. China, however, was different. "As everyone knows," Zhou asserted, "imperialism
came from the West." As a result, China could be a victim of imperialism
but not its perpetrator. And since imperialism was a uniquely Western
phenomenon, it followed that granting national republics as a show of
imperialist remorse and negation did not apply to China. Western powers, Zhou claimed, had embarked upon linear conquests far from their
own borders. But the spatial and human dimensions of China looked
more like an ever expanding and contracting amoeba, in which Han and
non-Han "naturally" mixed and merged.[12]

So went the rhetorical justification for Soviet affirmative action with
Chinese characteristics. Because China did not emerge from the Western
imperialist tradition, the only criteria capable of determining the proper

relationship with its minority peoples should derive from the lessons of Chinese history, not European or even Russian history. As for the lessons of Chinese history, Zhou claimed, they teach that the people of China have mixed and merged in a natural and harmonious fashion, eschewing the violent displacement so characteristic of Western history. It was precisely such violent displacement that had once forced the Bolsheviks to come up with the idea of establishing national republics, as a drastic tonic for a uniquely Western vice. But since China is a stranger to this vice, Zhou insisted, imbibing its tonic is unnecessary and counterproductive. As a result, granting independence or national autonomy to any non-Han peoples within China would be akin to forcing a healthy patient to take medicine for a disease he does not have—an analogy Communist leaders were fond of drawing. This, in turn, would weaken China's defenses against the future return of the ever-predatory Western imperialist powers.[13]

The logic of Soviet affirmative action with Chinese characteristics is also evident in the discussions that took place regarding the name to be applied to the new autonomous region in Xinjiang. Mao himself proposed *Xinjiang Autonomous Region*, preferring to omit formal mention of the Uighurs as its "steward." Prominent Uighurs in the Communist government, however, expressed far more concern at the inclusion of *Xinjiang* than the omission of *Uighur*. Burhan Shahidi apparently echoed the sentiments of many when he told Deng Xiaoping that "some of the ethnic groups in Xinjiang are not very fond of these two characters." What he meant was that *Xinjiang*—variously translated as "New Dominion," "New Territories," or "New Frontier"—connoted a relationship with the rest of China that could easily be construed as colonialist or imperialist. He proposed replacing it with *Tianshan*, the Chinese name for the "Heavenly Mountains" that divided the province into distinct northern and southern halves.[14]

Mao would have none of it. He insisted that *Xinjiang* remain. One month later, Deng Xiaoping duly broke the news to Uighur cadres. "The name *Xinjiang* does not contain any sense of an insult to the minority peoples, and therefore a change to *Tianshan* would be inappropriate," he wrote. As a concession, Mao agreed to the insertion of *Uighur*, so long as

Xinjiang retained its position at the front of the line. The end result was a curious amalgam. Though the new autonomous region "belonged" to the Uighurs, it was branded with a Chinese name that sounded much like those given to New World colonies in North America and Australia (e.g., New England, New South Wales). Mao's logic, of course, was irrefutable: since China is incapable of practicing imperialism, the name *Xinjiang* could not be interpreted as the rhetorical embodiment of an imperialist past. To agree to its omission would constitute a tacit admission that China was, in fact, capable of acting just like the Western imperialist powers. When stripped of its associated discourse, however, the new name merely represents one of many pragmatic attempts undertaken by Han statesmen during the twentieth century to reconcile contemporary "best practices" of empire imported from abroad with the domestic discourse of Chinese nationalism on which nearly every Han revolutionary had been weaned. *Uighur Autonomous Region* embodied the former, the retention of *Xinjiang* the latter.

If the Communist discourse on borderland "autonomy" skillfully elided any mention of the geopolitical pragmatism behind it—that the legacy of national humiliation lay behind the decision to eschew both a federation of republics and the right of secession—we are still left with the question of why Beijing decided to territorialize its own version of "autonomy." Neither Sheng Shicai nor the Nationalists had seen fit to do so, and the Communists clearly had no compunctions about adapting the Soviet model to suit "Chinese conditions." From a purely strategic point of view, it would seem that the ethnocultural model pursued by Sheng—also known as the Austro-Marxist platform—offered the least chance of separatism while retaining the discourse of progressive ethnopopulism. After all, cultural autonomy still provides the state with its coveted role as an evolutionary sponsor of substate nationalisms, while simultaneously denying the "beneficiaries" of such autonomy the administrative tools necessary to merge political activism with preexisting ethno-territorial categories. One suspects Beijing's reluctance to revive Sheng's program to be rooted in the *duban*'s execution of numerous Communist cadres (including Mao's brother), while aversion to the

FIGURE 5.1. The Xinjiang Uighur Autonomous Region, 1955. The new administrative divisions in Communist Xinjiang awarded seven nationalities a degree of regional autonomy at the county, prefectural, or regional level: Uighur (one region, five districts), Mongol (two prefectures, one county), Kazak (one prefecture, two counties), Hui (one prefecture, one county), Kyrgyz (one prefecture), Tajik (one county), and Sibe (one county). As was the case in the Soviet Union, much debate preceded the assignment of new administrative boundaries and their association with a nationality. The most contentious surrounded the designation of the Ili autonomous prefecture as "belonging" to the Kazaks, despite the presence of an urban Uighur demographic of long-standing political and economic weight. Uighur and Kazak cadres were both told they needed to emulate the Han in learning to balance the demands of political sovereignty and ethnic diversity. Cartography by Debbie Newell.

Austro-Marxist model might be attributable to its heretical status in the contemporary political culture of the Soviet Union.

Whatever the reason, the end product was an awkward ethnopolitical regime. It asked non-Han peoples to aspire to a national consciousness while settling for regional autonomy. As the sociologist Rogers Brubaker

has shown, for most people in most circumstances, there is likely to be
nothing at all provocative about this. The discourse of ethnopolitics is
far too abstract to figure much in the daily lives of most people, and it
usually takes a backseat to economic matters. There are, however, several circumstances in which ethnic conflict can rise to the fore, of which
two are relevant for our purposes here. The first is a sudden influx of
alien migration perceived by local residents as disruptive to preexisting economic relationships. The second is when the demographics of a
particular locale are no longer weighted in favor of a single ethnic group
but are instead split roughly between two or more groups of unequal
economic status.[15]

During the 1950s, these two conditions did not yet obtain in most
of Xinjiang. In the provincial capital, however, a sizable population of
Uighurs, Hui, and Kazaks did brush shoulders with the massive influx
of new Han migrants. The factory floors of Urumchi provided the backdrop. Close analysis of rare municipal party reports concerning modes of
interaction among the state and its Han and non-Han workers in Urumchi provide a suitable litmus test for the ethnopopulist discourse of the
new state.

UNVEILING AFFIRMATIVE ACTION IN URUMCHI

In October 1949, as the People's Liberation Army poured into Xinjiang,
a Nationalist officer in flight to India passed through the southern oasis
of Kucha. The local Han magistrate invited the officer into his home.
Once inside, the officer met his host's Uighur wife and two children. His
curiosity got the better of him.

"The Uighurs of southern Xinjiang are against Han men marrying
their women," he said. "But here you are, and you have gone and married a Uighur girl. How come they don't resist our immigration?"

His Han host shot back, "What is there for them to resist? All the children born here speak Uighur. Not only that, there are plenty of akhunds
who say openly in public that 'even if a hundred thousand Han come

out here, we will simply assimilate a hundred thousand Han. What are we afraid of?'"[16]

This exchange between a Nationalist officer in retreat and a lonely Han official in Kucha speaks to the ways shifting demographics can exacerbate or mitigate what is often thought of as ethnic conflict. As Brubaker discovered among Romanian and Hungarian communities in Transylvania, towns marked by a clear demographic majority weighted toward one ethnic group were least likely to become sites of ethnic conflict, even when local politicians from the majority group went out of their way to antagonize the minority community. By contrast, ethnic tensions and ethnic conflict were most likely to occur in places divided more evenly between two ethnic groups, particularly if such parity had been brought about by demographic trajectories experienced within living memory.[17] When the Han official in Kucha explained why local Uighurs did not oppose his marriage to a Uighur woman, he was giving voice to the first set of conditions, which had facilitated Mongol and Manchu rule before him. Simply put, an isolated handful of alien elites in no way threatens the socio-economic fabric of the community as a whole.

Indeed, for the duration of the Mao years and in some places right up until the present day, circumstances conducive to ethnic conflict have been absent from much of Xinjiang. The reason is simple: Han migration, managed on principles of difference familiar to China's imperial predecessors, was an intentionally segregated process. As a result, Han migration and its attendant capital investment—both embodied through the Xinjiang Production and Construction Corps—were largely funneled into agricultural reclamation sites or new industrial boomtowns located far from preexisting Uighur or Kazak communities. In this as in other matters, segregation was deemed the height of prudence. Thus a study of ethnopolitics after 1949 must focus not so much on the highly segregated and exclusionist *bingtuan*, but rather on places where representatives of different ethnic groups interacted and intermingled on a regular basis, under state supervision and with the possibility of state intervention. After all, though statistical charts quickly reveal the presence of majority-Han districts and counties throughout Xinjiang, it is not difficult to find entire cities and counties that have remained overwhelmingly Uighur, particularly in the south. Mao Zedong repeatedly butted heads with proponents of such a segregationist approach. Whenever the Chairman pursued one of his labor-intensive economic campaigns, he criticized the idea—apparently well entrenched—that non-Han peoples must be insulated from "disruptive" mobilization toward a socialist future.[18]

Prior to 1949, few if any oases in southern Xinjiang were home to a Han demographic exceeding 5 percent of the population. In most cases, the percentage was far lower, a realization belatedly cherished by those who ventured north in search of work after the Communist takeover. Upon experiencing difficult conditions in an Urumchi factory, a group of Uighur petitioners from Kashgar declared its intention to "go back home even if you put a bullet in our heads." Others expressed "discomfort" in the workplace by requesting a transfer back to what they referred to as the "pure Uighur" oases of the south.[19] As a result, it fell to Urumchi, with its 60/40 demographic ratio in favor of the Han, to serve as a bellwether for the government's ethnopolitical platform. That such a bellwether exists at all is quite new. Prior to 1949, no Han administration had been able to sustain its penetration to the ground level of society for more than a few years at a time. As such, the only organic ethnopolitical platform of any substance was that which had obtained among conservative elites, and it was upon this basis that claims to Chinese political legitimacy had long been made, in practice if not in name. Even when Osman Batur managed to recruit an ethnopopulist constituency following the imprisonment of Prince Ailin and other hereditary Kazak nobles, he proved quite willing to adopt the traditional title of khan and transfer his loyalty back to Urumchi once it became clear that Governor Wu was committed to both Prince Ailin and the old ethno-elitist order.

After 1949, however, the first traces of a stable, organically grown ethnopopulist constituency began to emerge in Xinjiang. This means that we can finally take stock of the state's claim to a narrative of political legitimacy in a non-Han land on the basis of the progressive ethnopopulist agenda long peddled—but never fully realized—in the region. Such a dramatic reorientation of our analytical priorities necessitates a paradigm shift of sorts. As one scholar has shown with respect to Soviet Kazakhstan, the vast majority of ordinary citizens typically do not assess the culturally alien state in terms of the "colonialist" abstractions so familiar to intellectuals, historians, and political elites. Instead, the critique from below tends to focus only on those aspects of state discourse relevant to the daily lives of upwardly mobile urbanites, who generally want to rise up through the system, not subvert it.[20] Thus, while political activists in Ili continued to promote geopolitical abstractions such as "Han colonialism" and "eggshell autonomy" well into the 1960s, Uighur smelters in the August 1 Steel Factory complained of far more pedestrian matters: dirty dormitories, pork-filled *baozi*, and a lack of on-the-job training.

On that note, let us take a closer look at what the first generation of Uighur, Hui, and Kazak "proletariat" in Xinjiang encountered in the factories of Urumchi. Before they ever set foot in the workplace, they would have been inundated with state-sponsored "development discourse" and the idea that "elder brother" Han were in Urumchi merely to train the non-Han peoples to take their places. The journalist Chu Anping painted a heartwarming portrait of this tutelage process. Not only did the Han "respect the local customs and unite with their fraternal ethnic neighbors," he wrote, but they also assumed an active and positive leadership role. When Uighur workers "enter the factory floor for the first time, it is apparent that they need constant care and attention from their Han coworkers, both in technical skills and in daily living." According to Chu, the Han did not shirk their responsibility. When one Uighur employee needed additional guidance outside normal work hours, her Han supervisor visited her dormitory and chatted until late into the night. On one occasion, when this same worker accidentally spent all her wages and was unable to purchase her next meal, her Han boss "purchased several dollars' worth of food tickets and delivered them" to her. As another Uighur worker put it, her Han manager routinely "treats me better than my own mother does."[21]

Woven into Chu's anecdotes is the silhouette of a pragmatic economic hierarchy that would consistently bedevil implementation of the state's ethnopolitical platform. Two irreconcilable priorities are in evidence here, resolved only in Chu's flight of literary fancy: while the Uighurs were supposed to be "masters of their own house" (*dangjia zuozhu*), that house could only be built with a massive influx of Han economic and technical assistance. As party secretary Wang Enmao put it several years later, during the first eight years of Communist rule, "the value of materials sent from the inner provinces to Xinjiang has amounted to two million tons." Meanwhile, he claimed, "Xinjiang has only sent a meager fifty thousand tons in return." The only reason Xinjiang had attained fiscal solvency for the first time in half a century, he continued, "is because the central government has invested an enormous amount of capital into Xinjiang's economy."[22] And since that investment naturally favored those with advanced skills and education undertaken in the official language of the new state, Han migrants to Xinjiang quickly became the new de facto masters of the house. Had these new Han migrants treated their non-Han understudies as Chu Anping's reports claimed they did, the disconnect between economic and ethnopolitical policies might not have been a problem.

Unfortunately, they did not. As the municipal branch of the Communist Party in Urumchi was soon to discover, the imperatives of industrialization left little time or energy for such altruism. After a series of non-Han strikes broke out at the October Automobile Repair Factory, July 1 Cotton Factory, and August 1 Steel Factory, the party carried out its own internal "ethnic policy inspection" (*minzu zhengce jiancha*). What they found was discouraging. Meetings were conducted exclusively in Chinese, while documents written in Uighur either "piled up" or "disappeared." In the factory, "none of the dispatches, announcements, door plates, slogans, or labor regulations are written in Uighur, and even some places with a 'danger' sign lack Uighur translation." Hiring decisions were based almost entirely upon the applicant's fluency in Chinese, a criterion that consigned one otherwise talented Uighur cadre to a demeaning career as a janitor. The interview process for Uighur and Kazak job applicants was often limited to a single question: "Do you understand speech or not?" (*ni dong bu dong hua*). In one case, an indignant reply was recorded: "We're humans, too, you know. How could we not understand speech?" By "speech," of course, the Han interviewers meant standard northern Chinese (Mandarin), the default language of all state-led economic activity. Despite repeated admonitions from the party, the only people who bothered to study Uighur, Kazak, Mongol, or Kyrgyz were Uighurs, Kazaks, Mongols, and Kyrgyz, a duty required of them by the newly "enlightened" government. The Han, free to ignore repeated admonitions that they study minority languages, could instead learn Russian or English, thus dramatically expanding their opportunities for professional advancement.[23]

For those Kazaks and Uighurs who did manage to land a job, the factory floor turned out to be an unusually hostile place. Libraries lacked even a single book not in Chinese, and work unit entertainment catered almost entirely to a Han audience. (In two factories, only 7 of 391 phonograph records were in Uighur or Kazak.) Contrary to Chu's heartwarming portrait of Han supervisors patiently cultivating Uighur understudies, "many Han cadres claim that ethnic cadres lack ability, cannot accomplish the work, and cannot communicate with them." Some work units were "unwilling to receive ethnic cadres transferred from other units, and they attempt to devise methods for getting rid of those they already have." No one wanted to devote precious time to training non-Han workers. "They believe incorrectly that minority cadres are all of a certain type, and completely shirk their leadership responsibility to assist them." Han treated non-Han with open contempt, "even to the point of despising them." Tricking Muslim colleagues into eating pork-filled *baozi* and then laughing at them in the cafeteria was openly tolerated, as was the quartering of pigs next to the Muslim dormitories. Han cadres "believe that ethnic cadres are dumb and suitable only for crude tasks." Another added that perhaps "another thirty years" of training might help. One Han worker said that he would "prefer to teach three Han rather than one Uighur" and that "a few are better than many, and none is best of all." In response, Kazak and Uighur workers chose to remove themselves from the workplace: extended sick leave and suspicious vacation time became frequent topics of discussion among Han managers.[24]

Not that all managers were Han. At the August 1 Steel Factory, the deputy director of production was a Kazak, one of several non-Han cadres who were said to "feel ill at ease in the workplace." The deputy director did not mince words: "Every day I go to my office, but there is no one I can talk to and nothing for me to do. So I sit at my desk all day and waste away. Everyone calls me deputy director, and this sounds swell. But in reality, I have nothing to do with the work that goes on around here. Sometimes I don't even know that the director has left for a business trip until after he returns, to say nothing of taking over in his absence." As a result, he chose to "spend most of the day at home rocking his baby," occasionally showing up at work just to "pull a few handles." It soon became apparent that Uighurs and Kazaks in positions of visible authority were usually "just for show." When one Uighur received a prestigious promotion from personnel to production, "he was extremely happy." Of course, that was before he learned he was expected to show up for work but not to do any work. When a colleague asked him if he was busy, he exploded in anger: "I'm busy as hell! I'm so busy I can't get all my work done!" Eventually he requested the revocation of his "promotion" and a transfer back to his more humble yet substantive work in personnel.[25]

These helicopter promotions of non-Han workers to positions of conspicuous but hollow authority did more than undermine the dignity of the recipients. They also generated considerable resentment among their Han colleagues, who "think that all achievements are theirs alone, and say that the revolution was made by the Han." To understand the perspectives of these recent Han arrivals, we should note that few had chosen to relocate to Xinjiang. In fact, in later reminiscences about their early days in the northwest, the two most common refrains emphasized their "dispatch" from the inner provinces and the considerable "hardship" they experienced as a result. In other words, most of them had been sent to Xinjiang against their will, to apply their advanced education and skill set to an environment deemed far more backward than the provinces from whence they came. As a result, in an ironic inversion of the state's affirmative action discourse, these Han migrants felt entitled to special treatment in Xinjiang. "In all of Kucha," bragged one Han accountant in the local bank, "you won't find a single person capable of doing the work I do."[26] In light of their perceived sacrifices and sufferings, the last thing these urban Han migrants wanted to see was Kazaks and Uighurs, often illiterate in Chinese, promoted to positions of privilege based purely upon the accident of their birth.

This disdain carried over into the workplace. "They do not respect the customs of the local ethnic groups," one report observed, "and view short hair and Han fashion as the definition of 'progressive,' while reading the Koran at funerals and doing *namaz* prayers are seen as backward." Han cadres were overheard to say things like "*Namaz* is something rich people do. You can do it all you like, but God won't give you a penny." In the workplace, Han openly criticized their non-Han colleagues for taking paid leave during religious holidays. "Who pays for your salary during such a long holiday?" asked one Han man who could not take such time off. In retaliation for such piecemeal demonstrations of respect, some Han went out of their way to denigrate their "undeserving" colleagues by ordering Uighur subordinates to transport pigs or tricking them into eating pork-filled *baozi*. No opportunity was missed to remind non-Han colleagues that all real and important tasks were reserved for the Han, regardless of what the state said. One insult pointed out that "the pilots of airplanes and drivers of vehicles and tanks are all Han. You guys aren't fit for such work."[27]

Faced with such dysfunction in the workplace, the party made a great show of official concern. Complaints from Han migrants were singled out and criticized as instances of "Han chauvinism," and attempts were made to solicit the opinions of Kazaks, Uighurs, and Hui. Yet few believed the party would make any sincere or sustained efforts at amelioration. "Talk won't solve anything," one man was heard to say after a meeting convened to discuss the issue. Another predicted that the ethnic inspection campaign "was just a passing wind" and that nothing would change. "While the ethnic policy inspection is going on, there are Uighur posters and Uighur-language films. After the inspection they'll all disappear." He was right. "On the first Sunday after the inspection concluded," the official report noted, "this is exactly what happened. Not only were there no Uighur-language films . . . but none of the announcements on the wall or in broadcasts were in Uighur . . . and all movies were projected exclusively in Chinese." The report concluded on a pessimistic note. "We believe that the chief cause of the problems listed above is that the party's ethnic policies are not being studied sufficiently, and most people have only a superficial understanding of them. Another reason is that most people concede only that our ethnic policies are important in principle, but then fail to undertake any tangible actions on the ground to implement them."[28]

The findings of the Urumchi Municipal Party Committee might be taken as an apt summation of the tensions inherent in the Soviet and Chinese versions of affirmative action. That is, nationality policies were important *in principle*, and an initial good faith effort would be made to realize them in official institutions and regulations. In reality, however, the desire to overtake the industrialized nations of the world as quickly as possible meant that economic development would always constitute an infinitely higher priority than issues of ethnopolitical import. And much as was the case under Jin Shuren two decades earlier, the demographic and economic imperatives of a developing Xinjiang oriented away from the Soviet Union inevitably required a massive influx of Han labor and capital. The difference after 1949, of course, was that Beijing was finally both able and willing to leverage its military and political resources to safeguard its investment. In an age in which national determination is valorized, however, the state needed to continue to maintain the pretense, however transparent, that the "natives" were the real stewards of progress in Xinjiang.

The more Beijing developed Xinjiang, however, the harder it became to camouflage the Han presence. In 1954, municipal authorities in Urumchi grew alarmed at a steady stream of unregulated Han migrants from the inner provinces. Some fled persecution, others called on relatives, but common to all was the misinformed perception that "money is easy to make in Xinjiang." Armed with an exaggerated sense of self-worth on the non-Han frontier, they refused offers of manual labor, instead demanding managerial cadre positions. When some took to begging

on the street, party authorities began to deplore the "extremely negative effect" imparted by these itinerant Han.[29] It was precisely with such
vagrants in mind that Yang Zengxin, hoping to alleviate indigenous fears
of unchecked Han migration, had once advertised Xinjiang's oxen as
"emaciated" and the local economy as "catastrophic." When that failed,
he drafted the worst of the Han migrants into a decrepit military establishment that effectively quarantined them away from the natives. With
the land at peace and the transportation infrastructure intact, however,
the Communist state no longer had any need of the old governor's tactics. A handful of illegal migrants notwithstanding, Beijing wanted nothing more than to resettle millions of Han workers to Xinjiang.[30] So long
as they skirted around long-established native communities, these Han
migrants offered few downsides: vulnerable, pliant, and expendable,
they could be used in appalling labor conditions without fear that their
discontent might be exploited by foreign powers.

The Communist state thus valued two types of Han migrants: urbanites for their education and technical skills, and peasants for endlessly
exploitable labor. Though it should not come as a surprise to see Beijing
leveraging its most readily available and least costly human resources
in Xinjiang, it is important to note the unintended consequence of such
demographic dependence: a non-Han populace that felt excluded from
the economic boom taking place right in its own backyard. The Urumchi
Municipal Party Committee was not ignorant of this sentiment. During
its investigation of select factories, it found that "minority workers are
very insistent on receiving political and technical training, and they hold
many opinions on these matters." Some of these opinions held that "we
have not done a sufficient job in nurturing minority cadres or in helping
them perform their tasks. They generally feel that they have titles but
no authority, are unable to perform in a managerial capacity, and thus
cannot accomplish any work." Much as was the case across the border
in Soviet Kazakhstan, discontent stemmed not from integration into a
culturally alien system, but rather from exclusion from that system and
its hierarchy of material rewards. According to the committee report,
one person expressed precisely this fear: "I don't care about any of the

other stuff. I'm only afraid that no one will teach me any useful skills."[31]

Similar refrains echoed well beyond the factory floors of Urumchi, in one of the few other regions to witness substantial interethnic mixing in Xinjiang. In May 1957, the party secretary in Ili, obliged by Mao's injunction to criticize the party's shortcomings during the Hundred Flowers movement, inadvertently gave voice to a wide swath of discontent among the people of his district. More than two years had passed since the designation of Ili as a Kazak Autonomous District, he observed, yet "not a single governing document has been issued in Kazak." Official signs were still written only in Chinese. Never mind highly placed non-Han cadres "just for show"; in Ili, many government and party offices—invariably the most important ones—still lacked even a single non-Han cadre. Industry, the lifeblood of the socialist economy, was dominated by migrant Han. "Some people say, 'This isn't a Kazak Autonomous District, it's a Chinese Autonomous District.'" One memorable critic characterized the system of regional autonomy as "eggshell autonomy" (*danke zizhi*). Plans to convene a meeting to discuss the issue were met, just as in Urumchi several years earlier, with jaded skepticism. "Whether we discuss it or not hardly matters," one Kazak cadre responded. "It's all the same in the end."[32]

In the summer of 1957, the Anti-Rightist Campaign revealed even more strident critiques of Chinese Communist policies in Xinjiang over the preceding decade. Saypiddin Azizi, the Uighur who succeeded Burhan Shahidi as the civil governor, took aim at unnamed critics of the regime in a lengthy speech later published in full. "Some people," he alleged, had called for an "independent Uighuristan or an East Turkestan Islamic Republic." Saypiddin himself received letters denouncing "Han party members who have stripped us of our land, our wealth, destroyed our religion, and turned the people of Xinjiang into homeless vagrants." Other anonymous critics characterized the arrival of Han migrants as a "natural disaster," described Han cadres as the new "landlord class," and branded all Han in Xinjiang as "colonialists." The natives of Xinjiang were "like slaves," subject to "assimilationist policies." Those who held real power in party and government "are all Han," while those non-

Han who accepted hollow positions of authority alongside them were "Han agents," "running dogs of the Han," or "ethnic Khitay [Chinese]." Despite Saypiddin's insistence that such sentiment was confined to a few egregious proponents, he acknowledged its prevalence throughout "government offices, industry, and schools."[33]

As is clear from these examples, Communist attempts to fashion a new narrative of Han political legitimacy on the non-Han frontier met with a great deal of resistance among those Uighurs and Kazaks who could still remember the inflated promises of previous decades. The pivot upon which nearly every critique of the new government turned was the success or failure of the state's new ethnopopulist platform. Ever since the 1930s, Han governors and Soviet consuls in Xinjiang had peddled such platforms in piecemeal fashion, with varying degrees of success and sincerity. By the 1950s, however, the Chinese Communists were finally expected to deliver tangible and sustained results on the ground. Had they done so, the discourse of "elder brother Han" help- ing to develop Xinjiang for the non-Han minorities might have evinced a viable staying power for many more decades. Ideally, from Beijing's perspective, charges of "Han imperialism" or "colonialism" would have searched in vain for a receptive audience in Xinjiang. But if the preceding analysis of Chinese Communist affirmative action in Urumchi and Ili is indicative of trends throughout Xinjiang in later decades, there is only one conclusion that the historian can reach: the ethnopopulist platform of the Chinese Communist state was hollow and insincere. Top party leaders were eager to pay it lip service but not to ensure its realization on the ground. As a result, the integrationist structural transformations undertaken on the ground in Xinjiang after 1949 have been continually plagued by the lack of an ethnopopulist discourse and constituency to match.

So long as the discourse of national determination is valorized in world politics, Han political and economic leaders in Xinjiang will feel the lack of a demonstrated record of ethnopopulist success capable of defusing aspirations among Uighur intellectuals for substantive politi- cal enfranchisement. The opportunity to develop just such a discourse arose in the first decade of the new state, but the state failed miserably to meet its own barometer for success. Beijing has been dealing with the consequences of this failure ever since. Outside China, however, Xinjiang has attained an international profile only over the past several decades, in stark contrast to the Dalai Lama and the Tibetans. In light of the fact that the Communist platform of ethnopopulism in Xinjiang crashed and burned almost immediately upon takeoff, amid a period of sustained and sometimes traumatic economic, demographic, and political transformations, this lack of international attention to Xinjiang during the Mao years begs explanation. We must therefore ask the following question: why has global awareness of Xinjiang, targeted for accelerated Han migration and economic development far earlier and far in excess of that aimed at Tibet, lagged so far behind that of its southern neighbor? Did no one hear the cries of disillusionment that accompanied the protracted birth pangs of Chinese affirmative action in Xinjiang? Or were other, more powerful forces at work, intent on silencing any attempt to draw global attention to the fate of China's largest remaining colony?

CHAPTER 6

THE XINJIANG
GOVERNMENT IN EXILE

IN JULY 1947, AN EMISSARY FROM THE TINY HIMALAYAN
princely state of Hunza met with a Chinese Nationalist consul in India.
During his meeting, the envoy "produced documentation proving their
former allegiance to us and requested the resumption of their status as
a dependency of China." Several months later, Mohammad Jamal Khan,
the mir of Hunza, sent another representative to Kashgar, with a letter
stating his desire to "restore our friendship of old." The envoy himself
had much more to say. Declaring that Hunza "was originally part of Chinese territory," he expressed a willingness to "return to China, for whose
people we have particular affection."[1] The backdrop for these sudden
overtures was the looming partition of India. The mir of Hunza faced a
difficult set of choices. Should he accede to Pakistan, to India, or attempt
to establish his own dominion? His efforts at soliciting the interest of
the Nationalist government in Xinjiang were intended to hedge against
potential threats from Pakistan or India, either of which might claim
Hunza for itself.

At first, the Nationalists failed to detect any ulterior motives in the
mir. After checking its files, the Ministry of Foreign Affairs learned that
Hunza had once sent tribute to Manchu—later Han—officials at Kashgar, the last recorded submission having occurred in 1935. Noting a
preponderance of British influence in the princely state, the ministry
duly added Hunza to its growing list of "lost territories" (sangshi tudi).
With the decolonization of the British Empire, however, came tantaliz-
ing opportunities for the Chinese. "Although they are a vulgar and rustic

people," observed a Nationalist official in Xinjiang, "they are capable of appreciating the majesty and virtue of the central government. As their annual submission of tribute has shown, they have not forgotten their ancestral nation." Before long, the ministry ordered its officials in Xinjiang to "dispatch a courier informing the Hunzans of the restoration of their tributary status" as a means of "respecting our sovereignty and securing our borderlands."[2]

From his office in Urumchi, Zhang Zhizhong did a double take. "Issuing a hasty order for Hunza to resume its imperial tribute does not seem to be the proper posture for a modern country to adopt," he wrote to Nanjing. What happened next is remarkable. In a response to Zhang's rejoinder, the ministry decided to abolish the "feudal system of submitting tribute and establish a Hunza Autonomous Region in its stead, under the jurisdiction of the Administrative Yuan." From Kashgar, Nationalist officials, parroting the progressive ethnopopulist rhetoric of the Soviets, praised the new relationship as capable of facilitating "our lofty policy of succoring and uplifting the weak and small peoples of the world." As part of this new plan, Mir Mohammad would become Commissioner (Zhuanyuan) Mohammad, and party and military officials would be sent to "participate in the government and act in an advisory capacity." Excitement within the Nationalist ranks was palpable. "If we are able to hold up Hunza as a precedent and broadcast the virtue of the central government to northern India," wrote one official from Kashgar, "then Ladakh may follow, and in light of the current conflict between Pakistan and India, perhaps even Kashmir."[3]

By early 1948, however, the mir's calculus had become all too clear. After throwing in his lot with Muslim insurgents fighting on behalf of Pakistan, Mir Mohammad reiterated his desire to initiate a relationship with China only upon "the old terms and bases, because the old terms are much more acceptable and respectable to both nations." These terms included a customary selection of "presents" from the Chinese government, "of which I hope you have got the list," along with various grazing, agricultural, and taxation rights in southern Xinjiang. To fulfill his end of the tributary bargain, the mir sent to Kashgar "a very small present

of shoes, which I hope you will accept." Ministry officials, perhaps wondering if someone was playing a cruel joke on them, closed the case. As
Bu Daoming, head of the West Asia Division, put it, the mir's requests
were "detrimental to our interests." Therefore, "we will not accede to
this request."[4]

If the Nationalists had emerged victorious from the Chinese civil war,
what sort of posture would they have adopted toward the non-Han borderlands? The curious twists and turns of the Hunza affair reveal much
regarding the evolving response of those Han administrators who continued to operate under the ideological umbrella of the Nationalist party.
From the perspective of the modern Chinese state, the goal was still—and
always had been—the consolidation of sovereignty and exploitation of
resources within lands imagined to have once been subject to the will
of the Qing court. In pursuit of this objective, the Nationalists had been
forced by unfavorable geopolitical conditions to adopt a bewildering
array of ethno-elitist and ethnopopulist platforms of difference in Xinjiang. In 1947, as the Hunza affair illustrates, they were still experiment-
ing with a range of ethnopolitical options, many bearing the imprint
of contemporary rivals. When the initial response from the Ministry of
Foreign Affairs was to "dispatch a courier informing the Hunzans of the
restoration of their tributary status," General Zhang Zhizhong, from
his office in Xinjiang, reminded the ministry that the revival of forms
of diplomacy once practiced by the Manchu emperors "does not seem
to be the proper posture for a modern country to adopt." Rather, the
proper posture was to delineate a form of "high-level autonomy" (gaodu
zizhi)—clearly related to the Communist blueprint for "regional autonomy" (diqu zizhi) already deployed in Inner Mongolia—as a demonstration of "our lofty policy of succoring and uplifting the weak and small
peoples of the world."

Despite such blatant borrowing of Soviet forms of ethnopolitical discourse, the Nationalists were obliged by their internal ideological schisms
to peddle forms of ethno-elitist difference, such as that championed by
one-time Governor Wu Zhongxin in Xinjiang. Thus the proposed Hunza
Autonomous Region, an obvious concession to the ethnopopulist plat-

form of the Soviets and Chinese Communists, would be presided over by Commissioner Mohammed, a Muslim king. Such flexibility would serve the Nationalists well after 1949, when geopolitical circumstances forced them into the most untenable position yet. In the midst of it all, however, they would continue to pursue the recrudescence of the modern Chinese state, a goal that, when viewed from the non-Han borderlands, effectively placed Nationalists and Communists in the same geopolitical camp. As this chapter will demonstrate through an analysis of the office of the Nationalist "governor" of Xinjiang from Taiwan, when faced with the united ethnopolitical front of two powerful Chinese metropoles, any alternative platform of difference, be it conceived in Xinjiang, Soviet Central Asia, or in the Middle East, was doomed to fail. A brief history of the Xinjiang government in exile will go a long way toward explaining why the refugee community from Xinjiang proved unable to construct a credible narrative of ethnopolitical legitimacy independent of the Chinese state. Their failure stands in stark contrast to the narrative put forth with considerable success by their Tibetan counterparts. It will also help explain why the Chinese Communists did not have to reckon fully with the failure of their ethnopopulist platform in Xinjiang during the 1950s until after their rivals on Taiwan could no longer speak for "free China."

A COLD WAR SCRAMBLE

In August 1947, the Soviet Union abruptly ordered the Chinese consulate in Semipalatinsk to shut its doors and cease operations. The Chinese ambassador in Moscow submitted a cryptic report on the situation. "Though their motives remain a mystery," he wrote to Nanjing in November, "rumor has it that an earthquake is expected in the Kazak capital [Almaty] sometime before 1950, and that there may be some relocation efforts. Thus it is possible that sensitive military or chemical installations will be transferred soon, and they do not want foreigners to spy on them."[5] The ambassador's reference to an "earthquake" may very well have been a form of prudent political doublespeak, particularly in light of what followed. Two years later, on August 29, 1949, the Soviets successfully tested their first atomic bomb just outside the city of Semi-palatinsk. Though there were no longer any Chinese diplomats stationed nearby to report on the matter, Douglas Mackiernan, a CIA operative stationed in neighboring Xinjiang, was able to determine, based on the atmospheric composition of prevailing winds, that an atomic blast had indeed taken place somewhere north of the Caspian Sea.[6]

Less than a month after the Soviets detonated their first atomic bomb in Kazakhstan, a steady exodus of Nationalist officials and soldiers, along with more than ten thousand anxious Kazak nomads and various other Communist irreconcilables, streamed south toward the Himala-yan passes, eager to exit the province before the arrival of the People's Liberation Army. Those fortunate enough to flee on wheels sped reck-lessly through local oases, plowing through donkeys and other livestock, whose intestines came to decorate the vehicles in macabre fashion. As they neared Tibet, motorized transport was abandoned, and everyone either struck out on foot or took mount, scaling snowy slopes in sub-zero temperatures. Pack animals slipped on a daily basis and fell to their demise, their splattered innards and mangled limbs traumatizing those who dared to look down. The elements were just as brutal, with lips and facial extremities peeling beyond all recognition. Numerous chil-dren froze to death, debilitating injuries were common, and few escaped chronic sickness. Some two to three months later, however, the survivors found themselves in Gilgit or Kalimpong, from whence they proceeded to Srinagar or New Delhi, many panhandling to make ends meet.[7] By 1952, some 2,300 Kazaks, 1,300 Uighurs, and several hundred Chinese refugees had managed to survive the flight into South Asia from Xinjiang.

As British and American diplomats in New Delhi and Isfahan were soon to learn, many carried fond memories of Douglas Mackiernan. Long an enigma, he is now tacitly acknowledged as the name behind the first star on the Memorial Wall at CIA headquarters, having been shot and dismembered by Tibetan border guards in April 1950. "I knew Mackier-nan very well, from the time he was in charge of a small detachment of army meteorologists," recalled an assistant to J. C. Hutchison, the Brit-

ish chargé d'affaires in Beijing, in 1950, "and always wondered why a
man with his exceptional qualities stayed on in Urumchi after the end
of the war."[8] We now know why: from 1945 until his death five years
later, Mackiernan seems to have cultivated extensive ties with potential
anti-Communist guerrilla warriors, the most famous of which was Kazak
chieftain Osman Batur, executed in 1951. The Chinese Communists were
convinced Mackiernan had spent his time dangling the prospect of significant American aid to disaffected nomads come World War III, and
said as much in reams of post-1949 propaganda.[9]

   With the benefit of archival hindsight, such charges are beginning to
appear less and less outlandish. Upon their arrival in Srinagar or New
Delhi, prominent Uighur and Kazak refugees invariably asked American and British visitors the same two questions: What had happened to
their good friend Douglas Mackiernan? And when was World War III due
to break out? Yolbars Khan, the onetime *ordabegi* (major-domo) of the
Hami khanate who had once parlayed his resistance to warlord Sheng
Shicai into an advisory post in the Nationalist government in Chongqing,
was canvassed soon after his arrival at the British embassy in New Delhi.
He "has reconciled himself to awaiting hopeful developments, among
which he seems (like so many other refugees) to include the possibility
of a third world war."[10] Husayin Taiji, the head of some three hundred
Kazak refugees in Srinagar, revealed extensive prior contact with Mackiernan, as well as considerable apprehension over whether he could still
leverage the latter's investment in him. "I am very much eager to hear
any news about Mr. Meckarneen who is, however, expected to have been
settled down in the free world," he wrote to John Hall Paxton, the former
U.S. consul in Urumchi, now posted to Isfahan. "I did my best to welcome and preceed him at Gas-kul, my dwelling place, where I got the
chance to treat and entertain him for five months as my only guest I have
ever had. I am still carrying his notes and an introduction as souvenir he
had written for me. I would be thankful to you if you be kind enough to
get me hear of him as soon as possible."[11]

   Just as the tragic fate of one past suitor came to light, however, another
suitor quickly stepped in to fill his shoes. This was the Nationalist gov-

ernment in Taipei, which soon issued numerous invitations for Kazak and Uighur refugee leaders to relocate to Taiwan. Delilhan Haji, the son of former Xinjiang minister of finance Janimhan, a Kazak chieftain executed by the Communists in 1951, relayed his invitation to sympathetic American diplomats. Speaking in "a cultured and well-modulated voice" to those who visited his camp in Srinagar, Delilhan—not to be confused with Delilhan Sugurbaev, the Soviet-sponsored general of the Ili rebellion—also sought advice from John Hall Paxton in Isfahan. "I received a letter from Formosa in which I have been invited to come to Formosa," he informed Paxton in admirable English, adding that the Nationalists had already agreed to send him funds and a passport for the journey. "But I afraid if I will go to Formosa, the Communists may reach there. Therefore I require your consultation weather I will go to Formosa or not."[12] Delilhan ultimately decided to remain in Srinigar, where he kept an open and sympathetic line of communication with Taipei. For Yolbars, however, who was then sixty-three years old and thus Delilhan's senior by some four decades, the prospect of a comfortable sinecure on Taiwan was most appealing. During an interview with British diplomats in New Delhi, Yolbars "stated his intention of going first to Kashmir to see the Sinkiang refugees there and then of continuing to Formosa where he was proposing to tell Chiang-kai-Shek of his mistake in giving arms to the Commander-in-Chief of Singkiang . . . who surrendered to the Communists, when he might have given them to Yolbas who fought the Communists."[13]

Also frequent participants in such meetings were Isa Yusuf Alptekin and Mohammed Emin Bugra, both of whom ranked high on the list of Xinjiang personages desired by the Nationalist government in Taiwan. Neither man expressed any interest in relocating to Taipei, however; they instead appear to have spent most of their time lobbying the Indian and Turkish governments to look after the welfare of the refugees in Kashmir. The most influential factor driving the various postures of Isa, Emin, and Yolbars toward Nationalist Taiwan appears to be their assessment of prospects for Xinjiang's geopolitical future. "We understand," wrote F. E. Cumming-Bruce, a British diplomat in the New Delhi embassy, "that

FIGURE 6.1. Yolbars Khan, governor of Xinjiang from Nationalist Taiwan, 1951–71. After the Nationalist government failed to convince Isa or Emin to take up the post of governor, Yolbars assumed responsibility for cultivating loyalties from Xinjiang refugees throughout South Asia and the Middle East. For two decades, he led the Nationalist assault on Isa and Emin's dissenting ethnopopulist narratives from Turkey, thus buttressing narratives of Chinese rule in Xinjiang put forth by the Communists. Zhongyang Yanjiuyuan Jindaishi Yanjiusuo Dang'an Guan, 119.51/0001, "Xinjiang xianfei qianhou qingxing baogao," 21.

whereas [Isa Yusuf] Aliptakin holds that an independent Turkestan is possible, Yolbas sees that such a state would be unable to withstand Soviet determination and that the only hope for Turkestan is to seek the protection of China, while endeavouring to secure the maximum degree of autonomy."[14] As a result, the Nationalists were able to recruit only one of these four coveted personages to Taiwan (though Delilhan, from his base in Srinagar, later proved willing to make official appearances at the occasional political conference in Taipei).

The failure to convince either Isa or Emin to take up residence in Taiwan did not sit well with many of the Nationalist faithful in Taipei, some of whom were not enamored of the geriatric Yolbars. Isa and Emin were learned, cosmopolitan Uighurs, in the prime of their careers, respected throughout the Muslim world, and thoroughly versed in the power of propaganda. By contrast, Yolbars was a product of the battlefield, and a parochial one at that. Until then, he had never set foot outside China. Furthermore, his well-known loyalty to the Nationalist government made his recruitment to Taiwan something less than a public relations coup. Of course someone like him would work for the Nationalists. In the mid-1940s, when the Nationalists finally succeeded in appointing a governor to Xinjiang, Yolbars leveraged his well-known loyalty to Chiang Kai-shek into reclaiming his former authority in Hami. Ever since his return, wrote one admiring Nationalist official at the time, Yolbars "has extolled the virtue of the central government to various leaders and . . . strenuously refuted the absurd proposals for independence and high-level autonomy."[15] By contrast, luring Isa or Emin—showcase ethnopopulists of the Nationalist platform during the 1940s whom Yolbars and Governor Wu disdained—to Taiwan would have allowed the Nationalists to parlay their recruitment into substantial political capital among Xinjiang refugees abroad.

Some top Nationalist officials in Taiwan were determined to pursue an alternative to Yolbars well into the 1950s, many years after he first set foot on the island. In November 1953, K. L. Rankin, the American ambassador in Taipei, solicited the views of foreign minister George Yeh regarding future Nationalist policy toward the non-Han borderlands, should the government one day succeed in retaking the mainland. Yeh took the occasion to excoriate Yolbars, calling him "ridiculous," "illiterate," and a "drag on the situation." Most importantly, Yeh charged, "he is quite unacceptable to Mehmet Emin BUGRA and Isa Yusuf ALPTEKIN, whom Dr. Yeh regards as among the real leaders of the Sinkiang people—despite their unfriendly attitude towards the Chinese Government. Dr. Yeh wished that these two men would come to Taipei but declared that, owing to Yalpus Khan's being here (and to other reasons), they would not come here."[16] Yeh's allegations—several of which were questionable—reflected the views of an influential faction within the National-

FIGURE 6.2. Isa Yusuf Alptekin, c. 1948. After serving as secretary-general (1947–49) for the Xinjiang provincial administration under the Nationalist government, Isa fled to India in 1949 and helped arrange for the resettlement of Uighur and Kazak refugees to Turkey. From his new base in Istanbul, Isa continued to lobby various world bodies to put pressure on both Chinese governments to recognize the aspirations of Uighur and Kazak peoples for an East Turkestan state in Xinjiang. Yolbars and other prominent Hui officials in Nationalist Taiwan rarely missed an opportunity to refute and rebut Isa's demands, most often by pointing out his extensive history of past cooperation with the Nationalist government. John Hall Paxton Papers (MS 629), Manuscripts and Archives, Yale University Library.

ist Party. The very next year, Chu Chia-hua, president of the prestigious Academia Sinica, published a series of letters he had exchanged with Mohammed Emin Bugra, in which he continued to implore his "misinformed" Uighur friend to take up residence on Taiwan, all the while somehow managing to avoid even a single reference to Yolbars, who by then had already been "governor" for three years.[17]

Xinjiang exile politics were contentious because there were so few men with the necessary credentials to serve as a convincing ethnopolitical representative for the province. Of the five former governors of Xinjiang who were still alive in 1950, two (Zhang Zhizhong and Burhan Shahidi) had defected to the Communists, one (Masud Sabri) was waiting to die in a Communist jail cell, and two (Wu Zhongxin and Sheng Shicai) had fled to Taiwan. Unfortunately for the Nationalists, the two ex-governors who had chosen to seek refuge in Taiwan were both ethnic Han. Quite apart from the obligation, ubiquitous in the age of decolonization, to elevate "indigenous" politicians to positions of conspicuous authority, both Wu and Sheng were effectively barred from participation in Xinjiang refugee politics for reasons entirely unrelated to their ethnicity. Wu Zhongxin, governor for two years dating from late 1944, was an implacable foe of both Isa and Emin, having long viewed them as "ambitious careerists" who had shrewdly played the race card to advance a separatist platform from within the party. As a result, if the goal was to lure Isa and Emin to Taiwan, Wu would be useless.

That left Sheng Shicai. The obligations of national determination notwithstanding, there is no reason an "enlightened" Han official could not play some substantive role on behalf of Chinese claims on Xinjiang, as former governor Zhang Zhizhong continued to do for the Communists after 1949. Sheng, for his part, had once been considered among the most "enlightened" Han officials to ever set foot in Xinjiang, having developed and sponsored numerous institutions of Soviet affirmative action during his eleven-year tenure as *duban*. That, of course, was all before 1937, the year when Sheng began to purge nearly everyone he had briefly enfranchised. Yolbars, in particular, dated his first period of exile from Xinjiang to Sheng's attempts to kill him in the mid-1930s, and the two men must have taken strict pains to avoid one another at party gatherings in Taipei. Former American consul John Paxton, during a visit to Hami in 1948, noted how Yolbars "continued throughout to extol the Chinese Government of the province since the overthrow of Sheng, for whom, alone of Chinese, Yolbars had no good word."[18]

Even for those more concerned about placating Emin and Isa rather than Yolbars, General Sheng was anathema. In the chaos of 1949, when eleven members of Sheng's extended family were brutally murdered as part of a revenge plot, Isa made a special trip to Lanzhou to console the perpetrators—recast in his account as "heroes"—and lobbied for clemency in the courts.[19] Throughout his remaining years on the mainland and well into the 1950s on Taiwan, Sheng grew accustomed to calls for justice whenever he attended a party conference. By the late 1950s, the uproar over Sheng's lack of accountability reached a peak, and some people suggested that he should "commit suicide to appease Heaven."[20] It was only the personal intervention of the Generalissimo that insulated Sheng from his detractors. Following his collaboration with Allen S. Whiting in 1958—with whom Sheng co-authored *Sinkiang: Pawn or Pivot?*—Sheng promptly dropped out of public life, changed his name, and began to carry a revolver, supporting himself on the 50,000 taels of gold he had siphoned from Xinjiang's coffers two decades prior. For such a man, there was no public or private role possible within the Xinjiang exile community. Instead, Sheng appears to have limited himself to accepting the occasional consultant gig for those in government or media who were looking for historical context to Soviet designs on Xinjiang.[21]

All of the above did not constitute an auspicious beginning for the borderland platform of the new regime on Taiwan. In the final analysis, the Nationalists had managed to procure only one aging Uighur dignitary, whose degree of literacy was dubious and whose loyalty had never been in question. Optimists within the party might also point to the tacit support of a young Kazak general in Srinagar, Delilhan Haji, who looked upon a veteran man-of-arms like Yolbars with reverence. Pessimists, however, could have noted Isa and Emin's considerable head start in the cultivation of refugee loyalties in Kashmir, as well as their extensive prior contacts throughout the Muslim world. How were Yolbars and Del-ilhan going to compete against Isa and Emin, who had mastered the art of Nationalist ethnopopulist rhetoric but were no longer constrained by party discipline?

RECRUITING KAZAKS

Once settled in Taiwan, Yolbars received for his daily paperwork a Nation-alist government seal demonstrably out of place in tropical Taiwan: Office of the Chairman of the Xinjiang Provincial Government (Xinjiang Sheng Zhengfu Zhuxi Bangongchu). This was a special office reserved specifi-cally for the chairman (governor) of Xinjiang alone, bereft of any claim to territorial administration. Three other provincial administrations oper-ated by the Nationalists after 1949—Taiwan, Fujian, and briefly, Yun-nan—all retained a living tax base and tangible clumps of land to look after.[22] Not so in the case of Xinjiang. The raison d'être for this office derived entirely from its symbolic power. By 1951, the dramatic plight of Uighur and Kazak refugees had caught the attention of Western media, culminating first in a lengthy *National Geographic* spread, and later in a highly embellished novelistic treatment, *Kazak Exodus*.[23] "The world is looking at developments in Xinjiang very closely," a planning com-mittee on Taiwan observed. It was Yolbars's job to ensure that whenever the global spotlight shone on Xinjiang, the Nationalists came out the better for it.

He began by sizing up his competition. The archival record in Taiwan opens in 1952, with letters to and from Isa and Emin, who by this point had left South Asia and relocated to Turkey. The extant missives, written in Uighur and translated into Chinese by Yolbars or his secretary, strain to maintain a façade of civility. "I served in the central government for thirteen years," Isa wrote to Yolbars in December. "Thinking back on it now, I accomplished absolutely nothing. It was all a waste of time. In the formulation of policy, the government never once consulted us, and it never adopted a single piece of our advice." Embittered by the glass ceiling experienced by non-Han figures such as himself within the Nationalist government, Isa used his correspondence with Yolbars as an opportunity to vent his dissatisfaction with Han rule in Xinjiang. "If I go to Taiwan, won't it be just like before? It is enough that you are there. Until I finish my work abroad, and until the central government recognizes our achievements, then there is nothing for me to do in Taiwan. It is better for me to stay here."[24]

"Here" was Istanbul. As it turned out, in the three years since 1949, Isa and Emin had been quite the industrious exiles. When they were not shuttling between New Delhi and Kashmir, they were crisscrossing the Middle East on fund-raising tours among Xinjiang refugee communities from an earlier era, when Sheng Shicai had taken aim at his province's Kazaks. One gold mine was Saudi Arabia, where some eight thousand refugees had long since integrated into local society and were eager to donate to Isa and Emin's cause. In 1951 alone, Yolbars learned, Emin had collected six thousand U.S. dollars in Saudi Arabia and an additional two thousand in Egypt, where the local press referred to him as the former "governor of Turkestan."[25] The funds were intended to help relocate several thousand Kazak refugees in Kashmir to Turkey as well as to publish anti-Communist propaganda from their new offices in Istanbul.[26] To speak for Xinjiang in the non-Communist world, Isa and Emin needed a Xinjiang constituency that would lend legitimacy to their words. Turkey, now the only Turkic-speaking nation not under Communist rule, fit the bill. Working tirelessly with representatives from multiple governments and charity organizations, Isa and Emin ultimately succeeded in securing asylum in Turkey for 1,734 Kazaks, along with several hundred Uighurs. The former settled in rural Anatolia, the latter in Istanbul.[27]

By the time Yolbars got his office in Taiwan up and running, Isa and Emin's resettlement plans for Turkey were nearly complete. Nevertheless, Yolbars still sent out feelers to the refugees, ensuring that some funds from the Association for Mainland Refugee Assistance were redirected to Kashmir. He also dangled the prospect of resettlement in Taiwan. Upon learning of the proposal to send Kazak nomads to a tropical island, a British clerk in India recorded a caustic observation: "The idea of sending Kazakhs to Formosa seems fantastic." Nevertheless, Yolbars was determined to make up for lost time, and in the three years from 1951 to 1953, he managed to direct US$16,000 to the refugees in Kashmir.[28] Two of them, Kali Beg and Hamza, duly began to parrot the rhetoric of the Nationalist government. Noting that 176 Kazaks and 13 Uighurs had already left for Turkey, Kali Beg announced that the remainder of his band, some 180 Kazaks, "swore an oath to remain behind in Kashmir and await orders to invade Xinjiang and eliminate the Communist bandits. We are loyal to party and state, and will follow the blue sky and white sun flag as we march forward."[29] Unbeknownst to Yolbars, however, these two Kazak chieftains had also been in touch with American and British authorities and seemed to be soliciting anyone with deep pockets.[30] In early 1952, Consul Paxton, from his office in Isfahan, was moved to send a personal check for almost three hundred dollars to the same Kali Beg and Hamza. "We have the pleasure to inform you that this amount was equally distributed by us amongst ourselves," Kali Beg wrote back in March. "So please accept our heartfelt thanks for this aid especially from the refugees of Kazaks 340 in number."[31]

At the same time that Yolbars and Kali Beg were exchanging letters, representatives from the Communist government on the mainland approached a large group of Kazak refugees in Pakistan. After a month of free banquets and regular allowances paid out in Russian rubles, a deep split emerged. Some refugees returned to the mainland by sea, while others were persuaded to recross the Himalayas on their own initiative. Isa, alarmed by the sudden overtures from Beijing and Taipei, attempted to reel Kali Beg back in. "The Turkish government has recently sent representatives to agitate among us, and they are inviting us to go to Turkey," Kali Beg informed Yolbars, referring to Isa and Emin's outfit in Istanbul. "But I was resolute and told them that my government is the Nationalist government, and that I will always be a citizen of the Republic of China." By late 1953, however, the allure of the resettlement deal in Turkey, brokered almost entirely by Isa and Emin, proved too much for the destitute refugees to turn down. Only Kali Beg and a hundred of his followers remained behind, in a final bid for Nationalist largesse. "People

from Xinjiang are scattered throughout many Muslim countries now,"
Kali Beg wrote. "If the central government ignores us, then it will have
a negative impact on foreign relations with the Muslim nations of the
Middle East, and they will begin to suspect that the government looks
down on the weak peoples of the world."[32]

Yet news of the resettlement of 1,734 refugees to Turkey had severely
undermined Kali Beg's declarations of loyalty to the Nationalist government in Taiwan. This in turn undermined Yolbars's ability to lobby on
their behalf. "In light of current financial difficulties," the Executive Yuan
in Taiwan announced soon after hearing of the resettlement in Anatolia,
"it will no longer be possible to provide relief funds to Xinjiang refugees
in India and Pakistan. At this time of hardship, we hope our compatriots
will be able to cultivate a spirit of 'overcoming all hardship' and look
after their own provisions." Though Yolbars scrambled to come up with a
formal blueprint to bring Kali Beg and his hundred followers to Taiwan,
the anticipated price tag (US$30,000) for their relocation was seen as too
high for the benefits of the publicity. Instead, the Nationalist government
decided—quite optimistically—that it could try to work through Isa and
Emin and attempt to foster symbolic declarations of loyalty from among
the resettled refugees.[33] Unwilling to admit that Isa and Emin had "won"
the opening round of Xinjiang refugee politics, certain voices within the
Nationalist Party, such as foreign minister Yeh, instead took to blaming
Yolbars for the exodus of nearly two thousand Kazaks—former citizens
of the Republic of China—to Turkey.

THE RIFT

The idea that the Nationalist government could simply work through
Isa and Emin was based upon a faulty assumption—namely, that the
interest was mutual. Once the refugees were settled in Turkey and the
prospect of additional aid from Taiwan diminished, serious doubts
began to surface. "Of course we are extremely excited about news of
an impending counterattack on the mainland," Emin wrote to Yolbars

in February 1953. "But never once did we receive a clear indication of
what the government's position will be regarding Xinjiang." To facilitate preparations for retaking the mainland, Emin demanded that Taipei
issue a clear statement regarding its "attitude" toward Xinjiang. "If the
government insists on being as stubborn as before and continues to view
Xinjiang as an inseparable province of China," he added, "then I assure
you that the disputes and disagreements will never end." Yolbars countered with vague assurances. "As far as I know, the government plans to
respect the opinions of local figures and implement regional autonomy,"
he replied. He then cautioned Emin not to let political ambitions cloud
his judgment. "You are an old veteran cadre of the party," he wrote, "and
you have served the central government for a long time now. You have
studied the dictates of our late premier [Sun Yat-sen] and know what
the fundamental policies of the party are. Surely you do not harbor any
misconceptions on that front." Instead, Yolbars tried to focus all attention on the Communist threat to their homeland. "Mutual suspicions and
individual pursuits will only serve to divide our strength."[34]

But the rift was clear, and Yolbars was quick to remind his detractors of Emin's continued "intransigence." Just three months after this
exchange, Yolbars submitted a comprehensive plan to the Ministry of
Foreign Affairs to raise the Nationalists' profile in the Middle East. He
now blamed the "conspiracy of Emin" for the way "two thousand of our
Kazak compatriots were seduced into adopting Turkish citizenship" and
elsewhere referred to "selfish and scheming individuals like Emin and
Isa." To make matters worse, the Communist government in Beijing had
begun to send formal Muslim diplomatic delegations to the Middle East,
an initiative that dovetailed with its interest in those refugees still living
in Pakistan. In response, Yolbars proposed a detailed list of counter-
measures. He suggested bringing some of the refugees from Turkey to
study in schools on Taiwan, staffing Nationalist embassies abroad with
Muslim personnel, sending an annual delegation to the World Muslim
Council, and participating in the hajj to Mecca. This last proposal met
with enthusiasm, and plans got underway to organize a pilgrimage to
Mecca the following year. Yolbars himself would headline the delega-

tion. In the meantime, in January 1954, Emin paid a visit to the Nationalist embassy in Ankara with his wife, not realizing that Yolbars had been
forwarding his letters up the Nationalist chain of command. Much to
Emin's surprise, the ambassador lashed out at him for "advocating Xinjiang independence and separation from the Republic of China." In no
uncertain terms, Emin was told that "the central government will never
grant you independence" and that "bad things" would happen to him if
he persisted in "pursuing such proposals abroad." Though the ambassador still forwarded Emin's request for $400 to Taipei, it was clear now
that any further largesse would come with tight strings attached.[35]

On July 17, 1954, with tensions running high, Yolbars, his son, and
three other prominent Hui officials boarded a plane for Egypt. Though
the Nationalist press touted this hajj delegation as an opportunity to win
over Middle Eastern leaders, the real goal was to bring Isa and Emin to
heel. Chiang Kai-shek approved additional relief funds for distribution
among Xinjiang refugees, and Yolbars vowed to convince Isa and Emin
to relocate to Taiwan.[36] On July 26, the long-awaited reunion took place
in Cairo. Yolbars handed Isa a goodwill gift of $2,000 and asked him
to come to Taiwan. According to Yolbars, Isa countered with a request
for another $10,000 as a Nationalist show of faith in his cause. Yolbars
must have demurred, because suddenly the gloves came off. "The government has never trusted me," Isa said, "instead giving power to Zhang
Zhizhong, Masud, and finally Burhan [the last three governors of Xin-
jiang]. Though I once received the post of secretary, still the government
did not trust me." Five years later, Isa was still smarting from an incident
in 1949 with Nationalist border guards, who had apparently detained
and roughed him up as he tried to flee the province. He now realized that
his service for the Nationalists in Xinjiang a decade prior had all been
a charade, and that Chiang Kai-shek had simply used him as a rhetorical counterweight to the Soviet puppet government in Ili. "The government fanned my hatred for communism and the Soviet Union, but then
let Xinjiang fall into their very hands. As a result, untold numbers of
anti-Communist youth were slaughtered and thousands of refugees fled
abroad. The government cannot shirk responsibility for this tragedy."[37]

Yolbars appears to have been taken aback by Isa's tirade, for his account contains no indication of a rebuttal. Not so two weeks later, when they met again in Mina, a town just outside of Mecca. This time Isa showed up with a host of refugees in tow. They immediately put Yolbars on the defensive. "We hear that you are destitute in Taiwan and have had to borrow money to make ends meet," Yolbars later recounted them as saying. "If you like, you can remain here with us and we will make sure that all of your living expenses are met. Rest assured that we have the means to take care of you." In addition, they blamed the loss of Xinjiang on the Nationalist failure to grant high-level autonomy to the province. This time, however, Yolbars came prepared with a rebuttal. "It is inappropriate to raise words of accusation at this time and place," the minutes record him as saying. "Unless we succeed in our goal of retaking the mainland, all talk of other matters is nothing more than hot air." If they wanted high-level autonomy in Xinjiang, Yolbars suggested, then they would have to earn it by deeds, not words. "I obtained my current titles as governor and commander of Xinjiang pacification neither before the loss of Xinjiang nor after arriving in Taiwan," he explained. "They were bestowed on me while I was in the mountains waging war on the Communists." If Isa wanted an official statement on high-level autonomy or independence for Xinjiang, Yolbars suggested, he and the refugees would first have to unite with the Nationalist government on Taiwan and work together for the liberation of the mainland.[38]

In the evening Isa returned for a third meeting. Yolbars did not even bother to record a detailed set of minutes for the occasion, noting merely that he "again complained about the government's lack of trust in him and revisited his abuse at the hands of the border patrol officer" in 1949. When Yolbars again visited Isa at his lodgings the next day, he found sixty refugees waiting. They must have had some choice words, for Yolbars immediately launched into a spirited defense of his past. "When Sheng Shicai leaned toward the Soviets and united with the Comintern," Yolbars said, "I fled to the central government and met high-ranking officials on Isa's introduction. The details of my service in the central government are well known to Isa, and he can vouch for me. I have never been bought off by the Han, and I am certainly not their running dog. Isa is in attendance here today. Go ahead and ask him whether or not this is true." One month later, upon his return to Taiwan, Yolbars hurried to debrief the Generalissimo. His conclusion was decidedly pessimistic. The goal of "preventing Isa and Emin from being used by others" would prove "very difficult to meet," he wrote. Over the course of four heated meetings in Egypt and Saudi Arabia, two things had become clear. First, Isa and Emin's "true colors" had emerged: they were now hostile to Han rule in general, be it in Nationalist or Communist guise. And second, Xinjiang refugees throughout the Middle East were fast falling under their wing, imbibing a narrative of ethnic conflict that elided the many contributions Isa and Emin themselves had once made on behalf of Chinese rule in Xinjiang.[39]

Faced with a propaganda war on two fronts, Yolbars quickly got to work. He renewed his correspondence with Kali Beg in Turkey, and through him learned of other former nomads in rural Anatolia who were either unhappy with the life of a farmer, annoyed at Isa and Emin, or both. Working through the Nationalist embassy in Ankara, Yolbars extended an offer of free university education for any disaffected refugees willing to study in Taiwan. Among the hundred or so volunteers was Kali Beg's own son. At the same time, Yolbars petitioned George Yeh, the Nationalist minister of foreign affairs, to build a new mosque in Taipei, in hopes of making a positive impression on visiting Muslim dignitaries. The hajj trips to Mecca became a near annual occurrence, though poor health and advanced age precluded Yolbars's inclusion. As for the rift with Isa and Emin, Nationalist authorities simply acted as though nothing had happened, continuing in the press to claim both men as allies. They combined their public silence on the "East Turkestan" issue with a slew of new propaganda from Yolbars's office, including *Frontier Culture* (Bianjiang wenhua), a monthly pictorial highlighting Uighur, Kazak, Tibetan, Hui, and Mongol loyalty to the Republic of China.[40]

The publication of *Frontier Culture* in October 1955 coincided with Beijing's designation of Xinjiang as the Uighur Autonomous Region. If Yolbars understood the modified Soviet calculus of the Chinese Communists on this front, his pronouncements in the press gave no indication. He went on public record denouncing the move as a "stepping-stone" to formal annexation of Xinjiang by the Soviet Union and claimed that Moscow had succeeded in "swallowing up" China's northwestern province. Aware only of Beijing's discourse but lacking eyes on the ground, Yolbars may actually have believed that Beijing "had to satisfy its master in the Kremlin." The Nationalist Ministry of Foreign Affairs, however, was less quick to jump to such conclusions. After thorough examination of an atlas recently published on the mainland, one official observed that "Yining, Tacheng, and Altay are all still present on the bandits' map." This official, thinking that perhaps Yolbars had based his comments on dubious intelligence gleaned from refugees, concluded that the comments in the press by Yolbars and other Nationalist officials were mere hyperbole, and that Xinjiang had not literally been "swallowed up" by Moscow. "Though Soviet ambitions in northern Xinjiang are well known," he wrote, "even the Communist bandits would not lightly give away a chunk of our national territory."[41]

It was this uncompromising aspiration for political and national sovereignty, a goal shared by Chinese Communists and Nationalists alike, that ultimately determined the fate of Chinese border politics during the Cold War. Simply put, neither Chiang Kai-shek nor Mao Zedong would willingly countenance the separatist activities of non-Han actors, be they in Turkey or Tibet. During the 1959 Tibetan uprising against the Communist government, the Generalissimo, while eager to exploit the revolt for his own aims, was unable to bring himself to support the goals of the rebels.[42] To do so would be to betray the ideal of national unity. It was the same with Xinjiang. In July 1956, when Yolbars issued a comprehensive report on the Middle Eastern activities of Isa, Emin, and the Chinese Communists, he made a telling assessment. "Taking advantage of their physical proximity," he wrote, Isa and Emin "frequently lure [the refugees] with promises of gain, threatening and cajoling them with considerable skill. From their bases of operation in Istanbul and Cairo, they publish journals and magazines, thereby swaying hearts and minds and influencing international opinion." The implications for Nationalist policies on Xinjiang were clear and surprising. "We should worry more about these activities than those of the Communist bandits."[43]

In other words, the threat of non-Han separatism was deemed of greater concern than that of a Communist regime committed to the protection of China's national sovereignty. To be sure, Yolbars kept meticulous tabs on the many cultural and religious delegations sent by the mainland to various Middle Eastern countries, and he often noted the participation of "the traitor Burhan." But these reports quickly became routine. Far more worrisome were indications that Xinjiang refugees in Turkey were lending a willing ear to the increasingly hostile ethnopopulist platform of Isa and Emin, who now ran the East Turkestan Refugee Association in Istanbul. These shifting dynamics were apparent in a letter sent to Yolbars in 1958 by a Uighur man who identified himself as Wahad. Once a lieutenant-colonel in the Nationalist army in Xinjiang during the 1940s, Wahad fled to Istanbul in 1949 and there came in touch with Isa and Emin's refugee community. In 1957, he wrote a letter to Chiang Kai-shek requesting a military pension. His plea apparently fell on deaf ears, for the following year he wrote a letter to Yolbars filled with violent imagery. "It is very difficult to get one's debts back from the Han," he wrote. "Unless you slit their throats you can't get anything." Referring to the Chinese staff at the Nationalist embassy at Ankara as "authoritarian Han," he lambasted the "many excuses they have for why they cannot help a Uighur compatriot." But the Han themselves, he continued, "have tons of money, travel to all the gorgeous places in the world, and live in beautiful Western houses." To enforce his claim for a military pension, Wahad stated his intention to murder an embassy employee. "Maybe if I do this, I can knock some sense into the Han." He signed off with a declaration that "it will be my glory to dispatch of such an enemy."[44]

It seems safe to say that Wahad's letter did not elicit much sympathy in Taiwan. Yet it must have been unsettling to see a former lieutenant-colonel in the Nationalist army transformed into a hate-spouting proponent of ethnic violence. This was a loyal Uighur who had once risked his life for the Nationalist cause. Once he arrived in Istanbul, however, where the close-knit Uighur community numbered in the hundreds, it would have been difficult to remain aloof from Isa and Emin's orbit, if for no other reason than the indispensability of their services in navigating the Turkish immigration bureaucracy. The lesson for Yolbars and the Nationalist government on Taiwan was clear: without vigorous counter-measures in relief funds, education, and propaganda, Xinjiang refugees throughout the Middle East would eventually begin to parrot the anti-Han discourse of Isa and Emin.

THE GLASS CEILING REVISITED

Despite the insinuations of Isa's refugees in Mecca, Yolbars appeared to be doing quite well for himself on Taiwan. In 1966, the *United Daily News* (Lianhe bao) reported on a thief who had broken into his home and stolen ¥200,000 worth of jewelry and other valuables, suggesting a life of considerable wealth and privilege.[45] Yet Yolbars, now entering his seventh decade, felt his age more than ever and was often confined to his desk. This, however, did not prevent him from continuing to attend official government functions, hosting the occasional delegation from Muslim countries, and arranging for more exchange students from Turkey. In 1960, one such student, Chengis Yarbağ, asked for more money to fund his studies. The Ministry of Foreign Affairs informed Yolbars that expenses for these refugee students were becoming "excessive." Still, the cost was worth it. "Since it is our nation's policy to take care of our border peoples, and seeing as Isa and Emin continue to raise the flag of independence at this time," the same memo observed, "we too will actively continue to cultivate the loyalty of our expatriate sons overseas for our own ends."[46]

Things changed again in the mid-1960s, when new developments began to alter the refugee landscape. First, in 1965, Emin died in Istanbul at sixty-four. Isa, who would live another three decades, now moved to exert even greater control over the exile community in Turkey. He immediately took the East Turkestan movement to a new level. In April

1965, he traveled to Mecca to make a presentation at the eleventh session of the World Muslim Congress. He asked the delegates assembled there to pass a resolution encouraging the Nationalist government on Taiwan to declare "East Turkestan" independent of China and to abolish the "colonial name" of Xinjiang. In addition, member nations were asked to commit to providing both tangible and moral support for Xinjiang refugees throughout the Middle East. When a representative from Syria seconded the motion, Nationalist spokesman Sun Shengwu immediately lodged a note of protest, invoking Congress prohibitions against involvement in politics. The next day the representative from Saudi Arabia, a staunch ally of the Nationalist government, rallied to Sun's defense, declaring that Muslims everywhere must adapt to the conditions of the country in which they live. In his notes, Sun recorded his satisfaction in seeing Isa pack up his briefcase to leave, only to be dissuaded by the Congress host.[47]

After the initial blindside, Sun Shengwu regained his composure. Several days later, he issued a rebuttal. "Mr. Isa was appointed by our very own government as secretary-general of the Xinjiang Provincial Government," Sun read. "Once the Communist Party began to occupy the mainland and Xinjiang, all the provincial leaders fled abroad. Except for a small number of ambitious careerists like Isa, the majority of them have continued to embrace the legal government of the Republic of China." It was here that recruiting Yolbars and two decades of funding the activities of his office paid huge rhetorical dividends. "In Taiwan we have set up an Office of the Chairman of the Xinjiang Provincial Government, and it is chaired by Yolbars Khan, a Uighur Muslim. This office provides relief aid and succor for dispersed refugees and draws up plans for the recovery of lost territory." The biggest blow to Isa's narrative of legitimacy, however, came when Sun divulged his extensive history of cooperation with the Nationalist government, a rhetorical strategy deployed to great effect by Yolbars during his spirited debate with Isa at Mina. "The political status of China's Muslims is not below that of any other Muslim nation," he concluded. "Indeed, Mr. Isa himself has now been nurtured and mentored by our government for more than three decades." In his report, Sun again recorded with relish the sight of Isa "folding up his briefcase and preparing to depart." In front of the assembly, however, Sun attempted to retain the moral high ground. He made a grand show of inviting Isa to come to Taiwan and "participate in the sacred task of resisting communism and recovering the mainland," and promised to submit his grievances to the Nationalist government for "consideration."[48]

Back in Taiwan, Yolbars was getting help from unexpected quarters. The disastrous famines of the Great Leap Forward (1958–61) and persecution campaigns on the mainland had resulted in a renewed crop of 701 refugees from Xinjiang. (In an unrelated incident in 1962, tens of thousands of Uighurs and Kazaks fled to the Soviet Union, where neither Beijing nor Taipei could attempt to win their loyalties.) These new refugees ended up in Pakistan and Afghanistan, neither of which recognized Taipei. One refugee in particular stood out from the pack, a man by the name of Sabik. In December 1963, two years after his escape from Xinjiang, he wrote a letter to the Nationalist ambassador in Ankara, who duly forwarded it to Yolbars. Sabik related the following story. A native of Yarkand in southern Xinjiang, he was once a member of several Nationalist Party organizations, including the local branch of the Uighur Association for Ethnocultural Advancement, a vestige of the Sheng era. Formerly a well-to-do man, he described repeated imprisonments after 1949, including the confiscation of US$60,000 in assets. During the famines of the Great Leap Forward, he claimed—most improbably—that starving Han had resorted to eating Uighur babies.[49] In 1961, following his wife's remarriage, he contacted relatives in Afghanistan and managed to flee as part of a trade caravan. Once in Kabul, the Afghan government pressured the refugees either to return to Xinjiang or to resettle in another country. After turning to the Americans for help, he was encouraged to get in touch with both Isa in Istanbul and the Nationalist embassy in Ankara.[50]

Yolbars sensed a golden opportunity. Sabik's background was not unlike that of Wahad, the one-time loyal Nationalist lieutenant-colonel turned violent anti-Han racist. Furthermore, because Sabik was from Yarkand, where Isa had once maintained an influential base of operations, Yolbars worried that the two men would quickly form a bond. When, for reasons that are unclear, Isa proved slow to respond, Yolbars sprang into action. "In this hour of need, when life and death hang in the balance," he wrote to the Ministry of Foreign Affairs, "Isa and Emin have abandoned these refugees. The political significance of a rescue effort undertaken by our government at this time would be considerable." Though Yolbars wanted to bring them to Taiwan, the ministry urged them to relocate to Turkey, which was now offering to pay relocation expenses. Events soon conspired to undermine this arrangement. First, Isa finally wrote back to Sabik, "scolding me for exchanging letters with Governor Yolbars." Suddenly aware of the deep schism that ran throughout the Xinjiang refugee community, Sabik informed Yolbars that he "no longer wanted to go to Turkey, since it will be hard to get along with my compatriots there if Isa is acting like this." Instead, Sabik asked Yolbars if he could help them travel to Saudi Arabia, where the Xinjiang exile community was more prosperous. But even that would prove difficult now. Alerted to Turkey's offer of resettlement, Beijing began to put pressure on Kabul to reverse its stance and let the refugees remain in Afghanistan. At least in this case, it seems, the Communists were more determined than the Nationalists to keep potential recruits out of Isa's reach.[51]

For his part, Yolbars, informed that his own government was unwilling to assume the burden of mass resettlement in Taiwan, saw little reason to help them relocate to Saudi Arabia, where the existing refugee community maintained extensive contacts with Isa. In Afghanistan, however, Sabik could continue to work on behalf of the Nationalist government as a covert agent among the steady stream of refugees who continued to file out of Xinjiang. With relocation efforts stalled, Kabul fast became the next battleground for Isa and Yolbars. According to Sabik, Isa sent his men to Afghanistan to spread rumors about the negative repercussions of carrying a Nationalist passport and further promised to sponsor free annual hajj trips for anyone who relocated to Turkey. They apparently also brought letters from refugees in Istanbul attesting to the luxurious life they were living under Isa's patronage. Yolbars countered by lodging urgent requests with his own government for relief funds to be distributed among Sabik's followers. It is not clear how much, if any, money was dispensed at this time, but something in Yolbars's overtures must have given many of the refugees pause; by 1967, when Isa finally succeeded in leveraging United Nations support for their resettlement in Turkey, only 235 of Sabik's 701 followers took up the offer. The remainder—how many in each case is not clear—either moved on to the Soviet Union, relocated to Taiwan, or simply remained in Kabul, where Sabik continued to speak on their behalf in his correspondence with Yolbars. In his documents, Yolbars began to refer to Sabik as "my secret agent and contact man in Afghanistan."[52]

For the next four years, Sabik was exactly that. The complex wheeling and dealing of the Xinjiang exile community need not detain us here, but suffice it to note that during these years Sabik seems to have served as a highly effective counterweight to Isa among the Middle Eastern exile community. Shuttling back and forth among Iran, Jordan, Saudi Arabia, Afghanistan, and Taiwan, he was entrusted with ever greater sums of money, numbers that peaked in 1969 with the deposit of US$25,000 in an Iranian bank account. Such large sums inevitably opened Sabik to accusations of graft, and—if the counteraccusations can be trusted—Isa's men never missed an opportunity to fan the rumor mill in Kabul. An investigation by Yolbars's son purported to clear Sabik of any wrongdoing and merely advised him to obtain a signed receipt whenever money changed hands. In 1969, the Xinjiang refugee population in Afghanistan suddenly swelled to 12,000, largely as a result of renewed chaos during the Cultural Revolution (1966–76). Yolbars gave Sabik his biggest task yet, flying him to Taiwan to draw up comprehensive blueprints that would provide this exile community with the necessary start-up capital to maintain a livelihood in Afghanistan. The archives for this time period are filled with requests for relief funds from newly arrived refugees. More often than not their wishes were granted, with gifts ranging anywhere from one to six hundred U.S. dollars apiece. With confidence running high, Yolbars, cognizant of his impending mortality, even offered his governorship to Isa, provided he assumed it on Taiwan.[53]

During the late 1960s, the momentum continued to shift in Yolbars's favor. By 1969, the son of former Xinjiang governor Masud Sabri (1947–48), once a devout follower of Isa, had broken off contact with his former mentor and informed Yolbars that he would like to visit Taiwan. With his coterie of covert agents across the Middle East growing fast, Yolbars decided that the time was ripe to spur his greatest ally into action. This was General Delilhan Haji, the one-time Kazak guerrilla warrior and son of the former minister of finance in Nationalist Xinjiang. Delilhan, who had remained in Srinagar but kept up a voluminous correspondence with Yolbars, declined numerous offers of relocation to either Turkey or Taiwan. He did, however, deign to fly to Taipei on several separate occasions in the 1950s and 1960s to participate in Nationalist Party congresses as a formal "representative" from Xinjiang. In possession of an Indian passport, Delilhan also made several trips to Afghanistan to liaison with Sabik and even took over the latter's responsibilities for a time when accusations of graft temporarily sidelined Yolbars's "secret agent."[54] That same year, however, Delilhan made his biggest move yet: he and his brother decided to abandon their home of nineteen years in Srinagar and spend their twilight years in Istanbul, Isa's home turf.

Neither Delilhan nor his brother, cut from the same ideological cloth as Yolbars, liked what they saw. The second generation of Kazak youth had been almost entirely assimilated into Turkish culture, and Uighur exiles in Istanbul enjoyed far better living conditions than their Kazak counterparts, confined as they were to the impoverished Anatolian countryside. Delilhan immediately blamed Isa, whom he accused of siphoning off UN aid money for his own personal use, all the while inflating his and Emin's roles in resisting the Chinese Communists in 1949. He reminded everyone of how Isa and Emin had fled Xinjiang long before the arrival of Communist troops, and how he, his father, Yolbars, and Osman Batur had waged a bloody struggle long after their departure. Fluent in Kazak, Turkish, Chinese, Urdu, and English, Delilhan wasted no time in contacting Turkish authorities and lobbying for better living conditions for the Kazak community.[55]

THE XINJIANG GOVERNMENT IN EXILE

    Delilhan was a cosmopolitan, experienced politician with an estab-
lished reputation among Kazak youth. They had grown up hearing tall
tales about the brave struggles of men like Delilhan, Osman, and Yolbars Khan. Isa, a complete stranger to the battlefield, had no rhetorical antidote to such a man. After Delilhan's arrival in Istanbul, a new
rift emerged within the exile community in Turkey, made possible in no
small part by Yolbars's efforts from Taiwan. Delilhan described Yolbars
and the Nationalist government in Taiwan in glowing terms and continued to sponsor student exchanges into the 1980s. When I met Delilhan
in Istanbul in 2008, he was eighty-seven years old and basking in the
reverent respect of the younger Kazak generations. (He has since passed
away.) The parents of these young Kazaks had moved from rural Anatolia
to urban Istanbul under his auspices, eventually striking it rich via the
manufacture of thermoplastic polymers. Now grossly outnumbering the
Uighur expatriate community in Istanbul and infinitely wealthier, these
third-generation Kazaks have elevated Delilhan and the long-departed
Osman Batur into a new pantheon of Xinjiang historical icons. They have
also gutted the East Turkestan Refugee Association of almost any association with its founder, who passed away in 1995. By and large, this
third generation of Kazak youth seemed unaware of the considerable
diplomatic legwork bequeathed their new patriarch by Yolbars Khan on
his island of exile.[56]

ONE CHINA, INDIVISIBLE

On the morning of July 27, 1971, at Taipei's Veterans General Hospital, Yolbars Khan passed away in his sleep. He was eighty-three years
old. Chiang Kai-shek wrote an inscription for his tomb lauding his many
decades of loyalty and service to the central government. Yet his services after the fall of the mainland were probably of greater import to
the Chinese state than anything he did before 1949. By the time of his
death, Isa's political ambitions had largely been frustrated, and the East
Turkestan Refugee Association could not claim anything close to an eth-

nopolitical monopoly over Xinjiang expatriate communities outside the Communist bloc. By maintaining a vigorous base of operations on Taiwan, Yolbars emitted a viable gravitational pull for anyone willing to pay lip service to the Nationalist ethnopolitical platform. That declarations of loyalty among the refugees were likely motivated more by poverty than by ideology is beside the point. Though Isa enjoyed a considerable head start in cultivating refugee loyalties and funded his activities with money from the United Nations, he proved unable to insulate his constituency from the overtures of two powerful and influential Chinese metropoles. In the end, Yolbars effectively denied a steady stream of impressionable migrants to Turkey, retained crucial loyalties in Afghanistan and Kashmir, and when the time was ripe, even infiltrated Isa's own de facto jurisdiction via proxy assault (Delilhan). Indeed, just two months before his death, the fruits of Yolbars's final labors were put on full display in the Nationalist press: Pakistan refugee Seyit Abdullah and his family of eight arrived in Taiwan to take up permanent residence on the island. Their portraits were splashed about in the newspapers.[57]

After the death of its chairman, the Office of the Chairman of the Xinjiang Provincial Government quickly withered away. Under Yao Daohong, Yolbars's eldest son, the office signed off on a letter to U.S. president Jimmy Carter in 1977 urging him not to normalize relations with the mainland government. Other than that, however, the archival record runs dry, and rumor has it that the bulk of the files were burned to avoid investigations of financial malfeasance. Then, in 1988, Yao submitted a routine application for a new government car, as permitted once every ten years. The proposed price tag of ¥600,000 attracted ministerial attention, and it was decided to shut down the office within a year. By this time the Xinjiang office was little more than a quaint curiosity of the Cold War, and several articles appeared in the newly democratic press poking fun at its past activities.[58] But it had been no laughing matter for the Generalissimo. During the twenty-two years that the Nationalist government on Taiwan had held the "China seat" in the United Nations, its "governor" of Xinjiang had played a crucial role in upholding Chiang's "one China" policy. Just as the Generalissimo's continued survival on

Taiwan guaranteed that the island would not fall victim to Washington's preferred "two Chinas" policy, so too did the Xinjiang government-in-exile help secure Chinese sovereignty—both Nationalist and Communist—over a historically non-Han, weakly integrated region.

In the form of Isa and Emin, the Nationalist Party encountered a credible threat to its narrative of Chinese political legitimacy in Xinjiang. It was all the more credible owing to the fact that Isa and Emin had originally developed their ethnopopulist platform under the auspices of the Nationalist government. No longer inhibited by the glass ceiling imposed by their Han patrons, Isa and Emin lacked only an ethnopolitical constituency in whose name they could speak. This they found in the first few years after the Communist takeover, shepherding some two thousand Uighurs and Kazaks to Turkey and establishing organizational linkages among the many more thousands of Xinjiang refugees scattered throughout the Middle East. Before long, the Nationalist government in Taiwan deemed Isa and Emin's political outfits in Istanbul to be a greater threat to China's territorial integrity than the Chinese Communists themselves, a judgment they also levied at Xinjiang expatriates receiving Soviet support in Tashkent.

Once it became evident that Isa and Emin would never relocate to Taiwan, Yolbars set out to sabotage their alternative narratives of ethnopolitical legitimacy. The consequences of Isa and Emin's inability to withstand the relentless assault levied against them from Taiwan and its ideological proxies in South Asia stand in sharp contrast to the fate of ethnopolitics in Tibet. After the Tibetan uprising against Communist rule in 1959, approximately 80,000 Tibetans fled with the Dalai Lama to India, where they set up a government of Tibet in exile. Less well known than the uprising itself is that the Nationalist administration on Taiwan, acting through its Committee for Tibetan and Mongolian Affairs in Taipei, also made overtures to the Tibetan leadership and offered assistance to the refugee community in Dharamsala. By and large, their overtures were rebuffed, and it was not until the late 1960s that any Tibetan political figures or students traveled to Taiwan to meet with Nationalist representatives. Offers of financial assistance, the construction of refugee schools in India, and invitations to travel to Taiwan were all declined. The Dalai Lama's personal fortune, estimated at nearly four million U.S. dollars, proved more than enough to sustain the Tibetan exile community.[59]

The only other person even remotely qualified to challenge the Dalai Lama's claim as spokesman for Tibet, the Panchen Lama, made the fateful decision to remain in China after 1959, where he publicly supported the Communist government. His subsequent persecution during the Cultural Revolution, combined with the failure of the Nationalists to recruit their own Tibetan eminence to Taiwan, meant that the Dalai Lama never had to endure a credible challenge to his leadership outside the communist bloc such as that experienced by Isa and Emin. Though the international reputation of prominent Xinjiang expatriates cannot be compared to someone of the Dalai Lama's stature, and the Islamic faith has never captured the sympathy of the Western world in the manner of an ostensibly "pacifist" Buddhism, still the comparison is illuminating. With regard to Tibet, the international community recognizes one very powerful, sympathetic, and credible expatriate spokesman. He stands in opposition to two Chinese metropoles, neither of which can claim much pride in its historical handling of the Tibet issue.

Regarding Xinjiang, however, neither the East Turkestan Refugee Association in Istanbul nor the legacy of the Xinjiang government in exile in Taiwan is widely known, if at all. And that is exactly how Chinese officials in Beijing and Taipei prefer it. As political scientist David Bachman notes, there exists today "no unified opposition and no widely agreed upon leader who is seen internationally (and even in China) as speaking for Uygurs or Xinjiang in the way that the Dalai Lama speaks for Tibet."[60] And yet, as the previous chapter demonstrated, the Chinese Communists failed utterly during the 1950s to implement a convincing discourse of ethnopopulism or to create the requisite non-Han ethnopopulist constituency in Xinjiang. So why did Isa and Emin prove unable to capitalize upon Beijing's systematic missteps in their homeland? As this chapter has shown, the answer lies not in Xinjiang or mainland China. Instead, we must look to Beijing's longtime island rival and a one-time major-domo of the Hami khanate to understand why the failure of ethnopopulism in early Communist Xinjiang did not capture global attention then as it does today. In this as in so many other matters of ethnopolitical import, the voices of Communist China and "free China" were curiously aligned.

CONCLUSION

W E END OUR STORY WITH A STATUE. A BRONZE STATUE, TO BE exact. For about a decade from the mid-1920s, it stood in a handsome two-story pavilion in Urumchi's West Park, a monument to traditional Chinese architecture. Standing on the second floor was a metallic bust of Governor Yang Zengxin, visible to all passersby.

In 1927, Nicholas Roerich, the peripatetic Russian philosopher and painter, passed through Xinjiang and recorded a dim view of its aesthetic qualities. "The collection of funds for the erection of the monument was conducted throughout the whole district by forced subscriptions," he observed. "And as a gift 'from the grateful population' appeared an ugly copper figure with gilded epaulettes and stars." Han visitors from outside the province were hardly more charitable. In the words of Xu Bingxu, the Chinese codirector of the Sino-Swedish Scientific Expedition, "The dress and appearance of the statue do not resemble the governor, and gold foil has been plastered all over the face. What a truly odd sight. Though the governor has many merits to his name as a result of his lengthy tenure in Xinjiang, a gesture such as this, which exults in a vain celebration of his achievements, seems most unnecessary."[1]

After Sheng Shicai rose to power, he removed the statue from the park and placed it in a locked storage closet in the Bureau of Transportation. Ten years later, Nationalist governor Wu Zhongxin stumbled upon it by accident. "I unlocked the door and went in to take a look. Inside I found a bronze statue of Yang Zengxin, about the height of a man. It exudes a majestic air. Gazing upon the statue, I was moved to reflect upon how Yang governed Xinjiang for seventeen years, keeping our borders peaceful and secure. His achievements cannot be denied. Therefore, I knelt

FIGURE C.1. Chinese Pavilion with Bronze Statue of Governor Yang Zengxin in West Park, Urumchi, c. 1927. Photograph by Owen Lattimore © President and Fellows of Harvard College, Peabody Museum of Archaeology and Ethnology, PM no. 2010.5.35197 (digital file no. 136590092).

and bowed three times, to show my respect."[2] The trail of documentation peters out after 1944. One suspects the statue remained in the same storage closet during the early Communist years, gathering dust much as it had during the era of Sheng Shicai. In all likelihood, it probably met with an ignominious end during a Maoist campaign: if not melted down to forge useless pig iron during the Great Leap Forward, it was probably trotted out for a public inferno during the Cultural Revolution, when so many other symbols of the imperial and republican past were destroyed.

Much like the legacy and fate of the Qing empire during the twentieth century, the bronze statue of Governor Yang Zengxin has long constituted an enigma. Historians know what distant observers have said about it—almost all of it negative—but we do not know much about its underlying substance. The reason men like Nicholas Roerich and Xu Bingxu, both outsiders to Xinjiang and its political scene, could not withhold criticism of Yang's statue was because they both expected something else. When the former deplored its gilded epaulettes and stars and the latter fixated on the vain indulgences of an acting official, they were comparing the statue unfavorably with idealized Western and Chinese aesthetic sensibilities. For Roerich, the addition of European military insignia on Yang's chest and shoulders sullied the architectural grandeur of the traditional Chinese pavilion in which the statue stood. For Xu, the very notion that an official should consent to the erection of a "living shrine" while occupying the office celebrated by that shrine smacked of cronyism and corruption. In traditional Chinese political culture, a renowned official may live to see the commissioning of a shrine celebrating his achievements after his departure from the jurisdiction in which it is built, or he may become a highly stylized and fabled "city-god" several centuries after his death. But he is not supposed to occupy the same office for seventeen years and then oversee the construction of his own living shrine while still holding that post.[3]

Yang's statue did not conform to either man's ideal. Instead, it was an amalgam of two political and cultural traditions fused into a Sino-Western hybrid whose true utility could be comprehended only by someone familiar with the politics of difference in Xinjiang. To put it another way, we might say that Governor Yang's statue was the physical embodiment of the historical argument this book has set forth: that is, the legacy of the Qing empire in twentieth-century Xinjiang obliged Han rulers in Urumchi to forge a new foundation of political difference. Drawing upon domestic precedents and foreign models, this new approach transformed modern China into a community of anxious administrators forced to deal with the legacy of multiethnic states in an era of national determination and decolonization. In crossing the 1911 and 1949 divides, we have identified important continuities in Chinese rule in Xinjiang. The strategies used by Han officials in Urumchi were neither especially Manchu nor Nationalist nor Communist, but were instead techniques drawn from the imperial repertoires of finance, defense, administration, and ideology that circulated freely among China's contemporary imperial rivals. Even when developments on the ground lagged far behind political discourse, Chinese officials still made it a point of pride to keep pace with the latest trends in ethnopolitical posturing.

The foregoing chapters have presented a narrative of modern China as an empire in transition whose political elites were obliged to meet similarly evolving threats with similarly evolving imperial repertoires. We began with Governor Yang and his selective revival of key conservative platforms from the high Qing era. Yang's revival of the discourse and structures of ethno-elitism, in which local Turkic *begs* and Chinggisid Muslim and Mongol princes retained their hereditary or divine rights to rule parts of Xinjiang, was a repudiation of premature attempts by the late Qing state to integrate Xinjiang into the rest of the country. When the Western discourse of the nation-state infiltrated Xinjiang during the Russian civil war and eventually served as the pretext to establish Outer Mongolia as an independent state, Yang's response was twofold. First, he developed a unique strain within the discourse of national humiliation to suggest that anyone who failed to treat Xinjiang differently from the rest of China would bear responsibility for its becoming "the next Outer Mongolia." Next, he responded to the collapse and reconstitution of imperial authority throughout Eurasia by attempting to insulate Xinjiang from any and all nationalist platforms, both those from the inner provinces, which valorized the "Yellow Race," and those from Soviet Central Asia, which promised to enfranchise the non-Han commoners of Xinjiang. He did this by refashioning the diplomatic institution of the Western consulate in his own image, directing his hard-won consulates in Soviet Central Asia to ensure that anyone inspired by Soviet affirmative action be barred reentry to the province.

When the continued inability of inner Chinese warlords to reunite the country led to a geopolitical crisis in Xinjiang—the assassination of Governor Yang in 1928 by agents of another warlord—Yang's successor, Jin Shuren, embarked on a wholesale repudiation of the politics of difference. His centralization and modernization initiatives very much resembled the late Qing drive to integrate the non-Han borderlands, a prolonged campaign again carried out in response to a geopolitical crisis. In Jin's case, however, the main difference was his entire lack of financial, political, or military support from the Chinese metropole. The late Qing state, however weak it may have seemed in the face of foreign aggression, had once supplied such support to its borderland officials, albeit in ever decreasing amounts. In quick succession, Jin managed to alienate the Incarnate Lama of Karashahr, the Soviets, and the Turkic peoples of Hami, both noble and commoner. When former retainers of Shah Maqsut rallied Turkic peasants against Jin's administration, they did so by invoking the idea of a "Chanto"—that is, Uighur—nation-state, borrowing this name from Chinese descriptions of the turbans some men wore on their heads. Soon the entire province was at war, with a bewildering array of national platforms on the lips of every belligerent.

In 1934, a Han warlord by the name of Sheng Shicai emerged triumphant from the wreckage of Yang and Jin. To gain the support of his non-Han subjects, many of whom had shed their blood to prevent the rise of another Han like him, Sheng had to meet demands within his province for demonstrations of support for national determination. In response, Sheng adapted the Soviet discourse and institutional structures of ethnopopulism, in which progressive and ostensibly elected representatives of the masses are placed into positions of government and expected to mobilize their constituents toward a more equitable and prosperous future. Chinese Comintern agent Yu Xiusong described

Sheng as having learned from the "only country in the entire world to have completely and correctly solved its nationality problems." From a somewhat broader historical perspective, Sheng was simply continuing under newly ascendant Han stewardship the millennia-long tradition of ethnopolitical engineering and posturing typical of China's many non-Han ruling elites in dynasties past.[4] Sheng's gambit worked, in spite of—or perhaps because of—his simultaneous importation of Stalinist police state tactics. These were eventually deployed to purge his administration of nearly all the non-Han peoples he had only so recently elevated into prominent positions of authority. Ultimately, however, Sheng's "purchase" of Soviet affirmative action blueprints saddled him with massive debts that neither he nor his Chinese Communist adviser Mao Zemin could ever fully repay. After Sheng took advantage of the siege of Stalingrad to shirk his obligations to the Soviets and return to the Nationalist fold, Moscow decided to reclaim its debts by directing an ethnopopulist Uighur and Kazak "national" insurgency against the new Chinese administration in the province. Not surprisingly, this insurgency, later glossed as the East Turkestan Republic, took as its strategic targets only those three districts in which the Soviets had once maintained heavy interests in industrial minerals (Altay), pastoral stock (Tacheng), and oil (Ili).

The Nationalist response was to raise the stakes of ethnopolitical patronage in wartime and postwar Xinjiang. Those within the party who admired an ethnopopulist approach—a camp that included Chiang Kai-shek—decided to meet Soviet sponsorship of Uighurs and Kazaks by elevating their own Uighur and Kazak figures to positions of visible authority in Xinjiang. Combined with the fruits of those who championed an ethno-elitist approach—chief among which was Governor Wu Zhongxin (1944–46)—the Nationalist cabinet of non-Han personages in Xinjiang during the 1940s effectively negated the novelty of Soviet-sponsored figures such as Ali Han Tore and Ahmetjan Qasimi. Never again would so much political agency be granted to the prince of the Kazaks (Ailin), the khan-wang of the Torgut Mongols (Manchuqjab), a Kazak *batur* (Osman), or ethnopopulists such as Masud Sabri, Mohammed Emin Bugra, Isa Yusuf Alptekin, and Burhan Shahidi. And it goes without saying that never again would the Chinese central government suffer Uighur officials in its political wing to publish journals that criticized the "tyrannical Chinese butchers" or advertised Xinjiang as the home of the "Turkestan nation," as General Zhang Zhizhong had once allowed. The reason for these bold Nationalist innovations was simple: in the postwar atmosphere of increasing demands for decolonization, the Nationalists had to prove their commitment to the emerging global discourse of "development" and "nurturing" of subaltern peoples the world over or risk tarnishing their narrative of ethnopolitical legitimacy in Xinjiang.

After 1949, it fell to the Chinese Communists to deal with this legacy of ethnopolitical "inflation" in Xinjiang. They did so by introducing one final adaptation to the Soviet affirmative action model: ethnocultural autonomy would be territorialized (unlike Sheng's Austro-Marxist interpretation), but it would not be institutionalized at the level of a republic, complete with the right of secession. The realpolitik calculus behind this innovation is evident in a speech given by Wang Enmao, party secretary of Xinjiang during the 1950s, to newly arrived Han cadres. To judge from the content of his speech, these men were far more familiar with Soviet ethnopopulist discourse—and its institutional embodiments just across the border—than with Chinese Communist adaptations. Noting widespread unease among Han cadres over the stated goal of making Uighurs the "masters of their own house" (*dangjia zuozhu*), Wang put his colleagues at ease: "The [Han] mistakenly believe that after the implementation of ethnic regional autonomy, they can go back home to the inner provinces. Some think the implementation of ethnic regional autonomy means that the responsibilities of ethnic cadres will increase, while those of Han cadres will decrease. What none of them realizes is that even after ethnic regional autonomy is put into practice, Han cadres still will not be allowed to go home. Our job of assisting the various nationalities of Xinjiang is a long-term mission."[5]

Elsewhere, Zhou Enlai justified the unprecedented waves of Han migration in the same language of "development" that the Nationalists before him had used. As for the Communist obligation to "nurture" the non-Han peoples of Xinjiang, Zhou could point to the institutionalization of ethnocultural and political privileges for fifty-five official non-Han nationalities, about half of which had only been "identified" by Communist ethnographers during the first five years of the new state.[6]

As evidenced by ubiquitous reports of ethnic tension and conflict on the factory floors of Urumchi, the Chinese Communists failed miserably to deliver on the promises of ethnopopulist affirmative action. At best, we might say that they delivered an emasculated version of ethno-elitism, one that masqueraded as ethnopopulism. That is to say, non-Han elites were still separated from "their" people and elevated into privileged positions of authority, but now without even the ability to wield that authority. All that mattered was that they stand in as a symbolic representation of the will of "their" people. Initially, however, the Communists had far less reason to worry about these ironic inversions than did the Nationalists. Unlike the Nationalists, they had both time and geopolitical circumstance on their side. They even had the assistance of a second Chinese metropole—the Nationalists in Taiwan—who assisted the mainland government in undermining any narrative of political legitimacy for Xinjiang that did not originate in Beijing or Taipei, both of which now evinced a more or less harmonious pursuit of common geopolitical and ethnopolitical goals. The end result was the creation of a "national empire" very similar to the state established by the Soviets just across the Eurasian border. Though no political elite or self-respecting Chinese nationalist today would employ such a term, marred as it is by the revolutionary discourse of an authoritarian—and most deplorable—form of power, this is precisely what has arisen from the ashes of the old monarchical empires: a vast state whose territorial and human heterogeneity must be nationalized to conform to new narratives of postrevolutionary political legitimacy.

The idea that an imperial entity could be defined, not undermined, by nationalism would have been familiar to the intellectuals of the late Qing era with which we began our study. In 1906, Ye Shanrong, editor of a family genealogy, envisioned the creation of a state capable of meeting the "tides of nationalism" (*minzu chaoliu*) that defined his age. Believing that his generation had already begun this process, Ye called his era "an age in which a national empire [*minzu diguo*] is being created."[7] It is not entirely clear what Ye meant by a "national empire," a novel term in his day. It combines the word for "nationality" (*minzu*) with the characters for a "state" (*guo*) presided over by an "emperor" (*di*). In reference to a type of state, Ye was likely simply describing the political status quo of his day, in which a Manchu emperor sat on the throne. But his use of "nationality" (*minzu*) is more specific: it is the idea that people should be organized on the principle of the "nation-state" (*guojia zhuyi de minzu*) as a means to wealth and power in the twentieth century. For someone who did not exercise actual political control on the ground, this is probably about as far as the concept was liable to be explicated at the time. But for this study, concerned as it is with Han administrators responsible for preserving the heterogeneous human and geographical landscape of the former Qing empire, Ye's formulation provides a striking premonition of just how the ideal of national determination would ultimately color the geopolitical calculus of Han administrators after the 1911 revolution.

The lands and peoples that compose the entity known as "China" are not today, nor have they ever been, a "nation-state." But they do constitute a state of many nations, each of which, including the Han, bears the imprint of deliberate ethnic manufacture by the state. If we follow Frederick Cooper in ascribing to such polities the designation *empire-state*—in lieu of *nation-state*—then we have already approximated what some Soviet scholars refer to as Moscow's "empire of nations."[8] But if the Soviet Union was an "empire of nations," composed of potentially detachable parts, then it makes sense to call the modern Chinese state a "national empire," defined by—but not divisible into—its fifty-six national components. Though anthropologists and historians of China have long recognized the hybrid nature of the modern Chinese state, few have attempted to trace in precise chronological detail the temporal and methodological contours of the evolution of this state throughout the late Qing, republican, and early Communist eras.[9] By telling just such a narrative here, we can attempt to situate the ethnopolitical history of China both within long-standing East Asian mainland traditions and within Eurasian and Euro-American innovations of much more recent vintage.

As a type of state, empires did not all disappear during the twentieth century. Instead, as we have seen in Xinjiang, some of them simply
redefined their institutional markers of difference from an ethno-elitist
to an ethnopopulist model. In other words, they got a nationalist make-
over. Before taking that fateful step, however, each empire made a point
of canvassing the imperial repertoires of every one of its rivals, selecting for modified deployment those tactics viewed as most suitable to
the unique conditions of its own imperial landscape. We might even
go so far as to say that the hallmark of a successful empire during the
twentieth century was the ability to deploy sufficient resources—and
imperial repertoires innovative enough—to maintain a monopoly on the
definition and sponsorship of categories of human difference, be they
in ethno-elitist or ethnopopulist guise. A state that could continue to
control the recognition and definition of its many peoples in nationalized forms was likely to subsist as some sort of a "national empire" or
"empire of nations." One that could not prevent its peoples from being
recognized and defined in national terms by rival metropoles was likely
to become a collection of putative "nation-states," however imperfectly
and artificially defined.

With the waning of Nationalist influence in world politics, the Chinese Communists have faced a host of new challenges in Xinjiang. After
all, for nearly four decades, the Nationalists had managed from Taiwan
to deflect foreign criticism of Chinese rule in Xinjiang by depriving dissenting Uighur ethnopopulists in Turkey of the support of "free China."
Beijing took full advantage of this extended reprieve, ensuring the complete integration of Xinjiang into China before Taipei lost what little
remained of its political clout in the United States and Europe. Ever since
the reform era, however, Chinese Communists have come face-to-face
with a delayed reckoning on the failure of their ethnopopulist platform
in Xinjiang during their first decade of rule. They have met this unwelcome increase in foreign scrutiny by once again adapting techniques
of rule from other multiethnic states considered more "advanced" or
"developed" than China, one of the few perks of a late-modernizing
state. Hence, Beijing has learned from the United States the utility of
discrediting non-Han dissent by suggesting transnational links to known

terrorist groups, while learning from France how to build upon the precedent of banning Muslim veils. As with Nationalist and Qing officials before them, the Communists have justified such measures by pointing to similar conditions, experiences, and responses within those very multiethnic states that deign to criticize Beijing. Any further adaptations to the foreign model are then conveniently justified through the discourse of special "Chinese characteristics."

Despite Beijing's opportunistic use of such tactics, it is likely that most future challenges to Chinese rule in Xinjiang will be forced to make creative use not of national discourses and structures but rather of those that are transnational in design and scope. The reason is simple. The twenty-first century was the golden age of nationalist discourses. As such, the conservative ethno-elitist empires in existence at the beginning of the century have all been transformed by the use and abuse of the geopolitical tool of the nation-state. Whether they became national empires, disbanded empires, or dismembered empires, each state made its own contribution toward raising the stakes in a global ethnopolitical arms race. There are now few discourses derivative of the ideal of the nation-state for which a rhetorical and institutional antidote has not already been devised. It is thus difficult to imagine any successful challenge to Chinese rule along the non-Han borderlands based upon an ethnopopulist discourse, or indeed any discourse related to national determination. If political dissidents want to challenge Chinese control in Xinjiang, they will need to come up with an ideology for which Han officials do not already have an answer bred from a century of intimate experience on the Chinese borderlands. In practice, this may augur a return to transnational appeals of religion or hereditary descent characteristic of the premodern era, but this time shorn of ethno-elitist pretensions and discourse.

Regardless of what happens in the future, it is clear what happened in the twentieth century. Indeed, had Chinese administrators proven unable to keep pace with the evolution of imperial repertoires after 1911, it is likely that every Han nationalist's worst nightmare would have come true. That Xinjiang did not become "the next Outer Mongolia" testifies to the pragmatic recognition of these administrators that China had not simply evolved—to paraphrase the words of intellectual historian Joseph Levenson—from a universal civilization to a nation in the world. If that had truly been the case, Han officials would not have been overly concerned with any part of the former empire outside of the inner provinces. On the contrary, even though most of them recognized that China was no longer the great "universal civilization" of yesteryear, they were far more bullish about what it had become than they are typically given credit for: an empire among empires, each of which was compelled to learn how to nationalize its empire before rival empires nationalized—and reoriented—it for them.

NOTES

INTRODUCTION

1 Wang Shunan, ed., *Xinjiang tuzhi*, vol. 6, 3952–53. My thanks to David Brophy for bringing this telegram to my attention.

2 Yang Zengxin, *Buguozhai wendu*, vol. 1, 186–90, 194–202.

3 Newby, *The Empire and the Khanate*; Millward, *Beyond the Pass*; and Millward, *Eurasian Crossroads*.

4 Millward, *Eurasian Crossroads*, 136–58; and Rowe, *China's Last Empire*, 209–12.

5 Kim, *Holy War in China*.

6 Zhongyang Yanjiuyuan Jindaishi Yanjiusuo, ed., *Zhong E guanxi shiliao: Xinjiang bianfang*, 14.

7 For an analysis of post-1911 Chinese discourse about the non-Han borderlands, see Leibold, *Reconfiguring Chinese Nationalism*.

8 Yang Zengxin, *Buguozhai wendu sanbian*, vol. 4, 2; Yang Zengxin, *Buguozhai wendu xubian*, vol. 1, 56–57; and Yang Zengxin, *Buguozhai wendu*, vol. 6, 3741.

9 On the "politics of difference," see Burbank and Cooper, *Empires in World History*.

10 Bulag, "Going Imperial," 260–95.

11 This is the Mongolian and Turkic name for the capital, as well as that used by Russian and British consular staff and almost all foreign travelers to the province. In light of the fact that the Chinese Communists also adopted an official Chinese version of this name after 1949 (*Wulumuqi* in pinyin and *Urumqi* in official, pinyin-inflected English), I will stick with the pre-1949 informal version throughout this study. In their communications to one another during the late Qing and Republican eras, Chinese officials usually referred to the city as Dihua ("to direct onto the right path" or "to civilize"). Informally, however, they too had other names for it: Xinjiang Sheng ("the provincial seat"), Hong Miaozi ("the red temple," so named for a prominent temple on a hill), and Shengshang ("at the provincial capital").

12 For previous studies of ethnic conflict in Republican Xinjiang, drawn from British and American archives, Russian archives, and open source Chinese narratives and news reports, see Forbes, *Warlords and Muslims in Chinese Central Asia*; Benson, *The Ili Rebellion*; David D. Wang, *Under the Soviet Shadow*; Barmin, *SSSR i Sin'tszian, 1918–1941*; and Barmin, *Sin'tszian v sovetsko-kitaiskikh otnosheniiakh, 1941–1949 gg*.

13 The term *imperial formation* is taken from Stoler et al., *Imperial Formations*.

14 On the phrase *empire of nations*, see Hirsch, *Empire of Nations*.

15 On *minzu diguo*, see the discussion in the Conclusion.

16 Burbank and Cooper, *Empires in World History*, 8.

17 Martin, *The Affirmative Action Empire*; Hirsch, *Empire of Nations*; and Edgar, *Tribal Nation*.

18 Mullaney, *Coming to Terms with the Nation*.

19 Porter, *The Absent-Minded Imperialists*, 8.

20 Owen Lattimore, *China Memoirs*, 26.

21 This was the fate that befell each of the individual contributors to Starr, *Xinjiang*.

22 For a summary of the affair, see Langfitt, "Why a Chinese Government Think Tank Attacked American Scholars."

1. IMPERIAL REPERTOIRES IN REPUBLICAN XINJIANG

1   Xie, *Xinjiang youji*, 125.

2   Qing Xuebu, ed., *Xuebu guanbao*, 463–64. My thanks to Eric Schluessel for bringing this source to my attention.

3   Liu Qin, *Wang Shunan shixue yanjiu*, 18–28.

4   Pelliot, "Trois ans dans la Haute Asie," 12.

5   Liu, *Wang Shunan shixue yanjiu*, 54, 59–60; and Mannerheim, *Across Asia*, 64.

6   Burbank and Cooper, *Empires in World History*, 3.

7   Mair, "The North(west)ern Peoples," 46–84.

8   Millward, *Beyond the Pass*, 158; Millward, "A Uyghur Muslim in Qianlong's Court," 438; and Wang Hui, *The Politics of Imagining Asia*, 157.

9   Barkey, *Empire of Difference*, 10.

10 Burbank and Cooper, *Empires in World History*, 13–14.

11 Yang Zengxin, *Buguozhai wendu*, vol. 1, 46.

12 Cannadine, *Ornamentalism*, 113.

13 Brophy, "Five Races, One Parliament?" 353–58.

14 Yang Zengxin, *Buguozhai wendu*, vol. 1, 113; and Mirsky, *Sir Aurel Stein*, 287.

15 For primary documents on the 1912 Hami uprising, see Yang Zengxin, *Buguozhai wendu*, vol. 1, 287–346. For an excellent secondary analysis of these and other related documents, see Li Xincheng, *Yang Zengxin zai Xinjiang*, 65–72.

16 Xie, *Xinjiang youji*, 245. Though the *beg* system was abolished on paper after 1884, it continued to function without significant modification on the ground.

17 Xinjiang Weiwuer Zizhiqu Dang'an Guan, ed., *Xinjiang yu E Su shangye maoyi dang'an shiliao*, 112–14.

18 Burbank and Cooper, *Empires in World History*, 14.

19 Eleanor Lattimore, *Turkestan Reunion*, 112.

20 Zhongyang Yanjiuyuan Jindaishi Yanjiusuo, ed., *Zhong E guanxi shiliao: Zhongdong tielu*, 148.

21 Xu, *Xu Xusheng xiyou riji*, 235.

22 Andreas, *Rise of the Red Engineers.*

23 Wakeman, "The Shun Interregnum of 1644," 91.

24 Mair, "The North(west)ern Peoples," 51–53; and Zhao, "Reinventing *China*," 1–28.

25 Mair, "The North(west)ern Peoples," 51–53; Mullaney, "Critical Han Studies: Introduction and Prolegomenon," 1–20; and Elliott, "Hushuo," 173–90.

26 Zhongyang yanjiuyuan jindaishi yanjiusuo, ed., *Zhong E guanxi shiliao: Xinjiang bianfang*, 245.

27 Yang Zengxin, *Buguozhai wendu*, vol. 1, 28.

28 Ibid., 35, 55.

29 Owen Lattimore, *High Tartary*, 85; and Yang Zengxin, *Buguozhai wendu*, vol. 1, 187.

30 Li Xincheng, *Yang Zengxin zai Xinjiang*, 174–75.

31 Yang Zengxin, *Buguozhai wendu*, vol. 1, 56, 122.

32 Yang Zengxin, *Buguozhai wendu sanbian*, vol. 2, 14–15.

33 Yang Zengxin, *Buguozhai wendu*, vol. 1, 74.

34 Li Xincheng, *Yang Zengxin zai Xinjiang*, 21–22.

35 Ibid., 129.

36 Yang Zengxin, *Buguozhai wendu xubian*, vol. 2, 53.

37 Ibid.

38 Dan, "Xinjiang lüxing ji," vol. 5, 2686.

39 Millward, "A Uyghur Muslim in Qianlong's Court," 427–58.

40 Garnaut, "From Yunnan to Xinjiang," 101.

41 Brophy, "Correcting Transgressions in the House of Islam," 276, 291.

42 Huang Wenbi, *Huang Wenbi Meng Xin kaocha riji*, 183.

43 Yang Zengxin, *Buguozhai wendu sanbian*, vol. 1, 6–7.

44 Ibid., vol. 2, 14.

45 Waijiaobu, ed., *Waijiaobu dang'an congshu*, vol. 1, 366.

46 Field diary entry for September 20, 1913. Papers of Sir Marc Aurel Stein, MS 215.

47 Xie, *Xinjiang youji*, 244–245.

2. COLLAPSE OF EMPIRES AND THE NATIONALIST THREAT

1 Esherick, *Ancestral Leaves*, 141.

2 For an exception to this long-standing trend, see Fuller, "North China Famine Revisited," 1–31.

3 Yang Zengxin, *Buguozhai wendu*, vol. 4, 1913.

4 Zhongyang Yanjiuyuan Jindaishi Yanjiusuo, ed., *Zhong E guanxi shiliao: E zhengbian yu yiban jiaoshe (yi)*, 13.

5 Yang Zengxin, *Buguozhai wendu*, vol. 4, 1925, 2040, 2052.

6 Zhongyang Yanjiuyuan Jindaishi Yanjiusuo, ed., *Zhong E guanxi shiliao: E zhengbian yu yiban jiaoshe (yi)*, 13.

7 Yang Zengxin, *Buguozhai wendu*, vol. 4, 1917–18.

8   Zhongyang Yanjiuyuan Jindaishi Yanjiusuo, ed., *Zhong E guanxi shiliao: E zhengbian yu yiban jiaoshe (yi)*, 15.

9   Yang Zengxin, *Buguozhai wendu*, vol. 4, 1981.

10 Zhongyang Yanjiuyuan Jindaishi Yanjiusuo, ed., *Zhong E guanxi shiliao: E zhengbian yu yiban jiaoshe (yi)*, 115, 120.

11 Zhongyang Yanjiuyuan Jindaishi Yanjiusuo, ed., *Zhong E guanxi shiliao: Xinjiang bianfang*, 293–94.

12 When Chinese archaeologist Xu Bingxu visited Urumchi in 1928, he met with Fan Yaonan, the provincial commissioner for foreign affairs, who informed Xu that "Xinjiang only maintains relations with the Ministry of Foreign Affairs and the Ministry of Finance. We have no dealings whatsoever with the Office of the President." Xu, *Xu Xusheng xiyou riji*, 195.

13 Yang Zengxin, *Buguozhai wendu*, vol. 6, 3625.

14 Yang Zengxin, *Buguozhai wendu xubian*, vol. 2, 11.

15 Luo, "Yang Zengxin, Feng Yuxiang zhijian de maodun he Xinjiang 'sanqi' zhengbian," 74.

16 Zhang Dajun, *Xinjiang fengbao qishi nian*, vol. 2, 666.

17 Zhongyang Yanjiuyuan Jindaishi Yanjiusuo, ed., *Zhong E guanxi shiliao: Xinjiang bianfang*, 193, 234.

18 Zhongyang Yanjiuyuan Jindaishi Yanjiusuo, ed., *Zhong E guanxi shiliao: E zhengbian (Zhonghua minguo jiu nian)*, 81.

19 Brophy "Tending to Unite?" 178–87.

20 Yang Zengxin, *Buguozhai wendu xubian*, vol. 9, 5.

21 Yang Zengxin, *Buguozhai wendu*, vol. 6, 3678–79.

22 Burbank and Cooper, *Empires in World History*, 9.

23 Yang Zengxin, *Buguozhai wendu xubian*, vol. 6, 3.

24 Zhongyang Yanjiuyuan Jindaishi Yanjiusuo, ed., *Zhong E guanxi shiliao: Zhongdong tielu, E zhengbian*, 129–30.

25 Yang Zengxin, *Buguozhai wendu xubian*, vol. 8, 24.

26 Yang Zengxin, *Buguozhai wendu sanbian*, vol. 1, 39.

27 Zhongyang Yanjiuyuan Jindaishi Yanjiusuo, ed., *Zhong E guanxi shiliao: E zhengbian (Zhonghua minguo jiu nian)*, 85; Yang Zengxin, *Buguozhai wendu xubian*, vol. 9, 4; Zhongyang Yanjiuyuan Jindaishi Yanjiusuo, ed., *Zhong E guanxi shiliao: Yiban jiaoshe*, 122; and Zhongyang Yanjiuyuan Jindaishi Yanjiusuo, ed., *Zhong E guanxi shiliao: E zhengbian (Zhonghua minguo jiu nian)*, 326. On developments in Soviet Central Asia, see Brophy, "Tending to Unite?"

28 On the death of Ma Fuxing, see Ma Fushou, "Yang Zengxin jianchu Ma Fuxing mudu ji," 72. For the view from the archives of the British consulate in Kashgar, see Forbes, *Warlords and Muslims*, 21–28.

29 Gao Jian and Zhao Jiangming, "Minguo qianqi Xinjiang shengyi hui yanjiu," 44.

30 Yang Zengxin, *Buguozhai wendu sanbian*, vol. 2, 14.

31 Ibid., 15–16.

32 Martin, *The Affirmative Action Empire*, 3. See also Edgar, *Tribal Nation*.

33 Zhongyang Yanjiuyuan Jindaishi Yanjiusuo, ed., *Zhong E guanxi shiliao: E zhengbian (Zhonghua minguo jiu nian)*, 81.

34 Yang Zengxin, *Buguozhai wendu sanbian*, vol. 4, 2; and vol. 2, 15–16.

35 Owen Lattimore, *High Tartary*, 211–12.

36 Yang Zengxin, *Buguozhai wendu sanbian*, vol. 4, 2, 18, 15.

37 Zhongyang Yanjiuyuan Jindaishi Yanjiusuo, ed., *Zhong E guanxi shiliao: E zhengbian (Zhonghua minguo jiu nian)*, 81.

38 Yang Zengxin, *Buguozhai wendu sanbian*, vol. 3, 27, 31–32. See also Xiaoyuan Liu, *Reins of Liberation*, 64.

39 Yang Zengxin, *Buguozhai wendu xubian*, vol. 2, 54.

40 Qutluğ Ḥaji and Yaʿqub Aḫund, "Kašğardan mektub," Terjüman, February 17, 1913, 2. Cited in David Brophy, "New Methods on the New Frontier: Jadidism in Xinjiang," *Journal of the Economic and Social History of the Orient* (forthcoming).

41 Zhongyang Yanjiuyuan Jindaishi Yanjiusuo, ed., *Zhong E guanxi shiliao: Xinjiang bianfang*, 34.

42 Yang Zengxin, *Buguozhai wendu sanbian*, vol. 1, 13.

43 Zhongyang Yanjiuyuan Jindaishi Yanjiusuo, ed., *Zhong E guanxi shiliao: Yiban jiaoshe*, 213.

44 Share, "The Russian Civil War in Chinese Turkestan (Xinjiang), 1918–1921," 414.

45 Brophy, "Tending to Unite," 317–53.

46 Field diary entry for October 18, 1930. Papers of Sir Marc Aurel Stein, MS 224.

47 Brophy, "Tending to Unite," 267–68.

48 Xinjiang Weiwuer Zizhiqu Dang'an Guan, ed., *Xinjiang yu E Su shangye maoyi dang'an shiliao*, 151–52.

49 Cai and Cai, "Qianding 'Yili linshi tongshang xieding,'" 70–78.

50 Brophy, "Tending to Unite," 165–67.

51 Zhongguo Di Er Lishi Dang'an Guan, ed., *Zhonghua minguo shi dang'an ziliao huibian—di san ji: Waijiao*, 725; and Zhongyang Yanjiuyuan Jindaishi Yanjiusuo, ed., *Zhong E guanxi shiliao: Yiban jiaoshe*, 322.

52 Zhongguo Di Er Lishi Dang'an Guan, ed., *Zhonghua minguo shi dang'an ziliao huibian—di san ji: Waijiao*, 725.

53 Zhongyang Yanjiuyuan Jindaishi Yanjiusuo, ed., *Zhong E guanxi shiliao: Yiban jiaoshe*, 267.

54 Xinjiang Weiwuer Zizhiqu Dang'an Guan, ed., *Xinjiang yu E Su shangye maoyi dang'an shiliao*, 231.

55 Huangfu, "Internalizing the West," 229, 262–74; and Larsen, *Tradition, Treaties, and Trade*, 95.

56 Yang Zengxin, *Buguozhai wendu sanbian*, vol. 5, 22.

57 The five Chinese consulates were located in Semipalatinsk, Almaty, Tashkent, Andijan, and Zaysan. From 1925 to 1931, the consul-general was stationed at the Semipalatinsk office. Thereafter the consulate-general was relocated to Tashkent. On paper,

Xinjiang's consulates were formally under the jurisdiction of the Chinese embassy in Moscow. In reality, however, the Chinese staff in the Moscow embassy knew virtually nothing about the personnel and daily affairs of Yang's five consulates. On one occasion, embassy staff in Moscow reported on a "suspicious" person—one of Yang's consulate employees—"masquerading" as a Chinese diplomatic "representative" during a visit to Moscow. See Yang Zengxin, *Buguozhai wendu sanbian*, vol. 1, 26–29.

58 Ibid., vol. 5, 26.

59 Ibid., vol. 1, 33.

60 Ibid., vol. 6, 52–53.

61 Ibid., 71–74.

62 I have drawn the details of Yang's daily routine from Guang, *Guang Lu huiyilu*, 52–53.

63 Xinjiang Weiwuer Zizhiqu Dang'an Guan, ed., *Xinjiang yu E Su shangye maoyi dang'an shiliao*, 236.

64 Chai, "Qi qi zhengbian qinjian pianduan," 76–77.

65 For an in-depth analysis of the July 7 assassination, see Jacobs, "Empire Besieged," 215–35. In Chinese, see Luo, "Yang Zengxin, Feng Yuxiang zhijian"; Fan, *Xinjiang "sanqi" zhengbian xie'an zhenxiang*; Chai, "Qi qi zhengbian qinjian pianduan"; and Luo, "Fan Yaonan zhuanlüe," 156–81.

66 Xu, *Xu Xusheng xiyou riji*, 264.

67 Ibid., 194.

68 Zhang Dajun, *Xinjiang fengbao*, vol. 5, 2614.

69 Xu, *Xu Xusheng xiyou riji*, 209.

70 Huang Wenbi, *Huang Wenbi Meng Xin kaocha riji*, 157.

71 Yang Zengxin, *Buguozhai wendu*, vol. 1, 188.

72 Field diary entry for January 1–2, 1931. Papers of Sir Marc Aurel Stein, MS 224.

73 Li Sheng, *Xinjiang dui Su (E) maoyi shi, 1600–1990*, 345–46.

74 Xinjiang Weiwuer Zizhiqu Dang'an Guan, ed., *Xinjiang yu E Su shangye maoyi dang'an shiliao*, 237.

75 Xinjiang Weiwuer Zizhiqu Dang'an Ju et al., eds., *Jindai Xinjiang menggu lishi dang'an*, 13.

76 Xu, *Xu Xusheng xiyou riji*, 235.

77 Liu Cao, Liu Jie, and Wang Xianhui, "Duo huofo zhi si," 48–54.

78 Chen Chao and Chen Huisheng, *Minguo Xinjiang shi*, 229–30; Fu, "Shilun Yang Zengxin zhuzheng Xinjiang shiqi de 'ruobing zhengce,'" 34; and Xinjiang Weiwuer Zizhiqu Jiaotong Shizhi Bianzuan Weiyuanhui, ed., *Xinjiang gonglu jiaotong shi*, 20–21, 24.

79 Field diary entry for October 3, 1930. Papers of Sir Marc Aurel Stein, MS 224.

80 Xie, *Xinjiang youji*, 87; and Lin Jing, *Xibei congbian*, 230–31.

81 Xinjiang Weiwuer Zizhiqu Dang'an Guan, ed., *Ma Zhongying zai Xinjiang dang'an shiliao xuanbian*, 61.

82 Brophy, "The Qumul Rebels' Appeal to Outer Mongolia."

83 Xinjiang Weiwuer Zizhiqu Dang'an Guan, ed., *Ma Zhongying zai Xinjiang dang'an shiliao xuanbian*, 110.

84 See Millward, *Eurasian Crossroads*, 188–206.

85 Brophy, "The Qumul Rebels' Appeal to Outer Mongolia," 334.

86 Xinjiang Weiwuer Zizhiqu Dang'an Guan, ed., *Ma Zhongying zai Xinjiang dang'an shi-liao xuanbian*, 88; and Zhang Dajun, *Xinjiang fengbao*, vol. 6, 3393–94.

87 Zhongguo Di Er Lishi Dang'an Guan, ed., *Zhonghua minguo shi dang'an ziliao huibian—di wu ji, di yi bian: Zhengzhi (wu)*, 506, 492.

3. RISE OF THE ETHNOPOPULISTS

1   Zhongguo Di Er Lishi Dang'an Guan, ed., *Zhonghua minguo shi dang'an ziliao huibian—di wu ji, di yi bian: Zhengzhi (wu)*, 484–85, 567.

2   Ibid., 522.

3   Ibid., 522, 486, 527, 523.

4   Ibid., 522–24, 544–46.

5   Ibid., 546, 574–77.

6   Cai Jinsong, *Sheng Shicai zai Xinjiang*, 126, 129–30.

7   Xinjiang Weiwuer Zizhiqu Dang'an Guan, 2-3-1156, 9–14.

8   Barmin, *SSSR i Sin'tszian, 1918–1941*, 84–86; and Xue, *Zhong Su guanxi shi (1945–1949)*, 211–13.

9   For a summary of the Soviet archival documents in question, see Xue, *Zhong Su guanxi shi*, 215. For a complete translation of the same documents into Chinese, see Shen, ed., *Eguo jiemi dang'an: Xinjiang wenti*, 2–3, 8.

10 Barmin, *SSSR i Sin'tszian, 1918–1941*, 116, 124–25.

11 Brophy, "Tending to Unite?" 6.

12 Xinjiang Weiwuer Zizhiqu Dang'an Guan, 2-2-105, 89–90.

13 RGASPI, f. 558 op. 11 d. 323, l. 1–28; and RGASPI, f. 558, op. 11, d. 323, l. 54–58.

14 Zhongguo Di Er Lishi Dang'an Guan, ed., *Zhonghua minguo shi dang'an ziliao huibian—di wu ji, di yi bian: Zhengzhi (wu)*, 559.

15 Zhang Dajun, *Xinjiang fengbao*, vol. 6, 3071; and Huang Jianhua, "Jin Shuren an tanxi," 47.

16 For a collection of facsimile reprints from *Frontier Bell* (*Bianduo*), one of the more prominent of these journals, see Jiang et al., eds., *Minguo bianshi yanjiu wenxian huibian*, vol. 2, 31–76.

17 Zhongguo Di Er Lishi Dang'an Guan, ed., *Zhonghua minguo shi dang'an ziliao huibian—di wu ji, di yi bian: Zhengzhi (wu)*, 527; and Luo, "Ai-sha xiaozhuan," 61–64.

18 Mao, "A Muslim Vision for the Chinese Nation," 373–95.

19 For a biased yet informative biography of Masud Sabri, see chapter 6 of Liu Xiang-hui and Chen Wuguo, *Yinmo Gebi de lishi suipian*, 176–219; and Luo, "Zhongsheng wuguo—minguo shiqi Xinjiang sheng di ba ren zhuxi Maisiwude de yi sheng," 60–64.

20 Zhang Dajun, *Xinjiang fengbao*, vol. 6, 3128; and Zhongguo Di Er Lishi Dang'an Guan, ed., *Zhonghua minguo shi dang'an ziliao huibian—di wu ji, di yi bian: Zhengzhi (wu)*, 561–65.

21 Zhongguo Di Er Lishi Dang'an Guan, ed., *Zhonghua minguo shi dang'an ziliao huibian—di wu ji, di yi bian: Zhengzhi (wu)*, 558.

22 Ibid., 559–60.

23 Zhongguo Di Er Lishi Dang'an Guan, ed., *Zhonghua minguo shi dang'an ziliao huibian—di wu ji, di er bian: Zhengzhi (si)*, 789.

24 Xinjiang Weiwuer Zizhiqu Jiaotong Shizhi Bianzuan Weiyuanhui, ed., *Xinjiang gonglu jiaotong shi*, 28–29; Cai, *Sheng Shicai zai Xinjiang*, 196–98, 207; and Zhu, *Xinjiang geming shi*, 25–29.

25 Forbes, *Warlords and Muslims in Chinese Central Asia*, 125–26; RGASPI f. 17 op. 162 d. 18, l. 170–72; RGASPI f. 17, op. 162, d. 19, l. 44; RGASPI f. 17, op. 162, d. 20, l. 26, 43, 51, 62–63; RGASPI f. 17, op. 162, d. 20, l. 115, 8, 18, 11–12, 181; and Zhongyang Yanjiuyuan Jindaishi Yanjiusuo Dang'an Guan, 110.19/0002, "Zhu Xin bian wu guan shiwu" [Affairs of the five consulates stationed along Xinjiang's borders], 40.

26 Brophy, "Tending to Unite."

27 Gongqingtuan Xinjiang Weiwuer Zizhiqu Weiyuanhui and Balujun Zhu Xinjiang Banshichu Jinian Guan, eds., *Xinjiang minzhong fandi lianhe hui ziliao huibian*, 9; and Brophy, "Tending to Unite," 371–85.

28 Gongqingtuan Xinjiang Weiwuer Zizhiqu Weiyuanhui and Balujun Zhu Xinjiang Banshichu Jinian Guan, eds., *Xinjiang minzhong fandi lianhe hui ziliao huibian*, 20, 183.

29 Xinjiang Weiwuer Zizhiqu Dang'an Ju et al., eds., *Jindai Xinjiang menggu lishi dang'an*, 50.

30 Gongqingtuan Xinjiang Weiwuer Zizhiqu Weiyuanhui and Balujun Zhu Xinjiang Banshichu Jinian Guan, eds., *Xinjiang minzhong fandi lianhe hui ziliao huibian*, 102.

31 Ibid., 100, 104, 107.

32 Xinjiang Weiwuer Zizhiqu Dang'an Ju et al., eds., *Jindai Xinjiang menggu lishi dang'an*, 146, 423.

33 Ibid., 151.

34 Ibid., 49–50.

35 Xinjiang Weiwuer Zizhiqu Dang'an Guan, 2–6–962, 13–14.

36 Xinjiang Weiwuer Zizhiqu Dang'an Ju et al., eds., *Jindai Xinjiang menggu lishi dang'an*, 80.

37 Martin, *The Affirmative Action Empire*, 21–22.

38 Xinjiang Weiwuer Zizhiqu Dang'an Guan, 2–6–962, 36, 100.

39 Xinjiang Weiwuer Zizhiqu Dang'an Ju et al., eds., *Jindai Xinjiang menggu lishi dang'an*, 264.

40 Ibid., 73.

41 Xinjiang Weiwuer Zizhiqu Caizheng Ting et al., eds., *Geming licaijia Mao Zemin*, 133.

42 Ibid.

43 Gansu Sheng Guji Wenxian Zhengli Bianyi Zhongxin, ed., *Zhongguo xibei wenxian congshu, er bian*, vol. 13, 183.

44 Ibid., vol. 11, 508; and vol. 10, 678.

45 Ibid., vol. 13, 131; vol. 10, 184; vol. 10, 95; and vol. 11, 134.

46 Zhonggong Hetian Diwei Dangshi Bangongshi, ed., *Kang Ri zhanzheng shiqi Zhonggong dangren zai Hetian*, 66, 63.

47 Hami Diqu Difangzhi Bangongshi and Hami Diqu Caizheng Chu, eds., *Mao Zemin yu Hami caizheng*, 189, 170.

48 Xinjiang Weiwuer Zizhiqu Dang'an Guan, 2–5–628, 51–52.

49 Ibid., 3–1–53, 67; and 2–6–933, 2–14.

50 Gongqingtuan Xinjiang Weiwuer Zizhiqu Weiyuanhui and Balujun Zhu Xinjiang Banshichu Jinian Guan, eds., *Xinjiang minzhong fandi lianhe hui ziliao huibian*, 129; and Xinjiang Weiwuer Zizhiqu Dang'an Guan, 3–1–53, 66.

51 Xinjiang Weiwuer Zizhiqu Dang'an Ju et al., eds., *Kang Ri zhanzheng shiqi Xinjiang ge minzu minzhong kang Ri mujuan dang'an shiliao*, 19.

52 Xinjiang Weiwuer Zizhiqu Dang'an Ju et al., eds., *Jindai Xinjiang menggu lishi dang'an*, 175, 192.

53 Hami Diqu Difangzhi Bangongshi and Hami Diqu Caizheng Chu, eds., *Mao Zemin yu Hami caizheng*, 329.

54 Xinjiang Weiwuer Zizhiqu Dang'an Ju et al., eds., *Kang Ri zhanzheng shiqi Xinjiang ge minzu minzhong kang Ri mujuan dang'an shiliao*, 204–5; and Xinjiang Weiwuer Zizhiqu Dang'an Guan, 2–6–933, 87.

55 Xinjiang Weiwuer Zizhiqu Dang'an Ju et al., eds., *Jindai Xinjiang menggu lishi dang'an*, 68.

56 Ibid., 66–67.

57 Ibid., 85.

58 Zhonggong Hetian Diwei Dangshi Bangongshi, ed., *Kang Ri zhanzheng shiqi Zhonggong dangren zai Hetian*, 22, 41–42, 55–56; and "Politburo decisions between 11 December 1937 and 21 January 1938," RGASPI F.17 op. 162, d. 22, l. 101–2.

59 Xinjiang Weiwuer Zizhiqu Dang'an Ju et al., eds., *Jindai Xinjiang menggu lishi dang'an*, 259–60.

60 Zhonggong Xinjiang Weiwuer Zizhiqu Weiyuanhui et al., eds., *Balujun zhu Xinjiang banshichu*, 38–40; and Zhongguo Di Er Lishi Dang'an Guan, ed., *Zhonghua minguo shi dang'an ziliao huibian—di wu ji, di er bian: Zhengzhi (si)*, 787.

61 Xinjiang Weiwuer Zizhiqu Dang'an Ju et al., eds., *Jindai Xinjiang menggu lishi dang'an*, 176.

62 Zhang Dajun, *Xinjiang fengbao*, vol. 8, 4330–31.

63 Zhonggong Xinjiang Weiwuer Zizhiqu Weiyuanhui et al., eds., *Balujun zhu Xinjiang banshichu*, 28; Kinzley, "Staking Claims to China's Borderland," 190–91.

64 Zhongguo Di Er Lishi Dang'an Guan, ed., *Zhonghua minguo shi dang'an ziliao huibian—di wu ji, di san bian: Zhengzhi (wu)*, 305.

65 Xinjiang Weiwuer Zizhiqu Dang'an Guan, 2–6–961, 52–53.

66 Zhang Dajun, *Xinjiang fengbao*, vol. 8, 4342–46.

67 Xinjiang Weiwuer Zizhiqu Dang'an Guan, ed., *Xinjiang yu E Su shangye maoyi dang'an shiliao*, 496–98, 502–6; and Kinzley, "Staking Claims to China's Borderland," 293–95.

68 Gongqingtuan Xinjiang Weiwuer Zizhiqu Weiyuanhui and Balujun Zhu Xinjiang Ban-

shichu Jinian Guan, eds., *Xinjiang minzhong fandi lianhe hui ziliao huibian*, 247, 337.

69 Gansu Sheng Guji Wenxian Zhengli Bianyi Zhongxin, ed., *Zhongguo xibei wenxian congshu, er bian*, vol. 11, 116.

70 Zhang Dajun, *Xinjiang fengbao*, vol. 9, 5193–95.

71 Cai, *Sheng Shicai zai Xinjiang*, 344; and Gao Sulan, "Zhanshi guomin zhengfu shili jinru Xinjiang shimo," 160.

4. RAISING THE STAKES IN NATIONALIST XINJIANG

1 Zhongyang Yanjiuyuan Jindaishi Yanjiusuo Dang'an Guan, 607.6/0005, "Xinjiang diaocha baogao."

2 Gansu Sheng Guji Wenxian Zhengli Bianyi Zhongxin, ed., *Zhongguo xibei wenxian congshu, er bian*, vol. 13, 64–65.

3 Ibid., vol. 10, 158–59, 302; and vol. 11, 261.

4 The standard accounts in English are Forbes, *Warlords and Muslims in Chinese Central Asia*, 163–228; Benson, *The Ili Rebellion*; and David D. Wang, *Under the Soviet Shadow*.

5 RGASPI F. 17, Op. 162, D. 37, ll. 76–78; and Barmin, *Sin'tszian v sovetsko-kitaiskikh otnosheniiakh, 1941–1949 gg.*, 75, 84, 71–72.

6 National Archives of the United States, Foreign Service Inspection Reports, Record Group 59, 2–3. I am indebted to Charles Kraus, who has allowed me to reproduce this quote from among his research materials.

7 Barmin, *Sin'tszian v sovetsko-kitaisikh otnosheniiakh, 1941–1949*, 75–78.

8 Waijiaobu, ed., *Waijiaobu dang'an congshu*, vol. 1, 196.

9 Ibid., 197.

10 Ibid., 195–96, 200–202.

11 Ibid., 202, 199, 204.

12 Barmin, *Sin'tszian v sovetsko-kitaiskikh otnosheniiakh, 1941–1949*, 76–77; and Xue, *Zhong Su guanxi shi*, 195–97.

13 Barmin, *Sin'tszian v sovetsko-kitaiskikh otnosheniiakh, 1941–1949*, 78, 84; and GARF, Fond R-9401ss, Opis' 2, Delo 95, ll. 334–38.

14 Zhongyang Yanjiuyuan Jindaishi Yanjiusuo Dang'an Guan, 110.19/0002, "Zhu Xin bian wuling shiwu," 36, 42; Waijiaobu, ed., *Waijiaobu dang'an congshu*, vol. 1, 238–40.

15 Waijiaobu, *Waijiaobu dang'an congshu—jiewu lei: Xinjiang juan*, vol. 1, 208–11, 224, 225, 228.

16 Ibid., 228.

17 Zhongyang Yanjiuyuan Jindaishi Yanjiusuo Dang'an Guan, 110.19/0004, "Su difang dangju dui wo Xin bian ge guan daiyu," 8, 17–18.

18 Ibid., 55, 78.

19 Zhongyang Yanjiuyuan Jindaishi Yanjiusuo Dang'an Guan, 110.19/0002, 122; and 110.19/0004, 32, 19.

20 Kinzley, "Staking Claims to China's Borderland," 246n132.

21 Barmin, *Sin'tszian v sovetsko-kitaiskikh otnosheniiakh, 1941–1949*, 76–77; Zhang Dajun, *Xinjiang fengbao*, vol. 9, 5198–5103; and Waijiaobu, ed., *Waijiaobu dang'an congshu*, vol. 1, 232.

22 Waijiaobu, ed., *Waijiaobu dang'an congshu*, vol. 1, 236, 247, 249.

23 Cai, *Sheng Shicai zai Xinjiang*, 394–96.

24 Ibid., 397.

25 Waijiaobu, ed., *Waijiaobu dang'an congshu*, vol. 1, 430.

26 Gansu Sheng Guji Wenxian Zhengli Bianyi Zhongxin, ed., *Zhongguo xibei wenxian congshu, er bian*, vol. 10, 146–47, 592–96.

27 Ibid., 254–58, 358–68; and vol. 11, 422–24.

28 Ibid., vol. 11, 373; vol. 10, 286, 702; vol. 12, 119; vol. 11, 425; vol. 10, 303; and vol. 12, 55–56.

29 Ibid., vol. 11, 72–74, 190–91, 431; and vol. 12, 57–62.

30 Ibid., vol. 11, 352.

31 Waijiaobu, ed., *Waijiaobu dang'an congshu*, vol. 1, 289.

32 GARF, Fond R-9401ss, Opis' 2, Delo 100, 270–72; and Xinjiang Shaoshu Minzu Shehui Lishi Diaocha Zu, ed., *Sanqu geming ziliao huibian*, vol. 5, 4–6.

33 Barmin, *Sin'tszian v sovetsko-kitaiskikh otnosheniiakh, 1941–1949*, 80–81.

34 GARF, Fond R-9401ss, Opis' 2, Delo 95, ll. 334–38; GARF, Fond R-9401ss, Opis' 2, Delo 95, ll. 352–59; and GARF, Fond 9401ss, Opis' 2, Delo 100, ll. 354–57;

35 Gansu Sheng Guji Wenxian Zhengli Bianyi Zhongxin, ed., *Zhongguo xibei wenxian congshu, er bian*, vol. 12, 332.

36 Ibid., vol. 10, 101, 116, 457; and Zhongguo Di Er Lishi Dang'an Guan, ed., *Zhonghua minguo shi dang'an ziliao huibian—di wu ji, di san bian: Zhengzhi (wu)*, 241.

37 Gansu Sheng Guji Wenxian Zhengli Bianyi Zhongxin, ed., *Zhongguo xibei wenxian congshu, er bian*, vol. 10, 354, 373, 424; and vol. 11, 629.

38 Ibid., vol. 10, 242; and vol. 11, 505.

39 Ibid., vol. 13, 146–47; vol. 11, 473; and vol. 10, 737.

40 Gonganbu Dang'an Guan, ed., *Zai Jiang Jieshi shenbian ba nian*, 306–7, 312.

41 Waijiaobu, ed., *Waijiaobu dang'an congshu*, vol. 1, 238, 254; and Gansu Sheng Guji Wenxian Zhengli Bianyi Zhongxin, ed., *Zhongguo xibei wenxian congshu, er bian*, vol. 10, 736.

42 Gansu Sheng Guji Wenxian Zhengli Bianyi Zhongxin, ed., *Zhongguo xibei wenxian congshu, er bian*, vol. 13, 95–96, 146.

43 Ibid., vol. 12, 199–200.

44 Zhongguo Di Er Lishi Dang'an Guan, ed., *Zhonghua minguo shi dang'an ziliao huibian—di wu ji, di san bian: Zhengzhi (wu)*, 449.

45 Gansu Sheng Guji Wenxian Zhengli Bianyi Zhongxin, ed., *Zhongguo xibei wenxian congshu, er bian*, vol. 13, 218, 378.

46 Ibid., 240–44, 516–18; and Xue, *Zhong Su guanxi shi*, 203–4.

47 Zhongguo Di Er Lishi Dang'an Guan, ed., *Zhonghua minguo shi dang'an ziliao huibian—di wu ji, di san bian: Zhengzhi (wu)*, 251, 262–63, 271, 278, 333, 337.

48 Gansu Sheng Guji Wenxian Zhengli Bianyi Zhongxin, ed., *Zhongguo xibei wenxian congshu, er bian*, vol. 13, 477.

49 Once it became apparent that the Soviets did not intend to uphold their end of the bargain—i.e., that Moscow not intervene in Chinese borderland politics—the Nationalists quickly retracted their recognition of an independent Mongol state. To this day, official government maps produced by the Republic of China on Taiwan still claim Outer Mongolia as part of Chinese territory. After 1949, the Chinese Communists continued to expect that the Soviets would return Mongolia to the Chinese fold. Mao was privately livid when they did not. He did, however, consent to formal recognition of the Mongol state during the 1950s, something the Communists would regret after the Sino-Soviet split. See Radchenko, "The Soviets' Best Friend in Asia"; and Luthi, *The Sino-Soviet Split*, 37, 41.

50 Zhongguo Di Er Lishi Dang'an Guan, ed., *Zhonghua minguo shi dang'an ziliao huibian—di wu ji, di san bian: Zhengzhi (wu)*, 265.

51 Ibid., 272, 281, 279.

52 Ibid., 277, 290.

53 Waijiaobu, ed., *Waijiaobu dang'an congshu*, vol. 1, 309.

54 Xue, *Zhong Su guanxi shi*, 227–29. The text of the request also appears in Soviet archives, dated September 15, 1945. See RGASPI F. 17. Op. 162, D. 37, ll. 150–51.

55 Zhongguo Di Er Lishi Dang'an Guan, ed., *Zhonghua minguo shi dang'an ziliao huibian—di wu ji, di san bian: Zhengzhi (wu)*, 325, 356.

56 Xue, *Zhong Su guanxi shi*, 231–32.

57 GARF, Fond 9401ss, Opis' 2, Delo 100; and GARF, Fond 9401ss, Opis' 2, Delo 100, ll. 354–57.

58 Ibid., 236; Barmin, *Sin'tszian v sovetsko-kitaiskikh otnosheniiakh, 1941–1949*, 58; and Xinjiang Sanqu Geming Shi Bianzuan Weiyuanhui, ed., *Xinjiang sanqu geming dashiji*, 6.

59 Zhongguo Di Er Lishi Dang'an Guan, ed., *Zhonghua minguo shi dang'an ziliao huibian—di wu ji, di san bian: Zhengzhi (wu)*, 291, 288, 269.

60 Ibid., 327.

61 Xinjiang Shaoshu Minzu Shehui Lishi Diaocha Zu, ed., *Sanqu geming ziliao huibian*, vol. 1, 7.

62 "Charges by Secretary General Aisabek of Chinese Oppression of the Natives of Sinkiang" November 20, 1947, National Archives of the United States, Department of State, Division of Chinese Affairs, 893.00 Sinkiang/11-2047.

63 Zhongguo Di Er Lishi Dang'an Guan, ed., *Zhonghua minguo shi dang'an ziliao huibian—di wu ji, di san bian: Zhengzhi (wu)*, 365; and Waijiaobu, ed., *Waijiaobu dang'an congshu*, vol. 1, 376.

64 Zhongguo Di Er Lishi Dang'an Guan, ed., *Zhonghua minguo shi dang'an ziliao huibian—di wu ji, di san bian: Zhengzhi (wu)*, 441, 443.

65 Ibid., 464–65.

66 Xinjiang Shaoshu Minzu Shehui Lishi Diaocha Zu, ed., *Sanqu geming ziliao huibian*,

vol. 1, 14; and Freeman, "Whose Martyr?" Some of these quotations are taken from draft translations of *Khan Tengri* articles provided to me by Ulug Kuzuoglu. The *Khan Tengri* journals are held at the Hoover Institution at Stanford.

67 Zhongguo Di Er Lishi Dang'an Guan, ed., *Zhonghua minguo shi dang'an ziliao huibian— di wu ji, di san bian: Zhengzhi (wu)*, 408.

68 Gansu Sheng Guji Wenxian Zhengli Bianyi Zhongxin, ed., *Zhongguo xibei wenxian congshu, er bian*, vol. 10, 196–97.

69 Ibid., 196.

70 Ibid., vol. 13, 482–85; and vol. 12, 82–83. For a short biography of Delilhan, see Xinjiang Sanqu Geming Shi Bianzuan Weiyuanhui, ed., *Xinjiang sanqu geming dashiji*, 11.

71 Gansu Sheng Guji Wenxian Zhengli Bianyi Zhongxin, ed., *Zhongguo xibei wenxian congshu, er bian*, vol. 11, 577–78; and vol. 12, 83, 152, 268–69.

72 Ibid., vol. 13, 389, 479.

73 Zhongguo Di Er Lishi Dang'an Guan, ed., *Zhonghua minguo shi dang'an ziliao huibian— di wu ji, di san bian: Zhengzhi (wu)*, 246, 424, 269.

74 Barmin, *Sin'tszian v sovetsko-kitaiskikh otnosheniiakh, 1941–1949*, 106; Zhongguo Di Er Lishi Dang'an Guan, ed., *Zhonghua minguo shi dang'an ziliao huibian—di wu ji, di san bian: Zhengzhi (wu)*, 360, 389; and Zhongyang Yanjiuyuan Jindaishi Yanjiusuo Dang'an Guan, 604.1/0001, "Xinjiang Zhong Su jingji hezuo fang'an," 2.

75 Masud's pending appointment and the Generalissimo's hand in the arrangement were leaked to the Western media about a month before he assumed his post. See Drake, "Chiang Backing of Turks Likely to Prove Costly," *Los Angeles Times*, May 1, 1947.

76 Drake, "Russ India Push Seen in Sinkiang," *Los Angeles Times*, June 15, 1947; and "Wei Maisiwude jiuren bensheng zhuxi Zhang zhuren yu sheng canyiyuan laihui hanjian," 24.

77 Quoted in Ondřej Klimeš, *Struggle by the Pen: The Uyghur Discourse of Nation and National Interest, c. 1900–1949* (Leiden: Brill, 2015), 201–2.

78 "Cong Maisiwude dao Baoerhan," 8.

79 My thanks to Hamit Zakir, David Brophy, and Eric Schluessel for their help in deciphering the Uighur calligraphy and its translation into English. On the ethnic initiatives of Zhang Zhizhong during the second half of 1947, see Jacobs, "How Chinese Turkestan Became Chinese," 545–91. I have revised some of my assertions from the original article, which mistakenly portrayed Uighur "resistance" as both undetected and disapproved by Nationalist authorities.

80 Xinjiang Shaoshu Minzu Shehui Lishi Diaocha Zu, ed., *Sanqu geming ziliao huibian*, vol. 6, 104; and vol. 1, 68–69, 75, 93–107.

81 Zhongyang Yanjiuyuan Jindaishi Yanjiusuo Dang'an Guan, 112.93/0001, "Mengjun qin Xin," 25; and Waijiaobu, ed., *Waijiaobu dang'an congshu*, vol. 1, 355.

82 Zhou Dongjiao, *Xinjiang shinian*, 301.

83 For the complex course of events leading up to and succeeding the Baytik incident, see Waijiaobu, ed., *Waijiaobu dang'an congshu*, vol. 2, 182–234.

84 Ibid., vol. 1, 343–44.

85 Xinjiang Shaoshu Minzu Shehui Lishi Diaocha Zu, ed., *Sanqu geming ziliao huibian*, vol. 1, 58–61, 101.

86 Waijiaobu, ed., *Waijiaobu dang'an congshu*, vol. 1, 361.

5. THE BIRTH PANGS OF CHINESE AFFIRMATIVE ACTION

1   Zhonggong Xinjiang Weiwuer Zizhiqu Weiyuanhui et al., eds., *Xinjiang heping jiefang*, 306.

2   For a summary of political events in Xinjiang during the 1949 takeover, including the fate of the ETR, see Jacobs, "Empire Besieged," 455–78.

3   Taylor, *The Generalissimo*, 141–335.

4   Zhonggong Xinjiang Weiwuer Zizhiqu Weiyuanhui Dangshi Yanjiushi, ed., *Zhongguo gongchandang yu minzu quyu zizhi zhidu de jianli he fazhan*, vol. 1, 68, 305.

5   Chiang, *China's Destiny and Chinese Economic Theory*, 39–40; and Zhongguo Di Er Lishi Dang'an Guan, ed., *Zhonghua minguo shi dang'an ziliao huibian—di wu ji, di san bian: Zhengzhi (wu)*, 398–99.

6   Xinjiang Sheng Di Yi Jie Renmin Daibiao Dahui Di Er Ci Huiyi Mishuchu, ed., *Xinjiang Weiwuer zizhiqu chengli tekan*, 177–390.

7   For an extended study of Nationalist geopolitical pragmatism amid uncompromising public discourse, see Hsiao-ting Lin, *Tibet and Nationalist China's Frontier*.

8   Bachman, "Making Xinjiang Safe for the Han?" 156, 176.

9   Waijiaobu, ed., *Waijiaobu dang'an congshu*, vol. 1, 365–66.

10 Hirsch, *Empire of Nations*.

11 Mullaney, *Coming to Terms with the Nation*.

12 Zhonggong Zhongyang Wenxian Yanjiushi and Zhonggong Xinjiang Weiwuer Zizhiqu Weiyuanhui, eds., *Xinjiang gongzuo wenxian*, 187–93.

13 Ibid.

14 Ibid., 94, 97–101; and Wang Enmao, *Wang Enmao wenji*, vol. 1, 226.

15 Brubaker et al., *Nationalist Politics and Everyday Ethnicity*.

16 Zhang Dajun, *Hengdu Kunlun san wan li*, 43.

17 An example of the former is Cluj-Napoca, home to an 80:20 ratio between Romanians and Hungarians, while the latter phenomenon was evident in Târgu Mureș, much closer to a 50:50 split. See Brubaker et al., *Nationalist Politics and Everyday Ethnicity*.

18 For Maoist discourse criticizing "discrimination" against the minorities in matters of socialist and economic development, see Zhonggong Zhongyang Wenxian Yanjiushi and Zhonggong Xinjiang Weiwuer Zizhiqu Weiyuanhui, eds., *Xinjiang gongzuo wenxian*, 141, 196–97.

19 Zhonggong Wulumuqi Shi Weiyuanhui Dangshi Gongzuo Weiyuanhui and Wulumuqi Shi Dang'an Ju, eds., *Zhongguo gongchandang Wulumuqi shi weiyuanhui wenjian xuanbian*, 354, 639.

20 Dave, *Kazakhstan*.

21 Chu Anping, *Xinjiang xin mianmao*, 227–34.

22 Wang Enmao, *Wang Enmao wenji*, vol. 1, 305.

23 Zhonggong Wulumuqi Shi Weiyuanhui Dangshi Gongzuo Weiyuanhui and Wulumuqi Shi Dang'an Ju, eds., *Zhongguo gongchandang Wulumuqi shi weiyuanhui wenjian xuanbian*, 75, 298, 353–54, 392, 464, 536.

24 Ibid., 574–78, 625, 637, 671.

25 Ibid., 670.

26 Ibid., 334, 354–55; and Quanguo Renmin Daibiao Dahui Minzu Weiyuanhui Bangongshi, ed., *Xinjiang Weiwuer zizhiqu ruogan diaocha cailiao huibian*, 95.

27 Zhonggong Wulumuqi Shi Weiyuanhui Dangshi Gongzuo Weiyuanhui and Wulumuqi Shi Dang'an Ju, eds., *Zhongguo gongchandang Wulumuqi shi weiyuanhui wenjian xuanbian*, 334, 354–55, 392, 536, 671.

28 Ibid., 671–72.

29 Ibid., 488–92.

30 On plans developed in 1958 for the resettlement of an additional two million Han migrants to Xinjiang, see Zhonggong Zhongyang Wenxian Yanjiushi and Zhonggong Xinjiang Weiwuer Zizhiqu Weiyuanhui, eds., *Xinjiang gongzuo wenxian*, 202–3, 206, 210.

31 Zhonggong Wulumuqi Shi Weiyuanhui Dangshi Gongzuo Weiyuanhui and Wulumuqi Shi Dang'an Ju, eds., *Zhongguo gongchandang Wulumuqi shi weiyuanhui wenjian xuanbian*, 670–71.

32 Zhonggong Yili Hasake Zizhizhou Weiyuanhui Dangshi Yanjiushi and Yili Hasake Zizhizhou Dang'an Ju (Guan), eds., *Zhongguo gongchandang Yili Hasake zizhizhou weiyuanhui zhongyao wenjian xuanbian*, 435–36.

33 Saifuding [Saypiddin Azizi], *Jianjue fandui difang minzu zhuyi, wei shehuizhuyi de weida shengli er fendou!*, 12, 26–28, 36, 38, 41.

6. THE XINJIANG GOVERNMENT IN EXILE

1 Waijiaobu, ed., *Waijiaobu dang'an congshu*, vol. 2, 25, 51, 27.

2 Ibid., 21–22, 24–25.

3 Ibid., 24, 28.

4 Ibid., 62–63, 76, 84, 90, 117–24.

5 Zhongyang Yanjiuyuan Jindaishi Yanjiusuo Dang'an Guan, 110.11/0001, "Zhu Xie-mi lingguan chexiao," 45.

6 Laird, *Into Tibet*, 81–90.

7 Zhang Dajun, *Hengdu Kunlun san wan li*, 44–45, 74–76, 86–87, 124.

8 "A Report on Conditions in Sinkiang Prepared by Mr. O.C. Ellis," November 15, 1950, British National Archives, Far Eastern Department, FO 171/92207, Enclosure 2, 2.

9 Jacobs, "The Many Deaths of a Kazak Unaligned," 1291–1314.

10 "Record of Interviews with General Yolbas Beg, former Governor of Hami in Sinkiang, at New Delhi," April 3, 1951, British National Archives, Far Eastern Department, FO 171/92207.

11 "Letter from Husayin Tayji to Mr. J. Hall Paxton," January 23, 1952, National Archives of the United States, Department of State, Office of Chinese Affairs, 350.4.

12 "Notes on the Kazak refugees in Kashmir" and "Letter from General Dalil Khan Haji to J. Hall Paxton, February 2, 1952," National Archives of the United States, Department of State, Office of Chinese Affairs, 350.4.

13 "Record of Interviews with General Yolbas Beg," FO 171/92207.

14 Ibid.

15 Zhongguo Di Er Lishi Dang'an Guan, ed., *Zhonghua minguo shi dang'an ziliao huibian—di wu ji, di san bian: Zhengzhi (wu)*, 466.

16 K. L. Rankin to Walter P. McConaughy, November 5, 1953, National Archives of the United States, Department of State, Office of Chinese Affairs, 350.4.

17 Chu Chia-hua, *Taiwan and Sinkiang (Formosa and Chinese Turkistan)*.

18 "Travels in Southern and Eastern Sinkiang," September 20, 1948, National Archives of the United States, Department of State, Office of Chinese Affairs, Sinkiang file 893.00.

19 Ma Zhiyong, "Xinjiang junfa Sheng Shicai yuefu yijia bei sha zhi mi."

20 Zhang Murong, "Li jiang hou de 'Xinjiang wang' Sheng Shicai."

21 For a complete account of the afterlife of Sheng Shicai, see Jacobs, "Empire Besieged," 380–84.

22 In the case of Fujian, this meant only a handful of offshore islands, while in the case of Yunnan, it was limited to jurisdiction claimed by defeated Nationalist general Li Mi in Burma.

23 Clark, "How the Kazakhs Fled to Freedom," 621–44; Lias, "Kazakh Nomads' Struggle against Communists"; and Lias, *Kazakh Exodus*.

24 Zhongyang Yanjiuyuan Jindaishi Yanjiusuo Dang'an Guan, 109/0005, "Xinjiang nanmin yiju Tuerqi," 108.

25 "Governor of Turkestan Has Escaped from Russia and arrived in Cairo," November 4, 1953, British National Archives, Far Eastern Department, FO 371/106523.

26 Zhongyang Yanjiuyuan Jindaishi Yanjiusuo Dang'an Guan, 109/0005, 113–18, 239–42.

27 Ibid., 227–35.

28 "Kazakh Refugees," October 12, 1951, British National Archives, Far Eastern Department, FO 371/92897; and Letter from Orville L. Bennett to Dr. George A. Fitch, March 24, 1955, National Archives of the United States, Department of State, Office for Refugees, Migration, and Voluntary Assistance.

29 Zhongyang Yanjiuyuan Jindaishi Yanjiusuo Dang'an Guan, 109/0005, 129–30.

30 Godfrey Lias conveyed their overtures to Winston Churchill in *Kazak Exodus*, 229.

31 Letter from Kali Beg and Hamza to J. Hall Paxton, March 13, 1952, National Archives of the United States, Department of State, Office of Chinese Affairs, #6p Sinkiang. I am indebted to Charles Kraus, whose prior research in these archives first alerted me to the existence of these documents.

32 Zhongyang Yanjiuyuan Jindaishi Yanjiusuo Dang'an Guan, 109/0005, 175–80, 171, 110.

33 Ibid., 152.11/0048, "Xinjiang sheng zhengfu ji Zhongguo huijiao xiehui zhi guomin waijiao huodong," 30; and 109/0005, 216–19, 229, 246–47, 256.

34 Ibid., 109/0005, 109, 120–121.

35 Ibid., 152.11/0048, 21–22; 109/0005, 226, 239–42; and Letter from Yolbars Khan to Mr. George Fitch, Far East Director of the Committee to Aid Refugee Chinese Intellectuals, July 1955, National Archives of the United States, Department of State, Office of Chinese Affairs, #6p Sinkiang.

36 Zhongyang Yanjiuyuan Jindaishi Yanjiusuo Dang'an Guan, 105.22/0005, "Juyu feibang chaosheng tuanti qianzheng; zhu Sha dashiguan zhoubao," 89–90, 95–96, 110, 119.

37 Ibid., 157–58.

38 Ibid., 158–59.

39 Ibid., 159–60.

40 Zhongyang Yanjiuyuan Jindaishi Yanjiusuo Dang'an Guan, 109/005, 246–47, 251–53; 112.22/0003, "Tuerqi jizhe fang Tai; lü Tuerqi huaqiao fang Tai; lü Bajisitan huaqiao Shabulei; Aisha zhangzi Mulade fang Hua; Zhong Tu youhao xiehui," 28–31; and 152.11/0048, 111–14.

41 Ibid., 152.11/0048, 186–93; and 119.5/0001, 228.

42 Taylor, *The Generalissimo*, 505–6.

43 Zhongyang Yanjiuyuan Jindaishi Yanjiusuo Dang'an Guan, 152.11/0048, 124.

44 Ibid., 107/0001, "Tuerqi renwu zhi; Xinjiang ji Wahede shenqing zhengjian; Xinjiang ji Sudan shenqing zhengjian; Xinjiang ji Palati xueli shengqing zhengjian," 61, 107–9.

45 *Lianhe bao*, March 9, 1962; January 30, 1963; June 25, 1963; and February 25, 1966.

46 Zhongyang Yanjiuyuan Jindaishi Yanjiusuo Dang'an Guan, 112.22/0003, 34–35.

47 Ibid., 152.11/0045, "Huijiao renshi Sun Shengwu yu Xiao Yongtai," 40–43, 46–48.

48 Ibid., 152.11/0045, 61–66.

49 Though it is now clear that cannibalism was a common strategy of survival in many regions of China during the Great Leap Forward, there are several reasons for considering this claim suspect with regard to Xinjiang. First, Xinjiang suffered perhaps the least of any region in China during the Great Leap Forward, to the point where it soon became a net exporter of grain to other regions in China. On this point, see Li Danhui, "Dui 1962 nian Xinjiang Yi-Ta shijian qiyin de lishi kaocha," 486–514. Second, in those rural areas where starvation might have occurred in Xinjiang, the state maintained strict segregation between Uighur and Han communities, the latter tightly insulated within military colonies.

50 Zhongyang Yanjiuyuan Jindaishi Yanjiusuo Dang'an Guan, 119.5/0001, "Zhiliu Afuhan Xinjiang nanmin," 11–12.

51 Ibid., 14–20, 51–53, 96–100.

52 Ibid., 101–7, 150–53, 220, 225, 242–50. See also "Information: Refugees: From East Turkestan," November 17, 1967, to October 17, 1968, British National Archives, Far Eastern Department, FO 95/15.

53 Zhongyang Yanjiuyuan Jindaishi Yanjiusuo Dang'an Guan, 119.5/0001, "Jiuji Xinjiang nanbao" and "Zhiliu Afuhan Xinjiang nanmin," 47–48; and 119.5/0002, "Jiuji Xinjiang nanbao."

54 For those activities Delilhan carried out on behalf of Yolbars, including correspon-

dence between the two men, see Zhongyang Yanjiuyuan Jindaishi Yanjiusuo Dang'an
   Guan, 119.5/0002, 13–15, 156–59; 119.5/0001, "Zhiliu Afuhan Xinjiang nanmin," 249;
   119.5/0001, "Jiuji Xinjiang nanmin," 104, 163–65; 112.22/0003, 40–41, 96–99; 109/0005,
   137–39; and *Lianhe bao*, May 26, 1960.

55 Svanberg, *Kazak Refugees in Turkey*, 172–74.

56 Ibid.; Jacobs, "The Many Deaths of a Kazak Unaligned," 1304–12; and author interviews, Istanbul, April and May 2008.

57 *Lianhe bao*, July 28, 1971; and Zhongyang Yanjiuyuan Jindaishi Yanjiusuo Dang'an
   Guan, 162.5/0001, 154–55.

58 *Lianhe bao*, May 20, 1988; May 31, 1991; and December 28, 1991.

59 Chen Ming-hsiang, "Zangbao zai Tai shenghuo zhuangkuang diaocha ji fudao cuoshi
   zhi yanjiu."

60 Bachman, "Making Xinjiang Safe for the Han?" 182.

CONCLUSION

1 Roerich, *Altai-Himalaya*, 280; and Xu, *Xu Xusheng xiyou riji*, 198.

2 Gansu sheng guji wenxian zhengli bianyi zhongxin, ed., *Zhongguo xibei wenxian congshu, er bian*, vol. 10, 302, 158–59.

3 On "living shrines" in Chinese political culture, see Schneewind, "Beyond Flattery,"
   345–66.

4 Prior to the twentieth century, the delineation of ethnic identities and institutionalization of ethnic hierarchies was nearly always undertaken by the non-Han conquerors
   of northern hybrid states such as the Northern Wei, Tang, Liao, Jin, Yuan, and Qing.
   For one of the earliest examples of ethnic engineering in Chinese history, see Elliott,
   "Hushuo."

5 Wang Enmao, *Wang Enmao wenji*, vol. 1, 173.

6 Mullaney, *Coming to Terms with the Nation*.

7 Esherick, *Ancestral Leaves*, 108; and personal communication with Esherick to confirm
   the usage of *minzu diguo* in the original Chinese source.

8 Cooper, *Colonialism in Question*.

9 See, for instance, Harrell, *Cultural Encounters on China's Ethnic Frontiers*; Gladney, *Dislocating China*; Rhoads, *Manchus and Han*; Litzinger, *Other Chinas*; Mackerras, *China's
   Ethnic Minorities and Globalisation*; McCarthy, *Communist Multiculturalism*; and Mullaney, *Critical Han Studies*.

GLOSSARY OF CHINESE CHARACTERS

Ahmetjan Qasimi 阿合買提江
Altay 阿爾泰

Bianjiang wenhua 邊疆文化
biantong 變通
Bu Daoming 卜道明
Buguozhai wendu 補過齋文牘
buluo 部落
Burhan Shahidi 鮑爾漢

canzan 參贊
chantou 纏頭
Chiang Kai-shek 蔣介石
Chu Anping 儲安平
Chu Chia-hua 朱家驊

danke zizhi 蛋殼自治
daoyin 道尹
de 德
Delilhan 達里力汗
Deng Liqun 鄧力群
di 帝
Dihua 迪化
diqu zizhi 地區自治
dongbei zhi xu 東北之續
duban 督辦

Fandihui 反帝會
fanshu 藩屬
fazhan Xinjiang wenhua 發展新疆文化
Feng Yuxiang 馮玉祥
Feng Zuwen 馮祖文
Fu Bingchang 傅秉常

ganma 幹嘛
Gao Boyu 高伯玉
gaodu zizhi 高度自治
Guang Lu 廣祿
Gucheng 古城
guo 國
guochi 國恥
guojia zhuyi de minzu 國家主義的民族

Hami 哈密
Hong miaozi 紅廟子
Huang Musong 黃慕松
Huang Wenbi 黃文弼
huaxia 華夏
Hui 回

Ili 伊犁
Isa Yusuf Alptekin 愛沙

Janimhan 賈尼穆漢

jiangjun 將軍

jimi 羈縻

Jin Shuren 金樹仁

jiuguo 救國

juedi 絕地

junchan zhuyi 均產主義

Karashahr 焉耆

kebing 客兵

Khobdo 科布多

Khoja Niyaz Haji 和加尼牙孜

kongcheng ji 空城計

Kulun zhi xu 庫倫之續

Lianhe bao 聯合報

Liankui 聯魁

Lifanyuan 理藩院

Liu Mengchun 劉孟純

Liu Wenlong 劉文龍

Liu Zerong 劉澤榮

liyong Meng Ha Hui Chan wei zhuyi 利用
    蒙哈回纏為主義

Lu Xiaozu 魯效祖

Luo Wen'gan 羅文榦

Ma Fuxing 馬福興

Ma Hushan 馬虎山

Ma Shaowu 馬紹武

Ma Zhongying 馬仲英

Manchuqjab 滿楚克札布

Mao Zemin 毛澤民

Masud Sabri 麥斯武德

minzu 民族

minzu chaoliu 民族潮流

minzu diguo 民族帝國

Minzu Wenhua Cujinhui 民族文化促進會

minzu zhengce jiancha 民族政策檢查

Mohammed Emin Bugra 伊敏

Mou Weitong 牟維潼

neisheng 內省

ni dong bu dong hua 你懂不懂話

Osman 烏斯滿

Prince Ailin 艾林君王

qi shi you bu neng 其勢有不能

Qing 清

Qiu Zongjun 邱宗浚

Sadiq 司的克

sangshi tudi 喪失土地

sanqu geming 三區革命

Saypiddin Azizi 賽福鼎

Shah Maqsut 沙木胡索特

Sheng Shicai 盛世才

shengshang 省上

shudi 屬地

Sun Shengwu 孫繩武

Sun Wendou 孫文斗

Tacheng 塔城

tebie qingxing 特別情形

Timur 鐵木爾

titai 提台

Tsetsen Puntsag Gegeen 多布棟策楞車敏

Turfan 吐魯番

Urumchi 烏魯木齊

wai Meng zhi xu 外蒙之續
Wang Enmao 王恩茂
Wang Jingwei 汪精衛
Wang Shijie 王世杰
Wang Shunan 王樹楠
wanquan tongyi 完全同意
Wen Songling 聞松齡
Wu Zexiang 吳澤湘
Wu Zhongxin 吳忠信

Xie Bin 謝彬
xiexiang 協餉
Xinjiang sheng 新疆省
Xinjiang sheng zhengfu zhuxi bangong-
    chu 新疆省政府主席辦公處
Xinjiang shengchan jianshe bingtuan 新
    疆生產建設兵團
Xinjiang shengzhang 新疆省長
Xinjiang Weiwuer Zizhiqu 新疆維吾爾
    自治區
Xingxing Gorge 猩猩峽
Xizang zhi xu 西藏之續
Xu Bingxu 徐炳昶
Xu Shichang 徐世昌
Yang Zengbing 楊增炳
Yang Zengxin 楊增新
Yao Daohong 堯道宏
Yining 伊寧
Yolbars Khan 堯樂博士汗
yousheng 優勝
Yu Xiusong 俞秀松
Yuan Dahua 袁大化
Yuan Shikai 袁世凱

Zhang Chunxi 張純熙
Zhang Fengjiu 張鳳九
Zhang Peiyuan 張培元
Zhang Shaobo 張紹伯
Zhang Zhizhong 張治中
zhangguan 長官
Zhao Guoliang 趙國梁
zhimindi 殖民地
Zhongguo 中國
zhonghua 中華
zhongzu jiexian guoyu fenming
    種族界線過於分明
Zhou Bin 周彬
Zhu Ruichi 朱瑞墀
Zhu Shaoliang 朱紹良
zhuanyuan 專員
zongzu 宗族

BIBLIOGRAPHY

ARCHIVES

British National Archives. Far Eastern Department. London.

National Archives of the United States. Foreign Service Inspection Reports and Division of Chinese Affairs. College Park, Maryland.

Papers of Sir Marc Aurel Stein. Bodleian Library. Oxford.

Russian State Archive of Socio-Political History (RGASPI). Translated by Gary Goldberg for the Cold War International History Project, Wilson Center Digital Archive.

State Archive of the Russian Federation (GARF). Translated by Gary Goldberg for the Cold War International History Project, Wilson Center Digital Archive.

Xinjiang Weiwuer Zizhiqu Dang'an Guan [Archives of the Xinjiang Uighur Autonomous Region], Urumqi, China.

Zhongyang Yanjiuyuan Jindaishi Yanjiusuo Dang'an Guan [Archives of the Institute of Modern History, Academia Sinica]. Waijiaobu [Ministry of Foreign Affairs]: Yaxisi [West Asia Division], Renshichu [Personnel Department], and Tiaofasi [Legal Division]. Nankang, Taiwan.

PUBLISHED ARCHIVAL COLLECTIONS IN CHINESE

Gansu Sheng Guji Wenxian Zhengli Bianyi Zhongxin, ed. 2006. *Zhongguo xibei wenxian congshu. Er bian* [Collection of documents relating to northwest China. Series two]. Vols. 10–16. Beijing: Xianzhuang Shuju,

Gonganbu Dang'an Guan, ed. 1991. *Zai Jiang Jieshi shenbian ba nian: Shicongshi gaoji muliao Tang Zong riji* [At Chiang Kai-shek's side for eight years: The diary of Tang Zong, a high-level diplomat in the intelligence office]. Beijing: Qunzhong Chubanshe.

Gongqingtuan Xinjiang Weiwuer Zizhiqu Weiyuanhui and Balujun Zhu Xinjiang Banshichu Jinian Guan, eds. 1986. *Xinjiang minzhong fandi lianhe hui ziliao huibian* [An edited collection of materials on the United Anti-Imperialist Society of the Xinjiang Masses]. Wulumuqi: Xinjiang Qingshao Nian Chubanshe.

Hami Diqu Difangzhi Bangongshi and Hami Diqu Caizheng Chu, eds. 1992. *Mao Zemin yu Hami caizheng* [Mao Zemin and public finance in Hami]. Wulumuqi: Xinjiang Renmin Chubanshe.

Quanguo Renmin Daibiao Dahui Minzu Weiyuanhui Bangongshi, ed. 1956. *Xinjiang Wei-wuer Zizhiqu ruogan diaocha cailiao huibian* [Edited collection of materials from several investigations carried out in Xinjiang Uighur Autonomous Region]. Beijing: Neibu Ziliao.

Shen Zhihua, ed. 2013. *Eguo jiemi dang'an: Xinjiang wenti* [Uncovering the secrets of Russian archives: The Xinjiang issue]. Wulumuqi: Xinjiang Renmin Chubanshe.

Waijiaobu, ed. 2001. *Waijiaobu dang'an congshu—jiewu lei: Xinjiang juan* [The Ministry of Foreign Affairs documents series—border affairs: Xinjiang files]. 2 vols. Taibei: Waijiaobu.

Xinjiang Shaoshu Minzu Shehui Lishi Diaocha Zu, ed. 1959. *Sanqu geming ziliao huibian* [Edited materials on the Three Districts Revolution]. 8 vols. Wulumuqi: n.p.

Xinjiang Weiwuer Zizhiqu Dang'an Guan, ed. 1994. *Xinjiang yu E Su shangye maoyi dang'an shiliao* [Historical documents on commerce and trade between Xinjiang and Russia/Soviet Union]. Wulumuqi: Xinjiang Renmin Chubanshe.

——. 1997. *Ma Zhongying zai Xinjiang dang'an shiliao xuanbian* [Selected historical documents pertaining to Ma Zhongying in Xinjiang]. Wulumuqi: Xinjiang Renmin Chubanshe.

Xinjiang Weiwuer Zizhiqu Dang'an Ju, Zhongguo Shehui Kexueyuan Bianjiang Shidi Yanjiu Zhongxin, and "Xinjiang tongshi" Bianzhuan Weiyuanhui, eds. 2007. *Jindai Xinjiang menggu lishi dang'an* [Historical documents on the Mongols in modern Xinjiang]. Wulumuqi: Xinjiang Renmin Chubanshe.

——. 2008. *Kang Ri zhanzheng shiqi Xinjiang ge minzu minzhong kang Ri mujuan dang'an shiliao* [Historical documents on donations by the various ethnicities of the Xinjiang masses during the anti-Japanese war of resistance]. Wulumuqi: Xinjiang Renmin Chubanshe.

Xue Xiantian, ed. 1996. *Zhong Su guojia guanxi shi ziliao huibian* [An edited collection of historical materials pertaining to Sino-Soviet relations]. Beijing: Shehui Kexue Wenxian Chubanshe.

Yang Zengxin. 1921 [1965]. *Buguozhai wendu* [Records from the Studio of Rectification], 6 vols. Taibei: Wenhai Chubanshe.

——. 1926. *Buguozhai wendu xubian* [Records from the Studio of Rectification: Additional compilations], 14 vols. Shanghuan: n.p.

——. 1934. *Buguozhai wendu sanbian* [Records from the Studio of Rectification: Three compilations], 6 vols. n.p.

Zhang Yuxi, ed. 2000. *Xinjiang pingpan jiaofei* [The suppression of bandits in Xinjiang]. Wulumuqi: Xinjiang Renmin Chubanshe.

Zhonggong Hetian Diwei Dangshi Bangongshi, ed. 1995. *Kang Ri zhanzheng shiqi Zhonggong dangren zai Hetian* [Chinese Communist Party members in Khotan during the period of the anti-Japanese war of resistance]. Wulumuqi: Xinjiang Renmin Chubanshe.

Zhonggong Wulumuqi Shi Weiyuanhui Dangshi Gongzuo Weiyuanhui and Wulumuqi Shi Dang'an Ju, eds. 1998. *Zhongguo gongchandang Wulumuqi shi weiyuanhui wenjian xuanbian (1949 nian–1955 nian)* [Edited selection of documents from the Chinese Communist Party Urumchi Municipal Committee (1949–55)]. Wulumuqi: Xinjiang Renmin Chubanshe.

Zhonggong Xinjiang Weiwuer Zizhiqu Weiyuanhui, Dangshi gongzuo weiyuanhui, and Zhongguo renmin jiefangjun Xinjiang junqu zhengzhibu, eds. 1990. *Xinjiang heping jiefang* [The peaceful liberation of Xinjiang]. Wulumuqi: Xinjiang Renmin Chubanshe.

Zhonggong Xinjiang Weiwuer Zizhiqu Weiyuanhui, Dangshi Gongzuo Weiyuanhui, and Zhonggong Wulumuqi Shi Weiyuanhui Dangshi Gongzuo Weiyuanhui, eds. 1992. *Balujun zhu Xinjiang banshichu* [The Eighth Route Army office in Xinjiang]. Wulumuqi: Xinjiang Renmin Chubanshe.

Zhonggong Xinjiang Weiwuer Zizhiqu Weiyuanhui Dangshi Yanjiushi, ed. 2000. *Zhongguo gongchandang yu minzu quyu zizhi zhidu de jianli he fazhan* [The Chinese Communist Party and the establishment and development of the ethnic regional autonomy system]. 2 vols. Beijing: Zhonggong Dangshi Chubanshe.

Zhonggong Yili Hasake Zizhizhou Weiyuanhui Dangshi Yanjiushi and Yili Hasake Zizhizhou Dang'an Ju (Guan), eds. 2001. *Zhongguo gongchandang Yili Hasake zizhizhou weiyuanhui zhongyao wenjian xuanbian (1950 nian 4 yue–1957 nian 12 yue)* [Edited selection of important documents from the Chinese Communist Party Ili Kazak Autonomous District Committee]. Yining: Yili Zhou Dangwei Dangshi Yanjiushi.

Zhonggong Zhongyang Wenxian Yanjiushi and Zhonggong Xinjiang Weiwuer Zizhiqu Weiyuanhui, eds. 2010. *Xinjiang gongzuo wenxian xuanbian (1949–2010 nian)* [An edited selection of documents concerning party work in Xinjiang (1949– 2010)]. Beijing: Zhongyang Wenxian Chubanshe.

Zhongguo Di Er Lishi Dang'an Guan, ed. 1991. *Zhonghua minguo shi dang'an ziliao huibian—di san ji: Waijiao* [Collection of archival materials concerning the history of the Republic of China—vol. 3: Foreign relations]. Nanjing: Jiangsu Guji Chubanshe.

——. 1994. *Zhonghua minguo shi dang'an ziliao huibian—di wu ji, di yi bian: Zhengzhi (wu)* [Collection of archival materials concerning the history of the Republic of China—vol. 5, no. 1: Politics, pt. 5]. Nanjing: Jiangsu Guji Chubanshe.

——. 1998. *Zhonghua minguo shi dang'an ziliao huibian—di wu ji, di er bian: Zhengzhi (si)* [Collection of archival materials concerning the history of the Republic of China—vol. 5, no. 2: Politics, pt. 4]. Nanjing: Jiangsu Guji Chubanshe.

——. 1999. *Zhonghua minguo shi dang'an ziliao huibian—di wu ji, di san bian: Zhengzhi (wu)* [Collection of archival materials concerning the history of the Republic of China—vol. 5, no. 3: Politics, pt. 5]. Nanjing: Jiangsu Guji Chubanshe.

Zhongyang Yanjiuyuan Jindaishi Yanjiusuo, ed. 1960 [1984]. *Zhong E guanxi shiliao: E zhengbian yu yiban jiaoshe (yi) (Zhonghua minguo liu nian zhi ba nian)* [Historical materials on Sino-Russian relations: The Russian revolution and general diplomacy (1) (1917–19)]. Taibei: Zhongyang Yanjiuyuan Jindaishi Yanjiusuo.

——. 1960 [1983]. *Zhong E guanxi shiliao: Xinjiang bianfang (Zhonghua minguo liu nian zhi ba nian)* [Historical materials on Sino-Russian relations: Xinjiang border defense (1917–19)]. Taibei: Zhongyang Yanjiuyuan Jindaishi Yanjiusuo.

——. 1968. *Zhong E guanxi shiliao: E zhengbian (Zhonghua minguo jiu nian)* [Historical materials on Sino-Russian relations: The Russian Revolution (1920)]. Taibei: Zhong-yang Yanjiuyuan Jindaishi Yanjiusuo.

———. 1968. *Zhong E guanxi shiliao: Yiban jiaoshe (Zhonghua minguo jiu nian)* [Historical materials on Sino-Russian relations: General diplomacy (1920)]. Taibei: Zhongyang Yanjiuyuan Jindaishi Yanjiusuo.

———. 1974. *Zhong E guanxi shiliao: Zhongdong tielu, E zhengbian (Zhonghua minguo shi nian)* [Historical materials on Sino-Russian relations: The Chinese Eastern Railway affair and the Russian Revolution (1921)]. Taibei: Zhongyang Yanjiuyuan Jindaishi Yanjiusuo.

OTHER PRIMARY AND SECONDARY SOURCES

Andreas, Joel. 2009. *Rise of the Red Engineers: The Cultural Revolution and the Origins of China's New Class*. Stanford, CA: Stanford University Press.

Bachman, David. 2004. "Making Xinjiang Safe for the Han? Contradictions and Ironies of Chinese Governance in China's Northwest," in Morris Rossabi, ed., *Governing China's Multiethnic Frontiers*. Seattle: University of Washington Press.

Bai Jiezhong. 1944. "Du Maisiwude xiansheng 'Jieshao Xinjiang de minzu'" [On reading Mr. Masud's "Introduction to the nationalities of Xinjiang"] *Tujue* 67: 16.

Barkey, Karen. 2008. *Empire of Difference: The Ottomans in Comparative Perspective*. Cambridge: Cambridge University Press.

Barmin, V. A. 1999. *SSSR i Sin'tszian, 1918–1941* [The Soviet Union and Xinjiang, 1918–1941]. Barnaul: Barnaul'skĭ Gosudarstvennyĭ Pedagogicheskiĭ Universitet.

———. 1999. *Sin'tszian v sovetsko-kitaiskikh otnosheniiakh, 1941–1949 gg.* [Sino-Soviet relations and Xinjiang, 1941–1949]. Barnaul: Barnaul'skii Gosudarstvennyi Pedagogicheskii Universitet.

Benson, Linda. 1990. *The Ili Rebellion: The Moslem Challenge to Chinese Authority in Xinjiang, 1944–1949*. Armonk, NY: M. E. Sharpe.

Benson, Linda, and Ingvar Svanberg, eds. 1988. *The Kazaks of China: Essays on an Ethnic Minority*. Uppsala: Almqvist and Wiksell International.

Bovingdon, Gardner. 2010. *The Uyghurs: Strangers in Their Own Land*. New York: Columbia University Press.

Brophy, David. 2010. "The Qumul Rebels' Appeal to Outer Mongolia." *Turcica* 42: 329– 41.

———. 2011. "Tending to Unite? The Origins of Uyghur Nationalism." PhD diss., Harvard University.

———. 2012. "Five Races, One Parliament? Xinhai in Xinjiang and the Problem of Minority Representation in the Chinese Republic." *Inner Asia* 14: 343–64.

———. 2013. "Correcting Transgressions in the House of Islam: Yang Zengxin's *Buguozhai wendu* on Xinjiang's Muslims," in Niccolò Pianciola and Paolo Sartori, eds., *Islam, Society and States across the Qazaq Steppe (18th–Early 20th Centuries)*, 267–96. Wien: Verlag der Österreichischen Akademie der Wissenschaften.

Brubaker, Rogers, Margit Feischmidt, Jon Fox, and Liana Grancea. 2006. *Nationalist Politics and Everyday Ethnicity in a Transylvanian Town*. Princeton, NJ: Princeton University Press.

Bulag, Uradyn E. 2006. "Going Imperial: Tibeto-Mongolian Buddhism and Nationalisms in China and Inner Asia," in Joseph W. Esherick, Hasan Kayali, and Eric Van Young, eds., *Empire to Nation: Historical Perspectives on the Making of the Modern World*, 260–95. Lanham, MD: Rowman and Littlefield.

Burbank, Jane, and Frederick Cooper. 2010. *Empires in World History: Power and the Politics of Difference*. Princeton, NJ: Princeton University Press.

Cai Jinsong. 1998. *Sheng Shicai zai Xinjiang* [Sheng Shicai in Xinjiang]. Zhengzhou: Henan Renmin Chubanshe.

Cai Jinsong and Cai Ying. 1985. "Qianding 'Yili linshi tongshang xieding' (ji 'Yining huiyi ding'an') de qianqian houhou" [The signing of the "Ili Provisional Trade Accord" (also known as the "Yining consultation resolution")]. *Xinjiang lishi yanjiu* 4: 70–78.

Cannadine, David. 2001. *Ornamentalism: How the British Saw Their Empire*. Oxford: Oxford University Press.

Chai Hengsen. 2005. "Qi qi zhengbian qinjian pianduan" [The brief account of an eyewitness to the July 7 coup], in Xiao Qian, *Kunlun caiyu lu* [Distinguished selections from the Kunlun]. Beijing: Zhonghua Shuju.

Chen Chao and Chen Huisheng. 1999. *Minguo Xinjiang shi* [A history of Republican Xinjiang]. Wulumuqi: Xinjiang Renmin Chubanshe.

Chen Ming-hsiang. 2002. "Zangbao zai Tai shenghuo zhuangkuang diaocha ji fudao cuoshi zhi yanjiu" [Research on the living conditions of Tibetans in Taiwan and suggestions for future measures]. Paper commissioned by the Committee for Tibetan and Mongolian Affairs and Tamkang University.

Chiang Kai-shek. 1947. *China's Destiny and Chinese Economic Theory*. New York: Roy Publishers.

Chu Anping. 1957. *Xinjiang xin mianmao* [The new face of Xinjiang]. Beijing: Zuojia Chubanshe.

Chu Chia-hua. 1954. *Taiwan and Sinkiang (Formosa and Chinese Turkistan)*. Taipei: Chinese Association for the United Nations.

Clark, Milton J. 1954. "How the Kazakhs Fled to Freedom." *National Geographic Magazine* 106, no. 5: 621–44.

"Cong Maisiwude dao Baoerhan: Zhe shi Zhang Zhizhong yishou daoyan de jiezuo" [From Masud to Burhan: a masterpiece directed by Zhang Zhizhong]. 1949. *Zhongguo xinwen* 8: 8.

Cooper, Frederick. 2005. *Colonialism in Question: Theory, Knowledge, History*. Berkeley: University of California Press.

Dan Qi. 2003. "Xinjiang lüxing ji" [Account of travels in Xinjiang], in Guojia Tushuguan Fenguan, ed., *Guji zhenben youji congkan* [Collection of old and rare travel accounts]. Vol. 5. Beijing: Xianzhuang Shuju.

Dave, Bhavna. 2007. *Kazakhstan: Ethnicity, Language and Power*. New York: Routledge.

Edgar, Adrienne Lynn. 2004. *Tribal Nation: The Making of Soviet Turkmenistan*. Princeton, NJ: Princeton University Press.

Elliott, Mark. 2012. "Hushuo: The Northern Other and the Naming of the Han Chinese," in Thomas S. Mullaney et al., eds., *Critical Han Studies: The History, Representation, and Identity of China's Majority*, 173–90. Berkeley: University of California Press.

Esherick, Joseph W. 2011. *Ancestral Leaves: A Family Journey through Chinese History*. Berkeley: University of California Press.

Fan Mingxin. 2001. *Xinjiang "sanqi" zhengbian xie'an zhenxiang* [The true story of the "triple seven" coup]. Pingdong: Fan Mingxin Kanyin.

Forbes, Andrew D. W. 1986. *Warlords and Muslims in Chinese Central Asia: A Political History of Republican Sinkiang, 1911–1949*. Cambridge: Cambridge University Press.

Freeman, Joshua L. 2011. "Whose Martyr? Lutpulla Mutellip and the Contingency of Canon Formation." Conference paper for "Beyond 'The Xinjiang Problem' Workshop," Australian National University, Canberra.

Fu Yang. 2001. "Shilun Yang Zengxin zhuzheng Xinjiang shiqi de 'ruobing zhengce'" [A brief discussion of Yang Zengxin's policy of a "weak army" during his tenure in Xinjiang]. *Xiyu yanjiu* 2: 32.

Fuller, Pierre. 2012. "North China Famine Revisited: Unsung Native Relief in the Warlord Era, 1920–1921." *Modern Asian Studies* (August): 1–31.

Gao Jian and Zhao Jiangming. 2005. "Minguo qianqi Xinjiang shengyi hui yanjiu" [Research on Xinjiang's Provincial Assembly during the early years of the Republic]. *Xiyu yanjiu* 3: 40–48.

Gao Sulan. 1997. "Sheng Shicai ru Xinjiang zhuzheng jingwei (minguo shijiu nian ~ ershisan nian)" [An account of Sheng Shicai's assumption of power in Xinjiang (1930–34)]. *Guoshiguan guankan* 22 (June): 135–54.

———. 2001. "Sheng Shicai yu zhonggong (minguo 26 nian zhi 31 nian)" [Sheng Shicai and the Chinese Communist Party (1937–42)]. *Guoshiguan xueshu jikan* 1 (December): 55–75.

———. 2008. "Zhanshi guomin zhengfu shili jinru Xinjiang shimo" [An account of the takeover of Xinjiang by the Nationalist government during the war years]. *Guoshiguan xueshu jikan* 7: 129–65.

Garnaut, Anthony. 2008. "From Yunnan to Xinjiang: Governor Yang Zengxin and his Dungan Generals." *Études orientales* 25: 93–125.

Gladney, Dru C. 2004. *Dislocating China: Muslims, Minorities, and Other Subaltern Subjects*. Chicago: Chicago University Press.

Guang Lu. 1964. *Guang Lu huiyilu* [Memoirs of Guang Lu]. Taibei: Wenxing Shudian.

Guo Shengli. 2010. "Xinjiang 'qiqi zhengbian' zhenxiang kaoshu" [An inquiry into the real story behind the "triple seven coup" in Xinjiang]. *Zhongguo bianjiang shidi yanjiu* 20, no. 1 (March): 36–47.

Harrell, Stevan, ed. 1996. *Cultural Encounters on China's Ethnic Frontiers*. Seattle: University of Washington Press.

Hirsch, Francine. 2005. *Empire of Nations: Ethnographic Knowledge and the Making of the Soviet Union*. Ithaca, NY: Cornell University Press.

Huang Jianhua. 1994. "Jin Shuren an tanxi" [An examination of the Jin Shuren case]. *Kashi shiyuan xuebao* 4: 46–50.

———. 1996. "Wu Zhongxin yu Maisiwude" [Wu Zhongxin and Masud Sabri]. *Xinjiang difang zhi* 3: 60–63.

———. 1999. "Wu Zhongxin zhaoxiang Wusiman de huodong" [Wu Zhongxin's efforts to urge Osman to submit]. *Xibei minzu yanjiu* 2: 241–47.

——. 2003. *Guomindang zhengfu de Xinjiang zhengce yanjiu* [Research on the Nationalist government's policies toward Xinjiang]. Beijing: Minzu Chubanshe.

Huang Wenbi. 1990. *Huang Wenbi Meng Xin kaocha riji* [The diary of Huang Wenbi during an expedition to Mongolia and Xinjiang]. Comp. Huang Lie. Beijing: Wenwu Chubanshe.

Huangfu, Zhengzheng. 2012. "Internalizing the West: Qing Envoys and Ministers in Europe, 1866–1893." PhD diss., University of California, San Diego.

Jacobs, Justin. 2008. "How Chinese Turkestan Became Chinese: Visualizing Zhang Zhizhong's *Tianshan Pictorial* and Xinjiang Youth Song and Dance Troupe." *Journal of Asian Studies* 67, no. 2 (May): 545–91.

——. 2010. "The Many Deaths of a Kazak Unaligned: Osman Batur, Chinese Decolonization, and the Nationalization of a Nomad." *American Historical Review* 115, no. 5 (December): 1291–1314.

——. 2011. "Empire Besieged: The Preservation of Chinese Rule in Xinjiang, 1884– 1971." PhD diss., University of California, San Diego.

Jiang Yasha, Jing Li, and Chen Zhanqi, eds. 2007. *Minguo bianshi yanjiu wenxian huibian* [A collection of documents for research on border affairs of the Republican era], vol. 2. Beijing: Quanguo Tushuguan Wenxian.

Kataoka, Kazutada. 1991. *Shinchō Shinkyō tōji kenkyū* [Research on Qing dynasty rule in Xinjiang]. Tokyo: Yū San Kaku.

Kim, Hodong. 2004. *Holy War in China: The Muslim Rebellion and State in Chinese Central Asia, 1864–1877*. Stanford, CA: Stanford University Press.

Kinzley, Judd. 2012. "Staking Claims to China's Borderland: Oil, Ores and State-Building in Xinjiang Province, 1893–1964." PhD diss., University of California, San Diego.

Klimeš, Ondřej. 2015. *Struggle by the Pen: Uyghur Discourse of Nation and National Interest, c. 1900–1949*. Leiden: Brill.

Kraus, Charles. 2010. "Creating a Soviet 'Semi-Colony'? Sino-Soviet Cooperation and Its Demise in Xinjiang, 1949–1955." *Chinese Historical Review* 17, no. 2 (Fall): 129–65.

Laird, Thomas. 2002. *Into Tibet: The CIA's First Atomic Spy and His Secret Expedition to Lhasa*. New York: Grove Press.

Langfitt, Frank. 2015. "Why a Chinese Government Think Tank Attacked American Scholars." *National Public Radio*, May 21.

Larsen, Kirk W. 2008. *Tradition, Treaties, and Trade: Qing Imperialism and Chosŏn Korea, 1850–1910*. Cambridge, MA: Harvard University Asia Center.

Lattimore, Eleanor Holgate. 1934. *Turkestan Reunion*. New York: John Day.

Lattimore, Owen. 1930. *High Tartary*. Boston: Little, Brown.

——. 1950. *Pivot of Asia: Sinkiang and the Inner Asian Frontiers of China and Russia*. Boston: Little, Brown.

——. 1990. *China Memoirs: Chiang Kai-shek and the War against Japan*. Tokyo: University of Tokyo Press.

Leibold, James. 2007. *Reconfiguring Chinese Nationalism: How the Qing Frontier and Its Indigenes Became Chinese*. New York: Palgrave Macmillan.

Li Danhui. 2006. "Dui 1962 nian Xinjiang Yi-Ta shijian qiyin de lishi kaocha: Laizi Zhongguo Xinjiang de dang'an cailiao" [A historical inquiry into the causes of the 1962 Yi-Ta incident in Xinjiang: Based on archival material from Xinjiang], in Shen Zhihua and Li Danhui, eds., *Zhanhou Zhong Su guanxi ruogan wenti yanjiu: Laizi Zhong E shuang-fang de dang'an wenxian* [Research on several issues in postwar Sino-Soviet relations: Based on archival documents from both China and Russia], 486–514. Beijing: Renmin Chubanshe.

Li Sheng. 1993. *Xinjiang dui Su (E) maoyi shi, 1600–1990* [A history of trade between Xinjiang and the Soviet Union (Russia), 1600–1990]. Wulumuqi: Xinjiang Renmin Chubanshe.

Li Xincheng. 1993. *Yang Zengxin zai Xinjiang* [Yang Zengxin in Xinjiang]. Taibei: Guoshiguan.

Lias, Godfrey. 1955. "Kazakh Nomads' Struggle against Communists." *Times* (London). February 17–18.

———. 1956. *Kazak Exodus*. London: Evans Bros.

Lin, Hsiao-ting. 2006. *Tibet and Nationalist China's Frontier: Intrigues and Ethnopolitics, 1928–49*. Vancouver: University of British Columbia Press.

———. 2009. "War, Leadership and Ethnopolitics: Chiang Kai-shek and China's Frontiers, 1941–1945." *Journal of Contemporary China* 18, no. 59 (March): 201–17.

Lin Jing. 1965 [1930]. *Xibei congbian* [Northwest miscellany]. Taibei: Zhongguo Wenxian Chubanshe.

Litzinger, Ralph A. 2000. *Other Chinas: The Yao and the Politics of National Belonging*. Durham, NC: Duke University Press.

Liu Cao, Liu Jie, and Wang Xianhui. 2006. "Duo huofo zhi si" [The death of the Incarnate Lama Tsetsen Puntsag Gegeen]. *Xiyu yanjiu* 2: 48–54.

Liu Qin. 2012. *Wang Shunan shixue yanjiu* [Historical research on Wang Shunan]. Tianjin: Tianjin Renmin Chubanshe.

Liu Xianghui and Chen Wuguo. 2007. *Yinmo Gebi de lishi suipian* [Fragments of history buried beneath the Gobi]. Wulumuqi: Xinjiang Meishu Sheying Chubanshe.

Liu, Xiaoyuan. 2006. *Reins of Liberation: An Entangled History of Mongolian Independence, Chinese Territoriality, and Great Power Hegemony, 1911–1950*. Stanford, CA: Stanford University Press.

Luo Shaowen. 1995. "Yang Zengxin, Feng Yuxiang zhijian de maodun he Xinjiang 'sanqi' zhengbian" [On the contradictions between Yang Zengxin and Feng Yuxiang and the July 7 coup in Xinjiang]. *Xibei shidi* 4: 67–83.

———. 1995. "Zhongsheng wuguo—minguo shiqi Xinjiang sheng di ba ren zhuxi Maisiwude de yi sheng" [A lifetime of injuring his nation: The life of Masud Sabri, eighth governor of Republican Xinjiang]. *Xinjiang difang zhi* 1: 60–64.

———. 1996. "Aisha xiaozhuan" [A brief biography of Isa]. *Xinjiang difang zhi* 2: 61–64.

———. 2007. "Fan Yaonan zhuanlüe [A short biography of Fan Yaonan]." *Hubei wenshi* 1: 156–81.

Luthi, Lorenz M. *The Sino-Soviet Split: Cold War in the Communist World*. Princeton, NJ: Princeton University Press, 2008.

Ma Fushou. 1987. "Yang Zengxin jianchu Ma Fuxing mudu ji" [An eyewitness account of Yang Zengxin's elimination of Ma Fuxing], in Miquan xian zhengxie wenshi ziliao yanjiu weiyuanhui, ed., *Miquan wenshi* [Miquan historical materials], vol. 1, 71–129. Miquan xian: Zhongguo Renmin Zhengzhi Xieshang Huiyi.

Ma Zhiyong. 2008. "Xinjiang junfa Sheng Shicai yuefu yijia bei sha zhi mi" [The mysterious case of the murder of Xinjiang warlord Sheng Shicai's father-in-law and his entire family]. *Wenshi tiandi* 9 (2008).

Mackerras, Colin. 2003. *China's Ethnic Minorities and Globalisation*. London: Routledge.

Mair, Victor. 2005. "The North(west)ern Peoples and the Recurrent Origins of the 'Chinese' State," in Joshua A. Fogel, ed., *The Teleology of the Modern Nation- State: Japan and China*, 46–84. Philadelphia: University of Pennsylvania Press.

Mannerheim, C. G. 2008. *Across Asia: From East to West in 1906–1908*. Helsinki: Otava Publishing.

Mao, Yufeng. 2011. "A Muslim Vision for the Chinese Nation: Chinese Pilgrimage Missions to Mecca during World War II." *Journal of Asian Studies* 70, no. 2 (May): 373–95.

Martin, Terry. 2001. *The Affirmative Action Empire: Nations and Nationalism in the Soviet Union, 1923–1939*. Ithaca, NY: Cornell University Press.

McCarthy, Susan K. 2009. *Communist Multiculturalism: Ethnic Revival in Southwest China*. Seattle: University of Washington Press.

McCord, Edward A. 1993. *The Power of the Gun: The Emergence of Modern Chinese Warlordism*. Berkeley: University of California Press.

McMillen, Donald H. 1979. *Chinese Communist Power and Policy in Xinjiang, 1949– 1977*. Boulder, CO: Westview.

Millward, James A. 1994. "A Uyghur Muslim in Qianlong's Court: The Meanings of the Fragrant Concubine." *Journal of Asian Studies* 53, no. 2 (May): 427–58.

——. 1998. *Beyond the Pass: Economy, Ethnicity, and Empire in Qing Central Asia, 1759–1864*. Stanford, CA: Stanford University Press.

——. 2007. *Eurasian Crossroads: A History of Xinjiang*. New York: Columbia University Press.

Mirsky, Jeannette. 1977. *Sir Aurel Stein: Archaeological Explorer*. Chicago: University of Chicago Press.

Mullaney, Thomas S. 2010. *Coming to Terms with the Nation: Ethnic Classification in Modern China*. Berkeley: University of California Press.

——. 2012. "Critical Han Studies: Introduction and Prolegomenon," in Thomas S. Mullaney et al., eds., *Critical Han Studies: The History, Representation, and Identity of China's Majority*, 1–20. Berkeley: University of California Press.

Newby, Laura. 2005. *The Empire and the Khanate: A Political History of Qing Relations with Khoqand, c. 1760–1860*. Boston: Brill.

Pelliot, Paul. 1910. "Trois ans dans la Haute Asie" [Three years in High Asia]. *Asie française* (January): 3–16.

Perdue, Peter C. 2005. *China Marches West: The Qing Conquest of Central Eurasia*. Cambridge, MA: Harvard University Press.

Porter, Bernard. 2004. *The Absent-Minded Imperialists: Empire, Society, and Culture in Britain*. Oxford: Oxford University Press.

Qing Xuebu, ed. 1980. *Xuebu guanbao* [Official bulletin of the Ministry of Education]. Vol. 3. Taibei: Guoli Gugong Bowuyuan.

Radchenko, Sergey S. "The Soviets' Best Friend in Asia: The Mongolian Dimension of the Sino-Soviet Split," Working Paper No. 42, Cold War International History Project, Washington, DC, November 2003.

Rhoads, Edward J. M. 2000. *Manchus and Han: Ethnic Relations and Political Power in Late Qing and Early Republican China, 1861–1928*. Seattle: University of Washington Press.

Roerich, Nicholas. 1929. *Altai-Himalaya; A Travel Diary*. New York: Frederick A. Stokes.

Rowe, William T. 2009. *China's Last Empire: The Great Qing*. Cambridge, MA: Harvard University Press.

Saifuding [Saypidin Azizi]. 1958. *Jianjue fandui difang minzu zhuyi, wei shehuizhuyi de weida shengli er fendou!* [Resolutely oppose local ethnonationalism, struggle for a great socialist victory!]. Wulumuqi: Xinjiang Renmin Chubanshe.

Schneewind, Sarah. 2013. "Beyond Flattery: Legitimating Political Participation in a Ming Living Shrine." *Journal of Asian Studies* 72, no. 2 (May): 345–66.

Share, Michael. 2010. "The Russian Civil War in Chinese Turkestan (Xinjiang), 1918–1921: A Little Known and Explored Front." *Europe-Asia Studies* 62, no. 3 (May): 389–420.

Shen Zhihua. 1999. "Zhong Su jiemeng yu Sulian dui Xinjiang zhengce de bianhua (1944–1950)" [The Sino-Soviet alliance and the shift in Soviet policy toward Xinjiang (1944–1950]. *Jindaishi yanjiu* 3.

Shi Lun. 2005. *Xibei Ma jia junfa shi* [A history of the Ma warlords in the northwest]. Lanzhou: Gansu Renmin Chubanshe.

Starr, S. Frederick, ed. 2004. *Xinjiang: China's Muslim Borderland*. Armonk, NY: M. E. Sharpe.

Stoler, Ann, Carole McGranahan, and Peter C. Perdue, eds. 2007. *Imperial Formations*. Santa Fe, NM: School for Advanced Research Press.

Svanberg, Ingvar. 1989. *Kazak Refugees in Turkey: A Study of Cultural Persistence and Social Change*. Uppsala: Almqvist and Wiksell International.

Taylor, Jay. 2009. *The Generalissimo: Chiang Kai-shek and the Struggle for Modern China*. Cambridge, MA: Harvard University Press.

"To Follow the Faith." 1951. *Time*, October 22.

United States Department of State. 1971. *Foreign Relations of the United States, 1947*. Vol. 7: *The Far East: China*. Washington, DC: Government Printing Office.

Wakeman, Frederic E., Jr. 2009. "The Shun Interregnum of 1644," in Lea H. Wakeman, ed., *Telling Chinese History: A Selection of Essays*. Berkeley: University of California Press.

Waley-Cohen, Joanna. 1991. *Exile in Mid-Qing China: Banishment to Xinjiang, 1758–1820*. New Haven, CT: Yale University Press.

Wang, David D. 1999. *Under the Soviet Shadow: The Yining Incident: Ethnic Conflicts and International Rivalry in Xinjiang, 1944–1949*. Hong Kong: Chinese University Press.

Wang Enmao. 1997. *Wang Enmao wenji* [Collected works of Wang Enmao], 2 vols. Beijing: Zhongyang wenxian chubanshe.

Wang Hui. 2011. *The Politics of Imagining Asia*, ed. Theodore Huters. Cambridge, MA: Harvard University Press.

Wang Shunan, ed. 1965 [1923]. *Xinjiang tuzhi* [Xinjiang Gazetteer]. 6 vols. Taibei: Wenhai Chubanshe.

"Wei Maisiwude jiuren bensheng zhuxi Zhang zhuren yu sheng canyiyuan laihui hanjian" [Letters between Commissioner Zhang and members of the provincial senate regarding the appointment of Masud as provincial chairman]. 1948. *Han haichao* 11: 24.

Whiting, Allen S., and Sheng Shih-ts'ai. 1958. *Sinkiang: Pawn or Pivot?* East Lansing: Michigan State University Press.

Xie Xiaozhong. 1923 [2003]. *Xinjiang youji* [An account of travels in Xinjiang]. Lanzhou: Gansu Renmin Chubanshe.

Xinjiang Sanqu Geming Shi Bianzuan Weiyuanhui, ed. 1994. *Xinjiang sanqu geming dashiji* [A chronology of the Three Districts Revolution in Xinjiang]. Wulumuqi: Xinjiang Renmin Chubanshe.

Xinjiang Sheng Di Yi Jie Renmin Daibiao Dahui Di Er Ci Huiyi Mishuchu, ed. No date. *Xinjiang Weiwuer Zizhiqu chengli tekan* [Special publication commemorating the establishment of the Xinjiang Uighur Autonomous Region]. No publisher.

Xinjiang Weiwuer Zizhiqu Caizheng Ting, Zhongguo Renmin Yinhang Jinrong Yanjiusuo, and Xinjiang Jinrong Yanjiusuo, eds. 1994. *Geming licaijia Mao Zemin* [Revolutionary financier Mao Zemin]. Wulumuqi: Xinjiang Renmin Chubanshe.

Xinjiang Weiwuer Zizhiqu Jiaotong Shizhi Bianzuan Weiyuanhui, ed. 1992. *Xinjiang gonglu jiaotong shi* [A history of transportation and public roads in Xinjiang], vol. 1. Beijing: Renmin Jiaotong Chubanshe.

Xu Bingxu. 1930 [2000]. *Xu Xusheng xiyou riji* [A diary of Xu Xusheng's western travels]. Yinchuan: Ningxia Renmin Chubanshe.

Xue Xiantian. 2003. *Zhong Su guanxi shi (1945–1949)* [A history of Sino-Soviet relations (1945–1949)]. Chengdu: Sichuan Renmin Chubanshe.

Yaoleboshi [Yolbars Khan]. 1969. *Yaoleboshi huiyilu* [Memoirs of Yolbars Khan]. Taibei: Zhuanji Wenxue Chubanshe.

Young, Ernest P. 1977. *The Presidency of Yuan Shih-k'ai: Liberalism and Dictatorship in Early Republican China*. Ann Arbor: University of Michigan Press.

Zhang Dajun. 1954. *Hengdu Kunlun san wan li* [Crossing the Kunlun Mountains at 30,000 li]. Xianggang: Yazhou Chubanshe.

———. 1980. *Xinjiang fengbao qishi nian* [Seventy years of turbulence in Xinjiang]. 12 vols. Taibei: Lanxi Chubanshe.

Zhang Murong. 2003. "Li jiang hou de 'Xinjiang wang' Sheng Shicai" [The life of "Xinjiang king" Sheng Shicai after leaving Xinjiang]. *Wenshi chunqiu* 11.

Zhao, Gang. 2006. "Reinventing *China*: Imperial Qing Ideology and the Rise of Modern Chinese National Identity in the Early Twentieth Century." *Modern China* 32, no. 1 (January): 1–28.

Zhou Dongjiao. 1948. *Xinjiang shinian* [A decade in Xinjiang]. Lanzhou: n.p.

Zhou, Minglang. 2010. "The Fate of the Soviet Model of Multinational State-Building in the

People's Republic of China," in Thomas P. Bernstein and Hua-Yu Li, eds., *China Learns from the Soviet Union, 1949–Present*, 477–503. Lanham, MD: Lexington Books.

Zhu Peimin. 1993. *Xinjiang geming shi (1933–1957)* [A history of the revolution in Xinjiang]. Wulumuqi: Xinjiang Renmin Chubanshe.

INDEX

administrative boundaries. *See* autonomy, administrative

affirmative action: Chinese Communist, 169–94, 234–35; Nationalists and, 101, 127; Sheng Shicai "purchase" of, 97*fig.*, 103–13, 125, 127, 134, 205, 233. *See also* ethnopopulism; nationality policies; Soviet affirmative action policies

Afghanistan, Xinjiang refugees, 219–22, 224

agriculture, 22; Altay, 122; famines, 219, 257n49; Sheng Shicai payment to Soviets, 108, 112; Uighurs, 80, 152; Xinjiang grain exports, 257n49; Xinjiang Production and Construction Corps reclamation projects, 175, 183

Ahmetjan Qasimi, 23, 154, 156, 162–68, 176, 233

Ailin, Prince, 61, 113, 123, 143–44, 159–62, 184, 233

Aksu: *daoyin* (circuit intendant), 53, 72; Ili rebellion, 148, 152–53

Ali Han Tore, 141–43, 147, 151–53, 156, 159, 233

Allied powers: empire dismantling after World War I, 33–34; World War II, 149, 171. *See also* Americans; Europe

Almaty: Chinese consulate, 245n57; earthquake, 198–99; Ili rebellion, 135

Altay, 118–25, 151*fig.*; arms, 38, 66, 120–21; autonomy/administrative

boundaries, 23, 52, 64, 84, 169; Chinese Communists, 215; *daoyin* (circuit intendant), 64, 121; Hami rebellion, 38; Ili rebellion, 137–38, 147–52, 151*fig.*, 158–63, 166–67, 170; Jin Shuren and, 80; mineral wealth, 121–22, 151*fig.*, 152, 161, 167, 233; minister *(zhangguan)*, 23, 52, 84; Mongols, 66, 119–21, 147, 166–67; Prince Ailin, 61, 113, 123, 143–44, 159–62, 184, 233; Russian civil war, 60–61, 94; Russian traders, 80; Sheng Shicai purges, 111, 113, 120–23; Soviet consulate, 134, 137; Soviet infiltration, 66, 121–22, 135; taxes, 67, 120; transport, 120; Yang Zengxin and, 23, 52, 64, 66, 67, 84, 120, 121; *zhuanyuan*, 148–49, 161. *See also* Osman Batur

Altay City, 120–22, 160–61, 167

Americans: ambassador in Taipei, 203; archival sources, 14; CIA, 199; consulate in Xinjiang, 149–50, 154–55, 205; dissent management, 237–38; and refugees from Chinese Communists, 199, 201; "two Chinas" policy, 224–25

Andijan, 62–64, 94, 135, 245n57

Annenkov, Boris, 39, 60, 61*fig.*

Anti-Imperialist Frontline (Fandi zhanxian), 106

Anti-Imperialist Society (Fandihui), 106–8, 116

Anti-Rightist Campaign, 192

Apresov, Garegin, 105, 111, 112

archival sources, 14–16, 130; Chinese, 14–16, 129, 172; Soviet, 14, 93–94, 96, 130–32, 142, 153; Taiwan, 14, 207, 221; Uighur-language source material, 14, 93. *See also* diaries; historians

aristocracy. *See* elites

Armenians, dependent intermediaries, 26, 31

armies: Hui, 26, 38, 63, 104; Ili rebellion, 135–43, 147–53, 167–68; Jin Shuren, 78–79, 82–87, 94; Kazak, 64; Mongols, 38, 60–61, 82; Nationalist, 90, 92, 95, 125, 138, 151–52, 216; New Armies, 5, 37–39; People's Liberation Army, 182, 199–200; Red Russian, 61, 142; Russian World War I manpower, 50; Sheng Shicai, 125, 133–34; Turbans, 63; warlord, 39, 78, 86–96, 103–4; Yang Zengxin resources, 38–39, 45, 48, 56, 78–79, 82, 120, 150, 191; Zhang Peiyuan, 92, 95. *See also* arms; military; soldiers; war

arms: Altay, 38, 66, 120–21; machine guns, 39, 51, 55, 56, 119, 140; Soviet atomic bomb, 199; Soviet-supplied in Xinjiang, 83, 92–95, 98, 103–4, 119, 137–38, 140–43, 148–52, 167. *See also* military

Association for Ethnocultural Advancement (Minzu Wenhua Cujinhui), 106–8; Mongol, 108, 116; Uighur, 132, 219

Association for Mainland Refugee Assistance, 208

atomic bomb, Soviet, 199

Austro-Hungarian empire, 33

Austro-Marxist ethnocultural autonomy, 105, 180–81, 234

autonomy, administrative, 170; Chinese Communist ethnopolitics, 25, 105, 173–82, 181*fig.*, 192, 214–15, 234–35; "eggshell autonomy," 185, 192; "high-level" *(gaodu zizhi)*, 170, 172, 197, 203, 213; lacking in Uighur Autonomous Region, 174; Sheng Shicai making no attempt with, 105; Yang Zengxin and, 23–25, 52–54, 54*fig.*, 58, 62–66. *See also* ethnocultural autonomy; national determination; regional autonomy

Bachman, David, 226

"back to the homestead" work teams, Anti-Imperialist Society, 106–7

"backward," 13, 33, 108, 188, 189

Bakich, Andrei, 60–61, 61*fig.*, 94

Barmin, V. A., 142

Baytik Mountains, Osman Batur camp, 166–67

begs, Turkic, 26, 29, 30*fig.*, 231

Beijing: journey from Urumchi to, 17. *See also* Chinese Communists; Manchu court; Qing empire

Beria, Lavrentii, 131, 142, 148, 153, 161

Beshir Wang, 85

Bolsheviks: Bolshevik revolution (1917–23), 49, 50, 54, 55, 69, 140; Ili Provisional Trade Accord, 71–72, 75, 80; learning about Xinjiang, 68. *See also* Russian civil war; Soviet Union

bomb, atomic, 199

British: archival sources, 14; Basutoland chief's visit, 27; chargé d'affaires in Beijing, 199–200; consul in Urumchi, 155; Empire, 10–11, 18, 38, 59, 83, 195; Hunza, 195; India, 18, 38, 83; India-based diplomats (1950s), 199–202; King George V, 27; and refugees from Chinese Communists, 199–202; and Tibet, 42

Brubaker, Rogers, 181–82, 183

Bu Daoming, 146, 197

Buddhism, 129, 226. *See also* Lamaists

Bulgin River, Osman Batur refuge, 124, 137

Burhan Shahidi, 31–32, 34; Chinese Communists and, 34, 47, 170, 205, 216; Nationalists and, 144–45, 157*fig.*, 216, 233; Xinjiang governorship, 47, 157*fig.*, 170, 192, 205, 212; and Xinjiang name, 179; Yang Zengxin and, 31–32, 34, 144–45

"camelgraph," 17

cannibalism, 219, 257n49

Carter, Jimmy, 224

censorship, media, by Yang Zengxin, 57

Central Daily News, 164, 165

chauvinism: Han, 8, 35–37, 107, 154–55, 166, 171–72, 189; Nationalist, 154, 164, 174; Russian, 37

Chiang Ching-kuo, 143, 147

Chiang Kai-shek, 36, 83, 88; *China's Destiny*, 172; diary, 124; ethnopolitics, 127, 147, 163, 166, 171–74, 233; funds for refugees from Chinese Communists, 212, 216; Ili rebellion, 150, 153–55, 163, 166; Jin Shuren trial, 36–37; Masud Sabri governorship, 163, 166, 176; "one China" policy, 224; and separatists, 212, 215; and Sheng Shicai, 95–96, 103, 124, 128–30, 138–39, 206; son, 143, 147; Wang Jingwei rival of, 91, 96, 127; Wu Zhongxin and, 146–47, 153; Yang Zengxin and, 76–77; Yolbars Khan and, 101, 201, 223–25

China: archival sources, 14–16, 129, 172. *See also* Chinese Communists; modern China; Nationalists; Qing empire; Xinjiang

China News, 163

China's Destiny, 172

Chinese Academy of Social Sciences, 15

"Chinese characteristics," 177–79, 234, 238

Chinese Communists, 10; affirmative action, 169–94, 234–35; cadres, 119, 179–80, 181*fig.*, 186–92, 211, 234–35; Central Committee, 169; challenges to, 237–38; Cultural Revolution (1966–76), 34, 221, 226, 230; early setbacks, 171; economics, 113–14, 177–78, 184; "empire of nations," 9, 177; ethnopolitics, 25, 47, 105, 169–94, 181*fig.*, 214–15, 234–35; ethnopopulism, 34, 177, 180, 184–85, 193–94, 197–98, 226–27, 234–35, 237; Great Leap Forward (1958–61), 219, 230, 257n49; Han members, 12, 104–5, 119, 187–92, 234–35; Han migrants, 40–41, 175, 182–93, 234–35; Hundred Flowers movement, 192; vs. imperialism, 106, 171, 178–79; Mao Zemin, 113–15, 119, 125, 180, 233; May 4th directive, 131; name for Urumchi, 241n11; narratives of political legitimacy, 46–47, 177, 184, 192, 235; National People's Congress, 172–73; Nationalists supplanted by, 169–72, 182–83, 199–200; People's Liberation Army, 182, 199–200; refugees from, 198–226, 202*fig.*, 204*fig.*; regional autonomy policies, 25, 105, 173–82, 181*fig.*, 192, 214–15, 234–35; Sheng Shicai purges, 119, 124, 180; Sino-Soviet split, 41, 252n49; Sixth Party Congress, 128; and Tibet, 171, 199–200, 215, 225, 226; Yan'an headquarters, 113–14, 119, 138, 171; Yang Zengxin statue, 230; Zhang Zhizhong and, 150, 205. *See also* Mao Zedong; People's Republic of China

Chinese consulates, in Soviet Central Asia, 135–37; Almaty, 245n57; Andijan, 135, 245n57; Semipalatinsk, 198–99, 245n57; Tashkent, 89, 99, 245–46n57; Yang Zengxin's, 65*fig.*, 68–74, 232, 245–46n57; Zaysan, 135–36, 145, 245n57

Chinese embassy in Moscow, 86–87, 127, 137, 150, 198, 246n57

Chinese-language schools, 5

Chinese-speaking Muslims. *See* Hui

Chongqing: Isa and Emin, 101, 146; Masud, 101, 146; Nationalist base, 124, 136, 138–39, 145–53, 200; Sheng Shicai, 129, 138–39, 200

Chu Anping, 185–86, 187

Chu Chia-hua, 205

CIA, 199

civil service examinations, 4, 18, 26, 42

Cold War, 198–207, 215, 224

colonialism, 10–11; Han, 41–42, 102–3, 118, 164–66, 185, 193; Nationalist, 164–65; nationality policies and, 178; ordinary citizens' assessments, 185; Sheng Shicai and, 106; Xinjiang as "colonial name," 218. *See also* imperialism

"colony" *(zhimindi)* of the inner provinces, Xinjiang as, 25, 40

Comintern, 94, 95, 105, 118, 232–33

communism. *See* Leninism; Marxism

Communist administrators. *See* Chinese Communists; Soviet Union

Confucianism, 32, 35, 36, 67, 87, 143–44

conservative ethnopolitics. *See* ethno-elitism

consulates: American in Xinjiang, 149–50, 154–55, 205; British in Urumchi, 155; Qing, 73; Western concept, 68, 74, 232. *See also* Chinese consulates; Soviet consulates

Cooper, Frederick, 236

Cultural Revolution (1966–76), 34, 221, 226, 230

Cumming-Bruce, F. E., 201–2

Dalai Lama, 194, 225–26

dance troupe, Zhang Zhizhong's, 164, 165*fig.*

Daoism, 75–76

daoyin (circuit intendant): Aksu, 53, 72; Altay, 64, 121; Kashgar, 111

Delilhan Haji, 201–2, 206–7, 222–23

Delilhan Sugurbaev, 159, 161–62, 167–68, 201, 222–23

Deng Liqun, 169, 171, 175

Deng Xiaoping, 179

dependent intermediaries, 21, 26–34, 30*fig.*, 144–45

"dependent territory" *(shudi)*, 4, 22

diaries: Chiang Kai-shek, 124; Wu Zhongxin, 15, 129, 141, 143, 145, 147

difference: discourse of, 7–8, 32–33; institutions of, 8, 10, 21–22, 25, 132, 177, 232–33, 258n4. *See also* ethnocultural difference; "politics of difference"

"disaster relief" campaign, 115–16

donation campaigns, 115–17

"double assimilation," 176–77

duban (military governor), 90; Sheng Shicai, 45–46, 83–84, 88–93, 97*fig.*, 103–23, 127–29, 137–39, 158–59, 162, 180, 205

Dunhuang, 60

Dushanzi, oil, 149, 151*fig.*, 152

earthquake: Almaty, 198–99; Lanzhou, 115–16

East Turkestan Refugee Association, 216, 223–24, 226

East Turkestan Republic, 86–87; Ahmetjan Qasimi president, 168; armies,

147–48, 168; boundaries, 151*fig.*; briefly independent, 83, 99–100; Chinese Communists and, 170; Ili as future capital of, 132; Ili rebellion, 139, 147–48, 151*fig.*; Isa Yusuf Alptekin and, 157*fig.*, 202, 204*fig.*, 214, 216, 217–18, 223–24, 226; Nationalists countering Soviets over, 157*fig.*, 169, 233; Osman Batur and, 159, 160, 161; Soviet support, 157*fig.*, 159, 161, 169; Three Districts Revolution, 170

economics: Altay, 121; Chinese Communist, 113–14, 177–78, 184, 186; currency, 79; donation campaigns, 115–17; education, 115; ethnopolitical discourse taking backseat to, 182, 190–92; exchange students, 217; extractive, 81*fig.*, 108; Jin Shuren, 79–80, 82–87, 125; language of, 187; military, 45, 48, 56, 78–79, 82–87, 92–95, 98, 103–4, 113, 115, 116, 191; Nationalist, 125, 150–51, 152, 166; rebel assets, 114–15; refugees from Chinese Communists, 208–24; "shared funds" *(xiexiang)* of "inner provinces" *(neisheng)*, 22, 79; Sheng Shicai, 103, 108, 112–17, 121–25, 233; Xinjiang Production and Construction Corps, 175, 183; Yang Zengxin, 20, 45, 48, 56, 78–79, 82, 150, 191; Yang Zengxin statue, 228; Yolbars' son, 224. *See also* agriculture; mineral wealth; modernization; taxes; trade; workers

education: Burhan Shahidi, 145; Sheng Shicai, 106–10, 115. *See also* exchange students; intellectuals; language; print culture; schools

"eggshell autonomy," 185, 192

Egypt, fund-raising for refugees, 208

elites, 33–34; glass ceiling for non-Hans, 207–8, 217, 225; Manchu bannermen,

4, 13, 22, 26, 38; Mongol, 4, 13, 22, 26, 29–30, 32, 38, 58, 82, 87, 231; non-Han nobility, 5, 8, 13, 22–32, 42, 58–59, 82–87, 91, 101–2, 105, 108, 112–13, 117, 129, 146, 200, 203, 226–27, 231–35; Turkic/Muslim nobility, 5, 22–32, 58–59, 82–87, 91, 102, 113, 200, 203, 226–27, 231, 232. *See also* chauvinism; ethnoelitism; Han; warlords

Emin (Mohammed Emin Bugra): death, 217; ethnopopulism, 101, 153–54, 157*fig.*, 164, 202*fig.*, 203, 207–17, 225, 233; Istanbul, 204*fig.*, 208–17; Nationalists and, 153–54, 157*fig.*, 164, 202–17, 202*fig.*, 233; refugee from Xinjiang, 172, 201–26, 202*fig.*

empire-state, 236

empires: "best practices," 13, 21, 180; British, 10–11, 18, 38, 59, 83, 195; collapse of, 49–88; dismembered after World War I, 33; divide and rule, 9; "empire of nations," 9, 177, 236, 237; institutionalization of difference, 21–22; modern China, 10, 12–16, 231, 236; modes of governance, 3–4; national empire *(minzu diguo)*, 9, 235–36, 237; northern and northwestern associations, 22; Ottoman, 9, 33, 59; "politics of difference," 9, 13–14, 33, 50, 231; repertoires of rule, 17–48, 68, 74, 87, 231, 237–38; transition from, 8, 9; as type of power, 9, 10; as type of state, 9, 10–11, 50, 236–37. *See also* Qing empire; Russian empire

ethnic chauvinism, Han, 8, 35–37, 107, 154–55, 166, 171–72, 189

ethnic classification, 10, 258n4. *See also* ethnocultural difference

"ethnic policy inspection" *(minzu zhengce jiancha)*, Urumchi factories, 186, 189–90 ethnic self-rule: and nation-state, 5, 13. *See also* national determination

ethnic tensions: demographics and, 183; Soviets remedying, 107; Urumchi factory workers, 235; Yang Zengxin deflecting, 37–41, 44, 46. *See also* rebellions; war

ethno-elitism, 13, 32–35, 88, 237–38; Chinese Communist, 34, 177; Huang Musong, 91, 98; Japan, 101; Jin Shuren repudiating, 77–79, 81*fig.*, 82, 175, 232; Khoja Niyaz, 86, 98; Luo Wen'gan, 98; narratives of political legitimacy, 33–34, 36, 41–48, 162, 168, 177, 184; Nationalist, 101, 129, 130, 168, 184, 197–98, 233; Sheng Shicai and, 109–10, 112, 117; Soviet, 160; Uighurs excluded, 99; Wu Zhongxin, 129, 143–46, 159, 172, 184, 197, 233; Yang Zengxin, 24*fig.*, 33, 46, 58, 61, 77–79, 82, 86, 96, 129, 231; Yolbars Khan, 86, 98. *See also* elites

ethnocultural autonomy, 128, 169, 180–81, 234; Austro-Marxist, 105, 180–81, 234; Chinese Communist, 234–35; Sheng Shicai and, 105–8, 112–13, 117, 180–81, 234. *See also* regional autonomy (*diqu zizhi*)

ethnocultural difference, 6, 11, 12. *See also* ethnic classification; ethnic tensions; *individual ethnic groups*

ethnopolitics, 32–33, 125, 130, 162–63, 231, 238; archives, 4; British in India, 18, 38; Chinese Communist, 14, 25, 47, 105, 169–94, 181*fig.*, 214–15, 234–35; "enlightened," 35, 37, 98–99, 130, 155, 162, 164, 166, 172, 187, 205; Nationalist, 37, 90, 98–99, 126–30, 143, 147, 154–58, 157*fig.*, 163–73, 177, 197, 223–24, 233–34; Sheng Shicai, 125, 128, 129–30;

Soviet, 130, 162, 173, 178, 197; Tibet, 225; Wu Zhongxin, 143, 147, 172; Yang Zengxin, 48, 82, 99–100. *See also* affirmative action; ethno-elitism; ethnopopulism; national determination; nationality policies; "politics of difference"

ethnopopulism, 13, 33–37, 68, 86, 89–126, 237, 238; Chinese Communist, 34, 177, 180, 184–85, 193–94, 197–98, 226–27, 234–35, 237; Han narrative of legitimacy, 46–48, 103, 106, 117, 168, 169, 192–94; Kazak/ Ili, 100–101, 120–24, 125, 145–47, 154–55, 157*fig.*, 162, 166–69, 233; narratives of political legitimacy, 34, 46–48, 103, 106, 117, 127, 158, 162, 167–69, 183–85, 192–94; Nationalists and, 46–47, 96–102, 128, 130, 145–47, 154–58, 157*fig.*, 168, 174, 196–98, 202*fig.*, 203, 207, 233; Sheng Shicai, 97*fig.*, 103, 105–8, 112–13, 117, 123–27, 129, 133–34, 177, 180, 232–33; Soviet, 13, 33–34, 37, 46, 58, 68, 94–95, 97*fig.*, 101, 127, 153, 157*fig.*, 159–60, 166, 168–69, 178, 196–98, 232–34; Uighur, 99–101, 145–47, 153–58, 157*fig.*, 164, 202*fig.*, 203, 207–18, 225, 233, 237. *See also* affirmative action; ethnic self-rule

eunuchs, 26, 31

Europe: governance modes of empires, 17, 18–19. *See also* Allied powers; British; France; Germans; World War I; World War II

examinations, civil service, 4, 18, 26, 42

exchange students: Xinjiang refugees, 217, 223; Xinjiang-Germany, 83; Xinjiang-Soviet, 103

"expert" knowledge, 34

extractive policies, 81*fig.*, 108. *See also* taxes

factory workers, Urumchi, 14, 184, 185–92, 235
famines, 219, 257n49. *See also* starvation
Fan Yaonan, 244n12
Feng Yuxiang, 7, 76, 78
Feng Zuwen, 135
food. *See* agriculture; famines; starvation
France: banning veils, 238; ethnopolitics in Vietnam, 18, 38
"free China," 198, 227, 237
Frontier Culture (Bianjiang wenhua), 214
Fu Bingchang, 137
Fu Zuoyi, 95
Fujian, 207

Gansu, 85; earthquake, 115–16; Han army conscripts, 83, 87; Hui, 42, 44, 86–92, 102, 104; Jin Shuren, 78, 101; Muslims, 19, 40, 42, 43; rebellions, 19, 40; warlords, 84–96, 102–4; Yang Zengxin background, 42, 43, 53; Zhang Zhizhong as northwestern commissioner, 156
Gao Boyu, 148–49
geopolitics, 49; army resources, 125; Chinese Communists, 20, 180, 198, 235; "eggshell autonomy," 185; ethnopopulism and, 201–2; "Han colonialism," 185; imperial "best practices," 13; imperial repertoires of rule, 21; Inner Asian conquest dynasty, 22; Jin Shuren, 78, 232; Kazak and Kyrgyz refugee crisis, 52; nation-state, 5, 13, 62, 231, 236, 238; national determination valorized in, 13, 93–94, 174, 190, 193–94, 231, 236; Nationalist, 47, 174, 197, 198, 201–2, 235; "politics of difference" in borderlands, 7; Russian civil war, 23, 50; and Sheng Shicai switch to Nationalists, 124; Soviet affirmative action, 69; Tibet receiving more attention than Xinjiang, 226–27;

"two Chinas," 235; warlord, 7, 50, 76, 232; World War I, 50; Xinjiang future (1950s), 201–2; Yang Zengxin assassination, 77, 232; Yang Zengxin's semiautonomous jurisdictions, 23, 62. *See also* revolution; war; West
Germans: dependent intermediaries, 26, 31; Jin Shuren trade, 83; after World War I, 33; World War II, 125, 127, 171
glass ceiling, for non-Hans, 207–8, 217, 225
governance modes, 3–6, 17, 20; European, 17, 18–19; Japanese, 3–4, 17; Soviet, 64–67; Xinjiang, 3–6, 17–48. *See also* "politics of difference"; repertoires of rule
government in exile: Tibet, 225–26; Xinjiang, 195–227
Great Leap Forward (1958–61), 219, 230, 257n49
Great War. *See* World War I
Guang Lu, 114
Gucheng, siege of (1921), 39
guilds, Han, 116
Guo Songling, 101

hajj, 211–14
Hami, 22, 23, 84–85; corvée labor, 28, 84; khanates, 23–29, 82–85, 91, 102, 113, 200, 203, 226–27, 232; land reform (1931), 102; rebel assets, 115; rebellions, 28–29, 38, 83–86, 94, 98, 100, 105–6, 125, 175; Shah Maqsut, 23, 27, 28–29, 83–85, 91, 232; Yolbars Khan *ordabegi* (major domo), 85, 200, 203, 226–27
Han, 11, 36, 170; chauvinism, 8, 35–37, 107, 154–55, 166, 171–72, 189; colonialism, 41–42, 102–3, 118, 164–66, 185, 193; crisis of political legitimacy, 162, 169; disgruntled peasants, 79, 84–85; "elder brother," 41, 185, 193;

Han (*continued*)

"exploited" but unmarked, 11; glass ceiling imposed on non-Hans, 207–8, 217, 225; guilds, 116; "heathen," 142; Isa and Emin vs., 100–101, 155, 205, 210–17; Japanese-trained, 83–84, 88, 97*fig.*, 101–2; migrants, 5, 40–41, 83–87, 175, 182–93, 234–35; narrative of ethnopopulist legitimacy, 46–48, 103, 117, 168, 169, 192–94; narrative of nation-state, 49; nationalism, 8, 35–37, 90; nationalization projects, 78; New Armies dominated by, 5, 37–39; newly defined, 36; non-Hans to learn from, 181*fig.*, 187, 234; refugees from Chinese Communists, 205; segregated, 183–84, 257n49; Xinjiang population percentage, 40, 184; Xinjiang Production and Construction Corps, 174, 183; Xinjiang Uighur Autonomous Region and, 181*fig.*; "yellow filth," 14–15, 86, 103

Han Fuju, 90

Han officials, 3–13, 17–91, 107, 238–39; alienation of Tibet and Outer Mongolia, 43; archival sources, 14–15; caps and sashes, 48; Chinese Communist, 12, 119, 187–92, 234–35; Comintern view of, 94, 118; in ethno-elitist alliance, 13; ethnopopulist role, 13, 46; governance modes, 3–6, 17–48; Hami peasants demanding, 84; vs. Han chauvinism, 36–37; Hunza and, 195; Ili Provisional Trade Accord, 71; Ili rebellion, 15, 130–53; Jin Shuren, 128, 175; nationalist threat, 11–13, 33–34, 36, 48, 67–68, 79, 236; Nationalists and, 90, 100, 157*fig.*, 182–83; Qing, 17–48, 53; and Russians and Soviets, 13, 20–21, 62, 70–71, 130–31; Sheng Shicai, 103, 105, 118–19, 124–25, 205; Urumchi

residents, 8, 12–13, 15, 18, 27–28, 231; Wang Shunan as, 26; in Xinjiang consulates, 104; Yang Zengxin, 26, 41–42; Yang Zengxin's management of, 23, 25, 29, 31–32, 42, 56–57, 63, 104–5, 129; after Yuan Shikai, 51

Hedin, Sven, 97*fig.*

Hirsch, Francine, 176–77

historians, 10–12, 15, 64. *See also* archival sources

Hokkaido, governance modes, 3–4

holy war, 5

Huang Musong, 91–92, 98, 99

Huang Wenbi, 44, 78

huaxia (civilized culture sphere), 36

Hui (Chinese-speaking Muslims): Gansu, 42, 44, 86–92, 102, 104; Jin Shuren ousters vs., 86–87; Ma Fuxing, 45, 53, 57, 58, 63, 94; Ma Zhongying, 86–96, 102–4; religious schools, 44; Russian, 62, 66; soldiers, 26, 38, 63, 104; Urumchi factory workers, 14, 185–89; in Xinjiang Uighur Autonomous Region, 181*fig.*; Yang Zengxin and, 38, 42, 44, 45, 63, 66; Yolbars Khan, 204*fig.*

Hundred Flowers movement, 192

hunting rights, nomad, 120–21

Hunza, 195–98

Hunza Autonomous Region, 196, 197–98

Husayin Taiji, 200

Hutchison, J. C., 199–200

Ili, 151*fig.*; activists in 1960s, 185; Annenkov, 60; autonomy/administrative boundaries, 23, 52, 105, 169, 181*fig.*; Bolsheviks and, 68; ethnopopulism, 100–101, 145–47, 154–55, 157*fig.*, 166–69; Kazak Autonomous District, 105, 192; Masud Sabri from, 99; mineral wealth, 151*fig.*, 233; New Armies, 37–38; Qing, 22; rebellions,

15, 28–29, 58, 130–70, 151*fig.*, 201; Soviet consulate, 134, 140, 151; trade hub, 152; in Xinjiang Uighur Autonomous Region, 181*fig.*; Zhang Peiyuan, 92

Ili Provisional Trade Accord (Soviet-Xinjiang), 71–72, 75, 80

Ili valley: Chinese Communists, 169; Ili rebellion, 139–42; Russian soldiers, 60; Sibe and Solon, 38

imperialism, 10–13, 163, 171; Anti-Imperialist Society, 106–8, 116; Chinese, 12, 58, 107; Chinese Communists vs., 106, 171, 178–79; Han, 193; Japan, 12; naming Xinjiang Uighur Autonomous Region (Xinjiang Weiwuer Zizhiqu) and, 179–80; Western, 12, 178–80. *See also* colonialism; empires

India: British Empire, 18, 38, 83; Hunza and, 195, 196; Masud Sabri, 100; refugees from Chinese Communists, 199–202, 204*fig.*; Tibet government in exile, 225–26

Inner Mongolia, 197

institutions, of difference, 8, 10, 21–22, 25, 132, 177, 232–33, 258n4

integrationist policies: Chinese Communist, 174–76, 193, 237; Jin Shuren, 81*fig.*, 232; Qing, 23–25, 28, 40, 81*fig.*, 174–76, 231. *See also* national unity

intellectuals: Han, 6; Ili rebellion, 134, 141–42, 153–56; and Sheng-Soviet alliance, 117; Uighur, 98–101, 153–58, 157*fig.*, 193–94, 203

Isa Yusuf Alptekin, 201–26, 204*fig.*; Chinese Communists and, 171–72; dance troupe, 164, 165*fig.*; death, 223; and East Turkestan Republic/Refugee Association, 157*fig.*, 202, 204*fig.*, 214, 216, 217–18, 223–24, 226; ethnopopulism, 99–101, 145–47, 153–56, 157*fig.*, 164, 202*fig.*, 203, 207–18,

225, 233; Istanbul, 204*fig.*, 208–23; Nationalists and, 99–101, 128, 145–47, 153–56, 164, 174, 202–22, 202*fig.*, 204*fig.*, 233; refugee from Xinjiang, 172, 201–26, 202*fig.*, 204*fig.*

Isfahan: Paxton, 200, 201, 209; refugees from Chinese Communists, 199–200

Istanbul: Masud Sabri, 99; Xinjiang refugees, 22, 204*fig.*, 208–23

Janimhan, 172, 201

Japan: governance modes, 3–4, 17; Han officials admiring, 19; Hans trained by, 83–84, 88, 97*fig.*, 101–2; imperialism, 12; Manchukuo, 6, 12, 101; "politics of difference," 101; Sino-Japanese War, 115; Twenty-One Demands to Yuan Shikai, 122; Wang Jingwei collaborating with, 127; World War II, 149, 171

Jews, 26, 31

Jin Shuren, 77–88, 96; Gansu, 78, 101; governor of Xinjiang (1928–33), 77–88, 81*fig.*, 91, 98, 99–100, 125, 175; Hami khanate abolished by, 29, 84–85, 102; Hami rebellion, 29, 38, 83–86, 94, 98, 100, 125, 175; Nationalists and, 37, 83–85, 88, 89–90, 91, 98–102, 127–28; ouster, 81*fig.*, 83–90, 144; "politics of difference" repudiated by, 77–79, 81*fig.*, 82, 175, 232; and Soviets, 83, 87–88, 94–95, 98, 125, 190, 232; trial, 37, 98–102, 127

Jin state, ethnic classification, 258n4

Jungaria, 94

Kali Beg, 209–10, 214

Karashahr, 29–30, 110; Han officials fleeing posts at, 118, 144; Incarnate Lama of, 82, 85, 232; Jin Shuren and, 38, 82, 83; Manchuqjab, 109–10, 113, 144, 172

Kashgar, 52–58, 62, 94; *daoyin* (circuit intendant), 111; Hunza, 195–97; Ili rebellion, 132–33, 134, 139; Ma Fuxing, 45, 53, 57, 58, 63, 94; and self-rule, 67–68; Soviet affirmative action, 70; Soviet consulate, 134

Kashmir: Nationalists and, 196; Xinjiang refugees, 201, 206–9, 224

Kazak Autonomous District, Ili, 105, 192

Kazak Exodus, 207

Kazakhstan: Almaty, 135, 198–99; atomic bomb, 199; Ili rebellion, 135; May 4th directive, 131; ordinary citizens' assessments, 185, 191–92; Soviet affirmative action, 64–67, 65*fig.*, 95, 127

Kazaks: Chinese, 65*fig.*, 66; Delilhan family, 159, 161–62, 167–68, 201–2, 206–7, 222–23; ethnopopulism, 120–26, 157*fig.*, 162, 233; Ili as Kazak Autonomous District, 105, 192; Ili rebellion, 130, 137–42, 147–48, 152–53, 157*fig.*, 158–68, 201; Janimhan, 172, 201; Kazak and Kyrgyz refugee crisis (1916), 50–55, 54*fig.*; military exclusion, 38; Nationalists and, 126, 143–44, 170, 207–10, 233; prepubescent marriages, 110; refugees from Chinese Communists, 199–222; Soviet nationality policies, 60–61, 64–67, 65*fig.*, 95, 168; Urumchi factory workers, 14, 185–90; Xinjiang expatriate workers in Russia, 65*fig.*, 74, 95; Xinjiang republican ethno-elitism with, 26, 29–30; Xinjiang Uighur Autonomous Region, 181*fig.*. *See also* Altay; Osman Batur

khan, Osman Batur title, 160–62, 184

Khan Tengri, 156

khanates, 22–30, 59; Hami, 23–29, 82–85, 91, 102, 113, 200, 203, 226–27, 232; Jin Shuren abolishing, 29, 84–85, 102

Khobdo, 22, 39

Khoja Niyaz Haji, 85–86, 94, 98, 100, 105–6, 111, 114, 128

Khorgas Pass, 71, 140

Khotan, 103; Hami rebellion, 83–86; Ili rebellion, 133; Ma Hushan, 103–4; Muslim nobility, 22, 23, 30*fig.*; school, 115; short-lived separatist state, 83, 99–100

Koktogay, 122, 152, 162, 167

Korea, 73

Kucha, 22, 23, 113, 115–16, 147–48, 182–83

Kudashev, Nikolai, 55

Kyrgyz: Kazak and Kyrgyz refugee crisis (1916), 50–55, 54*fig.*; in Xinjiang Uighur Autonomous Region, 181*fig.*

Kyrgyzstan, 95, 131

labor. *See* workers

Ladakh, 196

Lamaists: Dalai Lama, 194, 225–26; Incarnate Lama of Karashahr, 82, 85, 232; Incarnate Lama of Tacheng, 112; Panchen Lama, 226; Urumchi Lama temple, 108

language: Chinese-language schools, 5; Delilhan Haji skills, 222; factory, 186–87, 189–90; interpreters between people and rulers, 48; Kazak Autonomous District, 192; print culture, 107; Russian-language schools, 135; Uighur calligraphy, 164, 165*fig.*; Xinjiang name, 179

Lattimore, Eleanor, 31

Lattimore, Owen, 12, 31, 38, 57, 66

legitimacy. *See* political legitimacy

Lenin, V. I., 69, 94

Leninism, 49, 96, 169, 177–78. *See also* Bolsheviks; Marxism

Levenson, Joseph, 239

Liankui, 18

Liao state, ethnic classification, 258n4
Lin Jing, 84
Liu Mengchun, 157*fig.*
Liu Wenlong, 77
Liu Zerong, 150
Los Angeles Times, 163
Lu Xiaozu, 121
Luo Wen'gan, 92, 98
Lyuba, Viktor, 58

Ma Fuxing, 45, 53, 57, 58, 63, 94
Ma Hushan, 103–4
Ma Lin, 96
Ma Shaowu, 111
Ma Zhongying, 86–96, 102–4
Mackiernan, Douglas, 199–200
Manas River, Ili rebellion, 149, 151*fig.*
Manchu court, 35–36, 40; bannermen,
    4, 13, 22, 26, 38; fall (1911), 5; and
    Muslim khanates, 22; Yang Zengxin's
    audience with, 42. *See also* Qing
    empire
Manchukuo, 6, 12, 101
Manchuqjab, 109–10, 113, 144, 172, 233
Manchuria: Han officials, 12; Sino-Soviet
    Friendship Treaty, 149
Mannerheim, Gustaf, 20
Mao Zedong, 171, 183, 194; brother Mao
    Zemin, 113–15, 119, 125, 180, 233;
    Hundred Flowers movement, 192; and
    Outer Mongolia, 252n49; and segre-
    gationism, 184; and separatists, 215;
    Xinjiang name, 179–80
Mao Zemin, 113–15, 119, 125, 180, 233
Maqsut, Shah, Muslim prince of Hami, 23,
    27–29, 83–85, 91, 232
marriages, 23; Han-Mongol, 118; Han-
    Uighur, 182–83; prepubescent, 110
Martin, Terry, 46
Marxism: Austro-Marxist ethnocultural
    autonomy, 105, 180–81, 234; Marxist-
    Leninist dialectics, 96; Marxist-

Leninist principles of national
    determination, 169
Masud Sabri, 99–101, 128, 162–64, 171–
    72; Chinese Communists and, 172,
    173, 205; Nationalists and, 99–101,
    128, 145–47, 153–56, 157*fig.*, 163,
    166, 174, 176, 233; separatist rhetoric,
    100–101, 154–56, 163, 173; son, 222;
    Western media on appointment, 163,
    253n75; Xinjiang governorship, 99,
    156, 163–68, 170, 176, 212
May 4th directive, "national revival
    groups," 131
May 4th Movement, Treaty of Versailles
    linked to, 49
May 30th Incident, Northern Expedition
    linked to, 49
Mecca: hajj, 211–14; World Muslim Coun-
    cil, 217–18
media: Jin Shuren trial, 37; on Masud
    Sabri appointment, 163; on refugees
    from Chinese Communists, 207; Yang
    Zengxin censorship, 57. *See also*
    archival sources
migrants: Han, 5, 40–41, 83–87, 175,
    182–93, 234–35. *See also* refugees
military: economics, 45, 48, 56, 78–79,
    82–87, 92–95, 98, 103–4, 113, 115,
    116, 191; for Jin Shuren ouster,
    85–86, 89; Kazak, 66; Kazak and
    Kyrgyz refugee crisis (1916), 52–55;
    Manchu and Mongol bannermen, 4,
    13, 22, 26, 38. *See also* armies;
    arms; *duban* (military governor);
    soldiers
mineral wealth, Xinjiang: Altay, 121–22,
    151*fig.*, 152, 161, 167, 233; Soviets
    and, 103, 121–22, 152, 161, 167, 233;
    Xinjiang Tin Mines Agreement ("Sin-
    Tin" accord), 122. *See also* oil
Ming emperors, 26
minzu (minority nationality) regime, 10

minzu diguo (national empire), 9, 235–36, 237

minzu zhengce jiancha (ethnic policy inspection), 186, 189–90

modern China: empire, 10, 12–16, 231, 236; "empire of difference," 13–14; empire in transition, 231; historians, 10, 12, 15; national empire, 236. *See also* Chinese Communists; Taiwan

modernity, socialist, 46, 113, 177

modernization: cultural, 99; "primitive accumulation," 80; Xinjiang projects, 18–19, 78, 80, 83, 125, 232

Mohammad Jamal Khan: Commissioner (Zhuanyuan), 196, 198; mir of Hunza, 195–97

Mohammed Emin Bugra. *See* Emin

monarchy, 8, 51

Mongolian People's Republic, 120, 149

Mongols: Altay, 66, 119–21, 147, 166–67; Chinese imperialism against, 12; elites, 4, 13, 22, 26, 29–30, 32, 38, 58, 82, 231; and Han migrants, 40; Ili rebellion, 147; Khobdo invasion, 39; Lama temple in Urumchi, 108; Qing and, 38, 43; Russians and, 42, 60–62, 65*fig.*, 66–68, 82, 120; Sheng Shicai's ethnocultural institutions, 108, 109–10, 116; supranational civic ideology, 35; Torgut, 29–30, 38, 82, 85, 109–10, 113, 144, 233; Xinjiang Provincial Assembly, 32; in Xinjiang Uighur Autonomous Region, 181*fig.*. *See also* Outer Mongolia

Mou Weitong, 89, 90

Muccio, John, 131

Mullaney, Thomas, 46–47

Muslims, 4; brief rise and fall of an independent Islamic state, 4, 135–36; Chinese, 65*fig.*, 66; Chinese-language schools, 5; elites, 5, 22–32, 58–59, 82–87, 91, 102, 113, 200, 226–27,

231, 232; factory workers, 187, 189; Gansu, 19, 40, 42, 43; Hunza, 196, 198; Ili rebellion, 130, 134, 135, 141–42, 154–55; Jin Shuren ousters, 86–87; Mou Weitong on, 89, 90; Nationalists and, 29, 98–99, 146, 211–12, 217–19; "new method" schools, 67–68; Russian, 62, 64, 65*fig.*, 66, 71–72; and self-rule, 42, 58–59, 62, 67–68; Tibet's fate compared, 226; veils banned, 238; World Muslim Council, 211, 217–18; Xinjiang Provincial Assembly, 32; Xinjiang refugees from Chinese Communists, 203, 206–10; Yang Zengxin's legitimacy with, 42–44. *See also* Hami; Hui (Chinese-speaking Muslims); Turkic peoples

narratives of political legitimacy, 34, 88, 93–94; Chinese Communist, 46–47, 177, 184, 192, 235; conservative ethno-elitist, 33–34, 36, 41–48, 162, 168, 177, 184; Han ethnopopulist, 46–48, 103, 106, 117, 168, 169, 192–94; Nationalist, 46, 127, 158, 168, 170, 225, 234; progressive ethnopopulist, 34, 46–48, 103, 106, 117, 127, 158, 162, 167–69, 183–84, 192–94; refugee community, 198, 218, 225; Sheng Shicai, 46, 103, 106, 117, 130; Soviet, 46, 130; Yang Zengxin, 33–34, 36, 41–48

nation-state, 5–6, 9, 33–34, 59, 237; "Chinese nation-state," 12; empire-state instead of, 236; geopolitics, 5, 13, 62, 231, 236, 238; Han narrative of, 49; specter of, 13, 59

national determination, 11–12, 238; Chinese Communists and, 103–4, 168, 169, 171, 179, 190; geopolitical valorization of, 13, 93–94, 174,

190, 193–94, 231, 236; Han officials and threat of, 11–13, 33–34, 36, 48, 67–68, 79, 236; Marxist-Leninist principles, 169; Nationalists and, 86–87; Sheng Shicai and, 93–94, 103, 205, 232; Soviet support for, 64–68, 65*fig*., 79, 94–95; world political discourse of, 193; Yang Zengxin and, 41–42, 58–59, 62–68. *See also* ethnic self-rule; national liberation; national republics; nationalism

national empire *(minzu diguo)*, 9, 235–36, 237

National Geographic, 207

"national humiliation" *(guochi)*: Chinese Communists and, 47, 180; Nationalist discourse of, 47, 128, 129–30; Yang Zengxin and, 231

national liberation, 174; Chinese Communists and, 106, 169; Hami rebellion, 94, 100; Ili rebellion, 156, 164–65; Soviets and, 59–60, 64, 79, 94, 95, 134; Yang Zengxin and, 59–60, 63, 79. *See also* national determination; separatism

"national representative conferences," 105

national republics: Chinese Communist eschewing, 178, 180; Mongolian People's Republic, 120, 149; Soviets and, 64–70, 65*fig*., 94–95, 168, 178, 179. *See also* autonomy; East Turkestan Republic; national determination; People's Republic of China; Republic of China (1912–49)

"national revival groups," 131

"national salvation" *(jiuguo)* goal, 7–8

national sovereignty, 177–78, 215–16. *See also* national unity

national unity, 215–16, 223–27. *See also* integrationist policies; national sovereignty

nationalism, 81*fig*., 86–87, 238; Han, 8, 35–37, 90; Han officials and threat of, 11–13, 33–34, 36, 48, 67, 79, 236; national empire and, 235–36, 237; Soviet strategy with, 64–68, 65*fig*., 79, 94–95; Yang Zengxin vs., 24*fig*., 36, 58–59, 62–63, 67, 68, 79, 231–32. *See also* affirmative action; autonomy; national determination; national liberation

Nationalists, 49–88; "CC Clique," 164; chauvinism, 154, 164, 174; Chinese Communists supplanting, 169–72, 182–83, 199–200; Chongqing, 124, 136, 138–39, 145–53, 200; "clans" and "tribes," 143, 173, 177; ethnopolitics, 37, 90, 98–99, 126–30, 143, 147, 154–58, 157*fig*., 163–73, 177, 197, 223–24, 233–34; and ethnopopulism, 46–47, 96–102, 128, 130, 145–47, 154–58, 157*fig*., 168, 174, 196–98, 202*fig*., 203, 207, 233; government established by, 76; vs. Han chauvinism, 36–37, 154–55, 171–72; and Han migrants, 40–41, 83–85; and Hunza, 195–98; and Ili rebellion, 132, 133, 136, 138, 140–41, 143, 148–56, 161–68; and Jin Shuren, 37, 83–85, 88, 89–90, 91, 98–102, 127–28; Kazak recruitment for Taiwan, 207–10; and Muslims, 29, 98–99, 146, 211–12, 217–19; narratives of political legitimacy, 46, 127, 168, 170, 225, 234; "national humiliation" *(guochi)*, 47, 128, 129–30; and Osman Batur, 161–62, 166–67, 174, 233; "pacification commissioner," 90–91; plans for retaking mainland, 210–17; propaganda campaign (1930s and 1940s), 99; refugee funds, 212, 216, 217, 218; and refugees from Chinese Communists, 200–223, 202*fig*., 204*fig*.;

Nationalists (*continued*)
 Sheng Shicai and, 92–96, 97*fig.*,
 101–3, 124–30, 138–39, 200, 205–6,
 233; Sino-Soviet Friendship Treaty,
 149–51; and Soviets, 126, 138–39,
 146, 149–53, 163, 169, 176, 252n49;
 Taiwan (Republic of China), 12, 198,
 200–217, 202*fig.*, 237, 252n49; and
 Tibet, 215, 225–26; World War II,
 171; Wu Zhongxin disagreements, 15,
 37, 129–30, 145–47, 156; Xinjiang
 as province, 176; Yang Zengxin and,
 77, 129; Yolbars Khan and, 101, 200–
 225, 202*fig.*, 204*fig.*; Zhang Fengjiu as
 Xinjiang liaison, 87. *See also* Chiang
 Kai-shek; Wang Jingwei
nationality policies: Chinese Communist,
 172–73, 177, 190; Sheng Shicai,
 104–8, 124–25, 232–33; Soviet,
 95, 104–8, 190. *See also* affirmative
 action; ethnic self-rule; ethnopolitics;
 national republics
New Armies, 5, 37–39
New Delhi, refugees from Chinese Communists, 199–202
"new Qing historians," 10, 15
"the next Outer Mongolia," 6, 128,
 238–39
"the next Tibet," 6
Nilka County, 139
Nilka Pass, 75, 93
nobility. *See* elites
nomads: Altay, 67, 120–24; hunting
 rights, 120–21; resisting Russian conscription, 50; Sheng Shicai policies,
 108–9; taxes on, 67, 120
Northern Expedition, 49
"northern hybrid states," 21–22, 26,
 258n4
Northern Wei state, ethnic classification,
 258n4

Office of the Chairman of the Xinjiang Provincial Government (Xinjiang Sheng
 Zhengfu Zhuxi Bangongchu), Yolbars
 Khan, 207–24
oil: Dushanzi, 149, 151*fig.*, 152; Sheng
 and, 93, 121, 149; Soviet interests, 93,
 121, 149, 152, 233
Osman Batur, 123–25; Chinese Communists and, 172, 222; Ili rebellion,
 137–38, 143–44, 148, 158–68;
 khan title, 160–62, 184; Mackiernan
 and, 200; Nationalists and, 161–62,
 166–67, 174, 233; "nobody," 123,
 162; refugees from Chinese Communists and, 222, 223; *zhuanyuan* of
 Altay, 161
Ottoman Empire, 9, 33, 59
"outer dependency," 4, 22
Outer Mongolia, 85–86, 120–21; independent state, 12, 120, 149, 231,
 252n49; Mongolian People's Republic,
 120, 149; "national humiliation,"
 128, 129–30; Soviets and, 42, 60–62,
 65*fig.*, 66–68, 101, 120, 252n49;
 Urga, 6, 60–61; Xinjiang as "the next
 Outer Mongolia," 6, 25, 128, 238–39

"pacification commissioner," Nationalist,
 90–91
Pakistan: mir of Hunza and, 195, 196;
 Xinjiang refugees, 209, 219, 224
Panchen Lama, 226
Paxton, John Hall, 154–55, 200, 201,
 206, 209
Pelliot, Paul, 19
People's Liberation Army, 182, 199–200
People's Republic of China, 20; "double
 assimilation," 176–77; "empire of
 nations," 177; Han rulers, 12; name,
 171; national sovereignty, 177–78,
 215–16; *zhonghua*, 35. *See also* Chinese Communists

police/security agents, Sheng Shicai, 103, 114–15, 118, 125, 233

Politburo, Soviet, 94, 104, 131

political legitimacy: Han crisis of, 162, 169. *See also* narratives of political legitimacy

"politics of difference," 6–14, 176, 231; Chinese Communists and, 175, 176–77, 198; empires, 9, 13–14, 33, 50, 231; Jin Shuren repudiating, 77–79, 81*fig.*, 82, 175, 232; Nationalists and, 101, 198; Soviet tactics, 33–34, 160, 168; Wu Zhongxin, 143–46, 158, 172; Yang Zengxin, 6–9, 21, 31–32, 34–48, 62, 77, 84–85. *See also* ethno-elitism; ethnopolitics; ethnopopulism

population: Xinjiang, 3, 38, 40, 79, 184; Xinjiang refugees in Afghanistan, 221

Porter, Bernard, 10–11

"primitive accumulation," 80

prisons: Sheng Shicai purges, 114–15, 143–45, 159; Urumchi, 103

progressive ethnopolitics. *See* ethnopopulism

Provincial Assembly, Xinjiang, 32–33, 63

"public hygiene" campaign, 115, 116

purges: Sheng Shicai, 111–23, 143–45, 159, 180, 205, 233; Soviet Union, 111–13

Puyi, last emperor of Qing dynasty, 101

Qing empire, 3–5, 8–11, 232; *begs*, 29, 231; Chinese Communists and, 174; collapse, 52–58; constitution, 3; consulates, 73; Court for Managing the External (Lifanyuan), 22; ethnic classification, 258n4; extractive policies, 81*fig.*; Han officials, 17–48, 53; hub-and-spoke patronage network, 23; integrationist policies, 23–25, 28, 40, 81*fig.*, 174–76, 231; last emperor, 101; national empire, 235–36; "new Qing historians," 10, 15; repertoires of rule, 17–48, 68, 231; revolution ending (1911), 90; supranational civic ideology, 35; Xinjiang provincial status (1884), 4, 42, 173; Xinjiang "special conditions," 176; Yang Zengxin statue and, 230, 231. *See also* Manchu court

Qiu Zongjun, 112–13

Rankin, K. L., 203

Rebel Assets Committee, 114–15

rebellions, 89; Altay vs. Sheng, 121–25, 137–38, 158–59; Gansu, 19, 40; Hami, 28–29, 38, 83–86, 94, 98, 100, 105–6, 125, 175; Ili, 15, 28–29, 58, 130–70, 151*fig.*, 201; Tibet vs. Chinese Communists, 215, 225

Records from the Studio of Rectification (Buguozhai wendu), Yang Zengxin's, 7–8, 14, 19, 44, 63, 75–76

"red expert," 34

Red Russians. *See* Bolsheviks

refugees: Association for Mainland Refugee Assistance, 208; Bakich, 60; from Chinese Communists, 198–226, 202*fig.*, 204*fig.*; East Turkestan Refugee Association, 216, 223–24, 226; Ili rebellion, 149; Kazak and Kyrgyz crisis (1916), 50–55, 54*fig.*; Nationalist wars, 83; Taiwan recruitment of, 207–10

regional autonomy (*diqu zizhi*), 197; Chinese Communist, 25, 105, 173–82, 181*fig.*, 192, 214–15, 234–35; "eggshell autonomy," 185, 192; Hunza Autonomous Region, 196, 197–98; Kazak Autonomous District, 105, 192; Nationalists and, 196, 197–98, 211; semiautonomous regions under Yang Zengxin, 23–25, 52–54, 54*fig.*, 58, 62–66; Xinjiang Uighur Autonomous Region, 25, 69, 173–82, 181*fig.*, 214–15 religion: Confucianism, 32, 35, 36, 67, 87, 143–44; Daoism, 75–76; schools, 44. *See also* Buddhism; Muslims

repertoires of rule, imperial, 17–48, 68, 74, 87, 231, 237–38; Qing, 17–48, 68, 231; Russian, 20, 68, 74. *See also* governance modes

republic: Taiwan-based Republic of China, 198, 200–217, 202*fig.*, 237, 252n49. *See also* national republics; People's Republic of China; Republic of China (1912–49)

Republic of China (1912–49), 5, 10, 13, 17–55; Han officials "going imperial," 8; Ministry of Finance, 56; Ministry of Foreign Affairs, 53, 56; name for Urumchi, 241n11; Yang Zengxin governor of Xinjiang (1912–28), 19, 23–79, 24*fig.*, 82, 84–85; *zhonghua*, 35. *See also* Yuan Shikai, President of the Republic of China (1912–16)

revolution: Cultural Revolution (1966–76), 34, 221, 226, 230; ending Qing empire (1911), 90; ending Russian empire/Bolshevik (1917–23), 49, 50, 54, 55, 140; Three Districts Revolution, 170

roads: Altay lacking, 120; Jin Shuren construction, 83; Sheng-Soviet deal, 103

Roerich, Nicholas, 228, 239

Rome, Vatican Pope, 27

Russia. *See* Russian empire; Russians; Soviet Union

Russian civil war, 34, 231; Yang Zengxin and, 23, 29–32, 50, 55–56, 60, 71, 84, 144–45. *See also* Bolsheviks; Russian soldiers; White Russians

Russian empire, 4, 9, 20–21, 51–69; Kazak and Kyrgyz refugee crisis (1916), 50–55, 54*fig.*; repertoires of rule, 20, 68, 74. *See also* Russians

Russian soldiers, 26, 38, 58; Annenkov, 39, 60, 61*fig.*; Bakich, 60–61, 61*fig.*, 94; Ili rebellion, 135–42, 148; Jin Shuren ouster, 88, 90; Kashgar, 56; Kazak and Kyrgyz refugee crisis (1916), 52–55; machine guns, 51, 55, 56, 119, 140; Red, 60–62; Sheng Shicai support, 92–93; White, 26, 38–39, 56–61, 61*fig.*, 88, 90, 94, 135–42, 148. *See also* Russian civil war

Russians, 13, 29–30, 99; Altay, 80, 94, 121–22; on "camelgraph," 17; Kashgar, 62; Trans-Siberian Railway, 4, 27, 77; Turkestan, 50, 59, 62–63, 65*fig.*, 66, 71–72; on Yang Zengxin, 8. *See also* Bolsheviks; Kazakhstan; Russian civil war; Russian empire; Russian soldiers; Soviet Union; Uzbekistan; White Russians

Sabik, 219–22

Sadiq, 132–33, 134

Saudi Arabia, 208, 218, 220; Mecca, 211–14, 217–18

Saypiddin Azizi, 34, 192–93

schools: Chinese-language, 5; Khotan, 115; "new method," 67–68; for nomads, 109; religious, 44; Russian-language, 135. *See also* education

segregation, ethnic communities, 183–84, 257n49

self-rule, ethnic, 5, 13, 42, 58–59, 67–68, 124. *See also* national determination

semiautonomous regions, under Yang Zengxin, 23–25, 52–54, 54*fig.*, 58, 62–66

Semipalatinsk, 64, 71–72, 74, 92, 136, 198–99

Semireche, 53, 64, 66

senate, provincial, 146

separatism: East Turkestan Republic, 160; ethnopopulism defusing, 13, 180; Isa and Emin, 100–101, 205, 210–17; Khotan state, 99–100; Masud Sabri, 100, 163, 173; national sovereignty vs., 215–16. *See also* national determination; nationalism

Shaanxi: Han army conscripts, 83, 87; Mao Zedong, 171

Shanghai, Han officials, 12

Shapin, 132–33

"shared funds" *(xiexiang)* of "inner provinces" *(neisheng)*, 22, 79

Sheng Shicai, 45, 97*fig.*, 158, 208; administrative talent lacking, 95, 102, 117–18; and ethnocultural autonomy, 105–8, 112–13, 117, 180–81, 234; ethnopopulism, 97*fig.*, 103, 105–8, 112–13, 117, 123–27, 129, 133–34, 177, 180, 232–33; Japanese-trained Han, 83–84, 88, 97*fig.*, 101–2; and Jin Shuren's trial, 101–2; narrative of political legitimacy, 46, 103, 106, 117, 130; Nationalists and, 92–96, 97*fig.*, 101–3, 124–30, 138–39, 200, 205–6, 233; police/security agents, 103, 114–15, 118, 125, 233; purges, 111–23, 143–45, 159, 180, 205, 233; rebellions vs., 15, 28–29, 121–25, 130–39, 158–59; *Sinkiang: Pawn or Pivot?* (with Allen S. Whiting), 206; "soft-line" and "hard-line" policies, 110, 114; and Soviets, 92–98, 103–39, 205, 232–33; Taiwan, 205–6; warlord, 45–47, 83–84, 88, 95, 105, 117, 177, 200, 232; Xinjiang military governor *(duban)*, 45–46, 83–84, 88–93, 97*fig.*, 103–23, 127–29, 137–39, 158–59, 162, 180, 205; and Yang Zengxin statue, 228, 230

Shipton, Eric, 155

Sibe, 26, 38, 181*fig.*

Sino-Japanese War, 115

Sino-Soviet Friendship Treaty, 149–51

Sino-Swedish Scientific Expedition, 32, 228

slaves, 26

socialism: with Chinese characteristics, 177–79; Mao Zedong and, 184; modernity through, 46, 113, 177; Nationalists hostile to, 77; Sheng Shicai and, 96, 113; Yang Zengxin and, 68–69, 70, 74, 77

soldiers: Han, 5, 37–39; Hui, 26, 38, 63, 104; Ili rebellion, 135–42, 148–49, 152; imperial use of natives, 38; Kazak and Kyrgyz refugee crisis (1916), 52–55; refugees from Chinese Communists, 199; Sheng Shicai qualifications, 83–84, 88, 97*fig.*, 101–2; Xinjiang Production and Construction Corps, 174. *See also* armies; military; Russian soldiers

Solon, 26, 38

Soviet affirmative action policies, 46, 87–88, 163, 169, 231; Austro-Marxist line and, 105, 180–81, 234; with Chinese characteristics, 177–79, 234; Chinese Communists and, 169–94, 234–35; ethnopopulism, 13, 33–34, 37, 46, 58, 68, 94–95, 97*fig.*, 101, 127, 153, 157*fig.*, 159–60, 166, 168–69, 196–98, 232–34; national determination, 64–68, 65*fig.*, 79, 94–95; national liberation, 59–60, 64, 79, 94; national republics, 64–70, 65*fig.*, 94–95, 168, 178, 179; nationality policies, 95, 104–8, 190; Sheng Shicai "purchase" of, 97*fig.*, 103–13, 125, 127, 134, 205, 233; Yang Zengxin and, 65–74, 65*fig.*, 78, 231–32

Soviet consulates: Altay, 134, 137; Ili, 134, 140, 151; Kashgar, 134; Urumchi, 69, 80, 135–37, 140

Soviet Union: Altay prospectors from, 121–22; archival sources, 14, 93–94,

Soviet Union (*continued*)
96, 130–32, 142, 153; arms supplied in Xinjiang, 83, 92–95, 98, 103–4, 119, 137–38, 140–43, 148–52, 167; atomic bomb, 199; Chinese embassy in Moscow, 86–87, 127, 137, 150, 198, 246n57; "empire of nations," 9, 177, 236; historians, 10, 64; Ili rebellion, 15, 130–68, 170, 201; Jin Shuren and, 83, 94–95, 98, 125, 190, 232; migrant policies and, 40; more a "maker of nations" than a "breaker of nations," 10; narratives of political legitimacy, 46, 130; Nationalists and, 126, 138–39, 146, 149–53, 169, 176, 252n49; and Outer Mongolia, 42, 60–62, 65*fig.*, 66–68, 101, 120, 252n49; Politburo, 94, 104, 131; purges, 111–13; refugees from Chinese Communists, 219; Russian migrants, 41; Sheng Shicai and, 92–98, 103–39, 205, 232–33; Sino-Soviet Friendship Treaty, 149–51; Sino-Soviet split, 41, 252n49; "swallowing up" Xinjiang, 215; "swank," 131–32; trade with Xinjiang, 71–75, 80–82, 98; World War II, 124, 125, 233; Xinjiang expatriates, 14, 62, 65*fig.*, 70–74, 95, 104–5, 135, 225; Xinjiang as satellite of, 105; Yang Zengxin and, 60–75, 65*fig.*, 80, 231–32, 245–46n57. *See also* Bolsheviks; Russians; Soviet affirmative action policies

Spencer, Herbert, *The Study of Sociology*, 18

Srinagar, refugees from Chinese Communists, 199–201, 202, 206, 222

Stalin, Joseph: Ili rebellion, 148; and Jin Shuren, 94; May 4th directive, 131; police state, 103, 233; purges, 111; Sheng Shicai and, 96, 103, 105, 111, 138, 233; Sino-Soviet Friendship

Treaty, 149; Wu Zhongxin and, 140

starvation, 51, 150, 219, 257n49. *See also* famines

Stein, Aurel, 28, 48, 70, 79–80, 83

Stilwell, Joseph, 171

"strategies of difference," 6, 20, 21, 50, 101. *See also* ethno-elitism; ethnopopulism; "politics of difference"

Suiyuan, 95, 116

Sun Shengwu, 218–19

Sun Wendou, 136–37

Sun Yat-sen, 102, 164, 211

supranational civic ideology, 34–37, 41

Tacheng, 38, 89, 169; Bolsheviks and, 68; Chinese Communists, 215; Ili rebellion, 133–34, 147, 148–49, 170; Incarnate Lama of, 112; Lattimore, 38; mineral wealth, 151*fig.*; Mongol embrace, 66; Osman Batur conquest, 167; pastoral stock, 151*fig.*, 233; Russian civil war, 60–61; trade, 80, 152

Taiwan: archival sources, 14, 207, 221; Chinese Communists vs. imperialists over, 171; "free China," 198, 227, 237; governance modes, 3–4; Kazak recruitment, 207–10; Nationalists/Republic of China, 12, 198, 200–217, 202*fig.*, 237, 252n49; as province, 5; provincial administrations, 207; Taipei, 200–217, 202*fig.*; Yolbars Khan governor of Xinjiang from (1951–71), 202*fig.*, 203–7, 224

Tajiks, 181*fig.*

Tang dynasty, 4, 258n4

Tao Xisheng, 172

Tarbagatai, 22, 23, 38, 52

Tashkent: Ili rebellion, 135; Mou Weitong, 89; Russians, 62, 64; Xinjiang expatriates receiving Soviet support, 225; Yang Zengxin's consulates, 89, 99, 245–46n57

Tatars, 26, 31, 139–40. *See also* Burhan
Shahidi
taxes: by Jin Shuren, 79–81; Manchu, 5;
Muslim elites controlling, 22, 85, 196;
Xinjiang's base, 113, 207; by Yang
Zengxin on Altay Kazak nomads, 67,
120
Taylor, Jay, 171
telegrams, published, Yang Zengxin's
Records from the Studio of Rectification
(Buguozhai wendu), 7–8, 14, 19, 44,
63, 75–76
telegraph system, 17
telephony services, 83
Thousand-Buddha Caves, 60
Three Districts Revolution, 170
Tianshan, name, 179
Tibet, 11; Chinese Communists and, 171,
199–200, 215, 225, 226; Dalai Lama,
194, 225–26; government in exile,
225–26; lengthy estrangement, 12,
43, 62, 128; Mackiernan, 199; narrative of ethnopolitical legitimacy, 198;
Nationalists and, 128, 215, 225–26;
"pacification commissioner," 91; Xinjiang as ""the next Tibet," 6
Timur, 28–29
Torgut Mongols, 29–30, 38, 82, 85,
109–10, 113, 144, 233
trade: Ili Provisional Trade Accord, 71–72,
75, 80; Xinjiang-Soviet, 71–75,
80–82, 98
Trans-Siberian Railway, Russia, 4, 27, 77
transport: Altay, 120; camel paths, 27;
refugees from Chinese Communists,
199. *See also* roads; Trans-Siberian
Railway
Treaty of Versailles, 49
Triple Seven Coup, 76, 79
Tsetsen Puntsag Gegeen, 82
Turban Heads/Turbans, 38–39, 105, 232;
crossing Soviet border, 65*fig.*; Kashgar,

62, 63; Ma Fuxing and, 45, 63; racism
of name, 70; Russian, 62, 66; and self-
rule, 42, 59; Turkestan, 62; Xinjiang
expatriates working in Russia, 65*fig.*,
74
Turfan, 22–23, 31, 80, 84, 92, 113
Turkestan: Russian, 50, 59, 62–63, 65*fig.*,
66, 71–72. *See also* East Turkestan
Republic
Turkey: exchange students, 217; Nationalist embassy in Ankara, 212, 214, 219;
Xinjiang expatriates, 204*fig.*, 208–21,
224, 237. *See also* Istanbul; Ottoman
Empire
Turkic peoples: Andijan workers, 94;
begs, 26, 29, 30*fig.*, 231; corvée labor,
28, 84; entrepreneurs, 82; expatriates in Russia, 62, 72, 104–5; Khotan
militants, 99–100; nobility, 5, 22–32,
58–59, 82–87, 91, 102, 113, 200,
203, 226–27, 231, 232; pan-Turkic,
156, 164–65. *See also* Hami

Uighur Autonomous Archives, 14, 93
Uighur Autonomous Region (Xinjiang
Weiwuer Zizhiqu), Xinjiang, 25, 69,
173–82, 181*fig.*, 214–15
Uighurs, 11–12, 14, 105, 232; agriculture, 80, 152; Association for
Ethnocultural Advancement, 132,
219; calligraphy, 164, 165*fig.*; Chinese
Communist, 179; ethnocultural autonomy, 128; ethnopopulists, 100–101,
145–47, 154–58, 157*fig.*, 233–34,
237; Governor Yang's persecution
of, 14; Han chauvinism criticized by,
37, 171–72; Hui enmities with, 38,
45; Ili rebellion, 130, 135, 152–68;
intellectuals, 98–101, 153–58,
157*fig.*, 193–94, 203; Kucha, 182–83;
"masters of their own house" (*dangjia
zuozhu*), 186; Masud Sabri, 163–64;

Uighurs (*continued*)
military exclusion, 38; national
republics, 168; nationalist, 69;
Nationalists and, 126, 147, 154–58,
157*fig.*, 170, 233–34; pan-Turkic activism, 156, 164–65; prepubescent marriages, 110; refugees from Chinese
Communists, 199–223; refugees to
Soviet Union, 219; religious schools,
44; segregated, 183–84, 257n49;
in Soviet Union, 14, 70, 71–74, 95,
135–36; Urumchi factory workers,
14, 185–90; Xinjiang population
percentage, 38, 79; in Xinjiang Uighur
Autonomous Region, 174, 179–80,
181*fig.*. *See also* Burhan Shahidi; Isa
Yusuf Alptekin
Ungern-Sternberg, Baron Roman von,
60–61
United Daily News (Lianhe bao), 217
United Nations, 221, 222, 224
unity: national, 215–16, 223–27. *See also*
integrationist policies
Urumchi, 8, 12, 14; affirmative action,
182–94; battle for (1933–34), 88–96,
103–4; British consulate, 155;
demographics, 184; factory workers,
14, 184, 185–92, 235; Han officials
resident in, 8, 12–13, 15, 18, 27–28,
231; Ili rebellion, 148–55; journey to
Beijing from, 17; names for, 241n11;
New Armies, 37–38; "public hygiene"
campaign, 115, 116; Soviet consulate,
69, 80, 135–37, 140; Uighur Autonomous Archives, 14, 93; West Park,
228–30, 229*fig.*; Yang Zengxin statue,
228–31, 229*fig.*; Yang Zengxin's
authority outside of, 52. *See also*
Xinjiang
Uzbekistan, 127, 131, 135, 141–42, 153.
See also Tashkent

Vietnam, French ethnopolitics in, 18, 38
"virtue" (*de*), 35

Wang Enmao, 171, 186, 234
Wang Jingwei, 88, 91, 92, 127; ending
career in disgrace and ignominy, 100;
ethnopopulist message, 99, 171;
Jin Shuren and, 98, 100; and Sheng
Shicai, 95–96
Wang Shijie, 150–51
Wang Shunan, 18–20, 26
war: Cold War, 198–207, 215, 224; holy
war, 5; Sino-Japanese War, 115. *See
also* armies; rebellions; Russian civil
war; World War I; World War II
warlords, 7–8, 49, 77–78, 83; armies, 39,
78, 86–96, 103–4; Beijing, 45, 63;
Chinese Communists and, 170, 171;
"Christian," 76; era of (1916–28),
50, 77–78; Feng Yuxiang, 7, 76, 78;
Gansu, 84–96, 102–4; Guo Songling,
101; Jin Shuren vs., 82–83, 232; Ma
Zhongying, 86–96, 102–4; Nationalists incorporating, 170; Sheng Shicai,
45–47, 83–84, 88, 95, 105, 117, 177,
200, 232; Xinjiang information blockade, 17; Yang Zengxin and, 39, 56, 61,
63, 76–79, 83–85, 232
Wen Songling, 136
West: archaeologists and explorers to
Xinjiang, 20; Bolsheviks proving difference from, 178, 179; consulates,
68, 74, 232; governing dependent territories, 18; history of violent displacement, 179; imperialism, 12, 178–80;
media on Masud Sabri appointment,
163, 253n75; media on Uighur and
Kazak refugees, 207; nation-state discourse, 231; Nationalist threat, 170;
Tibet receiving more attention than
Xinjiang, 226; vicious wars unseen by,
83; Yang Zengxin statue, 230. *See also*

Allied powers; Americans; Europe
White Russians: exiled in Xinjiang,
31–32, 74; soldiers, 26, 38–39, 56,
58, 60–61, 61*fig.*, 88, 90, 94, 135–42,
148
Whiting, Allen S., 206
workers: education vs. helping out the
family, 109; Hami corvée labor, 28, 84;
Hui, 14; Kazak, 74, 185–90; Turban,
65*fig.*, 74; Turkic, 28, 62, 72, 84, 94;
Urumchi factories, 14, 184, 185–92,
235
world politics. *See* geopolitics
World Muslim Council, 211, 217–18
World War I: Allied powers dismantling
empires after, 33–34; Masud Sabri, 99;
Russian manpower shortages, 50
World War II: Burma theater, 171;
Germans, 125, 127, 171; Japanese
surrender, 149; Soviet Union, 124,
125, 233
Wu Peifu, 7
Wu Zexiang, 133
Wu Zhongxin, 129–30; diary, 15, 129,
141, 143, 145, 147; ethno-elitism,
129, 143–46, 159, 172, 184, 197,
233; Taiwan, 205; Xinjiang governor,
15, 37, 129, 139–63, 176, 203, 205;
and Yang Zengxin statue, 228–30

Xie Bin, 17, 29, 48, 56, 84
Xinjiang, 5, 17–55, 83; armies, 45,
48, 56, 78–79, 82–87; battle for
(1933–34), 88–96, 103–4; brief rise
and fall of an independent Islamic
state, 4, 135–36; Burhan Shahidi
governorship, 47, 157*fig.*, 170, 192,
205, 212; Chinese collapse in, 75–88;
as "colony" (*zhimindi*) of the inner
provinces, 25, 40; first-ever non-Han
governor, 47; global awareness of,
194; government in exile, 195–227;

Great Leap Forward (1958–61), 219,
230, 257n49; Jin Shuren governorship (1928–33), 77–89, 81*fig.*, 91,
98, 99–100, 125, 175; Kazak and
Kyrgyz refugee crisis (1916), 50–55,
54*fig.*; Masud Sabri governorship,
99, 156, 163–68, 170, 176, 212;
May 4th directive, 131; modernization projects, 18–19, 78, 80, 83, 125,
232; name, 179–80, 218; Nationalist,
87, 127–68; "the next Outer Mongolia," 6, 25, 128, 238–39; as "outer
dependency"/"dependent territory,"
4, 22; population, 3, 38, 40, 79, 184;
Provincial Assembly, 32–33, 63;
provincial status (1884), 4, 42, 173;
refugees from Chinese Communists,
198–226, 202*fig.*, 204*fig.*; Saypiddin
Azizi governorship, 192–93; Sheng
Shicai as military governor (*duban*),
45–46, 83–84, 88–93, 97*fig.*, 103–23,
127–29, 137–39, 158–59, 162, 180,
205; as Soviet satellite, 105; Soviet
trade with, 71–75, 80–82, 98; Soviet's
idea of two separate states, 94; "special conditions," 176; Wu Zhongxin
governorship, 15, 37, 129, 139–63,
176, 203, 205; Yang Zengxin governorship (1912–28), 19, 23–79, 24*fig.*,
82, 84–85; Yolbars Khan governorship
from Nationalist Taiwan (1951–71),
202*fig.*, 203–7, 224; Zhang Zhizhong
governorship, 156, 158, 163, 165–66,
196, 212. *See also* Chinese consulates; economics; ethnopolitics; Han;
Kazaks; Muslims; national republics;
Uighurs; Urumchi
Xinjiang Autonomous Region, keeping or
leaving out Uighurs, 179–80
Xinjiang Production and Construction
Corps (Xinjiang Shengchan Jianshe
Bingtuan), 174–75, 183

Xinjiang Tin Mines Agreement ("Sin-Tin" accord), 122

Xinjiang Uighur Autonomous Archives, 14, 93

Xinjiang Uighur Autonomous Region (Xinjiang Weiwuer Zizhiqu), 25, 69, 173–82, 181*fig.*, 214–15

Xinjiang Youth Song and Dance Troupe, 164, 165*fig.*

Xu Bingxu, 32, 228, 230, 244n12

Xu Shichang, 56

Yan Xishan, 7

Yan'an, Chinese Communist headquarters, 113–14, 119, 138, 171

Yang Zengbing, 28

Yang Zengxin, 3–4, 5–8, 24*fig.*, 42, 43, 87, 91, 231; accused of parochial and reactionary mindset, 17–18; and Altay, 23, 52, 64, 66, 67, 84, 120, 121; archival sources, 14; army resources, 38–39, 45, 48, 56, 78–79, 82, 120, 150, 191; assassinated (July 1928), 24*fig.*, 75–76, 81*fig.*; and Burhan Shahidi, 31–32, 34, 144–45; consulates, 65*fig.*, 68–74, 232, 245–46n57; daily routine, 75; deflecting ethnic tensions, 37–39, 44, 46; and dependent intermediaries, 27–33, 30*fig.*, 144–45; ethno-elitism, 24*fig.*, 33, 46, 58, 61, 77–79, 82, 86, 96, 129, 231; governance modes, 3–6, 17–48; management of Han officials, 23, 25, 29, 31–32, 42, 56–57, 63, 104–5, 129; and Masud Sabri, 99; Muslim concubine, 43–44; narratives of political legitimacy, 33–34, 36, 41–48; vs. nationalism, 24*fig.*, 36, 58–59, 62–63, 67, 68, 79, 231–32; "politics of difference," 6–9, 21, 31–32, 34–48, 62, 77, 84–85; *Records from the Studio of Rectification*

(Buguozhai wendu), 7–8, 14, 19, 44, 63, 75–76; Republican governor of Xinjiang (1912–28), 19, 23–79, 24*fig.*, 82, 84–85; retirement plans, 76–77; and Russian civil war, 23, 29–32, 50, 55–56, 60, 71, 84, 144–45; semiautonomous regions, 23–25, 52–54, 54*fig.*, 58, 62–66; and Soviets, 60–75, 65*fig.*, 80, 231–32, 245–46n57; statue, 228–31, 229*fig.*; "stratagem of the empty citadel" *(kongcheng ji)*, 77–78; tomb, 77; transferred to Xinjiang (1907), 26; Wang Shunan and, 19–20, 26; web of isolation, 56–57; and world outside Xinjiang, 56, 68–69, 244n12; Wu Zhongxin's diary on, 129

Yang Zuanxu, 67–68

Yangzi delta, 18–19, 83

Yao Daohong, 224

Yaqub Beg, 135–36

Ye Shanrong, 235–36

Yegnarov, General-Major, 142–43, 153

Yeh, George, 203–5, 210, 214

"yellow filth," Han, 14–15, 86, 103

"yellow race," nationalists valorizing, 24*fig.*, 232

Yining, 140–41, 215

Yolbars Khan, 202*fig.*; death, 223–24; governor of Xinjiang from Nationalist Taiwan (1951–71), 202*fig.*, 203–7, 224; Hami *ordabegi* (major domo), 85, 200, 203, 226–27; Hami uprising, 85–86, 94, 98, 100; and Isa and Emin, 202*fig.*, 203–22, 204*fig.*; vs. Jin Shuren, 85–86; Kazak recruitment for Taiwan, 207–10; and Nationalists, 101, 200–225, 202*fig.*, 204*fig.*; Office of the Chairman of the Xinjiang Provincial Government (Xinjiang Sheng Zhengfu Zhuxi Bangongchu), 207–24; refugee from Xinjiang, 172, 200–206, 202*fig.*

Yu Xiusong, 105, 106, 111, 232–33
Yuan Dahua, 3
Yuan Shikai, President of the Republic
 of China (1912–16), 55, 56; death
 (1916), 40, 49, 50, 51–52, 77; Japan's
 Twenty-One Demands to, 122
Yuan state, ethnic classification, 258n4
Yunnan: ethnic classification projects, 10;
 Nationalist provincial administration,
 207; Yang Zengxin background, 42, 45

Zaysan, 64, 135–36, 145, 245n57
Zhang Chunxi, 76
Zhang Fengjiu, 87
Zhang Peiyuan, 92–93, 95, 103–4
Zhang Shaobo, 29–30
Zhang Zhidong, 18
Zhang Zhizhong: Chinese Communist,
 205; Ili rebellion, 150, 152–56,
 161–68, 165*fig.*; northwestern com-
 missioner, 156; Xinjiang governorship,
 156, 158, 163, 165–66, 196, 212;
 Xinjiang as home of the "Turkestan
 nation," 234; Xinjiang Youth Song and
 Dance Troupe, 164, 165*fig.*
Zhao Guoliang, 71–72
zhonghua, 35–36
Zhou Enlai, 171, 178–79, 234–35
Zhu Ruichi, 53–55, 72
Zhu Shaoliang, 149–50
zhuanyuan, Altay, 148–49, 161
Zuo Zongtang, 40

Cultural Encounters on China's Ethnic Frontiers, edited by Stevan Harrell

Guest People: Hakka Identity in China and Abroad, edited by Nicole Constable

Familiar Strangers: A History of Muslims in Northwest China, by Jonathan N. Lipman

Lessons in Being Chinese: Minority Education and Ethnic Identity in Southwest China, by Mette Halskov Hansen

Manchus and Han: Ethnic Relations and Political Power in Late Qing and Early Republican China, 1861–1928, by Edward J. M. Rhoads

Ways of Being Ethnic in Southwest China, by Stevan Harrell

Governing China's Multiethnic Frontiers, edited by Morris Rossabi

On the Margins of Tibet: Cultural Survival on the Sino-Tibetan Frontier, by Åshild Kolås and Monika P. Thowsen

The Art of Ethnography: A Chinese "Miao Album," translation by David M. Deal and Laura Hostetler

Doing Business in Rural China: Liangshan's New Ethnic Entrepreneurs, by Thomas Heberer

Communist Multiculturalism: Ethnic Revival in Southwest China, by Susan K. McCarthy

Religious Revival in the Tibetan Borderlands: The Premi of Southwest China, by Koen Wellens

In the Land of the Eastern Queendom: The Politics of Gender and Ethnicity on the Sino-Tibetan Border, by Tenzin Jinba

Empire and Identity in Guizhou: Local Resistance to Qing Expansion, by Jodi L. Weinstein

China's New Socialist Countryside: Modernity Arrives in the Nu River Valley, by Russell Harwood

Mapping Shangrila: Contested Landscapes in the Sino-Tibetan Borderlands, edited by Emily T. Yeh and Chris Coggins

A Landscape of Travel: The Work of Tourism in Rural Ethnic China, by Jenny Chio

The Han: China's Diverse Majority, by Agnieszka Joniak-Lüthi

Xinjiang and the Modern Chinese State, by Justin M. Jacobs

www.ingramcontent.com/pod-product-compliance
Lightning Source LLC
Chambersburg PA
CBHW020459270326
41926CB00008B/668